# Decision Processes in Visual Perception

**ACADEMIC PRESS
SERIES IN COGNITION AND PERCEPTION**

*SERIES EDITORS:*
**Edward C. Carterette
Morton P. Friedman**
*Department of Psychology
University of California, Los Angeles
Los Angeles, California*

# Decision Processes in Visual Perception

**D. VICKERS**

*University of Adelaide*

ACADEMIC PRESS   New York  San Francisco  London
A Subsidiary of Harcourt Brace Jovanovich, Publishers

ACADEMIC PRESS INC. (LONDON) LTD.
24/28 Oval Road,
London NW1.


*United States Edition published by*
ACADEMIC PRESS INC.
111 Fifth Avenue
New York, New York 10003

Library of Congress Catalog Card Number: 79–50311
Vickers, Douglas
  Decision processes in visual perception.
  – (Academic Press series in cognition and
perception).
  1. Visual perception 2. Decision-making
I. Title
152.1'4    BF241    79–50311

ISBN 0-12-721550-6


Text set in 10/12 pt VIP Bembo, printed and bound
in Great Britain at The Pitman Press, Bath

# Preface

As is doubtless the case with most research, the impetus behind the work reported in this book has come from a number of different sources. In particular, I have been interested for some time in the relationships between the overall organization of a complex visual pattern by the perceptual system and the more molecular activity involved in the discrimination of differences in magnitude or intensity between two stimulus elements. In the former case, for example, there seems to be a predominant tendency towards the recognition of stimulus elements as being identical with respect to one or more dimensions, as in the perception of depth in two-dimensional gradient patterns consisting of many similar elements (e.g. Vickers, 1971). On the other hand, where there are very few elements, the tendency of the perceptual system seems to be towards differentiation, so that two lines of different length and width are discriminated with respect to those dimensions rather than perceived as being of the same length and width, but differently situated in depth. In between these two extremes, the processes of perceptual organization can be viewed as striking some kind of balance between the opposing tendencies of discrimination and identification. In consequence, it seems to me that one way of trying to decipher the functional relationships between simple psychophysical judgments and the more molar activities of perceptual organization would be to begin by studying the mechanisms underlying these two basic operations.

A second orienting factor has been the conviction that perception is unlikely to prove to be intelligible in terms of a multiplicity of highly specialized functions, each precisely ordered within a single unifying system. Rather, it seems to be more appropriately conceived as an accumulation of numerous adaptive refinements and modifications to the operation of a few fundamental principles. I feel it should be possible, therefore, to account for these basic functions in such a way that they might be realized by even a very simple organism.

To a large extent this book may be regarded as an exploration of these initial expectations. Although the theoretical framework developed in it is clearly a personal one, I have attempted throughout to show its relation to other approaches. In particular, I have tried to present alternative hypothesis as part of a logical sequence, even at the cost of not presenting an exhaustive evaluation of each. At the same time, I have tried to deal with the various notions in a concrete, intuitive way rather than by a purely mathematical treatment, which in any case I should be ill-equipped to sustain. I hope that the consequent loss of rigour may be compensated for by a wider accessibility of the argument to those interested in more molar problems of visual perception and human information-processing in general.

I began writing this book while on sabbatical leave at the Experimental Psychology Laboratory, University of Sussex, and I should like to thank Professor N. S. Sutherland for the facilities and the invaluable freedom from interruption which I enjoyed whilst there. The work reported in the book was financed throughout by the Australian Research Grants Committee, without whose support it would not have been possible. The extensive computer programming involved was carried out by Bob Willson, Peter Barnes and Roger Laws, for whose assistance and advice I am indebted. I am also grateful to Judy Fallon and to Helena van Ruth for transforming my pencilled sketches into finished diagrams, and to Margaret Blaber and Margaret Bruce, respectively, for typing the first and second drafts of the text.

Finally, I should like to express my gratitude to Professor A. T. Welford for his incisive comments and wise advice on the early drafts of some chapters. Without his continued encouragement over many years, the task of completing this book would have been much harder.

*April, 1979*                                        Douglas Vickers

# Contents

To Yvonne, and Marc and Anne

# I

## Simple Decision Processes

# 1
# Introduction

*What is a man but nature's finer success in self-explication? What is a man but a finer and compacter landscape than the horizon figures—nature's eclecticism?*
R. W. Emerson, "Essays" (Ser. 1, xii, p. 352.)

Within the dozen or so generations since Descartes examined the inversion of images by the lens of an eye excised from an ox, the study of responses by the vertebrate system to light falling on the retina has progressed from a delineation of its gross anatomy to the recording of electrical activity from a single cell in the cortex of a living cat. While such a dramatic improvement in the techniques of physiological measurement has undoubtedly led to a more detailed understanding of the mechanisms involved, it carries with it the risk that some of the more molar influences on the process of visual perception may be underrated or forgotten. Even at the behavioural level, with which most of this book is concerned, it is all too easy to lose sight of the importance of certain general principles in the concentration on experimental detail often needed to discern some pattern in a set of findings. Because of this, and because the theories developed in this book have been partly shaped by considerations beyond those of the immediately relevant data, it is useful to begin by recalling some of the most general and pervasive influences on visual perception.

## Process, Constraint and Structure

At least since the time of Aristotle, it has been appreciated that the ways in which men categorize the world have only a restricted validity. In particular, the habit of regarding certain aspects (such as flowers or nerve cells) as stable entities depends upon the grain of the time scale employed. Given a coarser grain (as in time-lapse photography), then, as William James remarks, "mushrooms and the swifter-growing plants will shoot into being

... [and] annual shrubs will rise and fall from the earth like restlessly boiling water springs" (1890, *1*, p. 639). On a still larger scale, even such "permanent" features as massive rock formations, can be seen to be not static entities, but *processes*, which occur in accordance with certain natural laws. From stellar bodies down through animal populations to cells, molecules and atoms, these processes are continuously changing in space and in time. Meanwhile, irrespective of the level, the behaviour of their constituent elements seems (from the inevitably limited viewpoint of any member of such a universe) to be neither completely determined nor completely random, but to be subject to the control of certain probabilistic *constraints*. It is the operation of these constraints that determines the character of any process. For example, as Weiss (1969) points out, a living cell remains the same, despite the continuous reshuffling and exchange of its molecular components; in the same way, a human society can retain its identity despite the turnover in population from birth, death and migration. In both cases, it is the constraints imposed upon these processes which determine their nature, structure and development.

A related insight, which was not emphasized in earlier associationist accounts of perception, but has since become widely recognized, is that *structure*, in the form of predictable relations among the distinguishable elements constituting a process, is omnipresent in the natural world. Any modern, illustrated encyclopaedia contains an abundance of striking examples, from both the organic and the inorganic world, of intricate structures imparted by the multiplicity of constraints controlling cellular reproduction and crystalline accretion. As well as these relatively familiar instances, however, structure may also appear when it is least expected, as in the layering effects observed when "random" numbers, generated by some computer programmes, are represented visually, or, as in Fig. 1, where apparently simple constraints produce an unexpectedly complex pattern. In a similar way, graphic artists may impart an elusive structure by the use of implicit constraints, as in the shapes shown in Fig. 2. Although the relevant constraints are often difficult to specify, the prevalence of detectable structure and regularity in nature has been eloquently described by a variety of thinkers, including the biologist D'Arcy Thompson (1917) and the poet Hopkins (1972), and has been studied in phenomena as diverse as the branching of blood vessels or the biography of a sand dune.

On this view, the structure of the elements composing some process may be regarded as providing a history of its growth or formation, as well as information about its composition and properties, the forces acting upon it, its interaction with other processes and its likely future development. For example, a swarm of parallel crevasses in the brittle surface of a glacier indicates the presence and direction of compression forces as the underlying

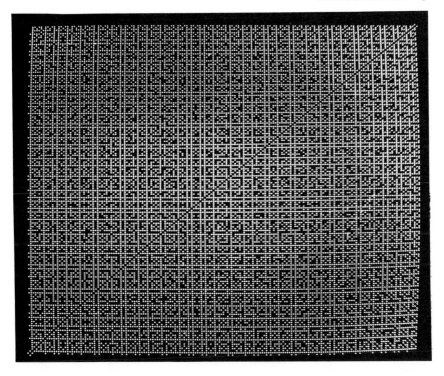

Fig. 1. The texture of the coordinates $x = 1$ to $180$, $y = 1$ to $180$. A point is plotted if its two coordinates have no common divisor. The resulting texture exhibits an interesting combination of regularity and randomness. Coordinates were generated by a PDP 8/E computer, plotted on a DEC VT8E video display and photographed. (The rectangularity is due to distortion in the display.) The demonstration was devised by Schroeder (1969).

flow is checked by some obstacle, while the jagged edges of the surrounding peaks reveal the source and direction of previous glaciation. On a smaller scale, the thickness, cross-section and economical design of earlier wrought iron implements constitute a legible signature of the operations performed by the blacksmith to bend, twist and beat a uniform bar of metal into a useful tool. Thus, the constraints which may be important in any particular case are diverse, and include the electrical forces which preserve the integrity of an atom, chemical reactions such as oxidation, electromagnetic effects, gravitational forces, the effects of heat and cold, processes of manufacture and erosion by wind and water.

In turn, the effects of these constraints can be classified for convenience into two main kinds. The first is concerned with the formation of elements,

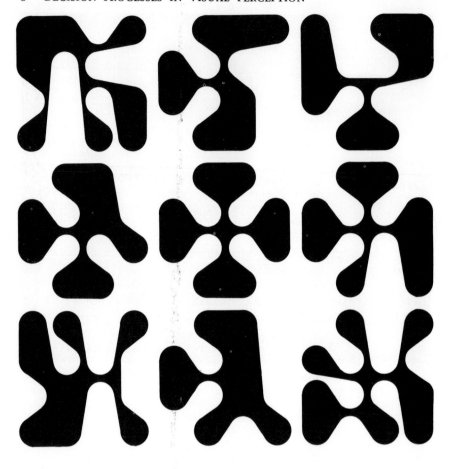

Fig. 2. "Gloopy figures", generated by looping lines around designated circles within a 4 × 4 array. The application of probabilistic constraints, such as symmetry, number of circles and maximum length of loop, gives rise to a set of shapes recognizable as a family. The technique is due to Hofman (1965).

that is, comparatively simple, unitary processes which recur throughout nature, such as atoms, molecules, crystals or cells. The second has to do with the linkage of these elements into more complex processes, such as the regular stacking of particles in a crystal, the spiral arrangement of stars in a galaxy, or the functional sandwiching of epidermal, palisade and mesophyll cells within a single leaf. It is true that, within certain broad limits, the classification of a process as an element itself or as a configuration of simpler elements is arbitrary, and the natural world may be regarded as a hierarchy, in which even highly complex processes, such as individual organisms, may be viewed as elements in an even more complex process, such as a social group. However, since the behaviour of elements in isolation may be quite different from that of a constellation of elements, the choice of descriptive level may have important practical consequences.

Irrespective of the level employed, however, it is evident that a knowledge of the constraints that determine a process is a key to our understanding of it. This seems to be particularly true in a world in which a multiplicity of interacting forces results in the appearance of only probabilistic constraint. One result of this, as has been pointed out by Leibniz, is that no two processes (be they peas, starfish, or fir trees) can be expected to be exactly alike, although the degree and form of the constraints controlling their production may remain constant. It would seem to be no accident, therefore, that responsiveness to such constraints among the majority of higher animals has depended upon their accurate transmission by an information-bearing medium with a few simple, invariant properties: the rectilinear propagation of light and the geometrically exact principles of reflection and refraction imply, among other things, that a reflecting surface will transmit precise and stable information concerning its structure and composition.

At the same time, the reflection of light is itself a process, in which the constraints jointly imposed by the geometrical relations between the source of light, the position and movements of the observer and the position, movements and rigidity of the object concerned all combine to impart a high degree of structure to the final focussed image. Thus, while the inherent organization of the object may be conveyed by the pattern of changes in the wavelengths and intensities of reflected (or refracted) light rays, the interaction between the relative positions of the light source, the object and the observer serves to produce a further set of geometrical transformations in the optical image. While these transformations are usually quite unrelated to the constraints responsible for the inherent structure of the object, they tend, within certain broad limits, to preserve the information specifying these constraints which is available in the image.

Before this information can be extracted by the observer, however, one further set of processes usually intervenes. This set includes variations in the availability of light from the source, the appearance or disappearance of intervening physical obstacles, certain movements of the light source, object, or observer, as well as variations in the arousal or attention of the latter. All these may serve to restrict the availability of the information in ways which are quite unrelated to its nature or significance. Thus, the process of visual perception may be construed as the attempt to respond differentially both to the spatial properties and to the inherent constraints in an object, as revealed in the limited and not completely predictable presentation of a structured optical image.

## *The Evolution of the Vertebrate Visual System*

Faced with the formidable complexity of such a process, one may well baulk. However, it is perhaps better not to approach the problem head on. After all, the vast and intricate complexity of the human visual system is not the result of a single design process, such as the prototype of a new digital computer, but the product of innumerable cumulative adaptations, occuring throughout the course of an evolutionary history of the order of one billion years. Each step in this long, slow evolution must represent the resultant in an interplay between environmental influences and the principles of genetic variation, and any evolutionary change must have consisted of a simple modification in the pattern of growth of the organism. One such modification, for example, seems to have been the production of more cortical cells, while recent microelectrode studies suggest that a related development has been a progressive refinement in the response of certain neural structures to sensory information.

Since the first modifications must have conveyed the most basic advantages, it is unlikely that they would be lost in the later development of the system. As Goodson argues, it seems inevitable that: "a few simple principles were crucial to adaptation among the most primitive forms of life, and that these same principles are still operative in the most complex evolutionary product: the human being" (1973, p. 2). If, as this implies, the later evolution of the visual system largely consists of the addition of structures successively refined in various ways, then a reasonable strategy for gaining insight into the overall system would be, first of all, to try to account for its most elementary achievements, those which the system must have been capable of in its earliest stages of evolution. At the very least, as Aristotle remarks: "he who sees things grow from their beginning will have the finest view of them." More than this, however, there is some hope that, if we can frame an account of these elementary abilities, we may use this as a building block in a more complex hypothesis capable of explaining more advanced achievements. It is with this possibility in mind that we turn now to consider, albeit briefly, the obscure origins of the vertebrate visual system.

Each single cell, as was first pointed out by Albrecht Haller about 1850, has three fundamental properties: "irritability", or sensitivity to outside agents such as light; "conductivity", or the ability to transmit excitation; and "contractility", with the help of which the cell body moves. Although the ability to respond to light may no longer be a universal property of organisms, it seems likely that all organic matter was originally photosensitive, and that only gradually did migratory aggregates of cells emerge as animals, which then became parasitic upon the photosynthetic produce of the plants.

With the emancipation of these animals from dependence upon light for energy, another basic characteristic of light—the fact that it travels in straight lines—acquired greater importance. This arose because the first primitive animals were probably sluggish creatures, inhabiting the lower depths of the warmer, shallow waters around the shores and scavenging among the debris of minute organisms that drifted to the sea bed. Since the approach of predators was generally signalled by shadows cast downwards, there existed a selective pressure for the cells forming the upper surface of the animal to develop into a strip of maximum photosensitivity. This gradually became more interconnected, and allowed the transmission of warning signals to other contractile cells to initiate some form of escape. The resulting segregation into three layers of specialist cells provided the basic recipe for vertebrate organization: a receptor system, a central nervous system, capable of comparing signals from different receptors, and an effector system which carried out the appropriate responses.

In his richly rewarding book on the vertebrate visual system, Polyak (1957) has suggested that the basic ingredients of the system were probably embodied in an organism resembling the hypothetical sketch in Fig. 3. Primitive though such an organism may appear, the gradient of response required to escape from predation (or from harmful levels of energy), together with the need to obtain energy, make it almost certain that it possessed the ability to perform an elementary brightness discrimination and to identify particular chemical emanations. Even single-celled organisms, such as the paramoecium, exhibit sensitivity to light and to chemicals, while a multicellular animal of comparable primitiveness, such as the flatworm, shows clear evidence of shunning light and tracking down food through chemoreceptors, as well as of possessing homeostatic control of such items as water content. For earlier organisms, which did not seek to preserve their internal integrity by the growth of a protective bark or shell, there would clearly be a strong selective pressure to develop differential responses of some flexibility. As Goodson remarks: "the first motile life elements must have been simple, homeostatic, negative-feedback mechanisms, and, considering the contexts in which they emerged, could not have been otherwise." He goes on to argue that the elementary processes of discrimination and identification would have been a prerequisite of evolution, as well as of survival, and concludes that "all living organisms, from the simplest to the most complex, reflect more or less elaborate variations of

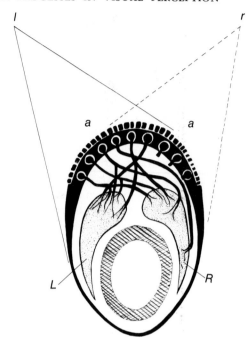

Fig. 3. Hypothetical organism from which elementary animals possessing the essential features of the vertebrate visual system seem likely to have developed. The photoreceptors at *a* are each connected to two main sets of muscle cells, *L* and *R*, responsible for movement. When the light at *l* is brighter than at *r*, the organism moves towards *l*. (Adapted from Polyak, 1957, p. 775, Fig. 436A).

[these] simple principles" (1973, p. 8). Since discrimination, identification and adaptive control are exhibited by human beings in countless different contexts in everyday life, this conclusion suggests that a natural constraint on theorizing would be to try to account for these primitive abilities in such a way that they are also capable of being realized by an organism comparable in complexity to that shown in Fig. 3.

## *The Roles of the Visual System in Human Evolution*

By interpreting the genetically programmed sequence of changes in the embryos of vertebrate animals as a cumulative record of past evolutionary stages, Polyak (1957) has reconstructed the major steps in the development of the vertebrate eye and visual system. As the photosensitive strip differentiated into two concave patches, and as its transparent skin thickened into a primitive lens, the organism of Fig. 3 would have become more mobile, venturing up from the sea bed to swim around in the middle depths. Even in such a diffusely lit environment, this increased mobility along each of the three major axes would exert a selective stress towards the development of shape recognition and constancy. Indeed, it seems likely that many of the basic processes of space perception were already highly developed in the early marine ancestors of the vertebrates.

Meanwhile, for an organism already heavily reliant on vision, the path towards more light, warmth, oxygen and food would naturally lead up from the sea bed to the upper regions of the water, and thence to the higher evolutionary possibilities opened up on land by the perfection of the visual system. Following the transitional amphibians, the development of a wide variety of animal types seems to have resulted from a period of biological stress, during which some animals decreased or abandoned their reliance on vision, while those that chose to live in the trees or the air became even more heavily dependent on sight. Among the latter were the ancestors of man. Although originally insectivorous, it is likely that they came to include fruit in their diet while foraging for the larvae of winged insects. In turn, the distinct advantage in recognizing fruit-bearing trees by their shape, bark and leaves would further strengthen their reliance upon vision, while the dramatic colour changes in ripening fruit would provide a strong inducement to develop colour sensitivity. Meanwhile, it seems plausible to suppose that the need to climb, grasp, examine and pick larvae and fruit was partly responsible for the specialization of hands as manipulative organs, while the activities of climbing, jumping and swinging through branches would give impetus to the development of good binocular vision. With a highly sensitive visual system and limbs constructed on a skeletal plan, in which a gradual increase in precision with each articulation allowed a great variety of movements, there would also arise an increasing need to coordinate the two systems. It is possible that it was partly in response to this need that the cerebral cortex began to develop.

At this stage it seems likely that man's development culminated in a situation in which an already abundant repertoire of abilities could interact in such a way that even a minute improvement in one could combine with others to produce a wide range of new possibilities. As man then began to make excursions from the forest into the rolling grasslands, his visual system would have become attuned to detecting slight movements, to spotting animals partly concealed by rocks or vegetation and to judging distances accurately over undulating and irregular terrain. It appears that he gradually began to improve the configurations of the sticks and stones he selected as weapons, a development made possible by the economy of control required for a skeletal structure, and by the precision of the visual information guiding his manipulations. When eventually man began to harvest fruit and cultivate crops, human society was achieved in much the same form in which it has persisted up to the present.

In tracing the development of man, it would be misleading to say that any one factor was responsible for his rise to predominance. It seems rather that his superiority arose from the conjunction of several mutually reinforcing factors, including his skeletal structure, upright posture, large cerebral cortex, social organization, his development of language, his use of tools and his reliance on vision. Though the exact sequence and interplay of these factors must remain obscure, it is salutary to speculate on the way these processes may have interacted. At the least, this exercise brings out the fact that the present human visual system is a product of a long and complex evolution, and embodies cumulative adaptations to a wide variety of different circumstances. As Goodson puts it: "every species incorporates within its morphology and process systems the effects of thousands of generations of interaction with particular segments of the environment" (1973, p. 3).

Thus, from the first simple discrimination between two brightnesses, or the identification of some vital chemical emanation, the primitive responses of the visual system have somehow been modified and refined so as to enable a differential response to be made to constraints of increasing precision in the structure of its surroundings. Indeed, the degree and complexity of its evolution would suggest that minute genetic variations have gradually permitted a differential response to practically any and every constraint that is present in the structured visual image. As the opening quotation from Emerson implies, the evolution of the visual system has been *eclectic*. For such a system to grow and develop, therefore, it must possess some especial design. For example, the cumulative character of the evolutionary process would suggest that the basic operations of the present human visual system may still be mediated by a small number of primitive responses, but that the execution and results of these responses have been progressively modified and refined by the piecemeal sensitization of the system to further constraints in the information available to it. As would appear to be the case, such a system would possess almost limitless flexibility and potential for further evolution. At the same time, unlike most complex systems manufactured by human technology, it seems to be an evolutionary prerequisite that it should not become incapable of functioning if even a minor process should fail to operate in the normal manner. As Simon (1962) has pointed out, each subsystem should be capable of functioning independently of—and even in competition with—the others. Before considering these implications further, however, it is instructive to look briefly at the role of the visual system in more recent human development.

## The "Scientific" Role of the Visual System in Recent Human Development

As we have seen, many different complex environments and demands have contributed to the evolution of the human visual system, and this, in turn, has equipped it to play a crucial role in more recent human development over the last 6000 years or so. For scientific cultures, at least, the visual system has been pre-eminent in the accumulation and transmission of knowledge and technology. In turn, the importance of the visual system within this context has encouraged some general attitudes in theorizing about the system itself. Before discussing these, however, it is perhaps useful to illustrate the fundamental importance of vision in the recent scientific development of man.

One instance in which the role of vision has been paramount, for example, is that of astronomy, the study of which is generally associated with the beginnings of a scientific and technological culture. Besides the evident involvement of vision in the observation of distant phenomena, it seems likely that the regularity of the movements of the sun and the stars were largely responsible for the acquisition of an explicit, communicable concept of time, while the orientation and paths of the heavenly bodies seem to have provided man with his early notions of geographical direction, and prompted the development of a simple Euclidean geometry. Of perhaps even greater consequence is the fact that the relative movements of the earth, moon, sun and planets presented man with a publicly accessible problem, which was sufficiently complex to stimulate deliberate scientific theorizing, but in which the phenomena were not characterized by a baffling unpredictability that promised no solution. Although the solution did not emerge for several thousand years, the impetus to observation and the liberation of thought eventually imparted by the theory of Copernicus brought about a permanent revolution in man's whole conception of the physical universe and of his own place in it. From this time on, following the discovery that a given translucent material possesses a constant refractive index, and the use of combined convex and concave lenses to construct the first telescope, man's conception of the universe was continually expanded, articulated and modified. However, until the development of the radio telescope in 1965, almost all the information on which man's understanding of the stellar universe was founded was wholly visual. Even today, the interpretation of galactic evolution still depends upon the perceptual organization of nebulous structures by a visual system that was originally developed merely to discriminate between two different bright-nesses.

The scientific role of vision has also been important at the other end of the scale and, since the seventeenth century, the refractive properties of lenses have been exploited to study the astonishing degrees of structure which are revealed when the images of both organic and inorganic matter are magnified. In particular, the ubiquity of minute structure to which the microscopic studies of Hooke and Leewenhoek first drew attention led, in the space of six or seven generations, to Virchow's formulation of the doctrine that all living matter was composed of cells, and that these were formed by the reproduction of other cells. As Ford remarks, once an understanding of the general structure and role of the cell had been achieved, "at one fell swoop it became obvious how animal and plant species grew and matured, how ova functioned . . . it became obvious how the disease process might function, how man himself was made" (1973, p. 99).

Meanwhile, developments in sciences based on the telescope and micro-scope, and in possibly every other intellectual discipline as well, were affected by another technological innovation which occurred at the begin-ning of the nineteenth century. Following the taking of the first successful photograph by Nicéphore Niépce, the ability to store, duplicate, transmit and analyse images, which accurately reproduced outline, structure, tonal values and colour found a multitude of applications. In microscopy, for example, techniques have been devised to record images formed by otherwise invisible radiations or to register information from radiation harmful to the human eye. Meanwhile, in submarine or extraterrestrial studies, photography is extensively used as a way of gathering detailed and readily assimilable information from an environment which is either inaccessible, or where man himself could not survive.

More recently, one further range of applications involving the minifying of images has emerged. Although originally employed primarily for military intelligence, "remote-sensing" techniques have found a growing number of civilian uses, such as photogrammetry, geologic charting, and agriculture and forestry surveying. It is now widely acknowledged that, at the expense of some loss of unimportant detail, remote-sensed imagery, taken from aircraft or satellites can provide an immediate, synoptic view of an area as a highly condensed, but quickly interpretable visual pattern. Indeed, as Alexander et al. pointed out in a recent review, the potential applications are "as diverse as the scenes that might be photographically recorded while overflying the entire world" (1974, p. 15). The same conclusion would apply to the numerous other techniques now available for obtaining and transforming visual images.

The extension of the visual system by means of the telescope, microscope, camera and remote-sensing platform has clearly given man access to information about processes that were either too distant, too small or too large, too numerous, complex, weak, intense, transitory, protracted, rapid or slow, dangerous, or too inaccessible to observe directly. While many of these technologies have ironically served to emphasize the superior capacity of the human perceptual system itself to process the resulting visual data, what seems of most immediate relevance is that, in all of these applications, the information in question has been acquired as part of a deliberate, usually cooperative, *scientific* activity, i.e. the information is needed for transmission to other individuals, for testing certain published (or communicable) hypotheses, or for storage until some future date. This intimate involvement of the visual system in the generation of scientific knowledge naturally invites us to think of the process of visual perception itself as a kind of prototype of scientific activity. Since the brain appears to take in limited amounts of fallible sensory information from the environment and to extract simple constants, relations, or patterns from it, so, it can be argued, the perceptual system resembles a scientist, who inspects data from a set of experiments and tries to arrive at a hypothesis to account for them, which will be as simple as possible, while still remaining consistent with all the observations. Thus, from Helmholtz onwards, the perceptual system has been regarded as a process of unconscious inference, or as a way of reducing or encoding visual data in the form of a hypothesis. Decisions between rival hypotheses have been compared to optimal statistical decision processes, and those between mutually consistent alternatives as embodying a principle of economy reminiscent of Occam's razor. For example, according to Gregory: "perception is not determined simply by the stimulus pattern; rather it is a dynamic searching for the best interpretation of the available data" (1966, p. 11).

Unfortunately, while this analogy has some suggestive and revealing aspects, there are a number of reasons, both general and specific, for considering that it may be misleading. Unlike the (ideal) scientist, for example, the visual system appears capable of sustaining mutually inconsistent hypotheses, either simultaneously or in quick succession, as happens in the viewing of paradoxical illustrations. Again, unlike the scientist, the visual system does not always appear to employ objective probability as a criterion for deciding between alternative hypotheses (as in the case, for instance, of the Ames' room demonstrations). Furthermore, unlike the scientist, decisions by the visual system between mutually consistent hypotheses of different degrees of parsimony frequently appear to introduce considerable distortion into the original data (e.g. Attneave and Frost, 1969; Vickers, 1971). Meanwhile, in testing between rival hypotheses, biasses and expectations appear to play an important role in perceptual decisions, which appear in turn to be made with a confidence that is at least partly determined by such considerations as the time available. This stands in marked contrast to the ideal statistical testing procedure, where every effort is made to reach unbiassed decisions with a certain predetermined minimum level of confidence.

It would be out of place to argue this view in more detail at this stage, but the reason for mentioning these objections here is to suggest that it may be misguided to look for a simple analogy between the process of individual scientific activity and that of visual perception. For one thing, unlike the scientist, the visual system may not be constrained by an overriding conceptual framework which precludes the maintenance of two contradictory hypotheses. Again, unlike the scientist, the visual system may not be concerned with objective, publicly verifiable truth, but as Hick (1952a) suggests, with *pragmatic* or useful truth, and its criteria of utility may be quite different from those guiding a scientist. For example, time may often be of crucial importance, while the requirement that only significant differences be reported may be irrelevant.

Perhaps the underlying reason that the analogy is misleading is that it involves a comparison between a complete system (the perceptual system) and an individual element (the ideal scientist) of a larger system (the scientific community). Indeed, it may be that a more appropriate comparison would be between the operation of the human perceptual system and the activity of a scientific community. In contrast to their ideal members, for example, scientific communities frequently entertain contradictory hypotheses, and allow bias and expectation to influence the prevailing view. Certainly, unlike the ideal behaviour of their individual members, that of a scientific community tends to be pragmatic, and it is this characteristic above all which seems peculiarly applicable to the process of visual perception.

## A Strategy for Research

Although admittedly general, the considerations outlined in this introductory chapter combine to suggest some constraints on any theory concerning the operation of human visual perception. In the first place, it has been argued that the natural world may be viewed as a multiplicity of processes, each controlled by natural laws, which, in their interaction, give rise to certain probabilistic constraints on the structure of each process. For convenience, these constraints may be classified into those which characterize the formation and maintenance of individual elementary processes, and those which govern the interaction and unification of several processes into a single larger process. Where a structured visual image, embodying these constraints, is available to an observing organism, the structure will be transformed by the geometrical relations between the light source, object and the observer. In addition, this structure may be obscured, fragmented, distorted, or otherwise disturbed by a number of intervening processes, controlled by constraints which are quite unrelated to those responsible for the inherent structure of the object, or to those transformations which specify its topography. A primary function of visual perception, therefore, may be understood as the task of responding differentially to the inherent structure and topography of an object, as detected in the limited and erratic presentation of the optical image reflected from it.

Despite the daunting complexity of such a process, it has been argued that one key to its understanding lies in tracing its evolution from the first differentiating and identifying responses of which the most primitive organisms must have been capable. While such an organism would have responded to only the most gross constraints in its environment, it seems likely that even this behaviour would have been subject to some regulative control. As the organism developed responses to more subtle constraints, it appears probable that its evolution would have consisted of the addition of further primitive response processes, resembling the original ones, but refined by progressive, minute modifications. Just as the ontogeny of an individual tends to recapitulate the evolution of its species, and as successive layers of sedimentation include fossil specimens of progressively greater antiquity, so the human visual system may be expected to embody a succession of progressively refined response subsystems, from the most primitive discrimination up to the most complex and specific recognition. Moreover, since the system has evolved in such a way as to exploit the constraints which operate in the natural world, so we may expect to find that the pattern of these constraints is, to some extent, embedded in the morphology of the perceptual process itself. At the same time, the eclectic addition of responses to more refined constraints, which makes the system so well equipped for its later scientific role, must, at each stage, have presupposed an already self-contained, fully functioning system. This, in turn, suggests that the present visual system may be more usefully thought of as a kind of loose society of similar, but independent, self-regulating individual units, rather than a unified system of interdependent specialized functions, such as is embodied in the ordered subroutines of most computer programmes.

If this general description has any validity, then the question immediately arises as to how it might be developed and tested in more specific ways. One answer seems to be that the least it does is suggest a somewhat different strategy from that which characterizes most current research on visual perception. In the first place, it implies that, if the subsequent evolution of the primitive system embodies the addition of progressively modified structures, which originally carried out simple discriminative and identifying functions, then a useful approach to the understanding of the developed system may be found in the study of the elementary discriminative and identifying capacities which have been retained. In the second place, it suggests that these basic functions must be explicable in terms of some simple process, capable of neurophysiological realization in an organism as elementary as that of Fig. 3. Thirdly, if the system is to survive, we should expect to find that even a simple process such as this could exhibit some adaptability within the lifetime of the organism, while, if it is to evolve, any development should consist of a simple change, such as a linkage into some rudimentary configuration, or a slight modification in the energy changes to which the elementary process is sensitive. Finally, if our theorizing is to capture the versatility of the human visual system, and be comparable in its evolutionary flexibility, it may be preferable to evolve our theorizing from a similar variety of constraints to that to which the system itself has become responsive, rather than to develop ever more accurate hypotheses concerning a limited number of features of the data. This means, for instance, that while the evidence to be considered in this book is primarily behavioural, at times neurophysiological and evolutionary factors will be considered. Such an eclectic process of theory development resembles a procedure of improving pattern recognition through feature testing over a wider sample of instances, rather than through the pursuit of greater precision in matching against a template. Indeed, as is perhaps now apparent, the strategy of theory development to be followed in this book is intended, to some extent, to mimic the evolution and operation of the process of visual perception itself.

# 2

# Early Models of Discrimination

*But it would be terrible if even such a dear old man as this could saddle our Science forever with his patient whimsies . . .*
William James (on Fechner) (1890, *1*, p. 549).

## *Introduction*

It was argued in the introductory chapter that the primitive organism depicted in Fig. 3 must have been capable of carrying out an elementary discrimination upon some single dimension, such as brightness, and that it was unlikely that such a basic adaptation would be lost in its later evolution. Indeed, a similar perceptual achievement is carried out by human beings in countless different contexts in everyday life. The handyman deciding between two shades of grey paint is performing a brightness discrimination, while the child hesitating about which slice of cake to choose is (usually) making some discrimination based on size. In general, any situation, in which an organism responds differently to the greater and the lesser of two stimuli (along whatever dimension they are measured), involves discrimination. However, if we are going to arrive at a satisfactory explanation of the underlying mechanism, then, as has also already been suggested, it seems necessary to try to frame our account in such a way that it is capable of being realized by an organism comparable in simplicity to the one in Fig. 3, as well as by a normally developed human being.

Bearing this constraint in mind, we now turn to look at some of the early systematic attempts to study this process within the field of human experimental psychology. After examining the development of the earliest "classical" model of discrimination as a rationale for the traditional psychophysical methods of determining sensory thresholds, we go on to consider a more recent model, derived from the theory of signal detection, and designed to overcome some of the shortcomings of the classical account. Evidence is then presented for a trade-off between speed and accuracy, which cannot be accommodated within either the classical or the signal detection hypotheses. Two kinds of alternative process are then examined: the first involving decisions based on some integrated function of a number of "inspections" of the sensory information available to the discriminating organism; the second based on an "optional-stopping" process, in which sensory information is not integrated over time, but is repeatedly inspected until some pre-set criterion is fulfilled.

## The Classical Model

As I have emphasized in the preface, the present book attempts to arrive at a unifying theory, rather than to supplant the excellent accounts of traditional theories to be found in such textbooks as Woodworth and Schlosberg (1954) or Corso (1967). Nevertheless, since we shall have frequent recourse to the terms and techniques of traditional psychophysics, it may perhaps save some time and misunderstanding if we begin with a brief résumé of the traditional psychophysical methods, before outlining the classical model and evaluating its usefulness.

### The Traditional Psychophysical Methods

The three basic methods by which the discriminative capacity of human observers have been traditionally measured were first formulated in "Elemente der Psychophysik" published in 1860 by the German physicist, Gustav Theodor Fechner, as a basis for his philosophical views concerning the relations between mind and matter. All three involve the comparison by an observer of a stimulus of variable magnitude with one of a constant or *standard* magnitude. For example, the standard $s$ may be a black, vertical line, similar to the left-hand line in Fig. 4, but 10 cm long and displayed 1 m from an observer, and at right angles to his line of sight. In this case, the experimenter's aim might be to study the ability of the observer to detect differences in length between this standard and another line of variable length $v$, as shown at the right in Fig. 4.

### The Method of Adjustment

The most natural of the traditional procedures is the *method of adjustment* ("reproduction" or "average error") in which the observer himself is free to adjust the variable (or "comparison") stimulus until it appears to be equal to the standard. Usually, the experimenter first sets the variable to a magnitude

S  V

Fig. 4. A typical discrimination display, in which the variable (*v*) is greater than the standard (*s*).

considerably lower than the standard, and the observer increases it gradually until the two appear equal. The experimenter then sets the variable to a value considerably higher than the standard, and the observer decreases it until the two appear equal. Over a series of ascending trials, the values at which the variable is judged equal to the standard can be averaged to provide a mean and standard deviation. Similarly, the descending trials, during which the variable is decreased, can provide a (possibly different) mean and standard deviation. Where these two means do differ, the range of stimulus values between them is termed the *interval of uncertainty (IU)*, and the midpoint of this range is usually taken as the *point of subjective equality (PSE)*. Where the two means are the same, of course, this single value is taken as the *PSE*.

## The Method of Limits

To avoid the problem that different observers tend to make their adjustments at different rates and engage in "backtracking" to varying extents, a second procedure is often preferred, namely, the *method of limits* (or "just noticeable differences"). In this method, the starting point and the size of the increments or decrements in the variable are controlled by the experimenter. At each step in either an ascending or a descending series, the observer reports whether the variable appears "less than", "equal to", or "greater than" the standard, and the experimenter notes the value of the variable at which the observer's response changes from "lesser" (or "greater") to "equal" (or to the converse).

As with the method of adjustment, it is clear that, unless the observer can discriminate perfectly, there will be a range of values of the variable, close to that of the standard, within which he will find some difficulty in reaching a judgment of "lesser" or "greater" and will be likely to say "equal". Such a region of indecision makes it likely (though not necessary) that the mean for ascending trials will differ from that for descending ones. However, even when the observer is forbidden to make "equal" judgments, but must opt for "lesser" or "greater", the means for ascending and descending trials may still turn out to be different. This has generally been "explained" as arising from two kinds of error on the part of the observer. The first of these, the *error of habituation*, is the tendency to persist in saying "lesser" in an ascending (or "greater" in a descending) series of trials. The second, the *error of anticipation*, is the converse tendency to change response too soon.

Because the amounts of error on ascending and descending trials may not be equal, the *PSE* is often found to be different from the value of the standard. If it lies above the standard, there is said to be a positive *constant error*, and, if below, a negative one.

## The Method of Constant Stimuli

A third procedure, designed to reduce the tendency towards errors of habituation or anticipation, is the *method of constant stimuli* (also referred to as the "method of right and wrong cases" or the "frequency method"). In this procedure, each of several values of the variable is presented many times by the experimenter for comparison with the standard, and the frequency of the different responses made by the observer is counted. Usually, the number of different values of the variable is quite small (e.g. between 5 and 11), usually they are chosen symmetrically above and below the standard, and usually they are presented in random order.

## *The Psychometric Function*

Although there are many different ways of analysing the data obtained by these procedures (e.g. Woodworth and Schlosberg, 1954; Guilford, 1954), perhaps the most common, and certainly the most useful for bringing out the concepts of the classical theory, is that of graphical representation. To illustrate this in the case of the method of constant stimuli, let us suppose that the task for an observer is to discriminate between the lengths of two lines similar to those in Fig. 4. When the variable ($v$) is much smaller than the standard ($s$), the relative frequency with which the observer will judge $v$ to be "greater" will usually be low, but will rise to about 50% as $v$ approaches equality with $s$, and become progressively greater as $v$ becomes objectively greater than $s$. As we consider different values of the difference ($v-s$) from large negative values (where $v$ is objectively much smaller than s), up, through zero, to large positive ones (where $v$ is objectively much larger), the relative frequency of each response (e.g. "$V > S$") can be plotted as a function of the value of the stimulus difference ($v$–$s$) judged by the observer. Following Urban (1910), such a curve has generally been termed a *psychometric function*.

## Two–category Judgments

Where an observer is allowed to make only two responses ("$V < S$" or "$V > S$"), then the two psychometric functions will be mirror images of each other, as illustrated in Fig. 5. In this case the *PSE* is defined as the stimulus difference at which we should expect the two responses to be made equally often. It is usually calculated by smoothing the curve, either freehand, or by some statistical curve-fitting method, to find the value of ($v$–$s$) at which 50% of the observer's responses would be of the form "$V > S$" (c.f. Woodworth and Schlosberg, 1954; Guilford, 1954). Since the two response

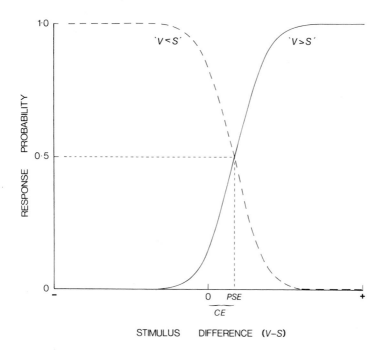

Fig. 5. Idealized psychometric functions for responses of the form "$V > S$" (solid line) and those of the form "$V < S$" (broken lines), plotted as a function of the difference between the hypothesized subjective magnitudes of the variable $V$ and the standard stimulus $S$. The distance from zero to the point of subjective equality (*PSE*) gives a measure of the constant error (*CE*).

curves are symmetrical, it makes no difference whether the *PSE* is calculated on the basis of the "greater" or the "lesser" judgments.

## Three-category Judgments

Where a third response category ("$V = S$") is allowed, then the frequencies of the "greater" and the "lesser" responses are no longer complementary, and their psychometric functions need no longer be symmetrical. Figure 6 shows a family of idealized response curves of the kind that might be expected in an experiment allowing the three categories of judgment. As in the case of a two-category judgment, it is possible to calculate the stimulus difference at which the response "$V > S$" can be expected on 50% of the trials. Similarly, the point at which the converse "lesser" response can be expected on half the trials can also be calculated. However, provided the

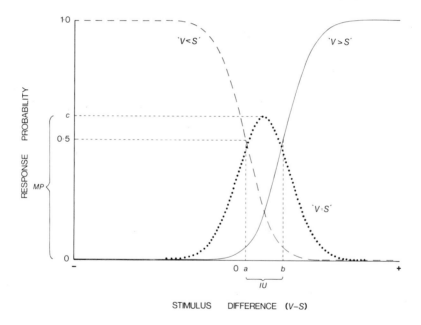

Fig. 6. Idealized psychometric functions when three response categories are employed. Responses of the form "$V > S$" are shown in solid lines, those of the form "$V < S$" in broken lines and those of the form "$V = S$" in dotted lines. The values $a$ and $b$ of the stimulus difference at which 50% of "lesser" and "greater" responses are made denote the respective *PSEs*, with the distance between them representing the interval of uncertainty (*IU*). The height *MP* represents the maximum probability of making an "equal" response. In this case the stimulus difference at which this occurs coincides with the midpoint of the *IU*, but this need not be so if the precision of the "greater" and "lesser" curves is unequal.

observer makes use of the intermediate (or "equal") category, as well as the two extreme categories, then these two points will be different. In the method of constant stimuli the range of $(v-s)$ values between these two points is termed the interval of uncertainty (*IU*), and by analogy with both the method of adjustment and the method of limits, the *PSE* is again taken as the midpoint of this range.

## The Psychometric Function, Thresholds and Noise

From the shape of the psychometric function it is possible to make some inferences about the nature of the underlying discriminative process. For example, if an observer were capable of discriminating perfectly, then we should expect that the psychometric function for responses of the form "$V > S$" should resemble the discontinuous step-function shown in Fig. 7a, irrespective of whether two or three categories of judgment were allowed. It is also possible to suppose that there might be a region of insensitivity around the value of the standard, in which case the response curves would be similar to those in Fig. 7b. Both sets of curves resemble the abrupt discontinuities in response that characterize, for example, the behaviour of many electronic components, particularly those used in digital computers. It is this kind of clear boundary between responses that is implied by the notion of a *limen* or *threshold*, originally derived from Leibniz by Herbart, who defined it as "those limits that an idea seems to overleap in passing from a state of complete inhibition to the state of a real idea" (Boring, 1950, p. 256). The notion is also typified by the all-or-none principle which governs the firing of the afferent nerve fibres, which ultimately provide the means by which sensory information is registered.

Despite these resemblances, however, Pierce and Jastrow found, as early as 1885, that the pattern of empirical response frequencies showed no evidence of the discontinuity implied by the notion of a definite threshold, but instead took the form of a continuous sigmoid curve. Figure 8 shows some similar results, obtained in a later extended study by Brown (1910), using 700 trials at each of 33 different stimulus differences. At least over the steepest part of the function in Fig. 8 there is a continuous, monotonic rise in the relative frequency of "greater" judgments, while the overall curve has a clear sigmoid shape. Although data from subsequent experiments are rarely as complete as these, they are, in general, consistent with this pattern (Urban, 1910; Guilford, 1954; Corso, 1967).

This smooth gradation of response probabilities as a function of objective stimulus difference $(v-s)$ was regarded as a fundamental law of psychophysics as early as Jastrow. According to Jastrow, the errors made at any value of $(v-s)$ could be regarded as "due to lapses of attention, slight

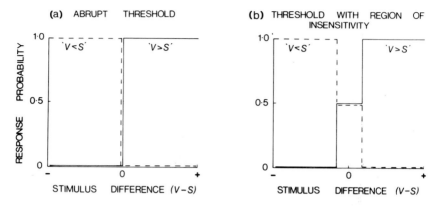

Fig. 7. Theoretically possible psychometric functions. Figure 7a shows the discontinuous function that would be expected in the two-category case if an observer were capable of perfect discrimination. Figure 7b shows the stepwise function that would be expected if an observer possessed a region of insensitivity around zero, but was capable of perfect discrimination outside this region. Responses of the form "$V > S$" are represented by solid lines and those of the form "$V < S$" by broken lines.

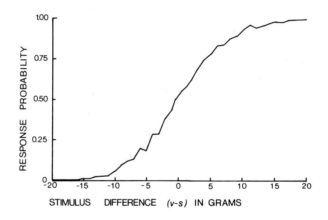

Fig. 8. An empirical psychometric function for responses of the form "$V > S$" obtained in a two-category discrimination study by Brown (1910). (The curve is redrawn from Woodworth and Schlosberg, 1954, p. 216, Fig. 8–10.)

fatigues, and all the other numerous psychological fluctuations that . . . may be said to have the effect of [increasing] the smaller stimulus or [decreasing] the larger" (1888, p. 284). A similar explanation was suggested by Cattell in terms of changes in the conductivity of neural pathways, rhythms in attention and "very numerous irregularities due to fatigue, interest, inhibition, etc." (1893, p. 287). Indeed, by the turn of the century Solomons could allude to "the well known fact of the variability of brain activity under identical stimuli" (1900, p. 234).

More recently, Welford (1965, 1968) has suggested that other central sources of disturbance might include the after-effects of cerebral activity, as well as random variations in the level of background activity due to other ongoing cortical processes. Besides these central variations, the neurophysiological work of Barlow (1956), Kuffler et al. (1957) and Barlow and Levick (1969a, b) has shown that spontaneous nervous activity can be recorded from retinal cells in complete darkness, so that, even at the earliest stages in the visual system, there may be "spurious excitations" or *neural noise*. There is, finally, an irreducible physical variability in any stimulus of nominally constant intensity (Hecht et al., 1942; de Vries, 1956).

## Noise and the Representation of Stimuli

While the vulnerability of the perceived stimulus to disturbance is now generally conceded, it is perhaps less commonly appreciated that the widely accepted description of these effects also originated with Jastrow. At any rate, Jastrow was one of the first to suggest that "the law that regulates the probabilities of the deviations by various degrees from the average . . . is the law expressed by the 'probability curve', which pictures the effect of a very large (strictly infinite) number of small causes, no one of which has of itself any decided influence" (1888, p. 285). Although attempts have been made subsequently to distinguish between the effects of different sources of noise (e.g. Gregory, 1956; Treisman, 1964), and although it can be argued that the distribution of effect might be more appropriately characterized by a Poisson distribution, Jastrow's original suggestion (that the combined effects arising from a multiplicity of independent sources of random variation should be closely approximated by a normal curve) has come to be generally accepted (Cattell, 1893; Boring, 1917; Tanner and Swets, 1954). According to this view, the sensory representations of two stimuli of different physical magnitudes can be described by two normal distributions of sensory effect, as illustrated in Fig. 9.

According to Thurstone (1927a, b), fluctuations in sensory effect occur *from one judgment to the next*, and each judgment is a function of the momentary "discriminal difference" $(V-S)$ between $V$ and $S$ on that trial. Where the original distributions of sensory effect are uncorrelated, have equal variances and are normal (as in Fig. 9), then, over a *series* of trials it can then be shown (e.g. Hays, 1963, p. 315) that the distribution of $(V-S)$ differences should also be normal, and should have a mean $\overline{(V-S)}$ equal to

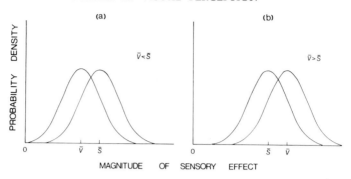

Fig. 9. Hypothetical probability density distributions of the magnitude of sensory effect corresponding to two stimuli $v$ and $s$. The distributions are normal, with means $\bar{V}$ and $\bar{S}$ and $\sigma_V = \sigma_S$. Figure 9a shows the case where $\bar{V} < \bar{S}$ and Fig. 9b the case where $\bar{V} > \bar{S}$.

$(\bar{V}-\bar{S})$, and a standard deviation $\sigma_{(V-S)} = \sqrt{2\sigma^2_V} = \sqrt{2\sigma^2_S}$ as illustrated in Fig. 10. (Where the distributions corresponding to $V$ and $S$ have unequal variances, then the value of $\sigma_{(V-S)}$ should be given by $\sqrt{\sigma^2_V + \sigma^2_{S'}}$ and, where they are also correlated, by the expression $\sqrt{\sigma^2_V + \sigma^2_S - 2r\sigma_V\sigma_{S'}}$ where $r$ is the coefficient of correlation. For the present, however, it is sufficient—and more convenient—to assume that the variances are equal, and that the sensory effects corresponding to the objective stimuli $v$ and $s$ are uncorrelated.)

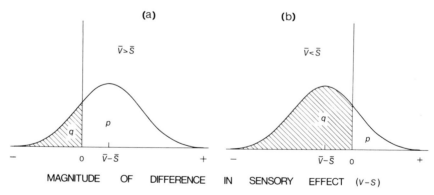

Fig. 10. Hypothetical probability density distributions of $(V-S)$ differences in the magnitude of sensory effect arising from two stimuli $v$ and $s$. Figure 10a illustrates the case where $\bar{V} > \bar{S}$ and Fig. 10b the case where $\bar{V} < \bar{S}$. The probability of a postive stimulus difference corresponds to the area $p$, while that of a negative difference corresponds to the shaded portion $q$, with $p + q = l$.

## The Phi–Gamma Hypothesis of Classical Psychophysics

The assumption that any stimulus of nominally fixed objective intensity is represented in the nervous system by a distribution of sensory effect, which varies randomly over time, has had profound consequences for the development of hypotheses about the processes of discrimination and identification. In particular, as outlined below in the so-called phi–gamma hypothesis of classical psychophysics, it has been used to explain both the shape and the steepness of the psychometric function obtained in two-category studies.

### The Phi–Gamma Hypothesis

If we accept the view summarized in the last section concerning the representation of sensory information, then the simplest hypothesis concerning the nature of the discrimination process is to suppose that, whenever the discriminal difference $(V–S)$ on a particular trial turns out to be negative, the observer decides that $V$ is less than $S$; otherwise, if the discriminal difference is positive, he decides that $V$ is greater than $S$. On this hypothesis, the probability $\varphi$ of making a response of the form "$V > S$" to a given stimulus difference $(v–s)$ corresponds to the (unshaded) proportion $p$ of the distribution of $(V–S)$ differences shown in Fig. 10, where the mean perceived stimulus difference $\gamma$ is measured in units of $\sigma_{(V–S)}$. As shown by Boring (1917), changes in the mean $\overline{(V–S)}$ will give rise to corresponding changes in $\varphi$, with phi function of gamma taking the form of a cumulative normal ogive.

The suggestion that psychometric data can be described in this way, though latent in the work of Fechner and Mueller, was first clearly formulated by Urban (1910). While Urban advocated the *phi–gamma hypothesis* because it gave a closer fit to empirical data than another arctan function with similar properties, it was Boring (1917) who girst gave the hypothesis a clear rationale. More recently, Guilford (1954) has given an account of various methods for calculating the value of $\sigma_{(v–s)}$, in terms of the physical units in which the stimuli are measured, using the proportion of responses of one kind made over a range of objective stimulus differences.

### Possible Restrictions and Alternatives

As Urban (1910) pointed out, and Thurstone (1928) has argued in detail, there might be some restriction on the generality of the phi–gamma hypothesis in cases where the magnitude of sensory effect ($V$ or $S$) is not linearly related to objective stimulus difference ($v$ or $s$). Where Weber's law holds, for example, a difference of 5 units between an $s$ of 100 and a $v$ of 95 will be more noticeable than the same difference between an $s$ of 100 and a $v$ of 105. Under such conditions, Thurstone points out, the psychometric function for the "greater" judgments should be positively skewed. This skewness should be removed, however, if empirical response frequencies are plotted against logarithmic values of the objective stimulus difference.

Some evidence for this modified phi–log–gamma hypothesis was presented by Fritz (1930), who claimed that data from Woodrow (1928) were given a closer visual fit by a phi–log–gamma function than by a normal ogive, and by Lufkin (1928), who argued that an asymmetrical Gram–Charlier frequency function gave a closer fit to Urban's data. Nevertheless, no direct quantitative comparison was actually provided by Fritz, whose graphical presentation seems consistent with Lufkin's conclusion that the normal ogive fitted the data almost as well as any type of skewed curve. In agreement with this, Guilford found a slightly, "but only slightly", better fit to a normal ogive when psychometric data were plotted on a logarithmic scale (1954, p. 146).

These findings reinforce the view that it is difficult to generalize, since the scale along which we measure physical events is to some extent arbitrary. They also support Thurstone's own contention that, when the Weber fraction is small (e.g. 0·02), the error in fitting the phi–gamma curve will also be small and will become serious only when the Weber fraction is larger (e.g. around 0·2). While a figure of 0·2 might be expected for taste, it is some 10 times higher than would be expected for judgments in the visual modality (Boring et al., 1948, p. 268).

Further support for the view that Thurstone's restriction is not important in this context is also to be found in a study of 630 differential thresholds by Fernberger (1949), which found no systematic difference between values of $\sigma_{(v-s)}$, calculated for the two extreme responses. Similarly, there seems to be no unequivocal evidence that the psychometric function shows consistent departures from the normal ogive (Corso, 1967). For the present, therefore, we seem to be justified in regarding the assumptions of normality, constant variance and a linear relation between objective stimulus difference and sensory effect as satisfactory approximations for the restricted range of values used in traditional determinations of a psychophysical threshold.

## Classical Measures of Discriminative Ability

As is perhaps now evident, the essence of the classical model of discrimination is contained in the phi–gamma hypothesis, which was developed to account for the pattern of errors made by an observer in discriminating between two stimuli according to one of the traditional psychophysical procedures. Because proneness to error was considered to be the main factor limiting discriminability, a considerable effort was expended by classical psychophysicists in an attempt to find some feature of the pattern of correct and incorrect responses which would provide a useful characterization of an observer's discriminative ability. To a great extent, therefore, the adequacy of the classical model may be judged by its success in providing a satisfactory rationale for adopting one particular measure, rather than another, as an index of discriminative capacity. It is with this in mind that we turn now to examine some of the traditional measures of the differential threshold.

## The Point of Subjective Equality

One of the simplest measures that can be taken from the psychometric curve is the point of subjective equality (PSE). Where only two responses are allowed, as in Fig. 5, this point marks the stimulus difference at which the observer can be expected to make 50% of "greater" responses and 50% of "lesser". If, following the phi–gamma hypothesis, normal ogives are fitted to the data, then the PSE is given either by interpolation on one curve or by the point of intersection of both curves.

According to the phi–gamma hypothesis, an equal proportion of "greater" and "lesser" responses will be made only when the sensory effect of the variable is on average equal to that of the standard, so that the mean of the distribution of $(V–S)$ differences is zero. In the absence of any factors influencing the observer to respond in a particular way, therefore, we should expect the PSE to coincide with an objective stimulus difference of zero. This, of course, suggests that the measure would be inappropriate as an index of discriminative capacity, since it leads us to expect the same value for all observers. In fact, the PSE rarely coincides with the zero stimulus difference. As we have already seen, if the PSE lies above the zero stimulus difference, there is said to be a positive constant error, and, if below, a negative one. These constant errors have traditionally been interpreted as a measure of biassing factors in the observer towards making one response rather than the other (Jastrow, 1888; Thurstone, 1948; Woodworth and Schlosberg, 1954). Until recently, however, no explicit way of accounting for this interpretation had been suggested in terms of the classical model of discrimination.

A further difficulty arises when we consider what happens to the PSE when an observer is allowed to make a third, intermediate category of response, such as "$V = S$", or "$V$ is like $S$". As is illustrated in Fig. 6, such a situation can give rise to two separate PSEs, for which no theoretical counterparts in the classical model exist.

## The Interval of Uncertainty and the Maximum Probability of an Intermediate Response

When three categories of response are allowed and two *PSE*s do occur, then, as is also shown in Fig. 6, there will be a range of stimulus differences between the two *PSE*s which is termed the interval of uncertainty (*IU*). The size of this interval naturally suggests itself as a measure of the readiness of an observer to give an intermediate judgment of "equal" or "like". If we further assume with Urban (1910) that the extent to which an observer makes "equal" responses is determined by his discriminative capacity, then, as Urban suggests, a good measure of the "accuracy of sense perception" should be provided by the size of the *IU* (or by any fixed proportion of that quantity). A second possible measure, which, as is illustrated in Fig. 12, is logically independent, but which Urban (1910) found to be perfectly correlated with the *IU*, is the maximum probability (*MP*) of an intermediate judgment (Fig. 6).

Unfortunately, while either the *IU* or the *MP* may, under certain conditions, be a valid indication of an observer's preference for an inter-mediate category of judgment, it is not clear on the classical approach that this should be so in general. To begin with, the classical account does not specify a mechanism by which "equal" responses eventuate. Instead, "equal" responses are often lumped together with "doubtful" ones under a general heading of "intermediate". However, it is not difficult to think of experiments where this identification would obviously be implausible (for example, where half the stimulus pairs are known by the observer to be objectively equal, and where the other pairs are clearly discriminable). As in the case of the constant error, the absence of an explicit theoretical account of the making of (and preference for) judgments of equality makes it impossible to interpret either the *IU* or the *MP* as unambiguous, alternative indices of the preference for an intermediate response.

Even if either the *IU* or the *MP* could be accepted as a valid measure of an observer's preference for an intermediate response, this preference might nevertheless be quite unrelated to his discriminative capacity. For example, in opposition to Urban, George (1917), argued that the inclusion of an intermediate category simply made it possible for an observer to adopt varying attitudes towards the task, while Thomson (1920) also argued that there may be a willingness or reluctance to give "equal" judgments, which is quite independent of an observer's discriminative capacity. According to Thomson, an assertive observer with poor discriminative ability could achieve an *IU* or *MP* of zero by never making intermediate responses, while a hesitant observer with fine discriminative power might produce a much higher measure simply through a greater tendency to respond "equal".

In agreement with this view, Angell (1907) was the first to speculate that a general tendency towards using or avoiding the intermediate category might be linked to a difference between "impulsive" and "deliberative" temperaments, rather than to discriminative ability. He also found that the frequency of intermediate judgments seemed to increase as a direct function both of the time spent on the task and of the range of stimulus differences. Even more strikingly, Fernberger (1914, 1931) found that the proportion of "like" judgments could be controlled quite precisely by instructions, and he suggested that this subjective factor constituted one of the main problems for psychophysics.

## The Coefficient of Precision

According to the phi–gamma hypothesis, the psychometric function obtained in a two-category task, employing the method of constant stimuli, should be accurately described by an ogive corresponding to the cumulative proportions of a normal curve, with mean $\mu_{(v-s)}$ and standard deviation $\sigma_{(v-s)}$. Several methods for calculating $\sigma_{(v-s)}$ have been developed (e.g. Guilford, 1954), and following the original work of Fechner (1966), either the measure $\sigma_{(v-s)}$ itself or the coefficient of precision $h(=1/1 \cdot 41\sigma_{(v-s)})$ have frequently been suggested as an index of discriminative capacity. Since, according to the classical model, the empirical value of $\sigma_{(v-s)}$ obtained under these conditions should correspond to the value of $\sigma_{(V-S)}$ (i.e. to the standard deviation of the underlying distribution of "discriminal differences"), the rationale seems clear and the interpretation plausible. The value of the related measure of precision $h$ will of course be inversely related to the extent of the supposed variability of the distribution of $(V-S)$ differences, and different degrees of precision (Fig. 11) can be taken to reflect differences in the noise which acts as a fundamental factor limiting discriminative capacity. As argued by Solomons, the index $\sigma_{(v-s)}$ "simply measures the range of this variability" (1900, p. 235).

Unfortunately for the simplicity of this interpretation, while the measure $\sigma_{(v-s)}$ appears to provide a useful measure of sensitivity, and while the constant error can be regarded as a measure of some bias towards making one response or the other, there is no element in the classical model which represents variations in bias and can explain how it operates. This deficiency is particularly serious in situations (such as those studied with the method of limits) where errors of anticipation and habituation may be of considerable magnitude. It is true that the effect of constant errors has not seemed so severe in studies employing the method of constant stimuli, due perhaps to a tendency by the observer to "keep his proportions of 'greater' and 'lesser' judgments relatively constant under changing conditions" (Guilford, 1954,

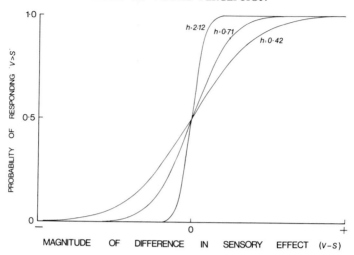

Fig. 11. Cumulative normal ogives, representing the proportion of positive $(V–S)$ differences as a function of the mean difference $(\overline{V–S})$ in sensory effect. The three curves show how the precision $h$ increases from 0·42 through 0·71 up to 2·12 as the value of $\sigma_{(V–S)}$ is reduced from 1·67 through 1·0 to 0·33.

p. 149), as well as to a deliberately designed imperviousness of the method to the effects of such non-sensory variables as order of testing (Clark *et al.*, 1967). Nevertheless, in the absence of a theoretical explanation for bias, it is no longer possible to assume, as is generally done, that bias affects only the positions of the psychometric curves along the scale of $(v–s)$ differences, but leaves their precision unchanged.

When only two categories of judgment are allowed, of course, the two psychometric functions are miror images of each other, and only one value of $\sigma_{(v–s)}$ need be calculated. However, as with the *PSE*, two independent measures of $\sigma_{(v–s)}$ may be calculated when the observer is allowed to make an intermediate response. The most straightforward solution would seem to be to average them, as was done by Culler (1926). However, when this was done, Culler found that the average value of $\sigma_{(v–s)}$ for the "greater" and "lesser" ogives in a three-category task was lower than the value for the same task when only two categories were allowed. On the assumption that threshold values should be as low as possible, he argued that the observer should be allowed to use three categories of response.

With the exception of Fernberger (1930), who argued for an experimental programme to determine the influences affecting "equal" responses, and of Kellogg (1930), who considered three-category judgments to be slightly more reliable in auditory work, most other workers have disagreed with Culler concerning the use of three categories. For example, Jastrow (1888) and Boring (1920) both argued that the only sure way of controlling variations in the tendency to make intermediate judgments was to exclude them altogether. In a similar vein, Thurstone considered that the use of a third category "might give an objective index of some characteristic of temperament [of the observer] . . . but not of his limen" (1948, p. 137), while Guilford concluded that "experience seems to show . . . that, for most purposes, two-category data are best" (1954, p. 140).

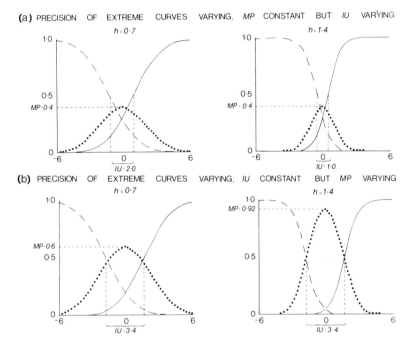

Fig. 12. Hypothetical psychometric functions for the three-category case. Responses of the form "$V > S$" are represented by solid lines, those of the form "$V < S$" by broken lines and those of the form "$V = S$" by dotted lines. Figure 12a shows how the $IU$ decreases as the coefficient of precision $h$ is increased, whilst holding $MP$ constant. Figure 12b shows how the $MP$ increases as $h$ is increased, whilst keeping $IU$ constant.

The controversy over the use of two or three categories of response is clearly symptomatic of the more general difficulties faced by the classical model in dealing with judgments of equality. Some of the more serious of these difficulties may be illustrated with a few examples, in which, for the sake of simplicity, it is assumed that both the "greater" and the "lesser" curves can be described by normal ogives of equal precision. When these restrictions are imposed, it follows that, if the $MP$ is held constant, and the precision of both the "greater" and "lesser" curves increased, then (contrary to Urban's implication) the $IU$ will decrease (Fig. 12a). Since the $MP$ has been held constant, the possibility therefore arises that the $IU$ may, in these circumstances, reflect changes in discriminative capacity rather than is bias. Conversely, if the $IU$ is held constant (Fig. 12b), then an increase in the precision of both extreme curves must necessarily result in an increase in the $MP$, and give rise to a similar problem. In each case, it seems that, while measures such as the $IU$, $MP$, or the constant error can be clearly defined and easily measured, the absence of an underlying theoretical referent leaves their interpretation uncertain. Until this is supplied, it is not possible to attempt an explanation of their significance and interrelationships, nor to account for Culler's finding that empirical measures of $\sigma_{(v-s)}$ derived from two-category tasks appear to be higher than those obtained in experiments which employ an intermediate response.

## An Explanation of Response Bias and Intermediate Judgments by Signal Detection Theory

Taken as a whole, the model of sensory discrimination outlined in the last four sections is "classical", not only in the sense of being traditional, but also in the sense that it offers an apparently simple, economical and integrated account of a basic perceptual judgment. The model is also attractive insofar as it seems capable of being realized by an organism as elementary as the one contemplated in Fig. 3.

Despite its appeal, however, the classical model suffers from a number of critical limitations. As we have seen, the most serious of these appears to be that there is no theoretical representation for bias on the part of an observer, nor any theoretical mechanism for the making of (and preference for) intermediate judgments. That these problems are not purely conceptual is demonstrated by Festinger's finding (1943a) that the $PSE$ was shifted upwards when observers were required, under "constant error" instructions, to guard against making "greater" responses incorrectly, and downwards when observers were told to be careful not to make "lesser" responses incorrectly. Nor are the difficulties confined to the process of discrimination: as is documented in Chapter 5, analogous problems arise in the traditional measurement of the absolute threshold, where their consequences are even more severe.

Indeed, it was in order to overcome these difficulties as they arose in the context of the absolute threshold, that Tanner and Swets (1954) developed the *theory of signal detection*, in which a measure of the observer's bias to make one or the other response is given a clear theoretical distinction from his sensitivity. As has already been emphasized, it is not the intention of this book to add to the many available accounts of established psychophysical procedures, and the reader seeking a detailed exposition of the theory may consult any one of several sources (e.g. Swets *et al.*, 1961; Hake and Rodwan, 1966; Green and Swets, 1966; Corso, 1967; McNicol, 1972). However, with the exception of the paper by Treisman and Watts (1966), the application of the theory to the study of discrimination has received less attention. It may therefore be useful to give a brief outline of their approach.

## A Signal Detection Model of Discrimination

The analysis proposed by Treisman and Watts (1966, pp. 443–444) is in fact very similar to the classical model, but instead of supposing that the proportion of "greater" and "lesser" responses is determined by a fixed boundary or "watershed" between positive and negative signal differences, they suggest that the observer is free to adopt, as a *cutoff*, any particular magnitude of positive or negative stimulus difference (Fig. 13).

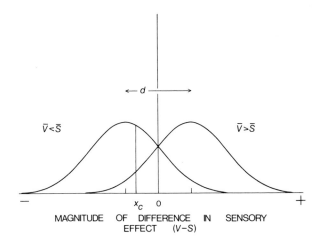

Fig. 13. Hypothetical probability density distribution of subjective $(V-S)$ differences consistent with a signal detection approach. The distribution with mean less than zero corresponds to the case where $\bar{V} < \bar{S}$, while that with a mean greater than zero corresponds to the case where $\bar{V} > \bar{S}$. Location of the cutoff $x_c$ above or below zero will produce bias in favour of one or the other response, leaving the discriminability $d$ (the distance between the two means) unaltered.

According to the general theory, the exact position of this cutoff would in principle be affected by an observer's knowledge of the *a priori* probabilities of the alternative responses, and of the distributions of sensory effect arising from the stimuli, as well as by the values and costs of making each response correctly or incorrectly. However, most experiments on discrimination have been deliberately designed to keep the *a priori* probabilities of the two responses equal, to balance the values and costs of the alternative responses and to make it impossible for an observer to know the distribution of sensory effect appropriate for any trial. Under these circumstances, there-fore, it is more realistic (and simpler) to think of the cutoff as corresponding to a particular value of perceived stimulus difference $(V-S)$ (as portrayed in Fig. 13), rather than strictly in terms of the value of a ratio between the likelihood that a particular difference might arise from the one situation (e.g. where $v$ is objectively greater than $s$) and that of the converse. Where the *a priori* probabilities of the responses are equal and the values and costs are balanced, we should expect an unbiassed observer to adopt a perceived stimulus difference of zero as his cutoff. In this case, the model is practically identical to the classical one.

## Bias

Where there is some biassing factor at play, then the cutoff may be shifted upwards or downwards. If only two responses are permitted, the position of the cutoff will coincide with the *PSE*. As shown by Treisman and Watts (and indeed implied by the phi–gamma hypothesis), a change in the relation between the cutoff and the mean of the distribution of perceived $(V-S)$ differences will shift only the *PSE*, leaving the precision of the psychometric curves unaltered. Thus the distance between the cutoff and a perceived stimulus difference of zero constitutes the exact theoretical counterpart to the constant error of classical psychophysics.

## Three-category Judgments

Where an observer is allowed to make "equal" responses, this intermediate category can be accounted for by supposing that the observer adopts not one but two cutoffs (Fig. 14). Stimulus differences falling below the lower cutoff give rise to "lesser" responses, those falling above the upper to "greater" and those between the two result in judgments of "equal". As in the case of two-category judgments, the positions of the cutoffs correspond to the respective *PSEs* for the psychometric functions of the "greater" and "lesser" judgments, with the *MP* of the "equal" responses lying midway between them along the *IU*. As again in the case of two-category judgments, the precision of the "greater" and "lesser" psychometric functions is affected only by the variability $\sigma_{(V-S)}$ in the underlying distribution of stimulus differences, so that changes in the positions of the cutoffs shift the extreme psychometric function upward or downward, but leave their precision unaltered. Finally, as the cutoffs are varied, the *MP* varies directly with the *IU*, as was found by Urban (1910), and is illustrated in Fig. 15.

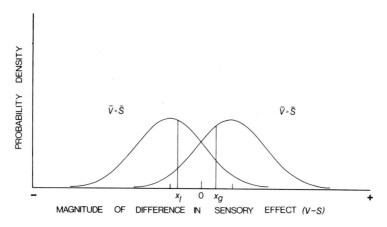

Fig. 14. Signal detection conceptualization appropriate for three-category discrimination.

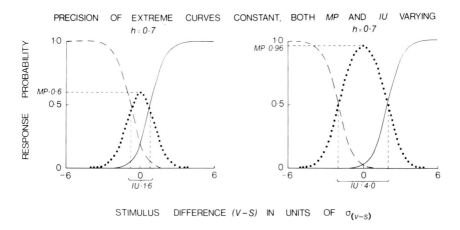

Fig. 15. Hypothetical psychometric functions for the three-category case predicted with a signal detection approach. Responses of the form "$V > S$" are represented by solid lines, those of the form "$V < S$" by broken lines and those of the form "$V = S$" by dotted lines. The figure shows how *IU* and *MP* both increase as the "greater" and "lesser" psychometric functions slide apart along the dimension of stimulus difference (*V–S*), whilst keeping the coefficient of precision *h* constant.

Besides giving a theoretical referent for variation in bias, the signal detection model clearly provides a plausible mechanism for the making of intermediate judgments. Moreover, this account seems to be in harmony with Solomon's insight (1900) that two stimuli must differ by more than the range of the variability in their sensory effect if the difference between them is to be detected with any certainty. Attractive though this conceptualization is, however, it leaves out of consideration one further aspect of discriminatory judgments, which has recently benefited from a renewal of interest and a recognition of its importance. To this we now turn.

## The Speed-Accuracy Trade-off

We have seen that, on both the classical model of sensory discrimination and on the one derived from signal detection theory, the precision of the psychometric curve is interpreted as an index of the discriminative capacity of an observer, with the implication that this in turn is determined by an inherent variability in the sensory representation of stimuli, and therefore constitutes a basic and constant factor limiting performance. As such, the measure $h$ (or $\sigma_{(v-s)} = 1/1\cdot41h$) should remain unaffected by changes in the observer's attitude towards a discrimination task, or by the time he takes to reach a judgment (within reasonable limits). These, of course, are empirical questions, on which there is now a considerable body of evidence, some of which we shall now examine.

### Accuracy and Time

Evidence that the slope of the psychometric curves may indeed depend upon the time taken by an observer was first presented by Garrett (1922). In an experiment measuring the differential threshold for lifted weights by the method of constant stimuli, Garrett found that values of the 75% threshold (averaged over the two psychometric curves) fell as the time allowed for each comparison was increased from 1·0, through 1·5, to 2·0 seconds, after which they rose again. Since the averaging procedure cancels out the effect of any constant error, these findings imply that the related measure $\sigma_{(v-s)}$ would also decrease as a function of the time spent judging the stimuli, at least up to periods of approximately 2·0 seconds (which is about the maximum time normally taken when no emphasis on speed is introduced by the experimenter). A similar improvement in accuracy was also found by Garrett in two further experiments on comparison of line lengths as viewing time was increased from 0·5 to 2·0, and from 0·2 to 2·5 seconds.

## Effects of Instructions

In an experiment which seems to be interpretable in very similar terms, Festinger (1943b) studied the effects of different sets of instructions on the errors made and on the time taken to respond, in a two-category study (again using the method of constant stimuli) of discrimination between the lengths of two simultaneously presented vertical lines. Festinger found that the precision of the psychometric functions for all five observers increased as the stress in instructions was changed from one of speed, through "usual" instructions (implying a compromise), to one emphasizing accuracy. He also found that, for all five observers, the rate at which mean response time increased from the largest to the smallest stimulus difference was lowest under instructions emphasizing speed and highest for those stressing accuracy.

Taken together, these two sets of findings suggest that an observer can somehow counteract the variability inherent in the internal representation of stimulus differences, but only at a cost of taking more time on average over his judgments (up to a possible limit of around 2·0 seconds). Supporting evidence for this view has also been obtained in a number of choice reaction tasks. For example, Howell and Kriedler (1963) and Fitts (1966) found that groups of observers under instructions to be accurate produced less errors, but had longer mean response times than others for whom the emphasis was on speed. Similarly, Pachella and Pew (1968) found that the lower the mean response time for a group of observers on a particular session, the higher was their proportion of errors.

Some evidence for the view that differences in performance between individual observers may also be at least partly explained by differences in the compromise adopted between speed and accuracy has already been obtained (Vickers et al., 1971). In our experiment, observers were asked to decide which of two regularly flashing lamps (one red and one blue) was set to come on more frequently. It was found that, when the times taken by each observer to make correct responses were averaged over all five sessions, there was an exact inverse correspondence between the rank orders of the mean response times and the corresponding total numbers of errors made. Observers could therefore be ordered from the fastest and most erratic to the slowest and most accurate.

In addition, when the total number of errors made by each of the five observers at each session was compared with the corresponding mean time for correct responses, there was a highly significant negative average rank correlation, whether data were averaged over sessions or over observers. Finally, when all 25 error totals were plotted together against the corresponding mean times for correct responses, the points were well fitted by a

single curve (Fig. 16), with highly significant linear and quadratic components and an appreciable, but not significant, cubic component.

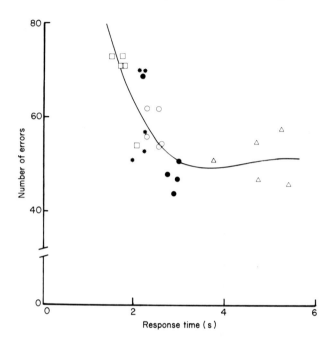

Fig. 16. Empirical speed–accuracy trade-off obtained by Vickers *et al.* (1971).
Different symbols denote mean data for each of 5 sessions by each of 5 observers.
The coefficients of the fitted third degree polynomial are 155·2, −0·76, 17·7 and
−1·3.

## A Speed-Accuracy Trade-off

Taken together, these three sets of findings suggest three main conclusions:

(i) Although there are undoubtedly important differences in the variability of the underlying distributions of sensory effect, our results (Vickers
*et al.*, 1971) suggest that differences in discrimination performance between
one observer and another may also be due to different compromises
adopted by each between accuracy and speed.

(ii) Variations from one session to another in the performance of an
individual observer can also be explained in terms of each observer's ability
to vary this compromise, either in response to the time allowed for
judgment or as a result of instructions.

(iii) When considered together, all our data (Vickers *et al.*, 1971) can be fitted by a single function. This suggests that, at least within the bounds of our kind of experiment (where the probability that an observer will encounter a particular stimulus event could be controlled quite precisely), the differences between the fast and the slow sessions of an individual observer are analogous to the differences between a fast observer and another slower one, and can be explained by supposing a *single underlying continuum* of differences in the compromise adopted between speed and accuracy.

Over the years a number of attempts have been made to characterize the form of this *speed–accuracy trade-off* in perceptual discrimination. For example, Philip (1936) carried out a painstaking series of studies, in which observers were required to discriminate between two sets of rhomboid perforations in a strip moving at different speeds, by tapping each "target" perforation of one kind through a viewing window. When the number of incorrectly tapped perforations was subtracted from those correctly tapped, it was found that the number of correct taps remaining (expressed as a proportion of the number of targets shown) bore a direct ogival relation to the time taken by the strip to move past the window. Similar results were obtained, both overall and at each level of discriminability, in a later experiment by Philip (1947), in which observers were required to discriminate between the relative frequencies of differently coloured dots, exposed tachistoscopically for five different durations ranging from 133 up to 668 ms.

As a result of Philip's earlier results and other indirectly related findings, Thurstone (1937) proposed that, with stimulus difference held constant, the relation between the time taken to make a judgment and its probability of being correct should be described by a normal ogive. However, in spite of the abundant evidence of a close relation between the time taken to make a discrimination and the accuracy of the eventual judgment, and despite suggestions of a similar relation in the case of absolute thresholds, little theoretical attention was paid to the speed–accuracy trade-off until the work of Hick (1952b) stimulated the theoretical and experimental analysis of choice reaction times. Nevertheless, within the context of discrimination, the implications of such a trade-off are of far-reaching significance, as soon becomes evident when an attempt is made to reconcile the effects with the signal detection model.

## Fixed Sample Decision Models

The major implication of the speed–accuracy trade-off for a theoretical account of the discrimination process is that an observer's performance seems to be open to influence by two separate subjective factors. Besides showing differences in *bias*, the observer seems capable of making judgments with varying degrees of *caution*. While bias differences should show up on the signal detection model as shifts in the position of the psychometric function along the dimension of stimulus differences, variations in caution should change the precision of the function and, on the signal detection model, would be indistinguishable from changes in the apparent sensitivity of the observer.

## Fixed Sample Models

In order to account for such an unbiassed improvement in accuracy, it seems that we must assume that an observer is somehow capable of adopting some strategy for increasing his sensitivity. A number of suggestions have been put forward as to how he might achieve this.

### Thomson's Urn Model

A solution to the problem seems to have been first proposed in a little known paper by Thomson (1920), which nevertheless has a claim to being the first statistical decision model of psychophysical judgment. Although Thomson's assumptions regarding sensory effect differ somewhat from those of Thurstone (1927a), their main import can be preserved if we continue to suppose that two stimuli give rise to a distribution of differences (as was shown in Fig. 10). If magnitude of stimulus difference is not taken into account, we can then assume, with Thomson, that the main sensory factors determining a judgment are the proportion $p$ of positive differences and the proportion $q = (1 - p)$ of negative differences. Where Thomson's *urn model* differs from the two we have examined so far is in its underlying assumption that the distribution of simulus differences is not a distribution over a series of separate trials, but *over successive instants within the duration of a single judgment*. This means that, instead of basing his decision upon a single observation of the perceived stimulus difference $(V-S)$, an observer might base it upon a number of observations $n$, with the value of $n$ varying with the degree of caution of the observer. In other ways, Thomson's account resembles the signal detection model, with changes in bias accounted for by making the "points of division" into the three response categories coincide with different values of the proportions of positive and negative observations included in a sample of $n$ observations.

### Crossman's Model

In a much later paper, which did a great deal to stimulate a renewal of experimental and theoretical interest in discrimination times, Crossman

(1955) put forward a similar proposal, namely, that the observer might make a series of observations of the stimulus differences, taking magnitude also into account, and average them. According to this hypothesis, the distributions in Fig. 10 would be replaced by sampling distributions of means (Hays, 1963, p. 193) (Fig. 17). As Crossman pointed out, their standard deviations (and hence the proportion of incorrect responses) should decrease as a function of the square root of $n$ (cf. Hays, 1963, pp. 202–203). If we also suppose with Crossman that each observation takes a constant time, and that observations are made at a steady rate, then the discriminability $d$ (corresponding to the difference in units of $\sigma_{(V-S)}$ between the means of the two distributions in Fig. 17) should increase as a linear function of the square root of $n$ or of time (cf. Green et al., 1957; Swets et al., 1959; Taylor et al., 1967). Crossman has also gone on to suggest that an observer might adjust the value of $n$ (or of time) so as to maintain a fixed proportion of errors.

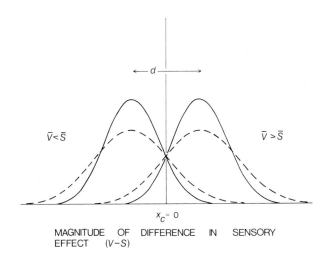

MAGNITUDE OF DIFFERENCE IN SENSORY EFFECT $(V-S)$

Fig. 17. Hypothetical probability density distributions of subjective $(V-S)$ differences when $\bar{V} > \bar{S}$, and when $\bar{V} < \bar{S}$. The broken lines represent distributions based on single observations, while solid lines denote distributions of the means of several observations. Increasing the size of the sample produces an increase in the discriminability $d$ of the two alternatives.

Similar proposals have been put forward a number of times. For example, Schouten and Bekker (1967) have suggested a *perceptual focussing* model, similar to a *confusion* model, previously suggested by Hammerton (1959), according to which the discriminability between two stimuli is determined by the area of overlap between their sensory representations. Schouten and Bekker further assume that discriminability increases as an exponential function of time and suggest that the observer attempts to keep his mean response time constant, accepting a higher likelihood of error when the time he takes falls short of this. As with Crossman's model and the urn process suggested by Thomson, the assumption that an observer can adapt the number of observations (or the time taken) to suit the overall difficulty of a task, or to meet the requirements for speed, allows us to incorporate the notion of a precisely quantifiable speed–accuracy trade-off into the signal detection model.

## Difficulties with a Fixed Sample Model

It would, of course, be possible to derive theoretical functions for various fixed-sample versions of the signal detection process, to relate the proportion of errors made to the time taken and to compare this relation with empirical results. However, a large number of experimental findings suggest that, irrespective of the outcome of such a comparison, models in which the observer is assumed to base a series of judgments upon a fixed number of observations, or upon a fixed error rate, are somehow wrong in principle. The difficulty is that, when the objective difference between two stimuli is varied randomly from trial to trial, there is no way in which an observer can predetermine a value for $n$ so as to spend a time commensurate with the difficulty of each discrimination and thereby maintain a fixed proportion of errors, irrespective of the size of the stimulus difference.

While it is not clear how this might be achieved by a fixed sample process, however, a large number of experiments in which stimulus difference has been varied from trial to trial, have indeed found that the proportion of errors is not constant, but is an inverse function of the size of the stimulus difference (Henmon, 1906; Lemmon, 1927; Kellogg, 1931; Johnson, 1939; Festinger, 1943a, b; Thurmond and Alluisi, 1963; Pickett, 1964, 1967, 1968; Morgan and Alluisi, 1967). Nor is this inverse relation due to observers settling down to an overall mean response time, independent of the size of each particular stimulus difference, and accepting that in consequence they will make more errors at the smaller differences. Not only do observers make more errors at the finer differences, they also take longer to discriminate them. As has already been pointed out (Vickers, 1970; Swensson, 1972), these findings are quite inconsistent with the notion that observers decide beforehand to take a fixed number of observations and then respond with a degree of accuracy related to the size of the stimulus difference.

## A Latency Function Alternative

We have seen that, since the proportion of errors in these experiments rises as stimulus difference is decreased, it follows on the signal detection model that observers cannot be adjusting the number of observations (or their response time) so as to keep this proportion constant. An alternative "explanation" for the increase in latency with reduced stimulus difference has been suggested by Gescheider *et al.* (1968, 1969) and consists of assuming that "the closer an observation is to the [cutoff], the more difficult it should be, and the longer it should take, for [an observer] to make his decision" (1969, p. 18). As Pike (1973) points out, the notion of a *latency function* decreasing with distance from the cutoff has been suggested by several writers (e.g. Bindra *et al.*, 1965; Bindra *et al.*, 1968; Audley and Mercer, 1968; Norman and Wickelgren, 1968; Thomas and Myers, 1972). However, the simplest advocacy of this hypothesis seems to be that of Gescheider *et al.* (1969), who suppose that decisions as to whether an observation falls below or above the cutoff are virtually error-free, but that those lying closer to the cutoff take longer to classify.

There are two obvious objections to this hypothesis, at least as applied within the context of discrimination (some more detailed difficulties are considered in Chapter 5). In the first place, it leaves the signal detection model once more incapable of accounting for the speed–accuracy trade-off discussed in the previous section, since differences in response time are now supposed to arise from a second, virtually error-free discrimination process. In the second place, this modification only succeeds in removing the problem one step further back: there still remains the problem of accounting for the hypothesized rise in response time as observations fall closer to the cutoff. (The *post hoc* nature of the explanation is brought out in the way in which Gescheider *et al.* (1969) needed to postulate a particular shape of function to explain their results). As I have already argued (Vickers, 1972a), the main problem is that this hypothesis seems to be an attempt to account for the rise in response time with decreased stimulus difference by transforming the effect into a theoretical assumption.

## An Optional-stopping Discrimination Process without a Memory

The difficulties encountered by the classical, the signal detection and the fixed sample models have served to precipitate, one by one, some of the most important features of the discrimination process. The occurrence of errors and the shape of the psychometric function imply that the sensory representation of stimuli is inherently variable. The prevalence and systematic behaviour of constant errors suggest that a second important feature is the operation of subjective bias. A further subjective factor, that of caution, is revealed in the speed–accuracy trade-off, which implies that an observer may, by taking longer, somehow counteract the inherent variability in the sensory representation of stimuli. Finally, the covariation of time and errors, as stimulus difference is randomly varied, shows that, without knowing beforehand the size of the stimulus difference he is going to be presented with, an observer can somehow tailor the number of observations to suit the discriminability of each stimulus pair, taking less time for larger differences. While this last ability only emerges from a particular experimental design, in which the stimulus difference is varied randomly from trial to trial, it is not merely an intriguing feature of performance, but perhaps a biologically necessary one. As Goodson (1973) points out, since an organism can withstand high energy levels better for shorter than for longer periods, then the more intense the energy (and hence the greater the sensory signal), the shorter should be the latency of response.

Despite the importance of this last feature, however, little attempt has been made (until recently) to formulate a mechanism for discrimination in which this was incorporated. One of the most useful steps towards this was first proposed by Cartwright and Festinger (1943). Although their model constitutes one of the first and most comprehensive accounts of psychophysical discrimination, its original statement was partly expressed in terms of Lewin's so-called "topological vector" theory (1935), which may explain to some extent its subsequent neglect by psychophysicists. Fortunately, for present purposes it is sufficient to outline a slightly simplified version of their hypothesis.

## The Model of Cartwright and Festinger

Cartwright and Festinger postulate the operation of a "restraining force", which prevents an observer from responding until he can be reasonably sure that his response will be correct. This restraining force can be thought of as corresponding to a region of "no-decision" extending from $k_l$ through 0 up to $k_g$ (Fig. 18). It is further assumed that an observer begins by taking an observation of the perceived ($V$–$S$) stimulus difference at that moment. If the difference lies below $k_l$ or above $k_g$, he responds "$V$ is less than $S$" or "$V$ is greater than $S$", respectively; if the difference falls between $k_l$ and $k_g$, he then takes another observation and continues until he encounters one which falls outside this region of no-decision. The original theory is perhaps unnecessarily complicated by the additional assumption that each value of $k$

varies randomly from moment to moment within each trial, thus giving rise to a distribution of "fluctuations in potency", which are the resultant of the value of the stimulus difference and that of the restraining force at each instant. In the present simplified version, the values of $k$ are assumed to remain constant throughout each trial, so that bias in responding can be accounted for by supposing that the values of $k_l$ and $k_g$ are unequal, and variations in caution by assuming that both values of $k$ can be reduced by instructions emphasizing speed or increased by instructions emphasizing accuracy.

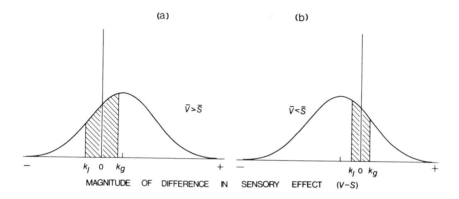

Fig. 18. Hypothetical probability density distributions of subjective $(V-S)$ differences in a model of the type proposed by Cartwright and Festinger (1943). Figure 18a shows the case where $\bar{V} > \bar{S}$, and Fig. 18b the case where $\bar{V} < \bar{S}$. The shaded area from $k_l$ to $k_g$ defines the region of no-decision.

Besides being designed to account for the empirical patterns of response frequency and time, the model is capable of making predictions about the subjective confidence with which a response is made. To account for the fact that the degree of confidence expressed in a judgment appears to be a direct, monotonic function of objective stimulus difference (Garrett, 1922; Johnson, 1939; Festinger, 1943a; Pierrel and Murray, 1963), Cartwright and Festinger proposed that confidence was a linear function of the difference in "potency" at the moment of a decision. This is tantamount, in our simplified version, to supposing that confidence ratings in responses of the form "$V < S$" and "$V > S$" are linear functions of the means of the truncated distributions of stimulus differences lying below $k_l$ and above $k_g$, respectively. Given that the values of $k$ are constant, and the variance in the distribution of perceived $(V-S)$ differences remains the same, then absolute confidence (irrespective of the response made) should increase as a direct function of the mean difference between $V$ and $S$.

## Predictions from the Model

In essence, the model resembles a signal detection account, in which the cutoff, defined as a single value, has been replaced by a range of values, with an associated interval of no-decision. As such, it accounts nicely for the empirical features of the discrimination process examined so far. The theoretical psychometric functions presented by Cartwright and Festinger (1943, p. 604) resemble those shown in Fig. 11, with the precision of the functions increasing as a direct function of $k$ (p. 609). Graphs of decision time against discriminability are also derived (p. 605), and account well for the observed increase in latency as stimulus difference is decreased. Finally, the model gives a good account of the trade-off between speed and accuracy, and of the finding that both errors and response time increase as stimulus difference is reduced. These advantages seem to be largely due to the fact that the model embodies an *optional stopping* rule, according to which an observer may respond immediately, if the evidence in favour of one alternative is sufficiently strong, or continue taking observations until this requirement is met.

Because the stopping rule employed by the model is defined as the encounter of a stimulus difference of a certain minimum magnitude, the model makes three further interesting predictions. Two of these seem at odds with common sense, but perhaps none of the three has ever been adequately tested:

(i) The first prediction is that, if the variance in the distribution of stimulus differences were increased, with values of $k$ and of the mean stimulus difference held constant, mean response time should decrease, since a greater proportion of stimulus differences will fall below $k_l$ or exceed $k_g$.

(ii) The second prediction is that (again with values of $k$ and mean stimulus difference held constant) an increase in variance should also produce an increase in mean absolute confidence (i.e. irrespective of the response made), since the means of the truncated distributions of negative and positive stimulus differences will be decreased and increased, respectively.

(iii) A third prediction hinges on the fact that differences in "potency" (and hence confidence ratings) are supposed to fluctuate randomly with time. According to Irwin *et al.*, therefore, an observer's confidence "should be independent of the duration of the decision process, since confidence is supposed to vary randomly with time, and no temporally cumulative effects are introduced" (1956, p. 261).

## Experimental Evidence

These predictions have been tested in a series of experiments by Irwin and Smith (1956) and Irwin *et al.* (1956), which employed an "expanded judgment" analogue of a psychophysical decision process, in which observers were shown numbers (representing sensory observations) printed on cards and drawn one at a time from large packs:

(i) In the first experiment of Irwin and Smith (1956), the means and standard deviations of the numbers varied from pack to pack and observers were required to indicate when they had decided that the mean of the whole pack was greater or less than zero. Contrary to the first prediction from Cartwright and Festinger's model, it was found that more observations (i.e. cards) were required for those packs in which the variance was larger. This finding is perhaps open to question, however, because it is uncertain that observers maintained the same values of $k$ for the packs with higher variance as for those with lower. Since each card was exhibited for approximately 2·5 s and between about 20 and 40 cards were inspected before a decision was made, observers had ample opportunity to increase the values of $k$ during the process of reaching a decision, in order to cope with a sample in which the standard deviation was almost four times as much as that characterizing a less variable sample.

(ii) The second prediction was tested in a superficially similar experiment by Irwin *et al.* (1956), in which the observer was presented with numbers on each of 20 cards, similarly drawn from packs with different means and standard deviations. In this experiment, the observer was asked to record after each card was shown: the number on the card; whether, on the basis of the cards shown, the mean of the whole pack was greater or less than zero; and, lastly, his confidence in this judgment. Contrary to the prediction, Irwin *et al.* found that, in all 16 of the possible comparisons, mean absolute confidence was greater for the pack with the smaller standard deviation.

Similar results were also obtained in a second experiment, in which observers were shown pairs of cards drawn simultaneously from two packs and asked to judge which of the two packs had the higher mean. However, as in the experiment of Irwin and Smith (1956), it is arguable that observers may have adopted higher values of $k$ for packs with a greater standard deviation. This would have the effect of reducing the "difference in potency" between the stimulus differences and the corresponding value of $k$ and would thus work against any decrease (or increase) in the means of the truncated distribution of negative (and positive) stimulus differences arising from an increased variability of the whole distribution.

(iii) Irwin et al. (1956) also tested the third prediction. Again, contrary to the prediction, they found that within each level of the standard deviation of the packs employed in both experiments, the observer's confidence was greater after the twentieth than after the tenth card inspected.

Audley (1964) has questioned these results on the grounds that the situation does not represent a true optional-stopping paradigm, in which the observer can call for as many cards as he wishes and make an assessment of confidence only after one final decision. Indeed it is true that, while Irwin et al. found confidence increased as more observations were taken, Henmon (1911) had found that, with discriminability held constant, judgments taking a longer time were made with less confidence. Similar results are reported by Audley (1964), in a task in which the observer could decide at any stage whether a stimulus sequence contained more red or green flashes, or was free to continue taking observations.

## Evaluation of the Model

In view of the criticisms which apply to the testing of the first two predictions, it would seem desirable to repeat these experiments, possibly speeding up the presentation of observations and emphasizing speed, while confronting observers with a range of less striking differences in variability and presenting them several times in random order. These modifications might make it more difficult for an observer to notice differences in the general "quality" of the observations with which he is presented and allow him less time to adjust to them by manipulating the values of $k_l$ and $k_g$. It would be interesting to see if such conditions produced the same results as those of Irwin et al. If they did, then this would imply (as was suggested in the introductory chapter) that the mechanism of discrimination may incorporate an inherent capacity for appropriately adapting the degree of caution to the prevailing quality of the sensory information with which an observer has to deal.

Meanwhile, in the case of the third prediction, it seems like that the apparent conflict between the results of Irwin et al., on the one hand, and those of Henmon and Audley, on the other, arises from the fact that the former experimenters forced observers to make judgments on the basis of a fixed number of observations, while the latter allowed them to adopt a true optional-stopping strategy. Indeed, a possible resolution of the conflict is presented in Chapter 6 (pp. 176–180), in which it is argued that each set of results is appropriate to its own particular experimental design.

Whether this resolution turns out to be a valid one or not, however, neither set of results agrees with the prediction of Cartwright and Fes-tinger's model that confidence should be independent of the duration of a judgment. As implied by Irwin and Smith, this defect in the model seems to stem from the fact that the decision process envisaged by Cartwright and Festinger is *memory-less*: an observer must simply wait until he encounters an observation of the requisite magnitude. If it should turn out, in agreement with Irwin and Smith and Irwin *et al.*, that an observer is capable of adapting some parameter of his performance in response to the general quality of the sensory information available to him, then this feature alone would disqualify the model from serious consideration.

A further disadvantage of this feature is that an observer, who (somehow) adopts high values of $k$ to deal with a series of particularly difficult discriminations, may have to wait for an indefinitely long time before encountering an observation of sufficient magnitude. However, even when two equal stimuli are presented and performance is otherwise relatively accurate, observers seem to be capable of responding in a time which is comparable to that for a moderately difficult discrimination (Kellogg, 1931; Johnson, 1939; Cartwright, 1941; Festinger, 1943b).

The absence of a memory also makes it difficult to extend the model to deal with three-category judgments, since the most obvious way of introducing the intermediate category would be to link it with observations falling between $k_l$ and $k_g$. In this case, however, one of the three alternative responses would invariably be elicited by the very first observation. Response time would then become independent of stimulus difference, which, besides being implausible, is contrary to experimental findings (Kellogg, 1931; Vickers, 1975). As with the other predictions, the root difficulty seems to be, as has recently been demonstrated by Schouten and Bekker (1967), that observers are capable of integrating information over time, and this is impossible for a model that is memory-less.

# 3

# Recent Models of Discrimination

*The deductions of Laplace and Gauss are of the greatest importance, but it should not be forgotten that the laws of nature cannot be invented; they must be discovered.*

Cattell (1893, p. 287)

## *Introduction*

At each successive stage in the development of the early models of discrimination traced in Chapter 2, a different ingredient was precipitated. Each of these ingredients seemed to be essential for a successful account of the process of differentiating between two stimuli along some particular dimension, and all are embodied in the models to be examined in the present chapter. All the models assume, for example, that an observer bases his decision upon a series of observations of momentary stimulus differences, which are perturbed by random noise from a multitude of different and independent sources, and are distributed as shown in Fig. 10. As in the model of Cartwright and Festinger, bias in favour of one or the other alternative is accommodated by supposing that the observer adopts unequal criteria, $k_g$ and $k_l$, for the "greater" and the "lesser" responses respectively, while the trade-off between speed and accuracy is explained by supposing that the observer can vary his degree of caution by raising or lowering the values of both $k_g$ and $k_l$. As also in the model of Cartwright and Festinger, the covariation of response time and errors as stimulus difference is changed is accounted for by supposing that the observer makes a series of observations of the stimulus differences one at a time and at a steady rate, until either of the criteria $k_g$ or $k_l$ is satisfied. However, unlike the memory-less model of Cartwright and Festinger, each of the models to be considered assumes that some or all of the observations taken by an observer are remembered. As will be seen, distinctions between the models stem mainly from differences in the amount and kind of information remembered, and in the exact specification of the stopping rule embodied in the criterion $k$.

The development of the present chapter is correspondingly simple, therefore, and consists in showing how the range of possible mechanisms is rapidly narrowed as the detailed structure of empirical constraint is brought into focus by the addition of further experimental findings. Before we embark on the scrutiny of particular models, however, it may be useful to comment briefly on a set of assumptions, common to all of the optional-stopping models, concerning the representation of "indecision" and the notion of an "observation".

## The Representation of Indecision and the Notion of an Observation

As in the model of Cartwright and Festinger, the state of indecision is thought of as an extended process of vacillation between two (or more) alternatives, with the final choice representing a resolution of two conflicting forces. In principle, the conflict might be between "tendencies of the will" and those of "association", between situations with different "valencies", as in Cartwright (1941), or between opposed "excitatory" and "inhibitory" forces (e.g. Hull, 1943; Spence, 1954). In practice, however, all the models considered in this chapter assume that the vacillations in question are embodied as changes in the stored representation of the sensory information and take place as a result of each new observation of the subjective stimulus difference $(V-S)$.

The notion of a series of "observations", "implicit", or "covert" responses is discussed by Audley (1960) and by Audley and Pike (1965), and, as we saw in the last chapter, it seems to be a necessary implication of both the speed–accuracy trade-off and of the concomitant rise in response time and errors as stimulus difference is reduced. Although these events remain hypothetical within the present context, they may be regarded as analogous to the so-called vicarious trial-and-error responses shown by animals which look back and forth between two stimuli before choosing between them (Muenzinger, 1938; Tolman, 1939), or to the "attending" or "observing" responses discussed by Wyckoff (1952). For the sake of generality, no specific interpretation of an "observation" is emphasized. Under certain circumstances, however, tentative identification might be attempted with observable responses, such as saccadic eye movements in the discrimination of complex visual patterns.

Where no overt responses are observable, but evidence suggests that the sampling of sensory information might nevertheless be discontinuous, I have suggested (Vickers, 1970) that the observation interval might be identified with the length of the "sampling time" or "perceptual moment", as discussed by Shallice (1964), and have estimated this from response time distributions to be about 100 ms. In two later experiments, my colleagues and I (Vickers *et al.*, 1972) presented observers with pairs of lines with such large differences in length that a single observation should have resulted in near perfect discrimination. We measured the stimulus exposure of *inspection time* needed for observers to reach a predetermined high level of accuracy and found this to be around 100 ms in both experiments. For the present, therefore, if we take into account the likely range of values of $k$ (estimated by such studies as Vickers *et al.* (1971) and Pike (1972)), and the fact that times for discrimination are usually between 0·5 and 2·0 s, it may be helpful to think of observations of visual stimuli, where the need for overt scanning is minimized, as taking place at a rate of about 10 per second.

Within the present context, then, an observation may be thought of as the inspection of a value of the subjective stimulus difference at a particular instant. In general, all the models to be considered assume that the decision process begins in a neutral, unbiased state, that each observation takes the same amount of time, that there are no empty intervals and that the observation in each interval favours either one or the other alternative, i.e. is either positive or negative. It should be emphasized, however, that, on the whole, these are not so much empirical assertions as simplifying assumptions, made for the sake of mathematical convenience. With these general considerations in mind, we may now turn to one of the first optional-stopping models of discrimination to embody some memory for sensory data.

## The "Runs" Model

One of the earliest optional-stopping models to incorporate memory derives ultimately from the work of Hull (1943) and was proposed by Spence (1954). Spence suggested that, if oscillatory inhibition varied randomly from moment to moment, then a response should be made only when the momentary effective potential (given by the difference between "excitatory potential" and "oscillatory inhibition") exceeded some reaction threshold. In an earlier paper, however, Taylor had argued that this was not necessarily the moment that a reaction would occur, since "the neurophysiological principle of summation of neural impulses suggests that, before a reaction can be evoked, reaction potential must exceed threshold in at least two successive units of time" (1950, p. 388).

Within the field of learning a similar criterion has been examined by Bower (1959) and by Estes (1960). Of more immediate relevance, Audley

(1960) has developed a *runs* model for discrimination, in which the criterion for a response can be expressed as the encounter of $k$ stimulus differences of the same sign *in succession*. If a run of $k_l$ negative differences is sampled, the observer responds "$V$ is less than $S$" and if $k_g$ successive positive differences are encountered, he responds "$V$ is greater than $S$"; otherwise he continues to inspect the stimulus differences until either criterion is satisfied. The model is thus a "partial" memory process, since the magnitude of the observations is not taken into account, and since the occurrence of an observation is stored only for as long as the inspected differences continue to be of the same sign.

## Predictions from the Runs Model

Given a particular value of the mean $(\bar{V}-\bar{S})$ and standard deviation $\sigma_{(V-S)}$ of the distribution of subjective stimulus differences, then positive and negative differences will be encountered in an independent, random sequence, with probabilities $p$ and $q = (1 - p)$ respectively. By specifying the unconditional probabilities that a run of $k_g$ positive or $k_l$ negative differences will first be encountered at the initial, and at each successive observation of such a sequence, it is possible to generate a distribution of the number of observations elapsing before each response can be expected to occur. The relative frequency with which each criterion can be expected to be reached first can then be calculated by summing these unconditional probabilities, while the mean, standard deviation, skewness and kurtosis of the distribution of the number of observations required for each response to occur can also be calculated from these distributions. The method of probability generating functions (Feller, 1968, Ch. 11) is useful in calculating these parameters, and has been employed in two studies (Audley and Pike, 1965; Vickers *et al.*, 1971, pp. 169–171) in the case of the runs model. Provided the model is an appropriate description of the discrimination process, then the means and standard deviations of empirical distributions of response times should be directly proportional to these theoretical means and standard deviations, since observations are assumed to occur at regular time intervals. Meanwhile the dimensionless measures of skewness and kurtosis, taken on the theoretical distributions, should correspond directly with the empirical values.

Thus, for any combination of the values of $k_g$ $k_l$, and $p$, it is possible to predict the relative frequency with which the hypothesized process will respond either "$V > S$" or "$V < S$", and also the distribution of times required to make each response. Detailed predictions for response probability and the mean, standard deviation, skewness and kurtosis of the response

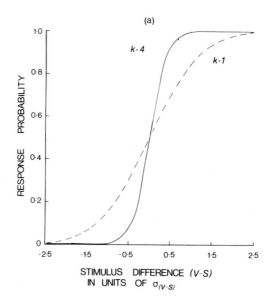

(a)

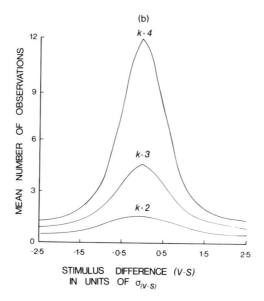

(b)

Fig. 19. The pattern of (a) response probabilities, and (b) mean response times predicted by a runs process for various values of $k$ $(= k_g = k_l)$. Predicted curves are for responses of the form "$V > S$".

time distributions have been presented (Vickers *et al.*, 1971, p. 153). Those for the probability of making a response of the form "$V > S$" and the mean number of observations taken, are shown in Fig. 19, plotted against values of the mean difference ($\bar{V}-\bar{S}$) between subjective magnitudes, measured in standard deviation units $\sigma_{(V-S)}$. As can be seen from Fig. 19a, the predicted psychometric function is a sigmoid curve, which increases in precision as the value of $k$ (assuming $k_g = k_l$) is increased. At the same time, as can be seen from Fig. 19b, the curve for response time is shifted up the $y$-axis and its range increased. Like the model of Cartwright and Festinger, therefore, the runs model can account for the speed–accuracy trade-off discussed in the last chapter.

As can also be seen from Fig. 19b, the mean response time function for any particular value of $k$ can be described as an inverted U-shaped curve, which is somewhat asymmetrical at low values of $k$, but becomes relatively more symmetrical as the value $k$ is increased (c.f. Audley and Pike, 1965, p. 223). Once again like the model of Cartwright and Festinger, therefore, the runs hypothesis can account for the concomitant rise in both errors and response time as stimulus difference is reduced. For example, where $\bar{V}$ is much greater than $\bar{S}$, then most of the ($V-S$) differences will be positive and it will not take many more than $k$ observations before a run of $k$ positive differences is encountered. Conversely, when $\bar{V}$ and $\bar{S}$ are equal, the probability of encountering a positive difference will be reduced from near unity to 0·5, and the number of observations which have to be inspected before encountering a run of $k$ of the same sign will in consequence be much higher.

## Evaluation of the Runs Model

While we have seen in the last chapter that empirical psychometric functions can be closely fitted by a normal ogive, the unreliability of empirical data points where observed response probabilities approach 0 or 1·0 means that the exercise of comparing the fit provided by a normal ogive and that provided by a similar theoretical function, such as that for the runs process, is not only difficult but of doubtful value. In the case of the runs model, where only integer values of $k$ are considered, a more useful comparison appears to be one between the shapes of empirical response time functions, plotted against the objective difference ($v-s$) between the stimuli, and those of the theoretical functions shown in Fig. 19b.

### Response Times

In making such comparisons, it is useful to remember that, on the theoretical curves of Fig. 19b, predicted times for responses of the form

"$V > S$" made at values of $(\bar{V}-\bar{S})$ at, or below, zero correspond to empirical times for responses of the same form made when the objective value of the difference $(v-s)$ between the stimuli is zero or negative. Since this will only occur when the variable is in fact equal to, or less than, the standard, such responses are classified as errors, both in the empirical and the theoretical case; conversely, points for "$V > S$" judgments located to the right of a stimulus difference of zero (whether subjective or objective) are classified as times for responses which are correct. Comparisons of times for correct and incorrect responses have customarily been made between the mean time for one response (e.g. "$V > S$"), made (correctly) at a positive stimulus difference of $x$ units, and that for the same response, made (incorrectly) at a negative stimulus difference of $-x$ units. Hence, symmetry in response time curves, such as those in Fig. 19b, indicates that the mean times for correct and incorrect responses are equal, while curves which are higher on the left indicate that times for a particular response made incorrectly are longer than when it is made correctly to a stimulus difference of the same absolute size.

If this is borne in mind, a survey of the relevant experimental evidence shows some marked discrepancies between theoretical and empirical response time functions. For example, Pike (1968) found that while response times for his faster observers fell on a symmetrical curve of the type predicted by a runs process with a high value of $k$ (e.g. $\geqslant 4$), data for his slower observers fell on an obviously asymmetrical function, in which times for incorrect responses were substantially longer than those for the same response made correctly. In this experiment, therefore, the empirically observed change from symmetry to asymmetry appears to be related to an increase in caution, while, in theory, the same change would be explained by the runs model as due to a decrease in $k$.

This conflict is not confined to Pike's experiment. Indeed Wollen (1963) was the first to report that an expected inverse relation between response time and frequency was confirmed in the case of slow responders, but broke down for those who were faster. Empirical confirmation of a change from a symmetrical to an asymmetrical response time function can also be found if we grade the relevant experiments from those emphasizing speed to those emphasizing accuracy. For example, in one of the simplest experiments on this issue, Hornsby (1968) instructed his observer to respond "as quickly as possible" to whichever of two (equally probable) lamps lit up on a particular trial. Hornsby found that over 2000 test trials conducted after 900 practice trials, there was no significant difference between the mean times for correct and incorrect responses, though their distributions did differ in shape. Again, in a two-choice task in which speed was emphasized, and in which—unlike other experiments of the set—the *a priori* probability of making each response was equal and constant, Laming (1968) found that times for incorrect responses were equal to, or less than, those for correct ones when the two shortest intertrial intervals were considered, though they were longer when data for the three longest intervals were examined.

At the other extreme, Kellogg (1931) tried to avoid "artificially shortening" judgment time by emphasizing accuracy and by not informing observers that their response times were being recorded. In both a two and a three-category discrimination task, Kellogg found that all five observers showed significantly longer times for incorrect than for correct responses, though times for the two classes of response were more similar for the faster observers. A similar inverse relation between the frequency of a response and the time taken to make it was obtained in a study of generalization gradients by La Berge (1961), who found that after observers were trained to an asymptotic level of accuracy, incorrect responses generally took longer than correct. As I have formerly pointed out (Vickers, 1972a), a large number of other experiments, in which accuracy has been emphasized (either through instructions, rewards, or the extreme difficulty of the task) have produced similar results (e.g. Cross and Lane, 1962; Pierrel and Murray, 1963; Pickett, 1967, 1968; Audley and Mercer, 1968; Pike, 1971).

Meanwhile, among experiments in which instructions have implied some compromise between speed and accuracy, the change from a symmetrical to an asymmetrical response time function is discernible in the difference between the individual empirical curves for less cautious and more cautious observers. For example, Henmon (1911) found that, for two observers, the time for errors were longer than those for correct responses, while for the third (the fastest and least accurate), there was no significant difference. If we make the reasonable assumption that differences in caution may be reflected either in accuracy or in the mean time for all responses, then more detailed confirmation of this trend may also be found in results obtained in our own experiments (Vickers et al., 1971). We showed that there was a significant positive rank order correlation between the total number of correct responses made by each observer and the coefficient of the slope of a straight line fitted to his response time data when plotted against objective stimulus difference ($v$–$s$). Further analysis by us of previously published data (Vickers, 1970) also showed a significant positive rank correlation between the coefficient of slope and the mean response time for individual observers. A similar trend is evident in the individual response time functions (Fig. 20), which were obtained in an unpublished experiment by myself and K. Domac, in which each of 8 observers was required to classify a series of 1600 lines as "longer" or "shorter".

As can be seen from Fig. 20, all these results suggest that the empirical function relating response time to discriminability (or, for that matter, to

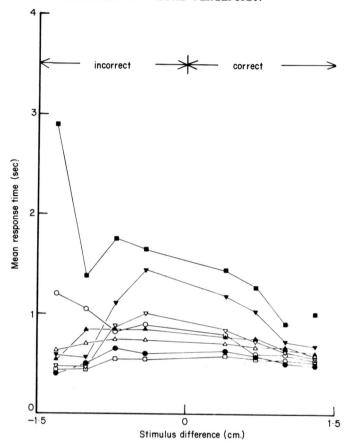

Fig. 20. Mean response times obtained in an unpublished experiment by myself and K. Domac. Individual curves represent data for individual observers (averaged for the two responses).

response frequency) is symmetrical when observers are fast and erratic, but becomes increasingly asymmetrical as observers take longer overall to respond in an effort to achieve greater accuracy. On the premiss that such changes in caution may be directly represented by variations in $k$, this pattern of results is directly opposite to the one predicted by a runs model, according to which response time functions should become more symmetrical as $k$ is increased.

It would of course be possible to go on to generate predictions for higher moments of the theoretical response time distributions, and to compare these with experimental data. (Indeed, this has already been done (Vickers *et al.*, 1971; Wilding, 1974) and substantial discrepancies have been found between predicted and obtained measures.) However, apart from adding to the evidence against the runs hypothesis, such comparisons do not throw much light on the reasons for the failure of the model. On the other hand, some other results which are more useful in this connection have been obtained in an analogue of the expanded judgment task encountered in the last chapter, and to these I shall now turn.

## Evidence on the Nature of the Remembered Information

In an experiment which constitutes a very direct test of the model, Sanders and Ter Linden (1967) presented regular sequences of flashes on two lamps, *A* and *B*, and recorded the time taken by observers to decide whether *A* or *B* was set to light up more frequently. Three types of sequence were employed, as illustrated in Table I: one type (*P*) containing 4 runs of 2 successive flashes of the same lamp within the first 13 flashes; a second (*Q*) containing 2 runs of 3; and a third type (*R*) containing 1 run of 5 in the same part of the sequence. Although observers did not generally respond to either the first or the second short run in a type *P* sequence, they did tend to respond before the fourth, although no runs longer than 2 were presented. Moreover, the number of flashes required to reach a decision increased from type *P*, through *Q*, to type *R*. Thus, although observers in this experiment did not respond to the first short run (suggesting that they operated with a higher level of *k*), they responded more quickly to a sequence containing several short runs than to one containing a longer run placed later in the sequence. In two further experiments, observers were also found to respond more quickly after a run placed later in an otherwise inconclusive sequence than when the run occurred earlier.

Although a general interpretation of these results is perhaps not immediately obvious, none of the results is consistent with the notion that

Table I. Sequences containing 2-item, 3-item, or 5-item runs employed by Sanders and Ter Linden (1967). (Reproduced with permission.)

Type P: 2-item runs: *A A* B *A A* B *A A* B *A* B *A A*
                         B *A* B *A* B *A* B *A* B B *A A A A A A* B B B A → etc.

Type Q: 3-item runs: A B *A* B *A A A* B *A* B *A A A*
                         B *A* B *A* B *A* B B *A A A A A A* B B B A → etc.

Type R: 5-item run: A B *A* B *A* B *A* B *A A A A A*
                       B *A* B *A* B *A* B B *A A A A A A* B B B A → etc.

observers make decisions by responding to the first run of observations of a particular kind which reaches or exceeds a predetermined critical length. More constructively, they suggest that the assumptions made by the runs hypothesis regarding the information remembered from a series of observations are inappropriate. In the first place, since the response to a run is a function of its position in the sequence, it appears that the memory for a binary sequence of events extends further back than the start of the most recent run.

More detailed confirmation of this comes from an experiment by Howell (1970), in which observers were required to predict, after each observation, which of two lamps would light up next. Over all 140 flashes the objective probability in favour of each lamp was 0·65, as opposed to 0·35 for the other. However, within each sequence, the probabilities within one "critical" block of 20 trials were either 0·50:0·50, 0·65:0·35, or 0·80:0·20. This critical block could occur early or late in the sequence. When asked during the task to estimate the proportion of events occurring in this critical block, observers gave estimates which were closely related to the actual proportion appearing within this block, provided the block occurred early in the sequence. However, when the critical block occurred later, estimates of the proportions of events approximated to the cumulative proportions over the entire preceding sequence.

Taken together with the findings of Sanders and Ter Linden, these results suggest that although observers retain some cumulative record of the relative frequency of events over an entire sequence of observations, they do not remember much information regarding the time of occurrence of these events. Other results also suggest that observers in this type of experiment do not store information about the sequential order of events. For example, in a similar study of the discrimination of the more frequent colour in a sequence of red and green stimuli, Audley reported that observers did not notice that, for some series, there was a regular alternation of three of one colour followed by two of another. According to Audley, observers did not "seem to be able to deal separately with the variability of the red and green runs, but [combined] this into one total impression" (1964, p. 30).

## The "Random Walk" Model

An alternative hypothesis, in which the detailed sequence of observations does not play a crucial role, is embodied in the *random walk* model, derived by Edwards (1965) from Stone (1960) and Wald (1947). According to

Edwards' version, the observer can be thought of as inspecting the stream of $(V-S)$ differences until the number of differences of one sign exceeds that of the other by a certain critical amount. Where $t_l$ represents the total number of negative instances inspected, and $t_g$ the total of the positive, then this model proposes that, as soon as $(t_g - t_l) \leqslant k_l$, or $(t_g - t_l) \geqslant k_g$, the observer responds "$V < S$" or "$V > S$", respectively (where $k_l$ and $k_g$ are integers such that $k_l \leqslant 0 \leqslant k_g$). As with the runs process, bias can be accounted for by supposing that the observer can operate with unequal absolute values of $k_g$ and $k_l$, while variations in caution can be accommodated by assuming that absolute values of $k_g$ and $k_l$ can be increased or decreased concomitantly. In contrast to the runs process, however, only the difference $(t_g - t_l)$ need be stored, and this can be continually updated as each new observation is taken. It is the excursions in the value of $(t_g - t_l)$ which, over a period of time, describe a "random walk". As has been shown by Edwards (1965), the attainment of a critical value of $(t_g - t_l)$ is tantamount to the achievement of a predetermined likelihood ratio. The model has the further attraction that it represents an optimal strategy in the sense that it ensures the attainment of a certain proportion of correct responses at a cost of inspecting, on average, the minimum number of $(V-S)$ differences.

## Predictions from the Random Walk Model

Given any particular value of $k_g$, $k_l$, and $p$ (the probability of encountering a positive $(V-S)$ difference), then, as in the case of the runs process, it is possible to derive a probability generating function (following Feller, 1968, p. 353, Eq. 5.7), which will permit the prediction of the relative frequency with which each response can be expected, the mean time taken to make it and the standard deviation, skewness and kurtosis of the associated distributions of response times (c.f. Audley and Pike, 1965, pp. 219–221). Graphs of these predictions for a range of values of $k_g$, $k_l$ and $p$ have been presented (Vickers et al., 1971, p. 153). Those for the mean, standard deviation, skewness, and kurtosis of the response time distributions are reproduced in Fig. 21.

Since the predicted pattern of response frequencies which we presented (Vickers et al., 1971) shows no interesting differences from that for the runs process (shown in Fig. 19), it seems unlikely that this feature of the empirical data would legislate for or against the random walk model as opposed to any other similar hypothesis. On the other hand, the predicted pattern of mean response times is more distinctive. As can be seen from Fig. 21a, the response time functions again constitute inverted U-shaped curves. However, unlike those for the runs process, the curves for the random walk

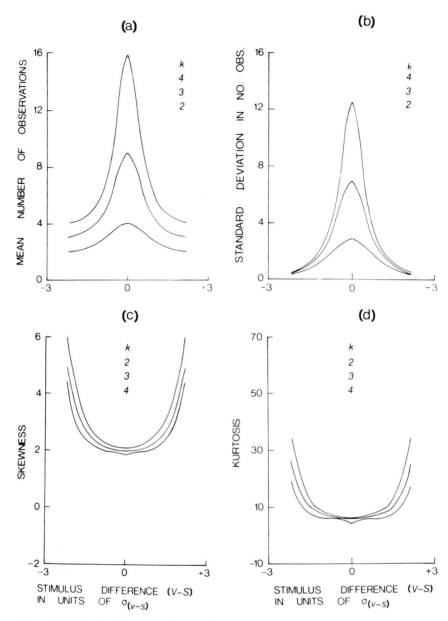

Fig. 21. Predictions from a random walk model for responses of the form "$V > S$" for various values of $k$ ($= k_g = k_l$), plotted against the hypothesized subjective difference between the stimuli $V$ and $S$. Figure 21a shows the pattern of the mean number of observations, Fig. 21b the standard deviation, Fig. 21c the pattern of skewness measures and Fig. 21d that for kurtosis.

model are symmetrical for all values of $k$ (assuming absolute values of $k_g$ and $k_l$ to be equal). Thus, according to the random walk model, the mean times for correct and incorrect responses should be the same. As can also be seen from Fig. 21, a similar symmetry characterizes the three remaining measures of standard deviation, skewness and kurtosis. In other words, according to the random walk hypothesis, the shapes of the response time distributions for correct and incorrect responses should be identical.

## Evaluation of the Random Walk Model

As with the runs process, the evidence relevant to an evaluation of the random walk model falls into two categories: one concerned with the agreement (or otherwise) between theoretical and empirical response time distributions; the other comprising a more direct investigation into the nature of the stopping-rule employed in simple discriminative decisions.

### Response Time Distributions

On the whole, empirical data do not support the prediction that mean times for correct and incorrect responses should be equal. Although mean times for correct and incorrect responses may be equal when observers respond quickly (e.g. Hornsby, 1968; Laming, 1968), the general trend (summarized on pp. 59–62) is for response time curves to become markedly asymmetrical as higher degrees of caution are exercised, with times for incorrect responses by slow responders being substantially longer than those for correct.

A similar discrepancy arises in the case of measures of skewness and kurtosis. While Figs 21c and 21d show that measures predicted by the random walk hypothesis should describe symmetrical U-shaped functions when plotted against stimulus difference, Wilding (1974) found no evidence of any quadratic components in the corresponding empirical data, while in several other studies (Vickers, 1970; Vickers et al., 1971; Wilding, 1974), a significant positive correlation between stimulus discriminability and both of these measures was found. As presaged by the study of Hornsby (1968), referred to earlier (p. 60), not only does the general form of the empirical response time functions differ from the theoretical, the predicted identity in shape between the distributions of times for correct and incorrect responses is not found empirically.

### The Nature of the Criterion Employed

In their experiments on discriminating between the frequency of occurrence of a binary sequence of probabilistic events, Sanders and Ter Linden (1967) obtained evidence suggesting that one source of these discrepancies might lie in the nature of the criterion. By varying the position in the sequence at which conclusive evidence was presented, Sanders and Ter Linden found that when observers reached a decision early in a sequence, the modulus $|t_g-t_l|$ between the total number of events of each kind which had been inspected was greater than when decisions were made later. On this basis, Sanders and Ter Linden suggested that if observers employ a random walk decision procedure, they may begin with high values of $k$ and progressively lower them as more observations are taken which do not result in a decision. A similar proposal has been put forward by Pickett (1968) in order to avoid the difficulty that the process might otherwise be "hung up" indefinitely on an inconclusive series of observations—an eventuality which is particularly likely when high values of $k$ are adopted in order to deal with what appears to be a low level of discriminability.

However, there are several strong objections to this alternative. For example, as Pike (1968, p. 174) points out, if the difference between fast, erratic responders and those who are slow and accurate is due to the former reducing $k$ at a higher rate, then fast observers should produce longer latencies for errors, while response time curves should become more symmetrical as the data for slower and more accurate observers are considered. As we have seen, this trend is in the opposite direction to that found empirically. Again, as has been pointed out (Vickers et al., 1971), this modification of the model would not predict the positive correlation generally obtained between kurtosis and discriminability.

Aside from these detailed discrepancies, such a modification would endow the mechanism with an undesirable degree of complexity, since assumptions would have to be made not only concerning the starting values of $k_g$ and $k_l$, but also about the point(s) at which they begin to decline, the rate(s) of decline and the nature of the function(s) relating the decline in $k$ to the number of observations inspected.

Other modifications are, of course, possible. For example, Laming (1968) has explored in detail the properties of a random walk process in which the magnitude of successive observations would also be taken into account by the decision process. Although such a modification seems intuitively plausible, the predictions for a process of this kind do not differ in any important respect from those where only unit increments are considered. Fortunately, there is in any case a simpler hypothesis, which appears to give a good account of the results of these experiments, and this I shall now consider.

## The "Recruitment" Model

A model with some interesting differences from either the runs or the random walk has been suggested by La Berge (1962). In an earlier paper, La Berge (1959) had considered a model, with some resemblances to that of Cartwright and Festinger, in which an observer could be thought of as sampling positive, negative, or neutral stimulus "elements" until the first positive or negative element occured. In order to adapt the model to the present context, the "neutral elements" of La Berge's early model could be identified with those observations falling within the region of "no-decision" in the model of Cartwright and Festinger, while the positive and negative elements can be taken to correspond to the positive and negative $(V–S)$ differences falling above the upper, or below the lower cutoff, respectively. In his later paper, La Berge (1962) presents a general recruitment model, in which an observer samples positive, negative, or neutral elements until he encounters a total of $k_g$ positive or $k_l$ negative elements.

Since the supposition of "sensory" criteria, distinguishing positive, negative and neutral $(V–S)$ differences (in addition to the "response" criteria $k_g$ and $k_l$), makes the model very unwieldy, and since the hypothesis that an observer recruits $k_g$ positive or $k_l$ negative differences by itself confers on the model all the requisite properties for an account of the general features of discrimination outlined so far, only the limiting case, in which there are no neutral elements, need be considered. According to this simpler hypothesis, then, an observer is pictured as taking observations of the series of positive and negative $(V–S)$ differences until he encounters a total of $k_g$ positive or $k_l$ negative differences, whereupon he responds "$V > S$" or "$V < S$", respectively.

Like the runs and random walk processes, the recruitment model simply registers the occurrence of a $(V–S)$ difference of a particular sign, and ignores its magnitude. Unlike the runs process, however, all occasions are remembered. Meanwhile, unlike the random walk hypothesis, on which this information is stored in a single bidirectional counter registering the current value of the difference $(t_g–t_l)$, the recruitment process assumes that the occurrences of positive and negative $(V–S)$ differences are stored in two separate counters, in each of which the total $(t_g$ or $t_l)$ can only increase up to the moment a decision is reached. This way of determining discriminative responses seems to correspond with a general feature of biological systems, termed "unidirectional rate sensitivity" or "rein control" (Clynes, 1961, 1969). Evidence for this type of control comes partly from the frequent asymmetries in the response of certain physiological systems, such as faster responses to increases than to decreases in blood pressure (Katona et al.,

1967), and partly from the apparent specificity of neuronal units to certain types of signal, as in the evidence for units sensitive to one direction only of change in pitch (Whitfield, 1967). In view of the apparent generality of this type of control, it seems plausible to suppose that the elicitation of opposed discriminative responses may be similarly controlled by separate, independent units, each of which is changed in a similar way by incoming evidence.

A further general advantage of the recruitment process is that the possibility of being "hung up" indefinitely over a series of inconclusive observations is avoided, without the need for any further assumptions (e.g. that values of $k$ diminish). If we suppose, for the sake of simplicity, that $k_g = k_l$, then, since the criterion for a response is a simple total of $k$ observations of one kind, an observer can never take less than $k$ observations before reaching a critical total. On the other hand, he will always have reached a decision by the time $(2k-1)$ observations have been inspected. Analogous limits also apply in the case where $k_g \neq k_l$. As in more molar, everyday contexts, the property of sampling a quantity of evidence which is proportional to the difficulty of each decision, while, at the same time, ensuring that some response will necessarily be made by a particular time, would seem to have some obvious biological advantages.

## *Predictions of the Recruitment Process*

Just as in the case of the runs and random walk models, it is possible, for any combination of the values of $k_g$, $k_l$ and $p$, to derive a probability generating function (following Feller, 1968, p. 165, Eq. 8.1), which will allow the prediction of relative response frequency and the mean and higher moments of the associated response time distributions (c.f. Audley and Pike, 1965, pp. 215–216). A detailed exposition of the model is given by La Berge (1962), and the main predictions are presented graphically in a later study (Vickers et al., 1971, p. 153). Those for the mean, standard deviation, skewness and kurtosis of the response time distributions are reproduced in Fig. 22.

Again as with the two previous models, the most distinctive aspect of these predictions concerns the mean response time functions. Whereas those for the random walk predict identical mean times for correct and incorrect responses, mean times predicted by the recruitment process show a monotonic decrease with increasing values of $(V–S)$, or of response frequency (c.f. Audley and Pike, 1965, p. 223), and imply that mean times for errors should always be longer. Meanwhile, as can be seen from a comparison of Figs 22a and 22b, standard deviations predicted by the recruitment process do not closely follow the mean (as they do on both the runs and random walk models). Again, unlike those for the runs and random walk models, predicted skewness measures clearly increase as a

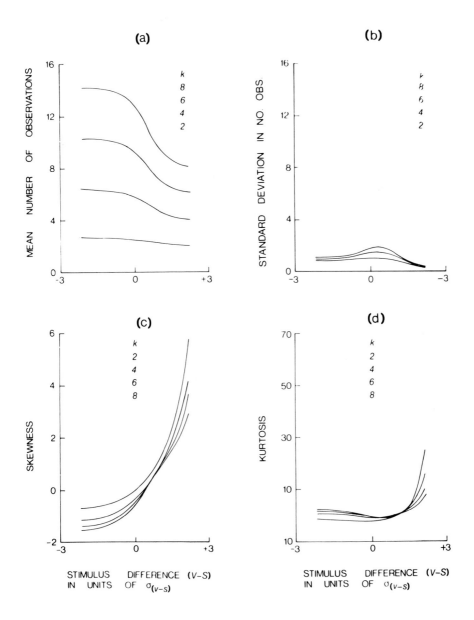

Fig. 22. Predictions from a recruitment model for responses of the form "$V > S$" for various values of $k$ ($= k_g = k_l$), plotted against the hypothesized subjective difference between the stimuli $V$ and $S$. Figure 22a shows the pattern of the mean number of observations, Fig. 22b the standard deviation, Fig. 22c the pattern of skewness measures and Fig. 22d that for kurtosis.

function of $(V-S)$, with measures for correct responses being predominantly positive, while those for errors are negative or zero (when $(V-S) = 0$ and $k = 2$). As Fig. 23 brings out, these contrasts represent some quite striking differences between the shapes of the predicted response time distributions.

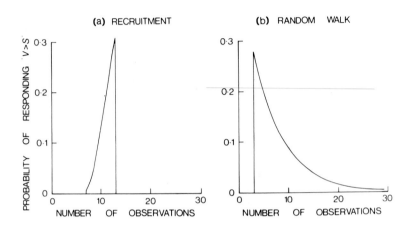

Fig. 23. Typical response time distributions predicted by (a) the recruitment, and (b) the random walk model. Distributions are for responses of the form "$V > S$" made *incorrectly* to a moderately large stimulus difference of $0·75\sigma_{(V-S)}$, with $k_g = k_l$, and taking values of 7 and 3 in (a) and (b) respectively.

## *Evaluation of the Recruitment Model*

Once again, the relevant evidence falls into two categories: the first concerned with aspects of the response time distributions; the second more concerned with the nature of the information upon which the observer bases his decisions.

### Response Time Distributions

*Mean response times.*   An immediately obvious discrepancy between theory and data is, of course, the one for mean response times. The identical times for correct and incorrect responses reported in some studies (Henmon, 1911; Hornsby, 1968; Laming, 1968), and the roughly symmetrical response time functions generated by the fast responders of others (Kellogg, 1931; Vickers, 1970; Vickers et al., 1971; Vickers and Domac (Fig. 20)) are all inconsistent with the monotonic decrease predicted by the recruitment process. Other discrepancies also occur in the case of the slow responders, where data for individual observers in my own experiments and those of Kellogg show a drop at low negative values of the objective stimulus difference. A similar tendency for mean times for slow responders to "tip back down" at low response probabilities has been noted by Pickett (1967, 1968) and by Wilding (1971, 1974).

In an attempt to modify the recruitment process to account for this kind of finding, Pike (1968, 1971, 1973) has suggested a *variable recruitment* process, whereby observers under a set for speed may operate with a value for $k$ which fluctuates from trial to trial. When $k$ is low and fluctuates in value from trial to trial, those trials on which it is low will produce a greater proportion of errors (taking a short time) than when $k$ is high. Conversely, trials executed with a low value for $k$ will produce fewer correct responses, so that, when these varying proportions are averaged, it can turn out that incorrect responses are equal to, or even slightly faster than, correct responses (Pike, 1968, 1971, 1973). Figure 24a, for example, shows the form of the response time function when $k$ takes values of 1 or 2 with equal probability. The change in the form of the empirical relations between response time and discriminability, as caution is increased, could be accounted for, according to Pike (1968), if it were supposed that fast responders used low values of $k$ which varied from trial to trial.

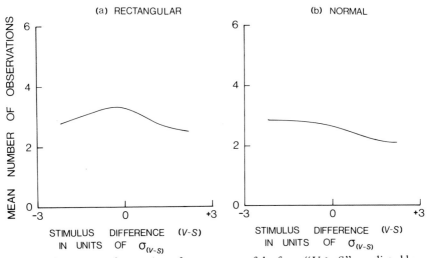

Fig. 24. The pattern of mean times for responses of the form "$V > S$", predicted by a recruitment process in which the value of $k_g = k_l$ varies randomly from trial to trial. Figure 24a shows the pattern when $k_g = k_l$ and takes the value 2 or 3 with equal probability. Figure 24b shows the pattern when $k_g = k_l$, and is normally distributed over successive observation intervals, with a mean of 2 and a standard deviation of 1.

There are, however, several objections to this modified recruitment model. In the first place, it involves the further assumption of a particular (rectangular) distribution for $k$. As can be seen from Fig. 24b, the assumption of a normal distribution for $k$ leaves the response time function little changed (c.f. Vickers *et al.*, 1971). In the second place, the recruitment model with higher (normally variable) values of $k$ does not give a good account of the shapes of response time functions for slow responders, which generally "tip back down", as was noted earlier. In the third place, Pike (1971) argues that an asymmetrical response time function would be predicted when an observer's criteria were stable and constant, as might be expected with well practised observers, who were quite sure of their criterion in terms of speed versus accuracy. However, the observers of Hornsby (1968) and Laming (1968) appear to have fulfilled these conditions, and yet have produced response time functions that are symmetrical. Moreover, results from several studies (Vickers, 1970; Vickers *et al.*, 1971; Vickers and Domac (unpublished)) show clearly that the tendency to produce symmetrical functions is related to a simple decrease in caution and becomes more marked towards the end of several sessions, by which time the observer is highly practised and has presumably reached a satisfactory compromise between speed and accuracy. Finally, as found in one of the studies (Vickers *et al.*, 1971) and argued below in more detail, the shapes of the response time distributions predicted by either the variable recruitment or the recruitment models show several marked discrepancies from those generally obtained in discrimination experiments. It would appear then that this modification does not fare better than the more economical hypothesis that values of $k$ remain effectively constant.

*Skewness and kurtosis.* Further evidence contradicting the simple recruitment hypothesis appears in the skewness measures for incorrect responses, which should be negative (with the single exception where $(V–S) = 0$ and $k \leqslant 2$, when the measure is zero). Table II presents the proportions of empirical distributions for both correct and incorrect responses which were found to be negatively skewed in a number of recent experiments I have conducted. In the case of the first three experiments, the distributions examined comprise times for correct (or incorrect) responses, irrespective of whether they were of the form "$V > S$" or "$V < S$".

Since none of the models to be considered in this book predicts that shewness measures should be greatly affected by the degree of caution assumed to be operating, this procedure seems to be acceptable. However, as a check, data are also given from an unpublished experiment which I conducted with R. Willson, which are based on distributions for correct and incorrect instances of each response, considered separately. In this experi-

Table II. The proportion of response time distributions with positive or negative skew obtained in a number of recent experiments. Correct and incorrect responses are considered separately and the total number of distributions examined in each case is also given.

| Experiment | Correct responses | | | Incorrect responses | | |
|---|---|---|---|---|---|---|
| | Number | % Positive | % Negative | Number | % Positive | % Negative |
| Vickers (1970) | 125 | 100 | 0 | 107 | 85 | 15 |
| Vickers, Caudrey and Willson (1971) | 125 | 96 | 4 | 95 | 83 | 17 |
| Vickers, Domac and Willson | 128 | 100 | 0 | 111 | 82 | 18 |
| Vickers and Willson | 500 | 99 | 1 | 140 | 78 | 22 |
| Pooled estimate | | 99 | 1 | | 81 | 19 |

ment, ten observers were presented with 620 circular arrays of randomly oriented line segments, similar to those shown in Fig. 25, and were instructed to press one of two keys as soon as they had decided whether the array as a whole appeared to be tilted in a clockwise or an anticlockwise direction with reference to the rectangular bars above and below each array. The arrays were similar to those used by Pickett (1968), but had a constant standard deviation of 15° from the mean orientation of the lines and 10 different mean orientations, ranging from −22·5° from the vertical (i.e. anticlockwise) to +22·5° (i.e. clockwise), in steps of 5°. As in the other experiments, observers were told to respond "as quickly and as accurately as possible", and to try to keep their performance stable. In the case of correct responses, the 500 distributions available for analysis represent the 5 distributions for each level of discriminability examined at each of 5 sessions for 10 observers for each of the 2 types of response allowed.

As can be seen from Table II, the results obtained when times for each response are analysed separately are virtually identical to those when times for both responses are considered together. In both cases, skewness measures for incorrect responses are positive in about 80% of instances, while the proportion for correct responses is almost 100%. This clear

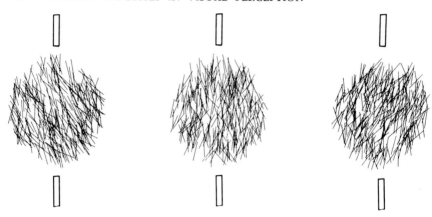

Fig. 25. Typical stimuli, consisting of randomly oriented line segments, used in an unpublished experiment by R. J. Willson and myself. The mean orientation of the segments in the left-hand stimulus is tilted anticlockwise from the vertical, that in the right-hand stimulus is tilted clockwise and that in the middle lies close to the vertical.

predominance of positive skewness measures for errors is also found in the results of each of the 28 individual observers represented in Table II (c.f. Vickers *et al.*, 1971, pp. 160, 163). It appears, therefore, that the sharply truncating effect of an absolute limit of $(2k - 1)$ observations, evident in Fig. 23, results in a theoretical distribution for incorrect responses with a distinctive, negative skew, which is to be found only infrequently among empirical distributions of response times.

## The Nature of the Remembered Information

The failure of the recruitment model to predict the nature of the response time distributions is somewhat disappointing in view of the economy with which it can account for the evidence concerning the nature of the information upon which observers appear to base their decisions. For example, when $k_g = k_l$, then, as we have seen, the theoretical range of the number of observations required to reach a decision extends from $k$ up to $(2k - 1)$. When a decision is reached after only $k$ observations, this means that all of them must be of the same kind, so that the modulus $|t_g - t_l|$ between the numbers of events sampled in favour of each of the two response alternatives will be at a maximum, namely $k$. Conversely, when a decision is not reached until after $(2k - 1)$ observations, the modulus $|t_g - t_l|$ will be reduced to a minimum of 1. Between these two extremes, it turns out that the greater the number of observations required (on average) to reach a decision, the smaller is the value of $|t_g - t_l|$ by the time a decision is reached. This feature accounts nicely for the decrease in empirical estimates of $|t_g - t_l|$ obtained by Sanders and Ter Linden as more observations were required, and dispenses with the need to postulate a complicated random walk process with diminishing values of $k$. Indeed, as Pike (1968a) has shown, if the value of the critical difference in a random walk model is assumed to decrease by 1 for every observation in excess of $k - 1$ without a response, then the model becomes exactly equivalent to a recruitment process.

a         b         c

Fig. 26. Examples of binary valued matrices with different transition probabilities. In (a) the transition probability is low (less than 0·5), in (b) it is medium (equal to 0·5) and in (c) it is high (greater than 0·5).

The simplicity of the recruitment process is very attractive, and, as Pitz implies, a process of this kind, in which the evidence for alternative responses is represented by a finite, small number of states, certainly "seems to fit the current Zeitgeist" (1970, p. 209). Nor is the model confined to stimuli composed of *sequences* of binary events. Figure 26, for example, shows three matrices of binary valued cells in which the unconditional probabilities that a cell will be black or white are equal, but in which the colour of each cell is related to that of the cell on its immediate left by a transition probability which can vary. A transition probability of 0·2, for instance, would mean that there was a chance of only 1 in 5 that any particular cell would be of the same colour as its neighbour. When this transition probability is low, as in Fig. 26a, then the matrix appears to have a fine-grained texture when viewed from a suitable distance. Conversely when the transition probability is high, as in Fig. 26c, the texture of the matrix appears coarse or "clumpy". In an experiment designed to exploit this distinction, Pickett (1967) presented observers with binary matrices of

this kind (constructed according to a range of different transition probabilities) and measured the time they took to classify the matrices as
"coarse" or "even", as well as their accuracy in making this discrimination.
Empirical response frequencies and times were found to be related to
transition probabilities above and below 0·5 in exactly the same way as
frequencies and times for apparently simpler discriminations have been
found to be related to stimulus differences above and below zero.

The most obvious application of the recruitment model to this task
would be to suppose that the observer scans the matrix in a random manner,
and inspects pairs of horizontally adjacent cells, adding 1 to a counter
(controlling the response "coarse") for each pair sampled of the same
colour, and adding 1 to a separate counter (controlling the "even" response)
for every dissimilar pair, making the appropriate response as soon as a
preset total $k$ is reached in either counter. With the exception of the times for
infrequent responses, which (as noted above) "appear to tip back down",
this interpretation would seem to give a reasonable account of the relations
between transition probability and response frequency and time, observed
by Pickett.

Unfortunately for this interpretation, Pickett also found that observers
became both faster and more accurate as the size of the matrix was increased
from $20 \times 20$ up to $120 \times 120$ cells. Such a change is inconsistent with a
simple reduction in $k$, and implies that the quality of the information
available from the larger matrices is somehow improved. If this is so,
however, then the application of the recruitment model proposed above
would seem to be mistaken since the chances of encountering a horizontally
adjacent pair of similar (or dissimilar) cells is independent of the size of the
matrix.

Since no other plausible explanation suggests itself, this finding, when
taken in conjunction with the discrepancies noted above in relation to
response times, and the good account nevertheless given of the results of
Sanders and Ter Linden, seems to indicate that the assumptions made by the
recruitment process concerning the nature of the remembered information
may be inappropriate in some small but significant way. At any rate, the
attempt to reconcile these findings suggests one further variant, to which
we now turn.

### An "Accumulator" Model

A few minutes' scrutiny of the stimuli in Fig. 26 is sufficient to suggest a
number of other kinds of information upon which an observer might base
his discrimination between "coarse" and "even" matrices. In particular, a
detailed comparison of the patterns shows that when the horizontal

transition probability is high (as in Fig. 26c), then the number of long horizontal runs of cells of the same colour is increased. Conversely, when the horizontal transition probability is low (as in Fig. 26a), the proportion of long, horizontal runs is reduced, but is increased in the vertical direction. Although Pickett used spots in place of black cells, thereby somewhat reducing the effect of these continuities, I have argued that it nevertheless seems plausible to suppose that his observers based their decisions on some predetermined accumulation of run lengths in either the horizontal or the vertical direction (Vickers, 1970). At the least, this hypothesis would explain the lawful relationships between transition probability and response time and frequency obtained by Pickett. Meanwhile, other evidence which would also point to such an interpretation is provided by a series of experiments, using similar patterns, in which Julesz found that discriminability was "based primarily on clusters of lines formed by points of uniform brightness" (1962, p. 84).

More strikingly, perhaps, the same hypothesis would explain Pickett's finding that both response times and errors decreased as more cells were added to the matrix. As is intuitively obvious, a short sequence length in the horizontal direction (as in the limiting case of only 2 cells) will limit the maximum length of the horizontal runs. On the other hand, provided that transition probability exceeds 0·5, a longer sequence should result in a distribution of runs with a somewhat greater mean length. In order to test this, 1000 sequences of each length used by Pickett were generated by computer for each of a range of different transition probabilities, and statistics calculated on the resulting distributions of run lengths. Some typical results are presented in Fig. 27, which shows how the mean run length for three different transition probabilities increases as the length of the sequence is extended from 20 (the shortest used by Pickett) up to 120 (the longest used by him). Although the increase in the mean length for horizontal runs is small, this increase would also take place in the length of the vertical runs for those matrices with a horizontal transition probability lower than 0·5. If we further assume, as argued above, that an observer accumulates several run lengths in order to attain a certain critical total magnitude, then the effect of a slight enhancement of mean run length as the size of the matrix is increased would be multiplied several times, and would appear to be sufficient to explain the general improvement in performance found by Pickett.

Meanwhile, this hypothesis would also remain consistent with the finding by Sanders and Ter Linden that the empirically estimated difference $|t_g - t_l|$ was lower when observers took longer to reach a decision. In the case of a binary sequence, the criterion of a total accumulated run length of $k$ events would have the same implications as the criterion of a simple total of

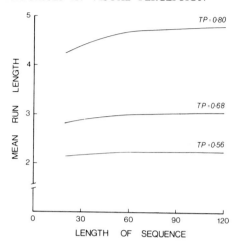

Fig. 27. Mean run lengths for different transition probabilities (*TP*) as a function of the length of a sequence of binary events. The curves are based on a computer simulation of the stimulus generation process employed by Pickett (1967).

$k$ events with respect to the value of $|t_g - t_i|$ at the moment the criterion is fulfilled. At the same time, the notion that the observer is accumulating a total run length, rather than looking for a run of a critical length, is sufficient to explain the results of Sanders and Ter Linden's third experiment. In this experiment (the design of which is outlined in Table I), responses to larger numbers of short runs occurring earlier in a sequence were compared with those to smaller numbers of longer runs presented later. As can be gleaned from Table I, and is clearly shown in Fig. 28, the constraints employed in generating these sequences have the incidental consequence that the total run length of $A$ events builds up more quickly in the early part of the short run ($P$) sequences than in the case of the long run ($Q$ and $R$) sequences. Provided the critical accumulated run length for some observers is 7 or less, therefore, the mean number of observations required for the whole group to reach a decision will be less for a type $P$ than a type $Q$ sequence, and less for a type $Q$ than a type $R$. In view of the independent evidence (c.f. Erlick, 1961) that clustering is also important in sequentially presented signals, these results would seem to show clearly that observers in this type of experiment base their decisions upon a certain critical magnitude of accumulated run length.

A somewhat similar proposal has in fact been put forward (Vickers *et al.*, 1971) to explain the results of our study of discriminating between the relative frequency of red and blue flashes presented in random sequence.

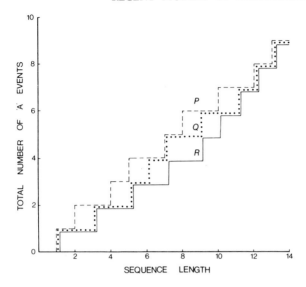

Fig. 28. Rate of accumulation of "A" events in the type $P$, type $Q$ and type $R$ sequences employed by Sanders and Ter Linden (1967).

However, we proposed that the perceived intensity of each individual flash might not remain constant, but might fluctuate normally from one observation to the next, with the observer's criterion being a certain accumulated intensity of red or blue. As Wilding (1974) pointed out, some very small discrepancies still remained between theoretical and empirical response time distributions, although these could be reduced or eliminated by assuming a greater variability in subjective flash intensity. However, the present hypothesis (that the observer accumulates runs of variable length, or some subjective representation thereof) appears to remove these discrepancies without the need to postulate an arbitrarily high degree of variability in the subjective intensity of each flash.

Besides the advantage of simplicity, the present hypothesis would lead us to expect the apparent close agreement among the results for experiments of the type carried out by Pickett, those in which sequences of binary events are presented, and those in which observers are required to discriminate between two continuously variable stimuli which vary along a single dimension, such as length. In effect, the agreement is to be expected in view of the similarity in the shapes of the distributions of the magnitudes of sampled events. For example, in the case of the probabilistic sequences employed in our study (Vickers et al., 1971) the distributions constitute a

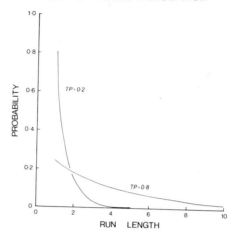

Fig. 29. Distribution of run lengths for two transition probabilities (*TP*) in stimuli of the type used by Pickett (1967).

discrete form of the negative exponential. As can be seen from the typical examples shown in Fig. 29, the distributions of run lengths to be encountered in Pickett's stimuli also conform to this description. In both cases they closely resemble the general form of the truncated distributions of positive and negative stimulus differences pictured earlier in Fig. 10. A considerable economy would be achieved, therefore, if we could suppose that, when an observer is required to discriminate between two stimuli which vary continuously on a single dimension, he bases his decision upon a certain critical magnitude of the accumulated positive or negative differences between their momentary subjective representations.

An *accumulator* model of this kind was first suggested (Vickers, 1967) as a way of accounting for the fact that, even when two signals are identical or very difficult to discriminate, observers do not continue to take observations indefinitely, but reach a decision in a time which is comparable to that for a discrimination of moderate difficulty (e.g. Kellogg, 1931; Johnson, 1939; Cartwright, 1941; Festinger, 1943a; Birren and Botwinick, 1955; Botwinick *et al.* 1958). As later outlined (Vickers, 1970), the model assumes that the observer accumulates the magnitudes of the positive and negative subjective ($V-S$) differences in two separate stores until the accumulated amount of positive difference $t_g$ reaches or exceeds a certain critical magnitude $k_g$, or until the amount of negative difference $t_l$ reaches or exceeds a (possibly different) critical magnitude $k_l$. If the accumulated total $t_g$ reaches $k_g$ first, he responds "$V > S$", and if the total $t_l$ reaches $k_l$ first, he responds "$V > S$". Otherwise he continues to take observations until either criterion is satisfied. As soon as a response is made, the totals $t_g$ and $t_l$ are reset to zero, and the process is ready to begin anew.

Expressed in this form, the accumulator model clearly has affinities with the recruitment process. As suggested by the data of Howell (1970) and Sanders and Ter Linden (1967), it accumulates information over the entire sequence, and, as implied by the results of Audley (1964), it does not store the order of the observations. Like the recruitment process, it also embodies the principle of "rein control" in two unidirectional counters. Unlike the recruitment process, however, the quantities stored are not unit increments, but continuously varying magnitudes, so that the model is not wasteful of information. Although the model falls into the class of "Generalized Accumulator" processes discussed by Audley and Pike (1965), the term *accumulator* has been kept for this specific model, since the other

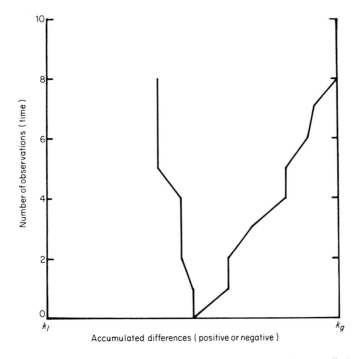

Fig. 30. The accumulator process conceived as a conditional random walk, in which a step to the left is taken on encountering a negative ($V$–$S$) difference and a step to the right if the difference is positive. A response of the form "$V > S$" or "$V < S$" is made when either of the accumulated positive or negative totals reaches or exceeds $k_g$ or $k_l$ respectively.

processes involve the counting or registration of unit increments, rather than the accumulation of varying quantities and, in any case, already have specific names. The name also has an immediate concrete analogy in a system of two capacitors or "accumulators", one of which accumulates randomly varying positive charges, while the other accumulates negative, until a certain total charge has been accumulated in one, whereupon it discharges.

The model also has analogies in the informal decision processes embodied in competitive games, such as squash, in which the period of service by each player contributes a randomly varying amount to his own individual score, with victory being accorded to the player whose score first reaches a certain prescribed total. Meanwhile, two more formal ways of conceptualizing the model are illustrated in Figs 30 and 31. In the first, the decision process is thought of as a kind of conditional random walk in which a step to the right is taken only if a positive $(V-S)$ difference is encountered, and vice versa. Within each observation interval, the magnitude of the step is determined by the magnitude of the sampled difference and, over a series of equal intervals, the first step of the walk to cross a boundary triggers the corresponding response. In the second, the model is conceived in terms of a flow diagram of the sequence of operations assumed to occur during the decision process and is largely self-explanatory.

As is perhaps now evident, the model has an appealing conceptual simplicity and derives a considerable plausibility from its capacity to explain a variety of qualitative experimental findings. For a more stringent test, however, we must examine the extent to which its more quantitative predictions match the features of empirical data.

## Predictions of an Accumulator Model

At this point we encounter a momentary setback, since, although the model is conceptually simple, the assumption that it operates on truncated distributions of continuously varying magnitudes makes its mathematical analysis extremely difficult.* In default of an analytical solution, I have presented detailed predictions from the model based on extensive computer simulations of the process (Vickers, 1970, 1972a). In these simulations a normal distribution of $(V-S)$ differences was generated, with mean $\overline{(V-S)}$ and standard deviation $\sigma_{(V-S)}$, which was intended to represent the distribution of subjective differences exemplified in Fig. 10. Positive and negative differences were randomly sampled from this distribution, according to the

---

* Since this chapter was written a more general random walk process has been formulated by Link and Heath (1975), and developed by Link (1975, 1978). However, this differs from the accumulator model, in which both walks proceed in opposite directions within the same trial, with movement along one precluding movement along the other (c.f. Link and Heath (1975) p. 81).

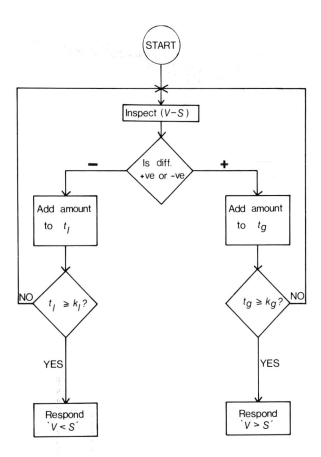

Fig. 31. Flow diagram of the sequence of operations envisaged in an accumulator model for two-category discrimination. The observer is thought of as separately accumulating positive and negative subjective $(V-S)$ differences, taking account of magnitude, until the accumulated quantity reaches or exceeds a critical amount $k_g$ or $k_l$.

sequence of operations specified in Fig. 31, until a preset total of positive or negative difference was accumulated, whereupon the appropriate "response" was recorded. This process was repeated over a large number of "trials" and statistics calculated concerning the relative frequency with which each "response" occurred, and the distribution of the number of observations required before the process reached a decision. Detailed results from a number of these simulations are presented below, where they are compared with the relevant experimental evidence.

## Response Probability

The pattern of response probabilities generated by an extensive simulation of the accumulator model is shown in Fig. 32. In this simulation the hypothesized process was presented with 2000 "trials" at each of 31 different values of the mean difference $(\overline{V-S})$, varying from $-3$ up to $+3$ in steps of $0 \cdot 2\sigma_{(V-S)}$. (For the sake of generality, the value of $\sigma_{(V-S)}$ is assumed throughout the book to be constant, and values of the mean $(V-S)$ and of the criteria $k_g$ and $k_l$ are expressed in common units of $\sigma_{(V-S)}$).

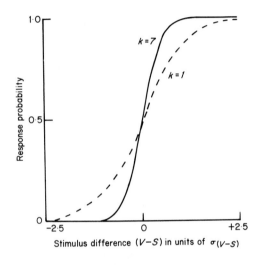

Fig. 32. The pattern of response probabilities generated by a computer simulation of the accumulator model for two-category discrimination for two values of $k_g = k_l$. The psychometric functions are for responses of the form "$V > S$".

As found empirically by a multitude of investigators since Pierce and Jastrow (1885), the probability of making a simulated response of the form "$V > S$" is a sigmoid function of the size of the stimulus difference. If $k_g$ and $k_l$ are assumed to be equal, then, as the value of $k$ is increased in the simulated process, so the precision of the ogives in Fig. 32 also increases, thereby providing the theoretical counterpart to the speed–accuracy trade-off discussed in the last chapter (pp. 40–43).

When the value of $k_g$ in the simulated process is not assumed to be equal to that of $k_l$, then either the precision of the ogives or the $PSE$ (or both) may vary. For example, when bias against the "greater" response is set up, as in Fig. 33, by increasing the value of $k_g$ from $(k_g = k_l = 2)$ up to $(k_g = 6, k_l = 2)$, then the psychometric function for "greater" responses increases in

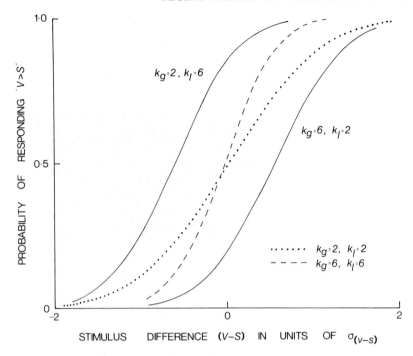

Fig. 33. Effects of bias on the probability of making responses of the form "$V > S$" in a computer simulation of the accumulator model of two-category discrimination for various combinations of the values of $k_g$ and $k_l$.

precision, and is shifted upwards along the $\overline{(V-S)}$ dimension. On the other hand, when this bias is reversed, so that $k_g = 2$ and $k_l = 6$, then the psychometric function retains its precision, but is shifted downwards along the dimension of stimulus differences. Although empirical data concerning the precision of the psychometric curves are not available, this shift seems to correspond directly with Festinger's finding (1943a) that the PSE was shifted upwards when observers were instructed to guard against making "greater" responses incorrectly, and downwards when they were told not to make the "lesser" ones incorrectly.

In an attempt to provide a general characterization of the psychometric functions in Fig. 32, the possibility was explored of fitting the curves by normal ogives. However, the fit produced by these was generally inferior to that produced by a logistic function of the form $y = [1 + \exp^{(-axk - bx)}]^{-1}$. It was found that a good approximation over a wide range of values of $\overline{(V-S)}$ and of $k$ was given by the constants $a = 0.4612$ and $b = 1.3026$, with $y$ interpreted as the probability of making a response of the form "$V > S$", $x$ as the stimulus difference measured in units of $\sigma_{(V-S)}$ and $k$ as the value of the criterion, with $k_g = k_l$.

Although the evidence summarized above would suggest that the normal ogive is as good an approximation to empirical psychometric functions as can be expected, the logistic function has several times been suggested as a useful alternative description of response frequencies (Berkson, 1944, 1953; Guilford, 1936; Luce, 1959; Bush, 1963; Ogilvie and Creelman, 1968). The proportion $P$ of "$V > S$" responses can be interpreted as the antilogit of $\lambda$, where $P = 1/1 + e^{-\lambda}$. The inverse function $\lambda = \log P/1 - P$ is known as logit $P$, tables of which are given by Berkson (1953) and Bush (1963). Where $\lambda = (ak - b)/x$, and the meanings of $a$, $b$, $k$ and $x$ remain as defined above, then this formulation has the advantage that an estimate of $k$ should be given by

$$\hat{k} = [x \log (P/1 - P) + 1\cdot3026]/0\cdot4612. \tag{1}$$

That is, if we know the stimulus difference $x$ and the response frequency $P$, the value of $k$ can be estimated in the same units as $x$. (The calculation of log $P/1 - P$ can be obviated by consulting the tables of logit $P$ in Berkson (1953) or Bush (1963)).

## The Speed–Accuracy Trade-off

While the predicted pattern of response probabilities by itself can hardly be regarded as decisive evidence in favour of the accumulator as opposed to any other process, when this is taken in conjunction with the pattern of associated response times, some clear support emerges for the kind of optional-stopping mechanism which the accumulator process implies. Figure 34, for example, shows some results from an extensive simulation of the accumulator process, in which each of four different values of the stimulus difference ($\overline{V-S}$) were presented 2000 times to the hypothetical process at each of 12 values of the criteria (with $k_g$ and $k_l$ being equal throughout). When plotted against the growing number of observations required by the process, as values of $k$ are increased, the percentage of correct responses falls on a negatively accelerated curve, which is different for each level of discriminability.

The most interesting feature of Fig. 34 is that the steepness of the curve relating percentage of correct responses to number of observations is a direct function of the difference between the stimuli being discriminated. Although this feature characterizes the predictions of all the optional-stopping models considered in this chapter and does not differentiate between them, it does serve to distinguish this approach from a number of other, more descriptive, hypotheses concerning the relation between accuracy and time.

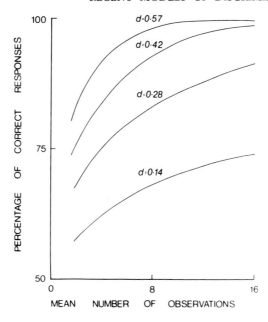

Fig. 34. Speed–accuracy trade-off functions observed in computer simulations of the accumulator model of two-category discrimination. Each curve shows how the percentage of correct responses made increases as the mean number of observations required to reach a decision becomes greater with higher values of $k_g = k_l$. The separate curves are for stimulus differences of mean value $d$, measured in units of $\sigma_{(V-S)}$.

For example, as mentioned in the last chapter, Thurstone (1937) proposed that, with discriminability held constant, the relation between the time taken to make a judgment and its probability of being correct should be described by a normal ogive. However, the relation between the slope of this ogive and stimulus discriminability remains unspecified. Much later, Schouten and Bekker (1967) suggested a "perceptual focussing model", according to which the logarithm of $(p_e/p_e + p_c)$ should be an inverse linear function of time, where $p_e$ represents the proportion of errors, and $p_c$ that of correct responses. At the same time, and on the basis of a similar, fixed-sample model, Taylor et al. (1967) deduced that the measure $d'^2$, calculated by taking the $z$-score corresponding to $p_c$, should be a direct linear function of time. Similarly, Pew (1969) has suggested that there should be a linear relation between log $(p_c/p_e)$ and response time. (In the two-alternative case, log $(p_c/p_e)$ is a linear transformation of $d'^2$.) Finally, starting from a different theoretical standpoint, Pachella et al. (1968),

Pachella and Fisher (1969), Swanson and Briggs (1969) and Pew (1969) have all found evidence in choice-reaction tasks that speed and accuracy are related according to Hick's law (1952b), whereby the time taken should be a linear function of the information $H_t$ transmitted by an observer's responses. According to Swensson (1972), this is tantamount in the two–alternative case to asserting a linear relation between response time and

$$H_t = 1 + [p_c \log (p_c) + p_e \log (p_e)].$$

Although all of these proposals predict that the empirical curve for percentage of correct response against time should be negatively acceler-ated, none of them predicts that the steepness of the curve should be a function of stimulus difference. However, a number of experiments do indicate that the slope of the trade-off function becomes steeper as dis-criminability is increased. For example, in a task in which observers were required to discriminate between the relative frequencies of differently coloured dots, exposed for various durations, Philip (1947) found that the proportion of correct responses for stimuli of intermediate discriminability increased as a more rapid function of exposure time than that for stimuli of very low discriminability. Meanwhile, highly discriminable stimuli were discriminated with nearly perfect accuracy, irrespective of the exposure interval used. More recently, Swensson has found that "increased stimulus difficulty (increasing similarity of the stimulus rectangles' length and width) clearly seemed to make trade-off functions less steep", while "unlike estimates of the trade-off slopes, the intercept estimates showed little systematic change with stimulus similarity" (1972, p. 27).

This description of empirical findings applies equally to the simulated trade-off functions in Fig. 34. Thus, although it seems unlikely that this aspect of performance will permit any further differentiation among the four main models considered in this chapter, the general pattern of experimental results is in good accord with the behaviour of the trade-off functions predicted by them. To this extent at least these data provide clear support for an optional-stopping process, like the accumulator, in which the average quality of successively sampled observations enters as an important parameter.

## Response Time and Stimulus Difference

When we turn to examine the pattern of response times predicted by an accumulator process as stimulus difference is varied, then some more precise distinctions become possible. These distinctions are most conve-niently dealt with by considering separately the times for correct responses only, before looking at the relation between the times for correct and those for incorrect responses.

*The relation between stimulus difference and the mean time for correct responses.* Although the general effect of variations in discriminability on the mean time for correct responses is well established, there has been comparatively little study of the precise nature of the function relating the objective difference between two stimuli to the time taken to discriminate between them. In an early study, Henmon (1906) found that, as objective difference was decreased arithmetically, judgment time appeared to increase geometrically. Some half a century later, Crossman (1955) considered several formulae and concluded that the rise in response time with reduced discriminability was best described by a "confusion function", according to which response time should be inversely proportional to the difference between the logarithmic values of the two stimulus magnitudes.

While this expression seemed to be consistent with a generally assumed logarithmic transformation of stimulus magnitude, and with Fechner's "difference formula" for the effective difference between two stimuli, I have already pointed out (Vickers, 1967) that this formula breaks down where discrimination is very difficult, as in my own experiments and in those of Birren and Botwinick (1955), and Botwinick *et al.* (1958). As was found in several other experiments (Kellogg, 1931; Pike, 1968; Vickers, 1970; Vickers *et al.*, 1971) and in numerous studies since, when discriminability is severely reduced, the rate of increase in the mean time for correct responses begins to level off.

Figure 35 shows the pattern of the mean number of observations required by the hypothetical process to reach a decision for different values of $k$, which was obtained in the simulation study already described in connection with response probability. As can be seen from the data for the response "$V > S$" made correctly (i.e. the portion of the curves to the right of a stimulus difference of zero), the mean value shows its most rapid change for stimulus differences between $1·5\sigma_{(V-S)}$ and $0·5\sigma_{(V-S)}$. As the stimulus difference exceeds $2·0\sigma_{(V-S)}$, or approaches 0, the rate of change becomes appreciably less. Thus this pattern conflicts with the formulations of Henmon (1906) and of Crossman (1955), but would appear to find ample empirical confirmation in the studies of Birren and others cited above.

*The times for correct and incorrect responses.*    While the above aspect does not distinguish among the four main models considered in this chapter, the relation between the mean numbers of observations for correct and incorrect responses clearly does. As we have seen (pp. 40–43), when observers respond quickly and are relatively inaccurate, then empirical mean times for incorrect responses are similar to those for correct, though their distributions differ somewhat in shape. However, as data for more

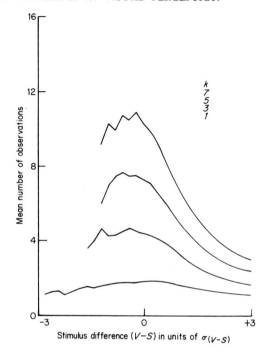

Fig. 35. The mean number of observations required by a computer simulation of the two-category accumulator process to make a response of the form "$V > S$" for various values of $k_g = k_l$.

cautious observers are considered, empirical response time functions become increasingly asymmetrical, although the times for errors still appear to "tip back down" when the probability of making an error is low. Although various features of this pattern are inconsistent with the predictions of each of the models previously examined, they all seem to correspond well with the behaviour of the simulated accumulator process depicted in Fig. 35. Thus, in addition to accommodating the implications of experiments by Audley (1964), Sanders and Ter Linden (1967), Pickett (1967), Howell (1970) and others regarding the nature of the information remembered and the criterion employed in reaching a decision, the accumulator model is clearly superior to the runs, random walk or recruitment processes in its detailed prediction of the rather complex interaction which appears to take place between stimulus difference, subjective caution and response time.

## The Shapes of the Response Time Distributions

The superiority of the accumulator process is further confirmed when we look at the higher moments of the response time distributions. For convenience, this examination can be broken down into a comparison of the predicted and obtained relations between stimulus difference and measures of skewness and kurtosis, followed by a more general comparison between the classifications of theoretical and empirical response time distributions.

*Measures of skewness and kurtosis.*    As we have already seen in several studies, it was found that there was a positive correlation between stimulus difference and measures of skewness and kurtosis for both correct and incorrect responses, with both measures remaining predominantly positive in the case of both correct responses and errors (Vickers, 1970; Vickers *et al.*, 1971; Wilding, 1974; Vickers and Domac (unpublished); Vickers and Willson (unpublished)). To varying extents, these findings are inconsistent with each of the runs, random walk and recruitment models. In contrast, however, this pattern corresponds exactly to that produced by the simulated accumulator process, which is presented in Fig. 36. As far as the detailed shape of the response time distributions is concerned, therefore, the accumulator would seem to have a clear superiority over the other alternatives.

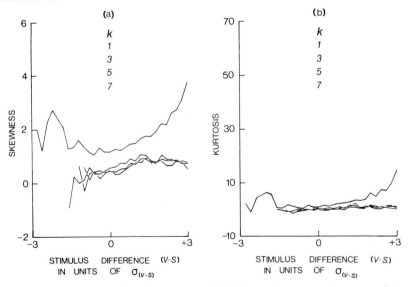

Fig. 36. The pattern of (a) skewness and (b) kurtosis measured generated by a computer simulation of the two-category accumulator model for various values of $k_g = k_l$. The curves shown represent measures for responses of the form "$V > S$".

*The classification of theoretical and empirical response time distributions.* Where $\mu_2$, $\mu_3$ and $\mu_4$ are the second, third and fourth moments about the mean, respectively, and where $\beta_1 = \mu_3^2/\mu_2^3$, and $\mu_2 = \mu_4/\mu_2^2$, it is possible to classify empirical and theoretical distributions into various types, according to the value assumed by $c$ in the identity $c = [\beta_1(\beta_2 + 3)^2]/[4(4\beta_2 - 3\beta_1)(2\beta_2 - 3\beta_1 - 6)]$. Where $c < 0$, a distribution is of Type I ("beta of the first kind"); where $0 < c < 1$, the distribution is of Type IV; where $c > 1$, the distribution is of Type II ("beta of the second kind"); and where $c \to \infty$, the distribution is of Type III (or "gamma"). In addition, for the ordinary gamma, an exact relation between the moments must hold, such that $\beta_2 = 3 + (3/2)\beta_1$ (Snodgrass *et al.*, 1967). Adjacent restrictions also apply to the generalized gamma (McGill, 1963; McGill and Gibbon, 1965), for which the following inequalities must be satisfied:

$$0 < \beta_1 \leqslant 4;$$

and

$$3 + (3/2)\beta_1 \leqslant \beta_2 \leqslant 3 + (27/2)^{\frac{1}{3}}\beta_1^{\frac{2}{3}}.$$

Values of $\beta_1$ for distributions generated by each of the four main models are shown in Fig. 37, plotted against $\beta_2$, together with the relations characterizing the gamma and the generalized gamma distributions, both of which have also been proposed as descriptions for empirical distributions of response time (e.g. McGill, 1963; Pike, 1973). For example, Pike (1973) has suggested that a recruitment process should be considered in which observations are made continuously, rather than at discrete intervals, since predicted standard deviations would then become much larger, and kurtosis would turn out to be positively correlated with discriminability. For this version of the recruitment process, he points out, the general form of the response time distribution is of the gamma type (Kendall and Stuart, 1968).

In order to test which of these descriptions most adequately capture the complex changes which occur in the shapes of response time distributions as stimulus difference and subjective caution are varied, values of $\beta_1$ and $\beta_2$ were calculated for the 878 distributions obtained in various studies (Vickers, 1970; Vickers *et al.*, 1971; Vickers and Domac (unpublished); Vickers and Willson (unpublished). For each experiment considered separately, plots of $\beta_1$ against $\beta_2$ were fitted reasonably well by straight lines, with intercepts of $-0.76$, $-0.93$, $-0.18$ and $-0.18$, and coefficients of $0.49$, $0.47$, $0.70$ and $0.57$ respectively. As can be seen from Fig. 37, the combined finding of a negative intercept and a slope of appreciably less than unity is unique to the accumulator process and, even then, applies only when values of $k$ exceed 3.

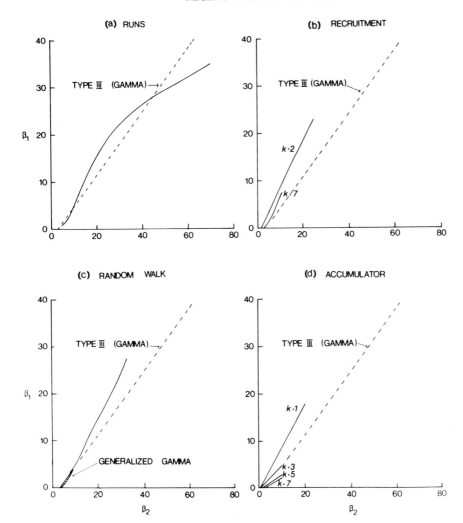

Fig. 37. Values of $\beta_1$ for (a) the runs, (b) the recruitment,(c) the random walk and (d) the accumulator models, plotted against corresponding values of $\beta_2$, together with the relations characterizing the gamma and generalized gamma distributions. For the accumulator process best fitting straight lines have been fitted to the results of a computer simulation.

Meanwhile, Table III shows the results of an attempt to classify the theoretical and empirical distributions into the various types distinguished above. The accumulator process is distinctive in that almost all of the

Table III. The percentages of response time distributions of each type obtained in a number of recent experiments, together with those obtained in extensive simulation of the accumulator process with 7 different values of $k_g = k_l$ ranging from 1 up to $7\sigma_{(V-S)}$.

| Experiment | $\beta$ Type I | Type IV | $\beta$ Type II | $\gamma$ Type III |
|---|---|---|---|---|
| Vickers (1970) | 2 | 92 | 4 | 2 |
| Vickers, Caudrey and Willson (1971) | 2 | 98 | 0 | 0 |
| Vickers, Domac and Willson | 2 | 83 | 15 | 0 |
| Vickers and Willson | 1 | 95 | 4 | 0 |
| Accumulator model | 1 | 96 | 3 | 0 |
| Empirical means | 1·75 | 92 | 5·75 | 0·5 |

simulated distributions (96%) fall into category IV, with a small number of exceptions occurring at the two lowest values of $k$ (1 and 2). As can be seen from the table, the empirical distributions fall into a very similar classification, with most of the distributions (92%) falling into category IV. The largest relative proportion of exceptions (15%) occurs in the experiment by myself and Domac (unpublished) and 13% of these were generated by the two fastest observers.

While it is clear that the type of empirical response time distribution generated by an observer may be affected by the degree of caution exercised by him, these data are probably representative of a fair range of degrees of caution. Although we cannot be sure that the range of $k$ (from 1 to 7) employed in generating the simulated distributions is exactly comparable to that employed by observers in these experiments, there are a number of indirect reasons for supposing that the two ranges are quite similar. (These reasons are mainly based on estimates of $k$ employed by observers in experiments, such as that of Vickers and Willson (unpublished) (c.f. Fig. 25), where the value of the "noise" added to the stimuli is independently known). In any case, the close correspondence between the proportions expected on the accumulator hypothesis and those obtained in a wide variety of different experimental tasks is remarkable. On the basis of the available data, the conclusion seems inescapable that, as far as the effects of bias, caution and discriminability on response probability and time are concerned, the behaviour of the accumulator model mimics that of the human observer in a very precise and striking manner.

## A Possible Neurophysiological Embodiment of the Accumulator Process

In view of the clear success of the accumulator model in accounting for both the qualitative and the quantitative features of human discriminative performance, it seems apposite to consider whether the model also remains consistent with some of the more general constraints mentioned towards the end of the introductory chapter. In later chapters, for example, we shall be concerned with the evolutionary potential of the accumulator mechanism, and with its capacity for self-regulation. Before examining these aspects, however, the argument of the first chapter makes it encumbent on us to ask whether this hypothetical process could conceivably be realised by an organism of the same order of complexity as the one illustrated above in Fig. 3.

If we bear in mind this elementary organism, which is faced with the problem of moving towards the lighter half of its limited visual field, then it does seem possible to transform the accumulator process into a neurophysiological version characterized by the requisite degree of simplicity. Indeed a mechanism capable of carrying out simple discriminations, and bearing a close resemblance to an accumulator process was first outlined by Landahl as early as 1938. A similar version, modified to suit our hypothetical organism and based on the well established neurophysiological principles of excitation and inhibition, temporal summation and threshold discharge, is illustrated in Fig. 38. Apart from the addition of two "accumulative processes", which summate signals over time before reaching a threshold and discharging, the version shown in Fig. 38 also corresponds to the schematic neural circuit outlined by Cornsweet for the primary processing of information from the retina of the horseshoe crab (1970, p. 295).

The system in Fig. 38 is exceedingly simple and consists of only two photoreceptors, four pathways, two input and accumulative processes and two sets of muscle cells, capable of producing movement in opposite directions. One pathway from each photoreceptor carries excitatory signals to the input process on the same side, while the other carries inhibitory signals to the contralateral input process. As a result of this arrangement, the input process labelled "$v > s$" will transmit excitatory signals only when the excitation from $v$ is greater than the inhibition from $s$; otherwise it will be inhibited and remain inactive. It seems reasonable to assume in addition that the strength of the excitatory signals from the "$v > s$" input is

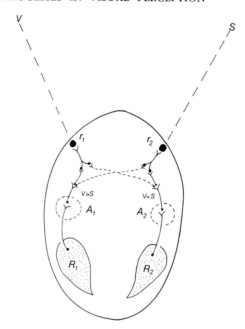

Fig. 38. Speculative realization of a simple organism similar to that shown in Fig. 3 and capable of embodying the essential features of an accumulator process of discrimination. Light intensities $v$ and $s$ are registered at photoreceptors $r_1$ and $r_2$, which send both excitatory (solid lines) and inhibitory impulses (broken lines) to two accumulators or storage centres $A_1$ and $A_2$. When the amount of excitation generated by $v$ is greater than that generated by $s$ then $A_1$ will receive an excitatory signal, while activity in $A_2$ will be inhibited by the greater inhibitory signal generated by $v$ and transmitted from $r_1$. The converse situation (i.e. $A_2$ activated, $A_1$ inhibited) will arise when the amount of excitation generated by $s$ is greater. The model assumes that excitation builds up in either $A_1$ or $A_2$ until a threshold is reached, whereupon the effectors $R_1$ or $R_2$ respectively, are activated. Such a simple organism would be capable of consistently moving towards the lighter (or darker) half of its visual field, i.e. of making an elementary brightness discrimination.

proportional to the difference between the amount of excitation from $v$ and the inhibition from $s$. Conversely, when $s$ gives rise to a signal of greater intensity than $v$, the input process labelled "$v < s$" will transmit signals proportional to the amount by which $s$ exceeds $v$.

As is perhaps now evident, the input processes are analogous to the positive and negative stimulus differences on which an accumulator model is supposed to operate. As in the model, the signals transmitted from each input process may be further assumed to accumulate in two separate centres until a certain critical level has been reached in one, whereupon a corresponding response (e.g. movement to the left or the right) is triggered. Such a process would behave in ways which are quite similar to the accumulator model outlined in this chapter. (For example, the time taken by the process would be inversely proportional to the difference in intensity between the two stimuli $v$ and $s$). Given this hypothetical neurophysiological embodiment, then, the accumulator model inferred from psychophysical studies of discrimination appears to be commensurate in complexity, as well as beguilingly similar in representation, to the elementary organism envisaged in the last chapter and pictured in Fig. 3.

# 4

## Models for Three-category Tasks and Judgments of Sameness and Difference

*If, then, we are dealing with mind as mind presents itself to us for examination, we cannot ignore these judgments . . . Our primary task, as psychologists, is to discover the processes of consciousness, not to force those processes into our ready-made channels.*

E. B. Titchener (1905, *vol.* II, part 2, p. 290).

It was suggested in the introductory chapter that, besides the ability to discriminate, even the most elementary organism of the kind shown in Fig. 3 would have possessed some capacity for recognizing identities between certain aspects of its environment. Similarly, at the human level, most experimenters who have trained observers in a "forced choice" discrimination procedure involving only two extreme categories of response, and employing stimuli which were very difficult to distinguish, would be inclined to agree with Titchener's conclusion that "doubtful and equal judgments do naturally occur; they are attested by introspection, and by the introspection of competent observers" (1905, p. 290). Although it is possible that an elementary organism might survive if its response repertoire were limited to purely comparative judgments, it is clear that the ability to perceive that two stimuli are effectively equal with respect to some particular dimension paves the way for powerful economies in the coding of sensory information. Indeed it is difficult to understand how such processes as generalization and recognition could operate without this facility. Meanwhile, the ability to make judgments of equality is obviously essential in countless practical contexts at the human level. (Carpentry would be a distressing occupation indeed if no two table legs ever appeared to be the same in length.)

As early as 1905, Titchener pointed out that it was "unscientific" to ignore these identification responses, while, in a later recognition of their importance, Fernberger (1930, 1931) argued that the subjective factors involved constituted one of the main problems for psychophysics. Although Fernberger urged an extensive experimental investigation of them, however, there has been something of a dearth of studies of the intermediate judgment. It will have been noticed, for example, that, although the classical psychophysical model was rejected in part because it failed to provide a theoretical mechanism for intermediate responses, none of the optional-stopping models outlined in the last chapter is capable, as it stands, of accounting for judgments of equality or sameness. Historically, at least, this omission does not seem to have stemmed from the opinion that intermediate judgments were unimportant, but from an early realization that they were influenced by a number of subjective factors in ways which were too complex to be encompassed by the classical theory (Jastrow, 1888; Boring, 1920; Thurstone, 1948; Guilford, 1936).

To some extent, therefore, the present chapter is intended to redress the omission of any treatment of intermediate responses from the previous one. For the sake of convenience in exposition, it is divided into two main sections. The first is taken up with three-category tasks, in which judgments of "greater", "lesser" and "equal" are allowed. The second and shorter section has to do with the superficially simpler judgments of "sameness" and "difference" (i.e. irrespective of which direction the "difference" takes). Although this organization means that we shall occasionally have to retrace our argument, it has the advantage of emphasizing the essential similarity of empirical findings and theorizing concerning these two types of judgment.

## Models for Three-category Tasks

Although no full-blown programme has yet materialized, there has lately been a quickening of interest in the intermediate response. As is to be expected, the recent development of theoretical models for three-category decisions has followed a similar course to that for two-category differential judgments. The first hypothesis we shall look at, therefore, is a signal detection account, in which the determination of alternative responses is largely accomplished by the preliminary classification of the inspected $(V-S)$ differences by means of two variable cutoffs. Following this, we shall consider a modification of one kind of optional-stopping process (the random walk), in which the intermediate response is made only if an extreme response does not eventuate by a predetermined deadline. Finally, we shall examine two possible modifications of an accumulator process, in which a critical amount of evidence for an intermediate response is attained by the accumulation of some function of the momentary positive and negative stimulus differences.

## *Signal Detection Accounts*

The general form of the psychometric functions typically obtained in three-category tasks has been illustrated earlier in Fig. 6. Meanwhile, some relevant empirical functions have been obtained in a set of recent experiments (Vickers, 1975), in which observers were required to decide whether the mean horizontal length of the randomly varying individual line segments in two square arrays, resembling those in Fig. 39, was greater in the left-hand or in the right-hand array, or was the same for both. Responses were made by moving the right forefinger from a wedge-shaped base to one of three keys set at the apex and at either side of the wedge.

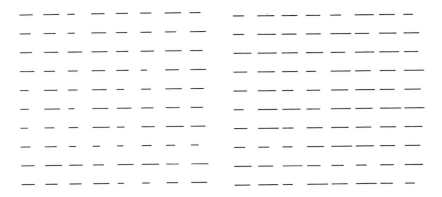

Fig. 39. Stimuli of the kind used in experiments on three-category judgments (Vickers, 1975). In this case the mean length of the horizontal line segments in the right-hand array is greater than that in the left.

Psychometric functions obtained in two of these experiments are shown in Fig. 40. Those in Fig. 40a represent means for five observers, each of which was presented with 220 pairs of stimuli in a random sequence in which the objective probability that the arrays were equal was quite low (0·09). Psychometric functions in Fig. 40b, on the other hand, are based on means for a second group of five observers, who carried out the same task over a similar number of trials, with the difference that the objective probability of encountering two equal arrays was much higher (0·5).

As can be seen from both Fig. 40a and 40b, the probability of making an "equal" response falls on a bell-shaped curve when plotted against the objective difference ($v$–$s$) between the left-hand and right-hand stimulus arrays. Although the observers in the two groups are different, the apparent increase in both *MP* and *IU* as the proportion of objectively equal stimuli is

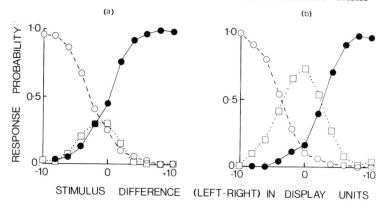

Fig. 40. The pattern of response probabilities obtained (Vickers, 1975) in two 3-category tasks. Figure 40a shows the results of experiment 1, in which the *a priori* probability of an "equal" response was 0·09, while Fig. 40b presents data for experiment 2, in which the *a priori* probability of the intermediate response was 0·50. Filled circles represent responses of the form "$V>S$", empty circles those of the form "$V < S$", and empty squares those of the form "$V = S$".

increased is consistent with Urban's finding of a perfect correlation between these two measures within the data for individual observers in the same condition. Meanwhile, the precision of the extreme curves does not appear to change greatly, which would suggest *as an initial approximation* that the pattern of change in the psychometric functions for three-category tasks might be restricted to that depicted earlier in Fig. 15.

## A Signal Detection Model of Three-category Decisions

It seems to have been in order to account for this type of pattern that, as has been outlined in Chapter 2 (pp. 36–40), both Greenberg (1965) and Treisman and Watts (1966) suggested a signal detection model, which is tantamount to a modification of Thurstone's law of comparative judgment (1927a, 1927b), to allow for the possibility of making an intermediate response. More recently, Olson and Ogilvie (1972) have proposed a more formal, but essentially similar version. While differing in detail, all these approaches resemble the one touched on in Chapter 2 and can be taken as supposing that, whenever the momentary value of the distribution of subjective $(V–S)$ differences exceeds a certain cutoff $x_g$, the observer responds "$V > S$". Conversely, when the value falls below a different cutoff $x_l$, he responds "$V < S$", and, if it falls between $x_g$ and $x_l$, he responds "$V = S$". According to this view, therefore, an increased tendency to make "equal" responses would signify a wider separation between the two cutoffs, while a reduced separation would give rise to the production of fewer intermediate judgments. The interval controlling the intermediate response is thus functionally equivalent to the region of "no-decision" in the model proposed by Cartwright and Festinger (1943).

As pointed out in Chapter 2, this three-category version of the signal detection model implies that the sole effect of an experimental treatment designed to increase the proportion of intermediate judgments should be an increase in both $MP$ and $IU$. The precision of the extreme psychometric functions, on the other hand, should remain unaltered (Fig. 15). Apart from the data shown in Fig. 40, however, no other empirical evidence is known which bears directly on this question.

It would seem that there is some need, therefore, for an experimental study, in which either the overall caution of an observer, or his relative bias towards making intermediate responses, is manipulated by means of appropriate instructions and *a priori* probabilities, with the specific aim of looking at changes in the measures of $MP$, $IU$ and in the precision of the extreme psychometric curves. Some grounds for expecting that the pattern of changes would not be restricted to that predicted by the signal detection model are to be found in the evidence for a speed–accuracy trade-off, summarized earlier (pp. 40–43), which shows clearly that observers in a two-category task may produce more or less precise psychometric curves by varying their degree of caution. If, as seems likely, a similar trade-off operates in the three-category case, then other patterns of change in the various psychometric curves would become possible, such as those illustrated in Fig. 12.

Although the small amount of data presently available on response probabilities appears to remain noncommittal on this point, the same is not true for the empirical pattern of response times. As pointed out in Chapter 2, the signal detection model for three-category decisions implies that times for each category of response should be equal and should be independent of stimulus difference. However, Fig. 41 clearly shows that the time taken to make intermediate judgments may be quite different from that required for extreme responses, while times for the latter increase markedly as the absolute value of the objective difference between the stimuli decreases. Since the proportion of errors also decreases, these data rule out any decision mechanism operating upon a fixed sample of data, and imply that the extreme responses at least are mediated by an optional-stopping process, in which the time taken is commensurate with the difficulty of the decision, even when this difficulty is not known beforehand. This feature of the data is evident also in the earlier study of Kellogg (1931), and clearly rules out

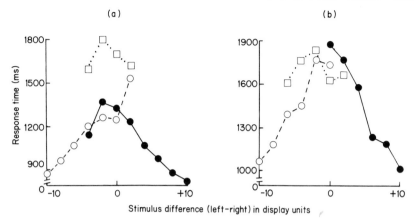

Fig. 41. The pattern of response times obtained (Vickers, 1975) in two 3-category tasks. Figure 41a shows the results of experiment 1, in which the *a priori* probability of an "equal" response was 0·09, while Fig. 41b presents data for experiment 2, in which the *a priori* probability of the intermediate response was 0·50. As in Fig. 40, responses of the form "$V > S$", "$V < S$" and "$V = S$" are represented by filled circles, empty circles and empty squares, respectively.

any approach on which responses are made following the sensory classification of a single observation.

## Optional-stopping up to a Deadline

### A Random Walk and Clock Model

Although no purely optional-stopping models have been suggested explicitly for the three-category case, it is not difficult to devise one by the simple modification of a timing process proposed by Sekuler (1965), Bindra *et al.* (1965) and Nickerson (1969) for signal detection and judgments of sameness and difference. This *random walk and clock* model is illustrated in Fig. 42. According to this hypothesis, the observer is thought of as making a series of observations at regular intervals of the normally distributed ($V$–$S$) differences. Positive and negative differences are stored separately, taking magnitude into account, until the quantity in one store exceeds that in the other by a predetermined amount $k_g$ or $k_l$, or until a critical time $t$ has elapsed, whereupon the observer responds "$V > S$", "$V < S$", or "$V = S$" respectively. Bias towards or away from making an intermediate response can be represented by lowering or raising the value of $t$, while increased caution can be primarily accounted for by increasing the values of

$k_g$ and $k_l$. However, since it is clear that the effects of increasing $k_g$ and $k_l$ may be at least partly offset by lowering the value of $t$, it is worth remarking that the predicted effects of bias and caution are interrelated.

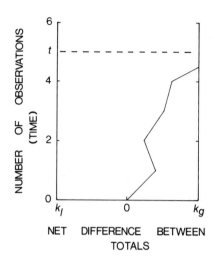

Fig. 42. Representation of a random walk and clock model for three-category judgment. A response of the form "$V > S$", "$V < S$", or "$V = S$" respectively, is made as soon as the net difference between the totals exceeds $k_g$ or $k_l$, or a deadline $t$ has elapsed. It is assumed that observations are made at a steady rate.

As outlined above, the mechanism for making the extreme judgments is essentially the same as the random walk process derived from the work of Stone (1960), Edwards (1965) and Laming (1968), and considered in Chapter 3. Meanwhile, the notion of a "neural clock" was first clearly formulated by McGill (1963), though the very first suggestion of some arbitrary criterion seems to have been made, in the context of two-category judgment, by Johnson, who pointed out that "people do not deliberate forever, even when two stimuli appear equal. They make a response after a while, even if only an arbitrary one. Something else, perhaps a 'giving up' process, must be considered" (1955, p. 373). More recently, a similar notion has underlain the use of "criterion times", which an observer is instructed to regard as a *deadline* for responding (e.g. Fitts, 1966; Ollman, 1966; Schouten and Bekker, 1967; Yellott, 1967, 1971; Pachella and Pew, 1968; Link and Tindall, 1971).

In order to explore the properties of this process, I carried out a number of computer simulations (Vickers, 1975) in which the hypothesized process was presented with sequences of normally distributed ($V$–$S$) differences, and the relative frequency of each "response" recorded, along with the number of "observations" taken to achieve it. Typical results, based on 1000 simulated trials at each of 19 values of the mean difference $(V–S)$ are reproduced in Fig. 43. As can be seen from Fig. 43a, the model produces appropriately shaped psychometric functions, with the exact pattern depending upon the values of $k_g$, $k_l$ and $t$. Meanwhile, as shown in Fig. 43b, times for an extreme response, made correctly, are identical to those for the same response, made incorrectly, to a stimulus difference which is equal in magnitude but opposite in sign. As is intuitively obvious, since intermediate responses are triggered "by default" only if no extreme judgment has been reached by the deadline $t$, these responses are everywhere slower than their extreme counterparts and take a constant time $t$, which is independent of stimulus difference.

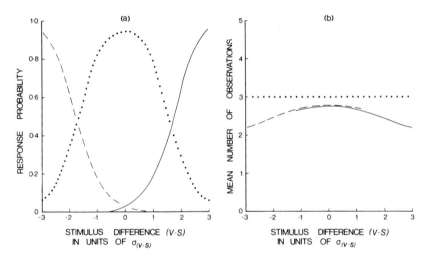

Fig. 43. Patterns of (a) response probabilities and (b) response times obtained in simulation of a random walk and clock model of three-category judgment. The solid line denotes responses of the form "$V > S$", the broken line those of the form "$V < S$", and the dotted line those of the form "$V = S$". In each case the value of $k_g = k_l = 5\sigma_{(V–S)}$ and the clock has a deadline of 3 observations.

An immediate difficulty with this model follows from its prediction that the times for intermediate responses should always be greater than those for the extreme categories. Although this prediction is confirmed in the study by Kellogg (1931), in which each of 7 stimulus differences, including zero, were equally likely, it is not borne out in other experiments in which observers were more likely to make intermediate judgments. For example, in contrast to the emphasis in Kellogg's experiment on finding a difference between the stimuli, Carlson *et al.* (1934) studied the relative times for intermediate and extreme responses under instructions which were designed to encourage the use of an "equal" category. These authors found that, when observers were "trained in an attitude in which the 'equal' judgment was accepted as a category equally valid and quite on a par with either of the categories of 'different' judgments", then there was no difference between the mean response times for the three categories. Meanwhile, in a converse study, Fernberger *et al.* (1934) repeated the experiment of Carlson *et al.* with the difference that they endeavoured to create an attitude on*the part of observers, which was designed to restrain them from making an "equal" response, except when absolutely necessary. Under these conditions, it was found that mean response times for "equal" judgments again became significantly longer than those for extreme responses.

These findings are echoed in the recent set of experiments I conducted (Vickers, 1975), some results of which are shown above in Figs 40 and 41. As can be seen in Fig. 40a, I found that, when observers were biassed against the intermediate category by the use of instructions explaining that only 1 in 11 pairs of stimuli were objectively equal, then the average *MP* was a low 0·30. Meanwhile, for individual observers, times for "equal" responses, made correctly, were greater in all 10 possible comparisons than those for extreme responses to a stimulus difference of zero. On the other hand, as in Fig. 40b and 41b when observers clearly understood that there were equal *a priori* probabilities of having to make an extreme or an intermediate response, the average *MP* rose to 0·73, while the times for the latter were shorter in 7 out of 10 comparisons (with 1 case equal). These results are consistent with Cartwright's conclusion that "the attitude not to give a judgment of 'equal' unless absolutely necessary slows down the judgment of 'equal' when it is made" (1941 p. 193). Contrary to the simple clock model, they imply that the relative times for intermediate and extreme responses depend upon the relative degrees of bias adopted by an observer towards these two categories of response.

## *Evidence against the Notion of a "Clock"*

As I have pointed out (Vickers, 1975), it is possible to go some way towards accounting for these findings if we suppose that the clock in question is not perfectly regular, but is subject to some random fluctuations in its operation. Figure 44, for example, shows the pattern of response times obtained in a computer simulation of a random walk process in which the clock was "noisy" (Vickers, 1975). In this simulation, both the mean value of $t$ and the values of the extreme criteria remain the same as those for the noise-free simulation, for which results have already been presented in Fig. 43. However, the time at which the deadline occurs now has a truncated normal distribution, with a standard deviation of two observations. Although intermediate responses (made incorrectly) to large stimulus differences remain infrequent, the most common situation in which they occur is one in which, by chance, the deadline occurs almost immediately the sequence of observations has begun. The result, as can be seen from Fig. 44, is that times for all intermediate responses now fall on an inverted U-shaped curve and remain well below those of the extreme responses at each of the corresponding stimulus differences.

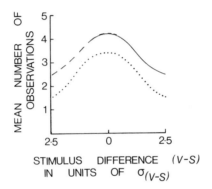

Fig. 44. Pattern of response times produced by a computer simulation of a random walk and noisy clock process. The solid line shows times for responses of the form "$V > S$", the broken line times for those of the form "$V < S$" and the dotted line those for responses of the form "$V = S$". The deadline in this case has a mean of 3 and a standard deviation of 2 observations.

Even with this modification, however, there are several grounds for unease at this approach. On a general level, the model is complicated by an extra parameter of $\sigma_t$ (the "noise" in the clock), and the value of $\sigma_t$ appears from preliminary simulation work to need to be suspiciously large (of the order of one or two observation intervals). Meanwhile, on a more specific level, the model predicts that intermediate responses will either all take more time than the corresponding extreme decision, or they will all take less. However, this prediction does not adequately describe the average results of my second experiment (shown in Fig. 41), nor the unpublished data for several individual observers which I obtained in a number of different studies. These all suggest that a strong encouragement to make "equal" responses produces times for that category which are less than those for extreme responses to a stimulus difference of zero, but remain comparable to the times for extreme responses to a stimulus difference of moderate size. The fact that a similar finding has been obtained in the case of "same" judgments by Bindra *et al.* (1968), and by Nickerson (1971), suggests that the random walk and clock model is wrong at least in detail.

At the same time, there are a number of grounds for questioning the notion that observers can control the length of time for which information is fed into the decision process (i.e. that they can choose to respond by a deadline). For example, Fitts (1966) suggested that mean overall response time in his experiments appeared to be simply a joint function of the difficulty of the decision and the degree of caution adopted by an observer. Although Pachella and Pew (1968) later argued, on the basis of a similar set of experiments, that it was necessary to suppose that observers operated also with a deadline, it is not clear that this assumption is necessary. Pachella and Pew demonstrated that observers working with the same payoff matrix for correct and incorrect, and fast and slow responses, produced different patterns of times and errors, depending upon whether a low criterion time of 360 ms was used to classify responses as fast and slow, or whether a high criterion time of 460 ms was employed. Rather than assume the operation of a deadline, however, it seems simpler to suppose that observers interpreted the payoff matrix differently, depending upon the criterion time employed, and adjusted their degree of caution (i.e. the values of $k$) accordingly.

Other experiments, which have been taken as evidence for the operation of a clock or deadline, can be similarly interpreted. For example, Link and Tindall (1971) reported that, when a 260 ms deadline for responding was imposed, response time no longer showed the generally found inverse relation with stimulus difference, but remained roughly constant for all levels of discriminability. However, as we point out (Vickers *et al.*, 1972), this conclusion is invalidated by the fact that Link and Tindall presented their stimuli in sub-blocks of 60 successive trials, all of equal discriminability. Under these conditions, an observer is left free to vary his degree of caution from one sub-block to another in order to maintain, as instructed, a stable mean response time for all degrees of discriminability. In addition, there is a second objection to this conclusion, which rests on the fact that the inverse relation between response time and discriminability did appear to hold for the longer deadline of 460 ms. With lower deadlines, an observer would be expected to adopt very low values of $k$. Under these circumstances, the slope of the inverse relation would be expected to be small, so that only minor adjustments to $k$ would be needed to reduce it to zero. It would seem highly likely, for instance, that it was minor adjustments of this kind, which were responsible for Schouten and Bekker's conclusion that an observer's "one and only freedom in a *series* of reactions is gradually to adjust his *mean* reaction time in order to settle for a personal compromise between speed and accuracy" (1967, p. 146).

Meanwhile, more positive evidence that observers must accumulate a predetermined amount of evidence before responding has been obtained in a series of experiments (Vickers *et al.*, 1972). In each of two experiments, we presented observers with pairs of lines of a constant, easily discernible difference in length and asked them to respond to the longer by pressing the left or the right-hand of two keys. The time for which the pairs were exposed was varied randomly from trial to trial, varying from 8 to 80 ms in one experiment, and from 12 to 120 ms in the other. Following Haber (1970), each stimulus was succeeded immediately by an appropriate backward mask to prevent further accumulation from stored memory traces.

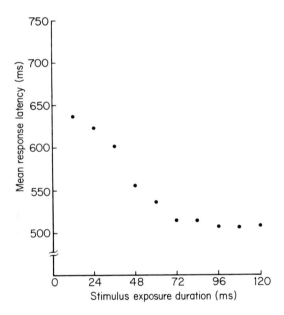

Fig. 45. Pattern of mean response times averaged over 10 observers (Vickers *et al.*, 1972, experiment 2), plotted against the duration for which discriminanda were exposed.

Had observers been capable of controlling the time for which information was fed to the decision process, the time taken should have been a direct function of stimulus exposure duration. Even if observers were not capable of using the appearance of the backward mask to halt the taking of further observations, they might be expected to take a constant time, equivalent, for example, to the response time at the longest stimulus exposure duration. Instead, as can be seen from Fig. 45, observers took longest to respond at the shortest exposure, and least time at the longest. These results strongly suggest that observers are incapable of adopting a deadline for responding, but need to continue taking observations even of non-informative, noise-produced stimulus differences, in order to achieve some predetermined critical amount of evidence. This interpretation is strengthened by the results of the third experiment in this study, in which a range of stimulus differences was exposed, each for 100 ms, and again with appropriate backward masking. Despite strong pressures to respond quickly and in a uniform time, response times were inversely related to the size of the stimulus difference. Like the results obtained with randomly varying stimulus exposures, this finding is inconsistent with the notion that observers can choose to decide by a deadline. However, both sets of findings are in harmony with the view that the observer must accumulate a predetermined amount of evidence in favour of one of the alternatives before a response can be initiated.

## An Accumulator Model of Three-category Judgment

The difficulties encountered above imply some positive recommendations for a more adequate account of the process of making three-category discriminations. For example, the inverse relation found between stimulus difference and the times for extreme responses implies that these at least are controlled by an optional-stopping decision mechanism, rather than following immediately from the sensory classification of a single observation. Meanwhile, as far as the intermediate responses are concerned, the effects of varying bias make it clear that these are not triggered by a noise-free clock. Indeed, the supposition of a neural clock seems unnecessary and uneconomical and is not supported by empirical evidence. Besides the general difficulty posed by the results of this study (Vickers et al., 1972), there is the more specific one that the shape of the function predicted for the times taken by intermediate responses is that of an inverted U, whereas the data which I obtained (Vickers, 1975) do not conform to this pattern. Although the notion is statistically unorthodox, all the evidence seems to suggest that observers are more likely to go through a positive process of accumulating information in favour of an "equal" judgment, rather than to make such a response simply by default.

## An Accumulator Model Employing an Inverse Function

A mechanism which seems to meet these requirements has been proposed (Vickers, 1975). In order to endow the process with the capacity to account for either three or two-category judgements, I supposed the extreme responses to be controlled by the accumulation of a critical amount of either positive or negative stimulus difference, as postulated by the accumulator model of two-category discrimination. Meanwhile, to account for Kellogg's (1931) finding that the times for "equal" responses appeared to increase as the difference between stimuli became greater, I proposed that evidence for the intermediate response was accumulated in the form of an inverse function of each stimulus difference inspected, irrespective of sign. According to this hypothesis, therefore, a response "$V > S$", "$V < S$", or "$V = S$" is made as soon as a critical total $k_g$, $k_l$ or $k_e$ is reached in any accumulator. A number of inverse transformations were considered, and the transformation $y = e^{-x^2}$ was chosen to avoid obvious difficulties in dealing with reciprocals. However, the pattern of predictions does not seem to be very sensitive to the transformation selected, largely because differences due to particular transformations can be offset to a large extent by manipulating the relative values of the criteria $k_g$, $k_l$ and $k_e$.

Unfortunately, while I have shown the general behaviour of this suggested process to be consistent with the data available, there remain some serious disadvantages with this idea. In the first place, although it is true that the performance of the model does not appear to depend critically upon the transformation chosen, the preference for any particular one remains quite arbitrary. Secondly, and more importantly, the inverting process discards useful information regarding the sign of the inspected differences. If we suppose, for example, that a series of inspected differences are all of the same size, this means that the rate at which the "equals" accumulator fills up will be the same whether the differences in question are all positive, all negative, or an even mixture of both. Clearly, however, we should expect this last type of sequence to be more effective in triggering an "equal" response.

## An Accumulator Model Based on the Sum Minus the Modulus

While the ingredients in a psychological theory are usually restricted to the immediately relevant data, there seem to be many instances where the addition of more remote constraints acts to precipitate a hypothesis which is then seen to be not only more elegant in the original context, but also to be serviceable in a much wider variety of situations. A case in point is provided by the present problem, where a remedy for the above deficiencies appears to follow from the recognition that further development of the model would be greatly facilitated if the evidence totals in all three accumulators were commensurable. Although it would be confusing to anticipate the argument, the further development of the accumulator principle in the second part of this book demonstrates that some considerable advantages accrue if the evidence for the "equals" outcome can be expressed in the same units (i.e. units of $\sigma_{(V-S)}$) as that for the "greater" and "lesser" decisions. If this is accepted (at least provisionally) as an additional constraint on theorizing, then the problem of selecting a suitable transformation becomes one of arriving at an expression which does not discard information and which preserves commensurability among the evidence totals for the intermediate and the extreme responses.

The solution to this more restricted problem appears to depend upon defining the conditions in which we should be most prepared to regard $V$ and $S$ as equal, and those in which we should be least willing to make an "equal" judgment. For example, if we assume for the sake of simplicity, that $k_g = k_l = k$, then the conditions under which we should be least prepared to make an intermediate response are clearly those where the evidence for one of the extreme responses is at a maximum, i.e. where all the evidence favours a "greater" response (with $t_g = k$ and $t_l = 0$), or where all the evidence favours a "lesser" (with $t_l = k$ and $t_g = 0$). Under these conditions the difference between $t_g$ and $t_l$, irrespective of sign, is at a maximum. Conversely, when this difference (i.e. the modulus $|t_g - t_l|$) is at a minimum, then we should regard an "equal" response as the most appropriate.

At the same time, however, it is obvious that we cannot specify this last condition alone as the criterion for making an intermediate decision, since the value of $|t_g - t_l|$ will be zero even before any observations have been taken (i.e. when $t_g = t_l = 0$). By a similar token, we should be less prepared to reach a judgment of "equal", when the condition that $|t_g - t_l| = 0$ arose after only a few observations than when it was based on a large number. As with other statistics, the reliability of $|t_g - t_l|$ as an estimate is a function of the number of observations upon which it is based. Some way has to be found, therefore, of taking this into account.

Since the desired condition for an intermediate response is one in which the modulus $|t_g - t_l|$ equals zero, it is fruitless to consider multiplying this expression by the number of observations. However, an alternative way of taking the same factor into account is to consider that the best evidence for an intermediate response occurs when $|t_g - t_l|$ is equal, or close, to zero, and when the sum $(t_g + t_l)$ is high. Since the sum $(t_g + t_l)$ is a direct linear function of the number of observations taken, we can specify the condition under which we should be prepared to make an intermediate judgment as that in which the sum $(t_g + t_l)$ reaches some critical value $k_e$ relative to the modulus $|t_g - t_l|$. In other words, the criterion for an "equals" response can be expressed as the condition where $(t_g + t_l) - |t_g - t_l| \geq k_e$. This expression enables us to arrive at a simpler reformulation of my model (Vickers, 1975). According to this version, a "greater" response is made if $t_g \geq k_{g'}$, a "lesser" if $t_l \geq k_l$ and an "equals" response if $(t_g + t_l) - |t_g - t_l| \geq k_e$, where $k_e$ is expressed in the same units of $\sigma_{(V-S)}$ as $k_g$ and $k_l$. A flow diagram of this process is shown in Fig. 46.

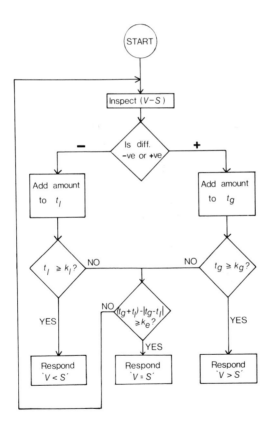

Fig. 46. Flow diagram of the sequence of operations envisaged in an accumulator model of three-category judgment, in which the evidence for the intermediate response is based on the sum minus the modulus of the evidence totals for the two extreme responses.

## General Properties of an Accumulator Model of Three-category Judgment

The hypothesis that the evidence for an intermediate response is represented by the sum of the evidence totals for the "greater" and the "lesser" responses minus their modulus, and that an "equal" decision is made when this quantity reaches or exceeds a critical amount $k_e$, has several advantages. In the first place, it explains the making of extreme judgments in terms of the same mechanism as was found in the last chapter to provide the most successful account of these responses in the two-category situation. In the second place, it accommodates the intermediate response by means of a similar accumulative mechanism, rather than by making the less economical supposition of a neural clock against which there seems in any case to be some strong evidence. In the third place, it eliminates an undesirable arbitrariness in the choice of an inverting function and fourthly, it does not waste information, so that, as we should expect, the rate at which the criterion $k_e$ is reached is faster when the inspected $(V-S)$ differences are an even mixture of positive and negative than when they are predominantly or exclusively of the same sign. Finally, and perhaps most importantly, the quantities accumulated for the three responses are commensurable. As is shown in the second part of this book, this property facilitates the making of straightforward "post-decisional comparisons" of the evidence in favour of each response alternative. This, in turn, enables simple adjustments to be made to criterion levels set for subsequent trials and enormously increases the flexibility of the model and its potential for further evolution.

These developments will be discussed in more detail later. For the present, we shall conclude this section with a brief summary of the properties of this revised accumulator model of three-category judgment, looking in turn at the patterns of response probability and time, and the effects of bias on the relative times for intermediate and extreme responses.

### Response Probability

As with the two-category process, the behaviour of the three-category model has been investigated by means of computer simulation. For example, Fig. 47 shows data for response probabilities obtained in one such simulation. In this study, 4000 trials of the proposed mechanism were simulated, in each of which the hypothetical process was presented with a normal distribution of stimulus differences possessing one of 21 different values of the mean $\overline{(V-S)}$, varying from $-2.5$ up to $+2.5$, in steps of $0.25$ $\sigma_{(V-S)}$. The data shown represent changes in the pattern of response probabilities, plotted against mean stimulus difference $\overline{(V-S)}$, as values of the criteria $k_g$, $k_l$ and $k_e$ are altered.

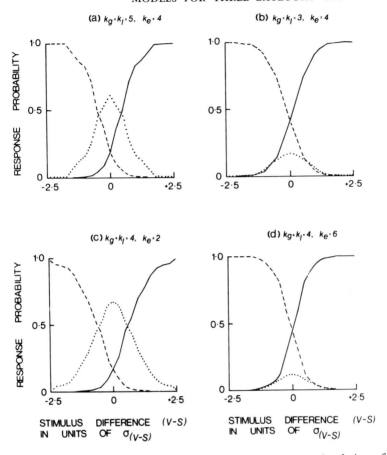

Fig. 47. Pattern of response probabilities produced by computer simulation of an accumulator model of three-category judgment, for various combinations of values of the criteria $k_g$, $k_l$ and $k_e$. Responses of the form "$V > S$", "$V < S$" and "$V = S$" are denoted by solid, broken and dotted curves respectively.

As can be seen from Fig. 47, the psychometric curves for the two extreme responses resemble those found for two-category discrimination, while the curve for intermediate responses resembles the bell-shaped function found by Kellogg (1931) and myself (Vickers, 1975). At the same time, small deviations from the ogival form can be detected in the shape of inflexions in the extreme curves where the proportion of intermediate responses is substantial (as in Figs 47a and 47c). Meanwhile, comparing Figs 47a with 47b, and 47c with 47d, it can also be seen that both *MP* and *IU* can be varied either by holding $k_e$ constant, and varying $k_g$ and $k_l$, or by fixing the latter and varying $k_e$. Empirical results exhibiting all these features have been obtained (Vickers, 1975) in experiments where the *a priori* probability of an intermediate response was varied, and data from two of these experiments are presented above in Fig. 40. If we suppose that changes in the subjective bias towards making an intermediate response are at least partly reflected in the relative criterion values for intermediate and extreme responses, then these experimental results would seem to be consistent with the pattern produced by the model.

MEASURES   OF   INTERMEDIATE   RESPONSES

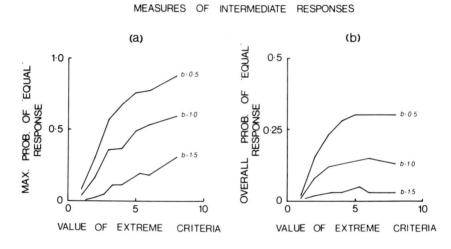

Fig. 48. The pattern of increases in (a) the maximum and in (b) the overall probability of an "equal" response, obtained in computer simulation of an accumulator model of three-category judgment for various values of the extreme criteria $k_g = k_l$. The separate curves are for different degrees of "bias" $b$, as evaluated by the ratio $k_e/k_g$.

Although there are as yet no relevant empirical data, it may be of some interest to pursue the behaviour of the model a little further. If we assume that values of $k_g$ and $k_l$ remain equal, and if we chose the ratio $k_e/k_g$ as a *purely arbitrary* measure of the bias $b$ towards making an extreme response, then the behaviour of the model can be summarized in terms of changes in the four traditional measures based on response probability. For example, Figs 48a and 48b show how *MP* and the overall proportion of intermediate responses vary as a function of the values of the extreme criteria, with $b$ as a parameter. As we should expect, the lower the value of $b$, the more likely it is that the process will make an intermediate response. However, Figs 48a and 48b also show that, whereas increases in $k_g = k_l$ up to about 5 produce increases in both *MP* and in the overall proportion of intermediate responses, the bulk of the effect of increasing $k_g = k_l$ still further occurs in the *MP*. Beyond the point where $k_g = k_l = 5$, any further increase in the caution with which extreme responses are made takes the form of an increase in the probability of a correct intermediate response, and a decrease in the probability of an incorrect one.

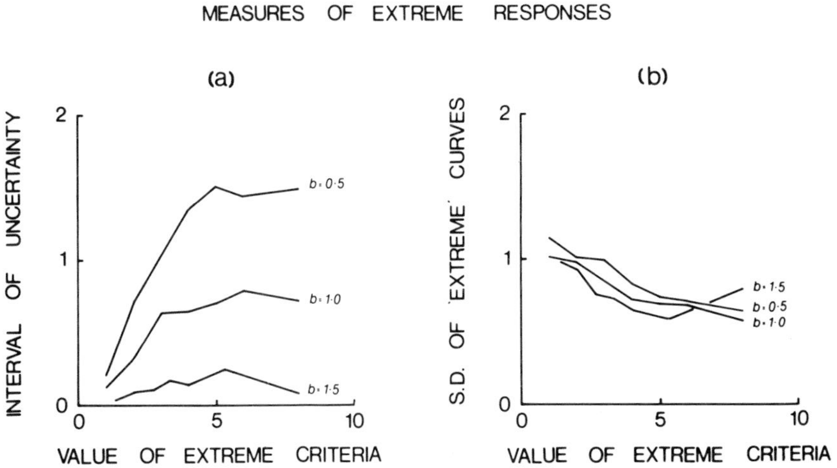

MEASURES OF EXTREME RESPONSES

Fig. 49. The pattern of changes in (a) the interval of uncertainty, and in (b) the standard deviation of the extreme psychometric functions, obtained in computer simulation of an accumulator model of three-category judgment for various values of the extreme criteria $k_g = k_l$. As in Fig. 48, the separate curves are for different degrees of "bias" $b$, as evaluated by the ratio $k_e/k_g$.

Turning to measures of the extreme responses, shown in Figs 49a and 49b, it can be seen that increases in caution up to the point where $k_g = k_l = 6$ result in substantial increases in the *IU*, with the greatest increase occurring where $b$ is lowest (0·5). Meanwhile, over the same range of $k_g = k_l$, the standard deviations of the ogives fitted to the extreme psychometric functions steadily decrease. However, although the standard deviations are generally lowest where $b$ is highest, differences in $b$ produce very little change in the standard deviations. As with the overall proportion of intermediate responses, little change is observed in either the *IU* or the standard deviation for increases in caution beyond $k_g = k_l = 6$. For criterion values higher than that, the major change seems to be in the direction of a more veridical distribution of the intermediate judgments.

In the absence of an established corpus of empirical data, the significance of these changes is simply that they do not conform to any of the three paradigms illustrated earlier in Chapter 2 (Figs 12 and 15). As such they emphasize the potential complexity of findings in this area, and the need to design experiments on a sufficiently ambitious scale. Meanwhile, the pattern of changes produced by the model is at least superfically consistent with the results of Urban (1910) and Fernberger (1931). For example, in subsequent analysis of data from an earlier experiment on lifted weights, Urban found that the $IU$ was perfectly correlated with the $MP$. This would be consistent with the pattern shown in Figs 48a and 49a, provided $b$ remains constant. However, it is not what we should expect from the two paradigms illustrated in Fig. 12 (a and b). Again, in a later series of experiments, also on lifted weights, Fernberger (1931) found that the $IU$ decreased with instructions minimizing the importance of the "equals" category, and increased when it was emphasized, while the standard deviations of the extreme psychometric curves showed little systematic change. These results are also in line with what we should expect from the proposed accumulator model. A comparison of Figs 49a and 49b shows clear effects of changes in $b$ on the $IU$, while the effect on the standard deviation of the extreme curves is very small by comparison with the variability we should expect in empirical data. While there is of course no evidence as yet that $b$ can be interpreted as a satisfactory, valid counterpart to subjective bias in three-category tasks, these correspondences between the behaviour of the model and that of the available data seem at least to be promising.

## Response Time

Meanwhile, typical patterns of mean response times produced by the simulated process are shown in Fig. 50. As is to be expected from the pattern of response probabilities, mean times for the two extreme responses closely resemble those for the "greater" and "lesser" responses in two-category discrimination, though there is some suggestion of an inflexion in the curve where stimulus difference is close to zero. As with two-category decisions, times for incorrect extreme responses are somewhat longer than those for correct, and the asymmetry in the response time functions increases as a direct function of the caution with which these responses are made.

Although the behaviour of the simulated process is clear enough, little data is known which bear on this last aspect. Very few errors of this kind were made by observers in the five experimental conditions that I studied (Vickers, 1975), though there was a slight preponderance of comparisons (86 out of 144) in which times for incorrect extreme responses were longer than those for the same response made correctly. A more definite conclu-

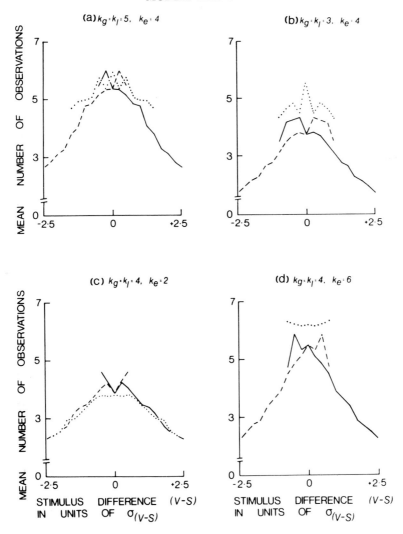

Fig. 50. The pattern of mean response times taken in computer simulation of an accumulator model of three-category judgment, for the same combinations of values of $k_g$, $k_l$ and $k_e$ as are represented in Fig. 47. Responses of the form "$V > S$", "$V < S$" and "$V = S$" are denoted by solid, broken and dotted lines respectively.

sion was reached by Kellogg, who found that "it takes longer without exception (on the average) to make a false judgment than it does to make a correct one" (1931, p. 74). Kellogg's data were perhaps clearer because no time pressure was put on the observers in his experiment, and it seems reasonable to suppose that they may have adopted rather higher degrees of caution in consequence.

While these findings are consistent with the proposed accumulator process, an apparent difficulty arises in the case of times for the intermediate judgment. As can be seen from Fig. 50, the times for "equal" responses by the simulated process remain more or less independent of stimulus difference when this is close to zero, but start to decrease when stimulus difference becomes appreciable. As it stands, this appears to be in conflict with Kellogg's finding (1931) that the times for intermediate judgments appeared to increase as stimulus difference became greater.

After failing to find a plausible transformation which would produce this effect theoretically, I carried out a series of experiments in order to explore the conditions under which such a direct relation might occur empirically (Vickers, 1975). Results were similar, whether observers were given a strong, medium, or weak bias towards the intermediate response, whether multi-element arrays or simple pairs of lines were used as stimuli, and whether the stimulus was terminated by a response or switched off after a constant interval. In all cases, the most economical description of the times for "equal" responses was that they remained largely independent of stimulus difference, with a tendency to decrease as stimulus difference became very large. I also noted a tendency for the intermediate response time function "to reach two maxima, one on either side of zero stimulus difference" (1975, p. 464), and the same phenomenon is evident in Kellogg's data (1931, p. 80, Fig. 3). Although the results of the computer simulation shown in Fig. 50 are difficult to capture by any simple characterization, they too exhibit a tendency for "peaks" to occur in the response time curve at a stimulus difference of about 0·5, beyond which point times for intermediate responses begin to fall again. In view of the complexity of possible findings illustrated in Fig. 50, it is quite possible, therefore, that both my results and those of Kellogg are consistent with the proposed model.

## The Effects of Bias on the Relative Times for Intermediate and Extreme Responses

As can be seen from Figs 50c and 50d, an increase in the bias towards the extreme category results in a substantial lowering of the times for extreme judgments, and a smaller reduction in the times for intermediate responses. An important consequence of this is that the relative times for intermediate and extreme responses depend to a large extent upon the degree of bias in favour of the extreme category: according to the degree of bias, times for "equal" responses at a stimulus difference of zero may be greater than, equal to, or less than the times for the corresponding extreme judgments.

As we have seen above (p. 108), this feature differs from the noise-free clock model, but agrees well with the data obtained by Kellogg (1931), Carlson *et al*. (1934), Fernberger *et al*. (1934), Cartwright (1941) and myself (Vickers, 1975). Like the pattern of response probabilities, and the shapes of the response time functions, this detailed aspect of the behaviour of the model corresponds nicely with the relevant experimental results. Taken in conjunction with the more general considerations outlined above as favouring an accumulator process, this close correspondence gives strong support for the present approach of attempting to account for a number of elementary information-processing abilities in terms of just one or two simple mechanisms. Accordingly, the remainder of this chapter is concerned with whether this approach can also be applied to a very closely related judgment, namely, that of sameness and difference.

## Judgments of Sameness and Difference

Although no systematic comparison of the two has ever been published, it is generally recognized that there is a close affinity between the three-category task and the decision as to whether two stimuli are the same or different. To a great extent, of course, this recognition is based on the fact that, when the stimuli in question differ along one particular dimension, then a three-category task can be converted into a same–different judgment simply by asking the observer to make the response "different" whenever the variable appears to be either greater or less than the standard, and to respond "same" when the two stimuli appear to be equal. Given this direct, logical relationship, it is not surprising that the tenor of empirical findings, and the development of theorizing concerning judgments of sameness and difference tends to reiterate that already encountered in the case of three-category decisions. Although I shall not dwell on these points of resemblance, the fact that the structure of this last section closely follows that of the previous one should by itself serve to bring out the remarkable consistencies between the two kinds of decision process. With this underlying aim in mind, therefore, I shall begin by summarizing some of the main empirical findings and commenting on the theoretical models suggested by them, before going on to consider how successfully an accumulator process might be applied to the same–different paradigm.

### *Response Probability and Signal Detection Accounts*

Figure 51 shows two typical examples of the pattern of response probabilities obtained in a same–different task, plotted against the difference between the stimuli being judged. The data were obtained by Nickerson (1971, experiment 1) in a study in which each of two observers was asked to report whether two sequentially presented tones were of the same or a different frequency. Since only two responses were permitted, the two curves are complementary. However, this redundant form of presentation was preserved in order to facilitate comparisons with the pattern of results obtained in three-category situations. For example, as is readily obvious, the probability of making a "same" response resembles the right half of the bell-shaped psychometric function typically obtained in three-category tasks, idealized examples of which are provided above in Figs 12 and 15. Meanwhile, the curve for "different" judgments is closely similar to the right half of the psychometric function for "greater" responses, also illustrated in Figs 12 and 15, with the possible difference that the portion of the "different" curve below the point of intersection appears, in Fig. 51a at least, to be slightly less steep than the portion above it. Finally, the variations between Figs 51a and 51b seem to be readily understandable as reflections of some difference in the relative readiness of the two observers to make the judgment "same".

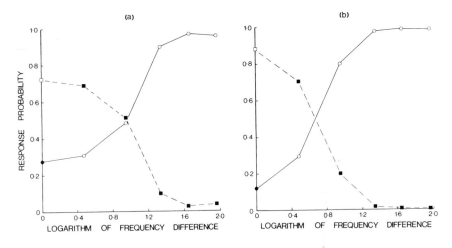

Fig. 51. Empirical response probabilities for two observers (a) and (b), obtained by Nickerson (1971) in a same–different task. Circles represent "different" responses and squares represent "same". Correct responses are indicated by empty and incorrect by filled symbols.

This pattern of results, of course, immediately invites interpretation in terms of the signal detection approach considered above for three-category decisions (pp. 103–105). All that seems necessary is to suppose that the response "same" is made under the same conditions as those for "equal", and that the response "different" is made whenever the decision outcome is either of the form "$V > S$" or "$V < S$". Certainly, these suppositions would account for the general shapes of the curves, as well as possible changes in the empirical pattern arising from differences in subjective bias. However, as with three-category tasks, this approach would not account for the finding that times for "different" responses have been found to be systematically related to stimulus difference, even when the amount of this difference is varied randomly from trial to trial (Nickerson, 1969, 1971). Nickerson's results echo those for extreme judgments in the three-category situation, as well as those for the two responses in the two-category case, and likewise imply the operation of an optional-stopping mechanism of the kind considered in Chapter 3 and in the preceding section of the present one.

## The Relative Times for "Same" and "Different" Responses and the Notion of a Clock

As in three-category tasks, it is commonly found that correct judgments of "same" (or "equal") tend to take longer than the alternative response (also made correctly). For example, Bindra et al. (1965) required observers to press one of two morse keys as soon as they decided whether pairs of successively presented tones were the same or different. The tones used were 1000 and 1060 cycles per second and were presented with equal probability, but in random order, in each of the following combinations: 1000–1000; 1000–1060; 1060–1000; 1060–1060. Under two, slightly different, sets of experimental conditions it was found that the mean times for judgments of "same", made correctly, were significantly greater than those for correct judgments of "different". In a similar experiment, this time employing several degrees of discriminability, Nickerson (1969) also used four equally probable tone pairs, AA, AB, BA and BB. Tone A was constant at 1001 cycles per second, while the other, B, was either 1004, 1010, 1023, 1045, or 1093 cycles per second. Under these conditions, Nickerson found that the mean time for "same", made correctly, was greater than that for correct "different" responses at all five levels of stimulus difference.

To account for such findings, Sekuler (1965), Bindra et al. (1965) and Nickerson (1969) have all proposed a "counter-and-clock" process, which corresponds to the random walk and clock model outlined in the previous section, with the exception that "different" responses are substituted for "greater" and "lesser", and "same" responses are regarded as equivalent to "equal". According to this model, an observer makes "different" responses by accumulating signal differences until a criterion amount of difference in either direction is achieved. On the other hand, "same" responses are triggered by the action of some internal clock, set to go off if a difference criterion has not been reached by a certain time *t*. Like "equal" responses, therefore, "same" decisions are made by default and should take longer than the slowest "different" decision, since no "different" response can take as long as *t* without the response "same" being triggered.

The difficulties with this notion are, as we should expect, the same as those encountered in the case of three-category tasks. Foremost among these is the evidence from experiments in which the mean time for "same" responses falls below that of "different" decisions. For example, Bindra *et al.* (1968) carried out two experiments in which observers were required to decide whether pairs of horizontal lines were of the same or different lengths. In cases where they were different, the difference was either large ("easy" condition), medium ("medium" condition), or small ("difficult" condition). Instructions and presentation time were also varied so as to encourage either a "speed" or an "accuracy" attitude on the part of observers. Finally, stimuli were presented either simultaneously or successively. Perhaps the most economical description of their several results would be to say that "same" responses, made correctly, tended to take times which were intermediate between those for easy "different" judgments (also made correctly) and those for difficult ones. The point of immediate importance is that the finding that mean times for "same" judgments may fall below those for "different" response is inconsistent with the notion of a noise-free clock.

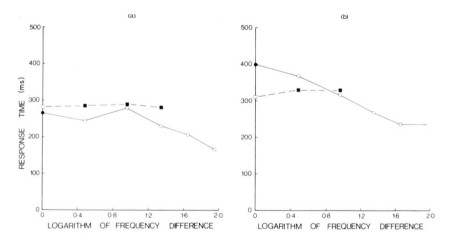

Fig. 52. Empirical response times for two observers (a) and (b), obtained by Nickerson (1971) in a same–different task. Circles represent "different" and squares represent "same" responses. Correct responses are indicated by empty and incorrect by filled symbols.

While it would not by itself account for this discrepancy between theory and data, one slight disadvantage with these results is that it is possible for some change in criteria to have occurred from one block of 40 trials at one level of difficulty to a succeeding block at another level. This confusing factor can be avoided if the level of difficulty is varied randomly from trial to trial, as was done by Nickerson (1971), using successively presented pairs of tones of 6 different frequencies. In two experiments, results for one observer did show "same" response times to be longer than those for "different" judgments. However, times for "same" responses by the second observer in each experiment, who showed a greater relative tendency to make incorrect "same" responses, were shorter than those for "different" responses when the discrimination was difficult. Meanwhile, for discriminations of moderate difficulty, times for both categories of response by this observer were almost identical. Figure 52, for example, shows the actual times obtained by Nickerson (1971) in his second experiment.

Similar results have been obtained in a recent unpublished study by S. Williams, using pairs of simultaneously presented line lengths, and her findings, together with those of Nickerson (1971), and Bindra et al. (1968), appear to rule out conclusively the possibility that "same" responses are triggered by some kind of pre-set neural clock. Although it would perhaps still be possible to suggest, as in the three-category case, that the clock in question may be noisy, the general objections already encountered to this modification would also apply in the case of same–different judgments: namely, the comparative advantages of commensurability, the evidence against deadline responding and the need to add a parameter with a suspiciously high value. Besides these arguments, there is the specific difficulty that the data do not appear to conform to the pattern predicted by a "noisy" clock. For example, the data of Nickerson (1971) presented in Fig. 52, show that, while "same" responses at low levels of discriminability may be faster than "different" ones, times for the two categories of response become virtually identical at higher levels of discriminability. A similar finding was reported by Nickerson for his first experiment, and, taken in conjunction with the discrepancies already noted in the three-category case, argues strongly against the supposition of a neural clock, noisy or otherwise.

## An Accumulator Model of "Same—Different" Judgments

The above criticisms clearly carry with them the obligation to show how an accumulator process might better account for judgments of sameness and difference. Fortunately, this is not difficult. Just as a three-category task can be converted into a same–different judgment by instructing observers to respond "same" whenever the stimuli appear equal, and "different" whenever the variable appears either greater or lesser than the standard, so the accumulator model for three-category decisions can be modified simply by a corresponding relabelling of its response outcomes. Thus there exists a morphological correspondence between changes in the task and modifications of the model. A flow diagram of the version for same–different judgments is given in Fig. 53 and can perhaps be taken as self-explanatory. In the remainder of this section, then, we shall examine briefly some of its main properties.

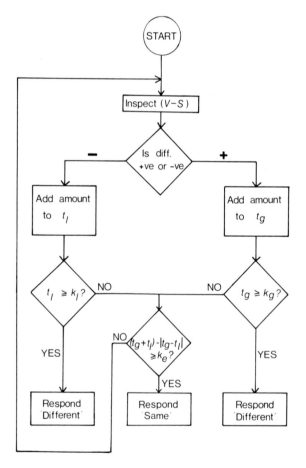

Fig. 53. The sequence of operations envisaged in an accumulator model for judgments of sameness and difference.

## General Properties of an Accumulator Model of "Same—Different" Judgments

Once again the main properties of the model have been investigated by means of computer simulation, with the descriptions which follow being based on a simulation study in which, for each combination of the values of $k_g = k_l$ and $k_e$, the hypothetical process was presented with 4000 distributions of stimulus differences with a constant standard deviation $\sigma_{(V-S)} = 1$, and 21 mean values ranging from $-2\cdot5$ up to $+2\cdot5$, in steps of $0\cdot25\ \sigma_{(V-S)}$. In this exploration of the behaviour of the model the restriction was followed that $k_g$ and $k_l$ should always be equal. Of course, this need not be assumed and some interesting predictions might follow if they were assumed to be unequal, which would be a natural supposition if the *a priori* probability of encountering stimuli where the variable was greater than the standard were different from the converse alternative. Since these possibilities far outrun the available data, however, we shall confine ourselves to the more mundane consideration of the patterns of response probabilities, times and the effects of changes in bias, in situations where it may be assumed that $k_g$ and $k_l$ are equal.

### Response Probability

Figure 54 shows the effects of varying discriminability on the pattern of response probabilities generated by the stimulated process for "same" and "different" judgments. The close resemblance between the empirical functions shown in Fig. 51 (which are based on positive objective differences only) and the corresponding right halves of the theoretical functions shown in Fig. 54a hardly needs to be dwelt upon. In the case of both the observers represented in Fig. 51, there seems to be a relatively strong bias towards making "same" responses and, indeed, the main value of the response probability measure at present seems to be limited to indicating some degree of bias, and thereby assisting in the interpretation of response times. It seems possible, however, that greater use could be made of the response probability measure. There are, for example, obvious close relationships between the measures *MP* and *IU* in same–different and in three-category tasks, and it seems worth exploring in the future whether such relations as those between the *MP*, the *IU* and the overall probability (*OP*) of a "same" response might turn out to provide some useful descriptions of performance.

### Response Time

Meanwhile, some typical patterns of response times produced by the

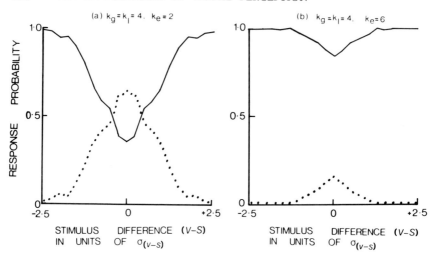

Fig. 54. The pattern of response probabilities produced by computer simulation of an accumulator model for judgments of sameness and difference. Responses of the form "different" and "same" are represented by solid and by dotted lines respectively. Figure 54a examplifies a bias towards making "same" responses, while Fig. 54b exemplifies a bias against the judgment "same".

simulated model are shown in Fig. 55. As in the case of response probability, the pattern of times generated for "same" responses is identical with the upper half of that produced for "equal" responses by the three-category process. Times for "different" responses are also very similar to those for correct "greater" (or "lesser") responses, except that they are modified at smaller stimulus differences by the progressive inclusion of more "different" responses based on incorrect "greater" or "lesser" decision outcomes: in other words by the occurrence of responses correctly classifying the stimuli as "different", although the difference registered by the decision process is in the opposite direction to that prevailing objectively. As can be seen from a comparison of Figs 50 and 55, this has very little effect on the response time curve for "different" responses, beyond the enhanced appearance of a "shoulder" in the curve between intermediate and low degrees of discriminability. In consequence, changes in the relative times for "same" and "different" responses are analogous to those outlined above for the three-category version, and are similarly determined by the degree of bias towards the "same" response.

So far as unidimensional stimuli are concerned, the detailed pattern of changes in the theoretical response time functions seems to be entirely consistent with the evidence already presented from Bindra *et al.* (1965,

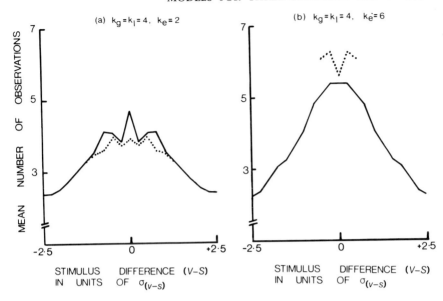

Fig. 55. The pattern of mean response times taken in computer simulation of an accumulator model for judgments of sameness and difference. Responses of the form "different" and "same" are represented by solid and by dotted lines, respectively. Figure 55a exemplifies a bias towards making "same" responses, while Fig. 55b exemplifies a bias against the judgment "same".

1968), Nickerson (1969, 1971) and the unpublished data of Williams. Considered as a whole, both theory and empirical data point to the conclusion that the time needed to make a "same" or a "different" judgment correctly is a joint function of bias and discriminability, as well as, perhaps, of the overall caution with which decisions are reached. For the present, therefore, it seems reasonable to conclude that same–different judgments seem to be mediated by the same kind of accumulator process which appears to underlie three-category judgments. Also consistent with this view is the finding by Bindra et al. (1968) of a trade-off between speed and accuracy which is quite in harmony with the present approach. In terms of an accumulator process, their data imply that a change of emphasis in instructions from one of speed to one stressing accuracy has been reflected by an increase in the criteria employed for both the "same" and the "different" accumulators—although the difference in response time at the most difficult level suggests that the "different" criteria may have been increased to a relatively greater extent. (Evidence in support of this interpretation is provided by the fact that markedly greater proportions of objectively different stimuli were mistakenly judged as "same" at this level of difficulty.)

## The Problem of Qualitatively Different Stimuli

One further experiment by Bindra *et al.* (1968) on the judgment of colours suggests that, under some circumstances, the relative times for "same" and "different" responses may not always depend mainly upon the relative bias in favour of each of the two categories of judgment. These authors presented observers with pairs of successively displayed coloured circles (red–red, red–blue, blue–red and blue–blue), and instructed them to respond "same" or "different" by pressing the appropriate key. Under two sets of conditions, it was found that mean times for correct "same" responses were less than those for correct "different" responses.

Although this finding need not be inconsistent with an accumulator process, if we suppose the value of $k_e$ to be set relatively low, it does represent an instance where it may be inappropriate to think of the process as operating upon positive and negative differences between stimuli arrayed along a single dimension. The specification of colours in terms of spectral frequency can be misleading, since a considerable amount of evidence in favour of either an opponent process or a trichromatic theory, as well as from phenomena such as the Purkinje shift, seems to indicate that the primary colours blue and yellow–red are registered by quite separate sensory channels (Cornsweet, 1970). Given this situation, an efficient strategy for the observer to follow would be to set up one accumulator for the energy detected by the red channel, another for that detected by the blue and a third for that detected by both, minus (as above) the modulus between them. If either the "red only" or "blue only" accumulators triggered first, then the observer would respond "same". On the other hand, if the "combined" accumulator reached its criterion level first, then the observer would respond "different". It should be noted that this method of operation is exactly analogous to the procedure for dealing with quantitatively different signals, except that the accumulator for dealing with combined inputs (e.g. positive and negative differences, or red and blue intensities) has now been used to control the response "different". We might therefore expect that the usual finding of somewhat longer times for "same" responses would also be reversed, as was indeed found by Bindra *et al.* (1968).

This interpretation is indeed superficially similar to that of Bindra *et al.*, who argue that stimuli that are "codable" (i.e. those which can be categorized by absolute judgment) yield a shorter latency for the decision "same", while "noncodable" stimuli (i.e. those requiring a reference stimulus for categorization) yield a longer latency for the decision "same" (1968, p. 121). However, according to the present approach, there is no important difference between the way that positive and negative differences (or excitatory and inhibitory signals) are accumulated and the way that other qualitatively different stimulus information is processed. All that need vary is the attachment of responses to decision outcomes. This means that, given qualitatively different stimuli of the kind used by Bindra et al. but a different kind of task, the observer might assign his responses to the decision outcomes in some alternative manner.

For example, if an observer is presented with a steady series of single flashes on either a red or a blue lamp and is asked to decide whether the lamps have been set to come on with the same or with different frequencies, then the assignment of responses would vary from that suggested for the experiment of Bindra et al. (1968). If we suppose amounts of excitation (corresponding, perhaps to run lengths) to be accumulated in "red", "blue" and "combined" counters, then it is evident that the prior filling up of either the "red" or the "blue" should trigger the response "different", while the "combined" accumulator should control the response "same". If we assumed that observers operated with a similar relative bias towards "same" or "different" to that pertaining in the experiment of Bindra et al., then we should expect times for "same" responses to be again longer, even though the stimuli are "codable" in their sense of the term.

A preliminary test of this hypothesis was carried out by me in an unpublished experiment, in which 6 observers made 150 judgments each as to whether sequences of red and blue flashes, appearing at a steady rate and terminated by the observer's response, were set to come on with equal or with different frequency. The red and blue flashes were presented in proportions of 30:70, 50:50 and 70:30, and the probability of each proportion was 0·33. For 9 out of the 12 possible comparisons, times for correct "same" responses were longer than those for correct "different" responses, while, for 5 out of the 6 observers, times for correct "same" responses were longer than those for incorrect "different" responses. While it is true that the relative bias towards "same" is likely to have been weaker in this experiment, since same stimuli occurred on only a third of all trials, it seems clear that it is not an inherent property of "codable" stimuli that "same" responses should take less time than judgments of "different".

This result is consistent with the view that both two and three-category discriminations, as well as judgments of sameness and difference, are mediated by a process of accumulating critical amounts of classified information. Only the information itself and the assignment of responses to the decision outcomes need be assumed to vary from one situation to another. The relative times for "same" and "different" responses will thus depend upon the relative bias towards these two categories, upon the overall caution of the observer, upon whether the stimuli are qualitatively or quantitatively different, upon the discriminability of the stimuli and upon the nature of the task.

This conclusion, in turn, goes some way towards explaining the finding that, in a large number of experiments, response times for "same" judgments turn out to be shorter than those for "different" judgments. The experiments in question were conducted by Nickerson (1965, 1967), Sternberg (1966), Posner and Keele (1967), Hawkins (1969), Bamber (1969), Briggs and Blaha (1969), Posner and Taylor (1969) and Posner et al. (1969), and all used multi-featured stimuli which were qualitatively different from one another. In contrast, experiments for which a reverse relationship has been found have all used quantitatively different stimuli (e.g. Bindra et al., 1965; Bindra et al., 1968; Nickerson, 1969, 1971). As it stands, therefore, the proposed accumulator model seems capable of accounting for the main features of same–different judgments and of explaining some otherwise puzzling results. In addition, the model outlined above seems to provide an explicit realization of a process first considered by Bindra et al., who considered (among others) the possibility that "there are two adders, one accumulating dissimilarity information, and the other similarity information" (1965, p. 1627).

# 5

## Signal Detection

*If we add to the burden on a man's back, straw by straw, he will, when sufficient straws have been added, become sensibly aware that the weight has increased as compared with some previous stage in the process. But at no point will he discern a difference between the weight he was previously carrying and the same weight as increased by only a single straw. Hence the successive straws must produce indiscernible differences in order to account, by their accumulation, for the difference which is ultimately noticed.*

G. F. Stout, (1938, 5th ed., pp. 301–302).

Although the piecing together of evidence concerning three-category decisions and same–different judgments has followed a somewhat prosaic course, the theoretical picture which is beginning to emerge is an exciting one. For example, one possibility suggested by the evidence is that the preliminary processing of sensory information may be conducted in two quite distinct stages. In the first, a large variety of neural systems, each specialized so as to respond to a particular feature of the environment, would be responsible for the qualitative analysis of sensory information. In the second, the information so classified would then be quantitatively evaluated by a very small number of simple decision processes. In turn, these processes may all operate in the same general way, storing the resultant activity from combinations of excitatory and inhibitory impulses until some threshold amount of activity is built up. To account for the difference between judgments with unidimensional and those with multidimensional stimuli, it is only necessary to suppose that the information accumulated may come from sources which are either qualitatively or, at least, topographically different. Meanwhile, differences between one task and another can be explained either by variations in the assignment of information to accumulators, or in the attachment of responses to decision outcomes.

If this line of theorizing is pursued, it points to the further possibility that a large number (perhaps all) of these simple decision processes may be carried out by a single, general-purpose elementary decision module, namely, the accumulator process which underlies three-category decisions. This process embodies both the discriminative and identifying responses which, it was argued in the inductory chapter, must have characterized the behaviour of even the most primitive of the first mobile organisms. By suppressing responses, or by varying the attachment of responses to decision outcomes, it is possible to account for other forms of judgment in terms of the operation of this same mechanism. For example, two-category discrimination can be accommodated either by assuming that no overt response is attached to the intermediate decision outcome, or by supposing that the criterion for that outcome $(k_e)$ is set so high that it is never reached in practice. Similarly, as we have seen, same–different judgments can be accounted for by supposing that the response "different" is normally attached to each of the "greater" and "lesser" outcomes, and is capable of being triggered by either. The possibility of such a mechanism would seem to be of fundamental importance, since it appears to have the potential for carrying out the basic computations involved in a wide variety of much more complex information-processing activities.

While the view that a great deal (if not all) of human information-processing may be mediated by a single, general-purpose decision module represents a hypothesis of dramatic simplicity and generality, it is not one which can be exhaustively substantiated in detail within the confines of a single book. At the same time, however, it seems incumbent to consider whether there are some other types of simple judgment which might be similarly accounted for. Before following out some further implications of this approach, therefore, this last chapter of Part I examines one further kind of simple judgment, which has traditionally received even more attention than discrimination. The judgment in question is that of signal detection, and we shall be concerned with the extent to which empirical findings and theorizing in this field echo these we have encountered so far. Although the establishment of these points of resemblance will involve some recapitulation of notions discussed earlier, the opportunity will be taken to expand on some aspects not developed before, while keeping discussion of those already dealt with to a minimum.

The organization of the present chapter is accordingly very straightforward. It begins with a brief discussion of the classical conception of the absolute threshold, and follows this with a more extended examination of several theories, all derived from the formal theory of signal detection. The third section then deals with some recent alternatives, generally referred to as "counting" models, and, finally, the fourth section presents the evidence for an accumulator model of signal detection and outlines some of its properties.

## The Classical Conception of the Absolute Threshold

As was outlined in Chapter 2 (pp. 27–28), classical psychophysics assumed that the neural representation of any incoming stimulus was superimposed upon a background of random neural activity, which, it was argued, could be expected to display a normal distribution of intensity over time. Some stimuli were sufficiently intense for their internal representations to be lifted over the "threshold" of consciousness, and some were not. According to classical psychophysics, the greater the intensity of a stimulus, the higher was the probability that its internal representation would exceed the threshold. Empirically, the "absolute threshold" was then defined as the minimum intensity of a given stimulus necessary for an observer to report its presence on a certain proportion (traditionally either 50 or 75%) of all trials.

## The Phi—Gamma Hypothesis

The classical conception is illustrated in Fig. 56. As objective stimulus intensity increased, so, it was assumed, the complete noise-plus-signal distribution would be shifted to the right, higher up the intensity axis. Those occasions on which the represented intensity exceeded the hypothesized threshold $l_c$ would give rise to a perception of the stimulus, while the proportion on which it did not (shown by the shaded area in Fig. 56) would remain unobserved. As was outlined in Chapter 2, the import of the classical theory was crystallized in the phi–gamma hypothesis, according to which the proportion of trials on which a stimulus would be observed should conform to the cumulative integral of a normal curve, with different points on this ogive corresponding to the successively larger proportions of the underlying noise-plus-signal distribution which exceeded $l_c$ as objective stimulus intensity was increased. In the opinion of classical psychophysicists, the absolute threshold $l_c$ had, in spite of its seeming strangeness, "a high teleological significance, as securing freedom from interruption" (Titchener, 1905, p. xciv).

## The Problem of Bias

While measurement of the 50 or 75% absolute threshold became widespread, several writers were actually aware of the likelihood that the threshold might be influenced by subjective factors. As early as 1905, in a discussion of differential judgments, Scripture asserted that "the chief interest of these experiments lies, not in finding a definite figure for the just noticeable difference, but in observing how this difference changes with the

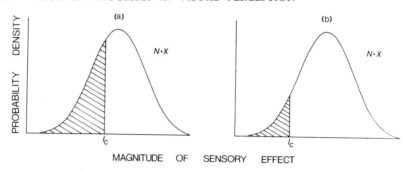

Fig. 56. Representation of the classical conception of the absolute threshold $l_c$. Figure 56a exemplifies the case of a high threshold and Fig. 56b that of a low threshold.

varying mental attitude" (p. 293). However, clear demonstrations of this point in the context of absolute thresholds did not appear until much later.

In one of the earliest examples, which followed upon the work of the Würzburg School (in which Külpe, Watt and others demonstrated the effects of set or attitude on various experiences), Knox (1945) studied the effects of variations in instructions on the flicker-fusion threshold (Ginsburg, 1970), as measured by the method of limits. He instructed two observers to respond to the first appearance of flicker when the flicker period was increased, and immediately upon its disappearance as the period was decreased. A second group of two observers were given similar instructions, except that emphasis was placed on the first appearance or disappearance of fusion. Meanwhile, a third group of two received neutral instructions, in which neither flicker nor fusion was stressed more than the others. Knox found that threshold flicker periods for the first group displayed a marked decrease over 10 successive days of practice, while flicker thresholds for the second showed a steady increase. In contrast, thresholds for the two observers who received neutral instructions remained quite stable over the practice sessions.

Similar effects on flicker-fusion thresholds have been demonstrated more recently by Landis and Hamwi (1954), Holland (1961) and Clark (1966). Analogous results for the detection of light intensities have also been obtained by Barlow (1956), who found that when an observer was told to report "possible or seen" flashes, the absolute threshold was lower than when he was told to report only those "definitely seen". As in the case of discrimination, these results testify to the operation of subjective biasing factors, which have no theoretical counterpart in the classical conception. The consequences too are similar, in that no firm interpretation can be placed on classical measures of detection ability, such as the *PSE* or the precision of the psychometric function.

## Approaches Based on Signal Detection Theory

Although these results may now seem unsurprising, and although earlier writers such as Thomson (1920) and Cartwright and Festinger (1943) had suggested theories capable of dealing with these complications, it was not until the work of Tanner and Swets (1954) that a theory was proposed, and generally accepted, which appeared to deal with the subjective aspect of detection in a readily intelligible manner. According to the formal *theory of signal detection*, proposed by Tanner and Swets, the observer takes an observation $x$ of the sensory events occurring within a fixed (usually narrow) interval of time, and makes a decision based on this observation as to whether the interval contained only random activity (i.e. "noise") or a signal as well. In terms of the theory, the probability that $x$ could have resulted from noise alone can then be represented by a normal distribution $n$, while the probability that $x$ might have arisen from the occurrence of noise-plus-signal can be similarly represented by a normal distribution $s$ (Fig. 57). The difference between the means of the two distributions is a direct function of the magnitude of the signal, and it is usually assumed that the two distributions have equal variances.

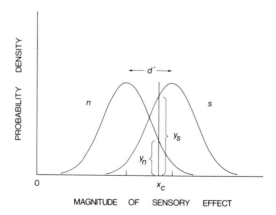

Fig. 57. Probability density distributions of the magnitude of sensory effect arising from noise ($n$) and noise plus signal ($s$) events, as postulated by the theory of signal detection. The distance $d'$ gives a measure of sensitivity, while the ratio between the heights of the ordinates $y_s/y_n$ at the cutoff $x_c$ yields a measure of the observer's bias $\beta$.

Given a particular observation, then, according to signal detection theory, an observer decides whether it arose from noise alone or from noise-plus-signal by adopting as a cutoff a critical observation magnitude $x_c$, classifying all observations greater than $x_c$ as "signal", and all those lower than $x_c$ as "noise" (or "nonsignal"). The outcomes of an observer's decisions may then be classified as "hits" $(S/s)$, "false alarms" $(S/n)$, "correct rejections" $(N/n)$, or "misses" $(N/s)$. The difference $d'$ between the means of the two distributions can be interpreted as a measure of the detectability of the signal, or (conversely) of the sensitivity of the observer, and is expressed by the algebraic difference between the $z$-scores for the two independent probabilities $p(S/s)$ and $p(S/n)$. These probabilities can also be used to infer the position of the cutoff, which is usually characterized by the ratio $\beta$ between the likelihood that $x$ arose from noise alone and that it resulted from noise-plus-signal, where $\beta$ is evaluated by the ratio $y_s/y_n$ between the ordinates at $x_c$ of the noise and noise-plus-signal distributions.

If we go on to assume that an observer attempts to maximize the expected value of his decisions, then it can be further shown that an optimal value for $\beta$ is given by:

$$\beta_i = \frac{p(n)}{p(s)} \cdot \frac{(V_{Nn} + C_{Sn})}{(V_{Ss} + C_{Ns})} \tag{5.1}$$

where $p(n)$ and $p(s)$ are the *a priori* probabilities of noise alone or noise-plus-signal, $V_{Ss}$ and $V_{Nn}$ are the values associated with hits and correct rejections, while $C_{Sn}$ and $C_{Ns}$ are the costs of false alarms and misses, respectively.

More detailed explanations of the theory of signal detection are abundant (e.g. Green and Swets, 1966; Hake and Rodwan, 1966; Corso, 1967; McNicol, 1972; Egan, 1976). For some time after its formulation, the theory gained a very general acceptance because it explicitly recognized the subjective element in detection, because it offered straightforward arithmetical procedures for calculating separate measures of bias $\beta$ and sensitivity $d'$ from data from appropriately designed experiments and because the "ideal observer", as defined by Eq. (5.1) provided a useful, and suggestive, standard against which human performance might be compared. It may be because the procedures for analysing data were so convenient that for some time little attempt was made to question or test the underlying assumptions of the signal detection theory. In any case, it is only recently that a number of papers have appeared which indicate that this approach suffers from some major limitations. We shall look first at two of these limitations, before going on to consider some modified models which have been developed to overcome them.

# Difficulties with the "Ideal Observer" Hypothesis

As generally understood, the ideal observer hypothesis implies that the human observer attempts to maximize the expected value of his decisions by adopting a value for the cutoff (or critical likelihood ratio) so that the measure $\beta$ corresponds closely to the optimal value as defined by Eq. (5.1) and is determined in the same way, and by the same factors (Williges, 1969, 1971, 1973; Embrey, 1975; Swets, 1977). Clearly, such a hypothesis represents a normative ideal to which human observers would be expected only to approximate and then only under appropriate conditions. However, the insight suggested by any normative model is reduced to the extent that human performance appears to deviate from that of the model, and there is a growing body of evidence which indicates that the extent of the divergence is sufficiently serious to abandon the hypothesis.

In the first place, the formulation of the cutoff in terms of a likelihood ratio assumes that the human observer has a good assessment of the descriptive statistics of the distributions of noise and of noise–plus–signal events. This assumption might seem justifiable in the restricted set of situations where the observer has ample opportunity to gain reasonable estimates of the characteristics of these distributions, but even here there appear to be some important qualifications. For example, when naive observers are asked to estimate an average value, they produce a variety of values which sometimes correspond to the mean, sometimes to the median and sometimes to the midrange (Spencer, 1963). Again, estimates of sample variances by human observers decrease as a function of the mean of the sample (Hofstatter, 1939; Lathrop, 1967), while different observers under different conditions may attach quite different weights to large and to small deviations (Hofstatter, 1939; Beach and Scopp, 1967).

Of course, the relevance of these findings to the ideal observer hypothesis may be questioned, since estimates of sensory information subject to rapid, internal variation may be more veridical than those of the externally varying stimulus values used in estimation studies. Against this, however, it has been found that the variance among estimates increases with both sample size and speed of presentation (Beach and Swensson, 1966; Spencer, 1961). If the ideal observer hypothesis is maintained nevertheless, these findings would seem at least to imply that the optimal cutoff adopted by a human observer may well be quite different from that predicted from an objective specification of the stimuli.

Other results also point to the conclusion that the location of the cutoff is not determined in an optimal manner as defined by Eq. (5.1). For example, a number of studies have failed to find significant effects on the observer's criterion following manipulations of the payoff matrix (e.g. Williges, 1971;

Guralnick, 1972; Smith and Barany, 1970), and Swets has concluded that the payoff matrix in an artificial laboratory experiment may not mean much to the observer. At the same time, in a more realistic situation he is likely to have "subjective values and costs too meaningful for them to be subject to easy manipulation" (1977, p. 17).

## The Relationship between Detectability and Time

If the detection of signals by human observers were a special instance of a process for which the signal detection account provided a general theory, then we should expect these observers to classify sensory events by adopting as a cutoff a critical likelihood ratio in accordance with the statistical features of signal and nonsignal events, and the relative costs and payoffs involved. As Smith (1972) points out, such a normative model makes extremely strong assumptions about the information processing capacities of the human observer, and, at the same time, aspires to goals which may be optimal in a narrow sense, but far from optimal for the complex situation in which the human observer operates. Indeed, it appears from the evidence cited above that human observers are not greatly affected by the costs and values specified by experimenters, and that they do not (or cannot) form veridical estimates of the statistical features of signal and nonsignal events.

Although these difficulties do not invalidate the theory as a descriptive model for human signal detection, they do restrict the range and level at which it may apply. In particular, they suggest that, if an observer does indeed classify sensory events by means of some cutoff, then the cutoff involved is realized in terms of some—much simpler—direct function of stimulus intensity. Certainly, a hypothesis of this kind seems necessary to provide a straightforward explanation of performance in experiments such as those of Gescheider et al. (1969), in which several different intensities are presented in random order with the result that the observer has no way beforehand of choosing a cutoff appropriate for a particular signal intensity.

While this alternative conceptualization has the merits of simplicity, it fails, as it stands, to account for the trading relationship between time and accuracy of performance—a relationship, according to Swets and Birdsall (1967), which is "largely ignored in experimental psychology, though central to most sensory, cognitive and motor performances" (p. 27). For example, in one of the earliest studies, Granit and Hammond (1931) showed that the critical cycle time for the detection of flicker (Throsby, 1962) decreased as a function of viewing time up to durations of at least one second. Since then, this finding has been confirmed several times, (e.g. Battersby and Jaffe, 1953; Huntington and Simonson, 1965; Anderson et al.,

1966). Although response times were not measured in these experiments, the range of stimulus exposures is similar to that employed in other psychophysical tasks which show evidence of a speed–accuracy trade-off (e.g. Garrett, 1922; Philip, 1936, 1947; Festinger, 1943b; Vickers *et al.*, 1971), and it seems reasonable to infer that the improvement in performance is at least partly due to a similar judgmental process. Indeed, it seems incontestable, as Boring pointed out half a century ago, that the time required to detect a stimulus "is one of the factors which, under a constant attitude, is a serial function of the stimulus, and a feasible subject for exact psychophysical investigation" (1920, p. 446).

In the case of signal detection this insight has been slow to germinate, so that even very recently Thomas and Myers could justifiably remark that "only a very few investigators have publicly taken cognizance of the fact that responses require time for their execution" (1972, p. 253). As a result, it is only recently that attempts have been made to measure response times in a signal detection task. Among the first to do so were Carterette *et al.* (1965), in a detailed study of the effects of varying the probability with which a 1000 cycle tone appeared embedded in a burst of noise. As might be expected, these authors found that the mean time taken to make either a "signal" or a "nonsignal" response was a decreasing function of the probability of a signal or nonsignal, respectively, with "signal" responses at high signal probabilities taking less time than "nonsignal" responses, and the reverse relation holding for low signal probabilities.

Less predictably, perhaps, Carterette *et al.* also found that there appeared to be an inverse relation across observers between response time and calculated values of $d'$. At about the same time, Sekuler (1965) studied the detection of a test stripe of variable duration, which was backward-masked after a fixed interval of 40 ms, and he too found a similar relation between the times for "signal" (or "nonsignal") responses and the probability of there being a signal (or nonsignal) trial. More importantly, Sekuler also found that plotted receiver operating characteristic (ROC) curves of "hits" against "false alarms" showed a shift upward along the negative diagonal as a function of test stripe duration, implying an increase in detectability over time, similar to the speed–accuracy trade-off found by Carterette *et al.* and already encountered in two and three-category decisions, and judgments of sameness and difference.

## A Fixed Sample Signal Detection Model

These and other similar results might be explained by the signal detection model if it were supposed that the observer did not base his decision upon a single observation, but upon some combination of observations (as was suggested by Crossman (1955) for two-category discrimination). Indeed, since the observer has a considerable amount of information potentially available to him concerning signal strengths, signal presentation probabilities and values and costs, Swets and Birdsall (1967) have considered the possibility that he might use this information to predetermine the number of observations on which he will base his decision in any trial. They then go on to suggest that, having fixed the size of the sample, the observer may base his decision on the product of the likelihood ratios for that number of observations. Such a process leads to the prediction that $d'$ should increase as a linear function of the square root of the number of observations taken in the sample (and hence of time, provided the observations are taken at a steady rate).

In the light of the difficulties discussed above, however, it seems unlikely that an observer would be capable of combining such precise information in this optimal manner. Indeed, Swets and Birdsall (1967) found clear differences between the distributions of times for "signal" and "nonsignal" responses, which is inconsistent with the notion of a predetermined sample size (and hence a fixed response time). Also in conflict with this hypothesis is the fact that, even when signal intensities are varied randomly within a single block of trials, the time taken to make "signal" responses still varies with signal intensity (Gescheider et al., 1968, 1969, 1971). This last result corresponds to the finding, presented in Chapter 2, that, when discriminability is varied randomly from trial to trial, both errors and response times continue to vary with the size of the stimulus difference. The implication too is similar: since the observer does not know the intensity beforehand, he has no way of predetermining an appropriate number of observations, so that the relation which persists between signal intensity and response time is presumably due to some other form of decision process.

## A Latency Function Signal Detection Model

As in the case of two-category discrimination, the simplest modification is to suppose that the observer does in fact base his decision on a single observation, but that the closer the observation lies to the cutoff the longer it takes to decide whether it is above or below. As was noted in Chapter 2, the notion of a latency function relating response time to distance from the cutoff has been considered by a number of writers, though the simplest form seems to be that proposed by Gescheider et al. (1969). In this form the hypothesis would be consistent with the generally observed increase in the time taken to respond "signal" as signal intensity is reduced (Gescheider et al., 1968, 1969, 1971; Emmerich et al., 1972). If, in addition, the latency function is assumed to be symmetrical on either side of the cutoff, and the cutoff lies between the means of the two distributions, as illustrated in Fig. 58, then the mean time for correct responses should be less than that for incorrect (Pike, 1973).

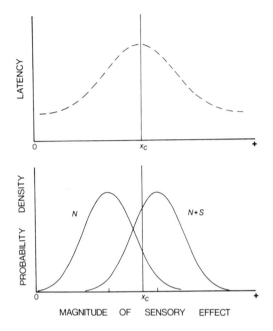

Fig. 58. Representation of the latency function hypothesis, where the latency function (denoted by the broken line in the upper diagram) is symmetrical about the cutoff $x_c$.

As in the context of discrimination, the latency function hypothesis is open to a number of objections. The first difficulty is that Gescheider et al. (1969) find it necessary to assume an additional "stimulus intensity component", which operates to produce an asymmetrical latency function. A second complication is that latency and distance from the cutoff cannot be regarded as simply interchangeable, since the form of latency-based ROC curves appears to vary with differences in the bias adopted by observers (Emmerich et al., 1972). Thirdly, even if latency is assumed to be a non-linear, asymmetrical function of the distance between an observation and the cutoff, the hypothesis cannot easily account for the discovery that times for incorrect "signal" responses may sometimes be lower than those for "signal" responses made correctly (Carterette et al., 1965; Pike, 1973; Pike and Ryder, 1973): it is not possible with this hypothesis for detection times to decrease unless there is an increase in the distance between the observation and the cutoff, and this is unlikely to occur in passing from a situation where there is a signal present to one where there is no signal.

A fourth limitation, already noted in Chapter 2, is that the hypothesis cannot account for the unbiased improvement in detectability that occurs as a function of time (Sekuler, 1965; Swets and Birdsall, 1967), since the only way of varying response time is by altering the position of the cutoff, thereby favouring one response at the expense of the other. As has already been pointed out, the latency function hypothesis is a description rather than an explanation, and complicating the hypothesis by the addition of further *ad hoc* latency components does nothing to elucidate the underlying decision process. What appears to be needed, as Koppell (1976) has recognized, is the specification of an underlying mechanism for which some kind of latency function would be an important property.

## *An Optional-stopping Process without a Memory*

One of the earliest attempts to specify such a process in the context of signal detection is that of Swets and Green (1961), who examined the possibility that an observer might adopt not one, but two cutoffs (Fig. 59). This model is very similar to one proposed for discrimination some thirty years ago by Cartwright and Festinger (1943), which was discussed in Chapter 2. If an observation falls above $x_s$ the observer responds "signal" and if below $x_n$, he responds "nonsignal"; otherwise, if the observation falls between $x_n$ and $x_s$, he continues taking observations until he encounters one which exceeds $x_s$ or falls below $x_n$. As was pointed out in Chapter 2, if the observer merely waits for a critical observation and rejects those falling in the region of no-decision, then no memory processes are assumed and no integration of information over successive observations is possible.

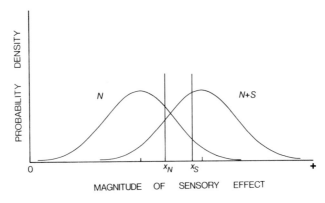

Fig. 59. Representation of a memory-less optional-stopping signal detection model, where the interval of no-decision is bounded by the cutoffs $x_s$ and $x_n$.

Swets and Green (1961) investigated this model in three experiments in which each observation interval was defined by the experimenter, and the observer was free after each observation to respond "signal", "nonsignal", or "continue" (to make observations). According to Swets and Green, observers showed no evidence of integrating information over successive observations, except where especially encouraged to do so. In particular, their distributions of terminating response times were roughly exponential in form, as would be expected from a memory-less mechanism (c.f. Broadbent, 1971, p. 291). Taken at face value, these results would suggest that an observer under normal conditions makes a response only when an observation falls outside the region of no-decision, and that he ignores all observations that fail to meet this criterion.

More recently, however, this conclusion has been questioned by Wolfendale (1967), who points out that Swets and Green plotted their graphs on a logarithmic scale, and that, when replotted on a linear scale, the graphs "show clearly that there is a progressive breakdown in the geometric form" (p. 155). Wolfendale himself tested the distributions of response times by an observer, who was required to detect a spot of reduced intensity within a circular background of white light, and found that they were not exponential in form. In the same vein, Swets and Birdsall (1967) have presented evidence that observers using a rating scale are capable of accumulating sensory information as effectively as if they were multiplying the likelihood ratios supposedly calculated by them for successive observations, though observers using a yes–no procedure appeared to use a somewhat less efficient procedure.

Taken in conjunction with the evidence for data accumulation in two-category discrimination, reviewed in Chapter 2, these results suggest that observers do not simply continue taking observations until one falls outside a region of no-decision. As has already been argued in Chapter 2, such a procedure would in any case be difficult to modify so as to account for the pattern of response times observed in three-category decisions by Kellogg (1931) and myself (Vickers, 1975), since the first observation would invariably fall into one of the three categories and hence trigger a response in a constant minimal time.

## The Neural Timing Model of Luce and Green (1972)

One process which still obeys the general logic of signal detection theory, but assumes complete integration of sensory information, and dispenses with the region of no-decision, is to be found in the neural timing model of detection recently proposed by Luce and Green (1972). According to these authors, signal intensity is represented at a hypothetical neural decision centre by several parallel, but independent, trains of impulses, each impulse being of very brief and constant duration. The variable of interest in this model is not a likelihood ratio, nor a direct representation of stimulus intensity by the number of impulses within a given time, but the interval between the arrival of successive impulses. On each channel these interarrival times (or IATs) are independent random variables conforming to a common exponential distribution, with an expected value that is a monotonic decreasing function of signal intensity. An observer's decisions are determined by rules, such as responding "signal" if the average over a fixed number of IATs is less than a certain critical value $x_t$, and responding "nonsignal" if the average IAT exceeds $x_t$. As an example, Fig. 60 illustrates the model where signals are arriving on one channel only. Since the more intense (signal) stimulus gives rise to shorter IATs the positions of the noise ($n$) and noise-plus-signal ($n + s$) distributions are the reverse of those found in the traditional signal detection model. In the version illustrated, a "signal" response is made if the average IAT is less than $x_t$, and a "nonsignal" response is made if it exceeds $x_t$.

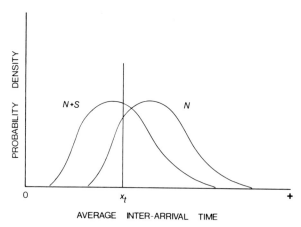

Fig. 60. Representation of the single channel neural timing model, where a "signal" response is made if the average inter-arrival time is less than $x_t$. (After Pike et al., 1974).

As has been pointed out by Pike et al. (1974) and by Pike and Dalgleish (1976), this model immediately leads to some qualitative predictions, which can be intuitively seen from Fig. 60. In the first place, the mean times (RT) for the four categories of response ("hits", "false alarms", "misses" and "correct rejections") should be in the order RT($S/s$) < RT($S/n$) < RT($N/s$) < RT($N/n$). Secondly, mean times for "signal" responses (whether correct or incorrect) should be lower than those for "nonsignal" responses (correct or incorrect). Thirdly, mean times for all responses on signal trials should be lower than the mean times for all responses on nonsignal trials. Finally, as the bias increases in favour of "signal" responses, then the mean times for all categories of response should increase. We shall briefly examine the evidence for each of these predictions in turn.

## Prediction 1

As the model stands, there are several gross discrepancies between its predictions and the available data. In the case of the first prediction, for example, it is true that the predicted rank ordering of mean times for the four response categories holds for all three observers in the experiment of Carterette et al. (1965), under the condition where signal probability was high (0·8), and also for observers 1 and 2 (who showed a bias towards making "signal" responses) even when signal and nonsignal trials were equiprobable. However, the order does not hold under the latter condition for observer 3 (who showed a bias towards making "nonsignal" responses), nor for any of the three observers when the probability of a signal was low (0·2). A very similar pattern is discernible in the results of Pike et al. (1974), which exhibit the predicted rank ordering when a deadline is imposed on "signal" responses (thereby encouraging a readiness to respond "signal"), but fail to do so for 3 out of 6 observers when a deadline (encouraging the opposite bias) is imposed on "non-signal" responses.

The divergence was further investigated by Pike and Dalgleish (1976), who encouraged such an attitude in their observers and found a quite different rank from the one predicted when the bias towards "nonsignal" responses was reinforced by a deadline. A general corroboration of these findings is provided by the data for observers 1 and 6 in my own experiment (Vickers, 1978), who showed the strongest bias towards "nonsignal" and "signal" responses respectively, though my results also imply that the detectability of the signal is an important additional factor in determining the eventual rank ordering of the mean times for the four response categories.

## Prediction 2

These findings suggest that this model is weakest where conditions favour a bias towards making "nonsignal" responses, and this conclusion is strengthened by an evaluation of the second prediction from the model, namely, that the mean time for "signal" responses (whether correct or incorrect) should be lower than that for "nonsignal" responses (whether correct or incorrect). This prediction is proved wrong as well by results obtained under conditions favouring a bias towards "nonsignal" responses, such as the data of Carterette *et al.* (1965) for the low signal probability of 0·2; contrary to the prediction, "nonsignal" responses took less time than "signal" responses in each of the six comparisons possible at this probability level.

The importance of bias in determining the relative times for "signal" and "nonsignal" responses also emerges clearly in the results of Pike *et al.* (1974), which confirm the prediction of the timing model in the case of five out of six observers when a deadline for "signal" decisions is imposed, but display the opposite relation for four out of six observers when a deadline is imposed on "nonsignal" responses. In turn, these findings are reinforced and sharpened by the data of Gescheider *et al.* (1968, 1969, 1971), which show that whether "signal" responses took more or less time than "nonsignal" depended upon both the probability of the signal and its level of detectability.

## Prediction 3

The weakness of the model under conditions favouring a bias towards "nonsignal" responses is further emphasized in the case of the third prediction, which states that the mean time for all responses on signal trials should be lower than that for all responses on nonsignal trials. This prediction is not borne out, for instance, by a calculation of pooled estimates from the data of Carterette *et al.* (1965, Table I), which show, in 5 out of 6 comparisons, that mean times for all responses on signal trials are greater than those on nonsignal trials, provided that signal probability is low (0·2). As in the case of the first two predictions, the third prediction is confirmed by the data of Pike *et al.* (1974) when a signal deadline is imposed, but is contradicted by their data for a nonsignal deadline. The results obtained by Pike and Dalgleish (1976) follow the same pattern, with mean times of 582 and 545 ms for "signal" and "nonsignal" decisions respectively, when a deadline is imposed on "nonsignal" responses.

## Prediction 4

The above results demonstrate the importance of both bias and detectability in determining the rank order of the various classifications of response times, and are quite inconsistent with the timing model, for which the order remains insensitive to these factors. A further conflict between theory and data arises in the case of the fourth prediction (that, as the bias in favour of "signal" responses increases, so the mean time for all responses should increase). This prediction is also clearly disproved—at least in the case of "hits"—by the data of Carterette *et al.* (1965), Gescheider *et al.* (1968, 1969,

1971), Pike *et al.* (1974) and Pike and Dalgleish (1976).

Other discrepancies between the neural timing model and the evidence have been noted by Pike *et al.* (1974) and by Pike and Dalgleish (1976), who consider several modifications to the model. These include various assumptions about different "residual time components" for "signal" and "non-signal" responses, the reintroduction of a region of no-decision (or "interval of uncertainty") and the abandonment of the timing model under some circumstances in favour of a "dual process". However, several of these modifications were quite unsatisfactory, and none was found by them to be completely adequate. No doubt further modifications might be considered, but any modified model is likely to be very unparsimonious, while its performance to date clearly suggests that further efforts in this direction would not be worthwhile.

## Counting Models

The models considered so far have all shared the assumption that events are classified by an observer through the single, direct application of some kind of variable "sensory" criterion to individual observations or to some group or combination of these observations. In addition, the no-decision model of Swets and Green (1961) and the neural timing process of Luce and Green (1972) have explored two ways of varying the number of observations (and hence the time) required to reach a decision, with the aim of accounting for both the speed–accuracy trade-off and the relationship which persists between response times and signals of randomly varying detectability. An alternative (and somewhat more direct) way of achieving the same end would be to make the attainment of a certain number of observations of a particular kind itself the criterion for a decision. Indeed Green and Luce (1973) suggest that observers may employ a "dual process" of timing on signal trials where there is a deadline, and counting on non-signal trials with a deadline. Clearly, it would be desirable to derive a more parsimonious explanation of the data, and the present section will examine the extent to which this can be provided by some variety of counting process. The models to be examined in this section postulate both sensory criteria for the classification of observations and response criteria for the reaching of decisions based on tallies of classified observations. Accordingly, they may be regarded as constituting a class of model quite distinct from the signal detection processes which we have just considered.

### Counter and Clock Models

In an attempt to formulate a model which would account for the apparent growth in detectability as a function of time, Carterette *et al.* (1965) have considered a model in which the criterion for a signal is a cumulative count of the number of times a given likelihood ratio has been exceeded, with this criterion varying (presumably decreasing) as a function of time. Sekuler (1965) has proposed a similar extension of McGill's proposal (1963), which embodies two neural counters, one of which accumulates only noise and the other of which accumulates either noise alone or noise-plus-signal, depending upon whether a signal is absent or present, respectively. When a signal is present, the counting rate in the second counter should increase and the quantities in the two counters should diverge. A decision to respond "signal" is made when the divergence has reached a certain critical value, while a decision to respond "nonsignal" is made if the accumulated divergence does not reach or exceed this critical value by a pre-set deadline $t$.

The notion of deadline responding has already been discussed in connection with three-category decisions and judgments of sameness and difference, and similar difficulties arise in the case of signal detection. Specifically, the notion of a deadline does not appear to be consistent with the finding that times to respond "nonsignal", either correctly or incorrectly, may be either greater or less than those to make "signal" responses, either correctly or incorrectly (Sekuler, 1965; Carterette *et al.*, 1965; Gescheider *et al.*, 1968, 1969, 1971; Pike and Ryder, 1973; Vickers, 1978), depending upon the *a priori* probability of a signal, the bias adopted by an observer and the detectability of the signal. As with three-category decisions or judgments of sameness and difference, it would be possible to suppose that the clock in question was noisy, but, besides adding another parameter, it again appears that the amount of randomness would have to be implausibly large in order to account for those occasions on which the time for "nonsignal" responses is substantially less than that for "signal" decisions (e.g. Carterette *et al.*, 1965; Gescheider *et al.*, 1968, 1969, 1971).

## The Counter Models of Pike (1973) and Pike et al. (1974)

### A Two Counter Model

In place of a clock, Pike (1973) has proposed a "multiple observations" model, in which a single cutoff classifies observations as "signal" or "nonsignal", two separate tallies are kept of the number of observations of each kind, and the appropriate response is made as soon as one of the tallies reaches or exceeds a certain critical number.

Unfortunately, this theoretical development seems to represent a retrograde step. In the first place, it is difficult to see how this approach could be extended to apply to judgments of sameness and difference or to three-category decisions, without the reintroduction of some additional process, such as a clock, to provide for responses in the "same" or "equal" category. In its application to two-category discrimination, the model would also encounter considerable contradictory evidence, since, for a fixed position of the cutoff, it has properties which correspond to the recruitment model of La Berge (1962), which we have already seen to be inadequate in this connection (Chapter 3).

Even within the context of detection, the model would appear to fail, since it predicts that times for correct responses should always be lower than those for incorrect, which is inconsistent with the results of Carterette et al. (1965) and of Gescheider et al. (1968, 1969, 1971). It is true that this last difficulty might be overcome by postulating unequal critical values for the counters, or by supposing that there is some variation over trials in the value of the critical count. However, the addition of these parameters to a model which already incorporates "sensory bias" in the position of the cutoff (which might equally well be susceptible to random variation), would rob the model of its initial simplicity. Whatever the reasons, Pike himself seems to have abandoned this line of approach in favour of a related, but more complex, alternative, to which we now turn.

## An Interval of Uncertainty Model

The model most recently considered by Pike et al. (1974) postulates two cutoffs, with an interval of uncertainty or no-decision between them. Observations falling above the upper cutoff are added to the "signal" counter, those falling below the lower cutoff are added to the "nonsignal" counter, while those falling within the interval of uncertainty are simply ignored. As in the previous model, observations are taken until the tally in one of the counters reaches a critical level, whereupon the appropriate response is initiated.

This model is obviously complex, since both bias and sensitivity measures may be affected by changes either in the positions of the two cutoffs or in the values of the critical tallies needed for a response, while the interactions between these "sensory" and "response" criteria make it difficult to extract simple predictions. However, two straightforward predictions made by Pike et al. (1974) are that the mean time for correct "signal" responses (or "hits") should be the same as that for "misses", and that the mean time for correct rejections should be equal to that for false alarms.

Neither of these predictions was borne out by the data of Pike et al. (1974), nor are they consistent with the results of Carterette et al. (1965). With signal detectability held constant and signal probability fixed at 0·5, the latter experimenters found hits to be faster than misses, and false alarms faster than correct rejections in the case of observers 1 and 2, who showed a bias in favour of "signal" responses. Meanwhile, the reverse relations were found to hold for their third observer,* who showed a bias towards "nonsignal" responses (Carterette et al., 1965, Fig. 3). The same pattern is evident in the results of Pike and Dalgleish (1976) before "corrections" are applied to account for various hypothesized "residual response components". Pike et al. (1974) also found difficulty in accounting for changes in the proportions of responses as deadlines were manipulated to favour slowness and accuracy in either "signal" or "nonsignal" responses.

In an attempt to account for the discrepancies between theory and data, Pike and Dalgleish (1976) postulate four basic additive and independent components of response time: (i) an overall input and output time; (ii) a decision time; (iii) a residual component in "non-deadline" conditions; (iv) a component varying inversely with the probability of response. These assumptions allow Pike and Dalgleish to apply corrections to their data which largely reconcile them with their theory. Nevertheless, these authors recognize that the model has become cumbersome and "very unparsimonious", and that some data, such as those of Carterette et al. (1965) remain recalcitrant.

## An Accumulator Model of Signal Detection

In the opinion of Pike and Dalgleish, the answer to these problems "lies in showing that a more general . . . model can account for the overall latency-probability relationship without the use of an extra component" (1976, p. 239). One possibility suggested by them is similar to the accumulator model of two-category judgment, with zero amounts being accumulated for observations falling within an interval of uncertainty, and observations falling outside contributing amounts which vary directly with their distance from this interval. According to Pike and Ryder (1973), a model in which variable amounts were accumulated to a criterion would have the added advantage of explaining their failure to find any evidence of the discontinuities in response time distributions which would be expected if detection were mediated by a simple counting process. In the light of their conclusions, and in view of the success of an accumulator process in accounting for the main features of other simple judgments, serious consideration of the application of such a model to detection would indeed seem to be inevitable. However, before embarking on an exploration of the potential of an accumulator process in this direction, one further considera-

---

* The rank order given by Carterette et al. in their Table I for observer 3 ("high" condition) does not correspond to the numbers it purports to summarize.

tion must be taken into account since it implies that one of the assumptions made by all of the models examined up to this point is inaccurate.

## Absolute and Relative Judgments

So far, the quantity represented along the decision axis has been supposed to be directly and completely determined by the intensity of the signal. An alternative view proposed by Macmillan (1971), is that this quantity is more appropriately conceived of as a change or difference between an observation (or observations) taken within the observation interval (or area) and an observation (or observations) taken outside. That is, the observer is thought of as deciding whether some carefully defined focal stimulus is the same as, or greater or less than, a certain background stimulus.

To test this possibility Ryder et al. (1974) studied the frequency of "signal" responses on occasional catch trials, when the level of background auditory noise was raised to a value reaching or exceeding that of the signal. If observers based their decisions on some direct function of signal intensity, then these incremented stimuli should give rise to "signal" responses. However, Ryder et al. found that the proportion of "signal" responses on incremented catch trials was lower than would be expected if observers were simply basing their judgments on some direct function of signal intensity. At the same time, the distribution of "nonsignal" responses on catch trials also differed from that on normal nonsignal trials, indicating that observers were nevertheless sensitive to the increase in the level of the nonsignal stimulus. Ryder et al. concluded that observers normally base their decisions on the difference between the focal and the background stimulus, but that they are also capable of a more direct appreciation of signal intensities by a process akin to absolute judgment. When catch trials are sufficiently distinctive, they may use this latter process as an alternative means of identifying the stimulus. However, when the detection task is more difficult, as in most of the experiments in the present context, then it appears that decisions based on the difference between observations of the focal and the background stimuli are likely to be more efficient.

## An Accumulator Model

Fortunately, the approach we have outlined to three-category decisions and to judgments of sameness and difference lends itself very naturally to this view. According to this approach, the observer in a signal detection experiment may be construed as attempting to decide whether a given focal stimulus is the same as, or greater (or less) than, the background stimulus along some specified dimension, such as brightness, length, weight, or loudness. As in the three-category or the same–different task, he may be conceived as continuing to inspect a stream of stimulus differences until some criterion is satisfied. The only difference is a minor terminological one, viz. the inspected differences in the signal detection case are not between a variable and a standard, but between the focal and the background stimulus. On this interpretation, the distinguishing feature of the signal detection paradigm is that, unlike same–different tasks, which typically present both increments and decrements in stimulus intensity, the former usually employs increments only. To apply the accumulator model to a situation of this kind all that is necessary is to attach a response of the form "signal" to the decision outcome "$V > S$" (i.e. "focal is greater than background"), and another of the form "nonsignal" to each of the other two logically possible decision outcomes (i.e. "$V = S$" or $V < S$"). When no decrements are presented, then the observer may in addition be supposed to set a very high criterion for the outcome "$V < S$". Other suppositions are possible, but this seems to be the most straightforward.

According to this view, both two and three-category discrimination, judgments of sameness and difference and signal detection would all be mediated by the same decision mechanism. In two-category tasks the intermediate response is assumed to be suppressed, in same–different tasks it is supposed that the response "different" is attached to both the "$V < S$" and the "$V > S$" outcomes, and in signal detection it is suggested that the "signal" response is attached to the "$V > S$" outcome, and the "nonsignal" response to both the "$V = S$" and the "$V < S$" outcomes. Since the latter would arise very infrequently (particularly with a high value of $k_l$), the signal detection task would usually resemble a truncated same–different task, in which the observer is thought of as deciding whether the focal stimulus is the same as, or greater than, the background.

This suggested similarity between the two tasks is indeed clearly borne out in two experiments by Bindra et al. (1965), in which observers were required to decide whether pairs of successively presented tones were of the same or a different pitch. In the first experiment, one response key was labelled "same" and the other "different", and observers were instructed to press the appropriate key after each stimulus pair. In the second experiment, one response key was labelled "yes" and the other "no". For one block of trials, observers were asked to press the appropriate key in answer to the question "are the tones the same, 'yes' or 'no'?", while, for the other block of trials, the question was "are the tones different, 'yes' or 'no'?". Bindra et al. found no difference in the pattern of errors between the two conditions of the second experiment, while in both experiments times for "same" judgments were longer than those for "different", whether these responses were given directly, or translated into the form of a "yes/no" answer to either question. This equivalence lends support to the hypothesis, put forward at the beginning of this chapter, that these (and perhaps other) simple judgments may all be mediated by a single decision mechanism, which can be applied to different tasks by suppressing one or more responses, or by varying the attachment of responses to decision outcomes.

## General Properties of an Accumulator Model of Signal Detection

Before considering any further implications of this last proposal we must obviously examine the accuracy with which the general features of detection performance are delineated by the model. The model is, of course, capable of yielding predictions concerning the effects of any combination of bias, caution and discriminability upon response frequency and time. As with the other simple judgments, however, attention will be focussed on those aspects only for which some relevant experimental data already exist.

### The Form and Position of the Psychometric Function

In general, the frequency with which an observer produces a "signal" response is an increasing function of objective signal intensity. Although some workers, such as Stevens et al. (1941) have argued that some form of step function would be more appropriate, most data relating detection frequency to signal intensity resemble the smooth sigmoid curve which characterizes response frequencies obtained with differential judgments (Woodworth and Scholsberg, 1954; Corso, 1967). Figure 62, for example, shows data from an experiment (Vickers, 1978), in which six observers were required to indicate on each trial whether or not the average height of an array of vertical line segments of randomly varying length and randomly positioned within a central square area, had been slightly increased. Typical stimuli are presented in Fig. 61 and illustrate incidentally the plausibility of supposing that an observer detects a signal by discriminating between a focal and a background stimulus. Figure 62a shows data for the observer who made the greatest proportion of "nonsignal" responses, while Fig. 62b shows data for the observer who showed the least bias in that direction.

The general form of these curves, and the shift downwards in the point of subjective equality with increasing bias towards "signal" responses, correspond well with the pattern predicted by the accumulator model. For example, Fig. 63 shows two typical patterns of response frequencies each generated by a computer simulation of 2000 trials of the proposed process, operating on a normal distribution of $(V-S)$ (or "focal" minus "standard") differences, with a mean $\overline{(V-S)}$, and a standard deviation $\sigma_{(V-S)} = 1$. For each simulation, eleven mean values of this distribution, varying from 0 up

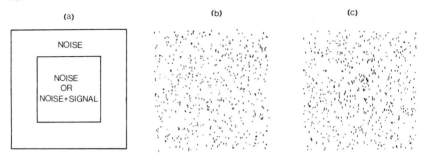

Fig. 61. Stimuli used in a signal-noise differentiation task (Vickers, 1978). The background noise consisted of a rectangular distribution of vertical lines of fixed mean height. A signal might or might not appear in the centre panel, indicated in (a), in the form of a slight increase in the average height of the lines. Figure 61b shows an example of noise alone, while Fig. 61c shows a typical "signal present" stimulus.

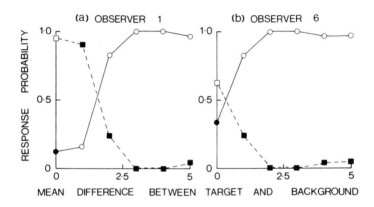

Fig. 62. Empirical response probabilities from a signal detection task (Vickers, 1978). Squares joined by broken lines denote "nonsignal" responses and circles joined by solid lines represent "signal" responses. Empty symbols represent responses made correctly and filled symbols those made incorrectly. The mean difference between the target and the background line segments is expressed in terms of the smallest unit increments on the Tektronix 611 display on which the stimuli were generated.

to $2 \cdot 5\sigma_{(V-S)}$ were presented to the hypothesized process. Figure 63a illustrates the pattern when the model is given a low value of $k_e$ so as to represent a bias in favour of the "nonsignal" response, while Fig. 63b illustrates the pattern when a high value is set for $k_e$. Although no attempts have been made to fit these theoretical curves to the data of Fig. 62, it is clear that the change in the empirical relation between detectability and response frequency as subjective bias is varied is well portrayed by the model.

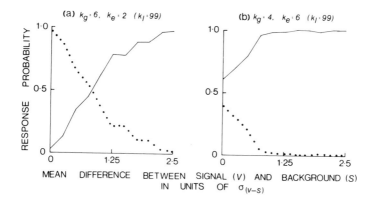

Fig. 63. Patterns of response probabilities produced in computer simulation of the accumulator model for signal detection. Data for "signal" responses are represented by solid lines and those for "nonsignal" by dotted lines. Figure 63a shows data for a case where there is a bias in favour of making "nonsignal" responses, and Fig. 63b those for a case where there is a bias against. (Since decrements in magnitude were not used, the extreme criterion $k_l$ has been given an arbitrary high value of 99, so that there were effectively no decision outcomes of the form "$V < S$").

## Stimulus Intensity and Response Time

Although the above account may be regarded as a somewhat elementary accomplishment on the part of any model, the testing of theory against data rapidly becomes more complex when the dependent variable of interest is that of response time. For instance, it appears to be generally accepted empirically that the mean time for correct detections decreases as the intensity of the signal increases (Gescheider et al., 1968, 1969, 1971; Grice, 1968; Murray, 1970; Teichner and Krebs, 1972). However, a number of studies suggest that at very low stimulus intensities, response time may well fall again (Gescheider et al., 1969, Fig. 2; Gescheider et al., 1971, Fig. 3; Teichner and Krebs, 1972, Fig. 4). A concrete instance is evident in Fig. 64, which presents the patterns of mean response times for those observers in my experiment (Vickers, 1978), for whom response probabilities have already been shown (Fig. 62). In Fig. 64a, the mean times for "signal" responses show a clear tendency to drop at the lowest signal intensity, with the mean time for false alarms appearing to drop still further. As I pointed out earlier, this last result is inconsistent with a latency function hypothesis. It is also inconsistent with all of the other models considered so far in this chapter.

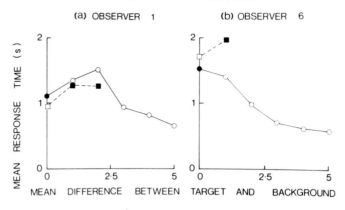

Fig. 64. Empirical response times from a signal detection task (Vickers, 1978). As in Fig. 62, squares joined by broken lines denote "nonsignal" responses and circles joined by solid lines represent "signal" responses. Empty symbols represent responses made correctly and filled symbols those made incorrectly. Figure 64a shows data for the observer who showed the greatest relative bias towards making "nonsignal" responses, and Fig. 64b shows data for the observer who showed the least bias in that direction. As in Fig. 62, the mean difference between the target and the background is expressed in terms of the smallest unit increments on the Tektronix 611 display on which the stimuli were generated.

In contrast, Fig. 65 shows the patterns of mean response times generated by the computer simulations of the accumulator model, for which the response probabilities have already been presented (Fig. 63). As with three-category decisions and judgments of sameness and difference, response times under certain circumstances do appear to reach a maximum above a stimulus difference or intensity of zero. This seems to be most likely to occur when the value of $k_e$ is set low (Fig. 63a) so that any "greater", "different", or "signal" responses must be made within a very short time if they are not to be "pipped to the post" by the "equals", "same", or "nonsignal" response. In the proposed accumulator process the probability of making a "signal" response is determined by the detectability of the signal, by the criterion $k_g$ and by the bias in criterion values. Although the complex interactions between these three parameters have yet to be teased out and studied in detail, the relative contribution made by each appears to depend on the values assumed by the others, with the result that the pattern of response times may change quite abruptly, or even reverse, following even small changes in one of them. It seems likely that the appearance of steps or inflection points in empirical curves of response probability may also be due to similar alterations in this intricate balance.

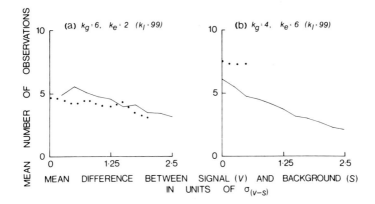

Fig. 65. Patterns of response times taken in computer simulation of the accumulator model for signal detection. As in Fig. 63, data for "signal" responses are represented by solid lines and those for "nonsignal" by dotted lines. Figure 65a shows data for a case where there is a bias in favour of making "nonsignal" responses, and Fig. 65b those for a case where there is a bias against. (Since decrements in magnitude were not used, the extreme criterion $k_l$ has been given an arbitrarily high value of 99, so that there were effectively no decision outcomes of the form "$V < S$").

## The Relation Between Detectability and Time

As we have seen in both Chapter 2, and the present chapter, the fixed sample statistical decision models proposed for both discrimination and detection predict that the index of detectability $d'$ should increase as the square root of the number of observations required to reach a decision (and hence of the time taken, provided that the observations are made at a steady rate). As we have also seen in Chapter 2, Taylor et al. (1967) made a direct test of this prediction by plotting against response time values of $d'^2$, which were calculated from a discrimination experiment by Schouten and Bekker (1967). Although data from one observer were well described by a straight line as predicted by the fixed sample model, average data for 10 observers fell on a smooth, but distinctly S-shaped curve.

Figure 66 shows the results of five separate simulations of the proposed accumulator model, each operating on a random series of equally probable signal and nonsignal stimuli. Each curve shows the rise in detectability as a function of the increase in the number of observations required to detect a stimulus of fixed objective detectability as the values of the criteria $k_g = k_e$ are increased in unit steps from two up to six (with $k_l$ made virtually inoperative by being set to 99). The curves all display an S-shaped form, which differs from that predicted by the fixed sample process, but resembles the empirical relation presented by Taylor et al. (1967).

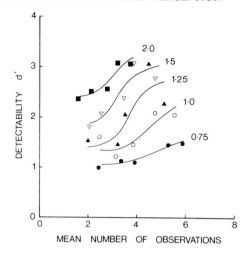

Fig. 66. Relations between $d'$ and the mean number of observations taken at different values of the criteria $k_g$ and $k_e$. The separate curves have been fitted by eye, and each represents data for a particular degree of discriminability, with a value for $(V–S)$ as shown.

For the sake of clarity the complete spectrum of curves obtained for each of ten levels of objective detectability is not shown, but the only important differences lie in the starting point and steepness of each. At intermediate levels of detectability, such as those illustrated in Fig. 66, there are marked increases in $d'$ as a function of number of observations. However, at very low and very high detectabilities the curves remain shallow, though they begin at low and at high values of $d'$ respectively. In all cases they retain an approximately sigmoid form. Although the comparison between theory and data must remain qualitative, it does suggest that the accumulator model can also be expected to yield a good quantitative description of the relation between detectability and response time.

## Times for Correct and Incorrect Responses

The close match between theoretical and empirical properties achieved so far by the accumulator process would lead us to prefer it to either the classical psychophysical or to the fixed sample signal detection model. The accumulator process also shows a similar superiority over the latency function hypothesis, even when we restrict our attention to an examination of the times for correct and incorrect responses, about which the latter hypothesis makes clear predictions. Irrespective of the form and symmetry of the assumed latency function, times for "signal" responses made correctly should be lower than those for "signal" responses made incorrectly. Similarly times for correct "nonsignal" responses should be lower than those for incorrect "nonsignal" responses.

While sufficient data are not available to test the latter prediction, the former is clearly proved to be erroneous by the data of Carterette *et al.* (1965), Pike and Ryder (1973) and myself (Vickers, 1978) for the observer showing greatest bias towards "nonsignal" responses. However, where $k_e$ is set low (Fig. 65a) so as to correspond to a similar bias, then the accumulator process predicts that times for "hits" at low detectabilities may indeed by higher than those for "false alarms". This agreement between the data and such a distinctive prediction would seem to be a telling point in favour of the accumulator over the latency function hypothesis.

In the above comparison we have examined the times for one response to two different stimuli. It is of course also possible to compare the times for different responses to the same stimulus (e.g. "hits" v. "misses", or "correct rejections" v. "false alarms"). As can be seen from Figs 63a and 65a, the accumulator model predicts that when there is a strong bias in favour of "nonsignal" responses, "hits" should generally take longer than "misses" and "correct rejections" may take about the same, or longer, than "false alarms". Conversely, when there is a strong bias in favour of "signal" responses, then "hits" should take less than "misses", while "correct rejections" should take longer than "false alarms".

These predictions closely resemble the data from my experiment (Vickers, 1978), which are given in Figs 64a and 64b for observers showing the greatest bias towards "nonsignal" and "signal" responses respectively. With the exception that, for observer 1, "correct rejections" are somewhat faster than "false alarms", the order of response times, and the dependence of this order on bias, are as predicted. In this respect, therefore, the accumulator also has a distinct advantage over the interval of uncertainty model, which, as we have seen, predicts that the mean time for "hits" should be equal to that for "misses", and that "correct rejections" should take the same time as "false alarms", irrespective of the degree of bias displayed by the observer.

## Times for "Signal" and "Nonsignal" Responses

One of the two remaining ways of partitioning and comparing the various categories of response in a signal detection task is to compare the times for all "signal" responses (correct or otherwise) with those for all "nonsignal" responses. As may be inferred from Fig. 65a, the accumulator model predicts that times for "signal" responses may be higher than those for "nonsignal" when there is a strong bias towards the latter response, but should be lower than those for "nonsignal" responses when there is a strong bias towards the former. As may be seen particularly in Fig. 65a, the objective detectability of the signal may also be important.

This general pattern of predictions corresponds closely with my own findings (Vickers, 1978) (Fig. 64). It is also confirmed by the data of Sekuler (1965), Carterette et al. (1965), Gescheider et al. (1968, 1969, 1971) and Pike and Ryder (1973). In this respect at least, therefore, the accumulator is clearly preferable to the counter-and-clock model, for which the mean time for "nonsignal" responses (correct or incorrect) must necessarily be longer than that for "signal" responses.

## Times on Signal and Nonsignal Trials

The remaining way of partitioning the response categories is to compare the times for all responses on signal trials with those on nonsignal (i.e. correct or otherwise). Given that a signal is presented, then Fig. 65b suggests that the accumulator model would predict that the mean response time for all signal trials will tend to be lower than for all nonsignal trials. This prediction coincides with that of the neural timing model and is confirmed by the data of Carterette et al. (1965) when signal probability is high, by that of Pike et al. (1974) and Pike and Dalgleish (1976) when a deadline is imposed on signal trials, and by my own data (Vickers, 1978) for the observer who shows the strongest bias, towards making "signal" responses (Fig. 64b). However, where there is a marked bias in the opposite direction, as occurs in Fig. 64a, then the mean predicted time for all signal trials (particularly at low levels of detectability) may be the same as, or even greater than, that for all nonsignal trials. This differs from the prediction of the timing model, but finds support in the results of Carterette et al. (1965) when signal probability is low, in those of Pike et al. (1974) and Pike and Dalgleish (1976) when a deadline is imposed on nonsignal trials, and in my own results (Vickers, 1978) for the observer showing the strongest bias in favour of making "nonsignal" responses (Fig. 64a).

## The Rank Order of Times for the Four Response Categories

One final feature with respect to which the accumulator and the neural timing model may be compared is the predicted rank ordering of mean times for the four response categories. Where there is a bias towards making "signal" responses, as there is in Fig. 65b, then the accumulator model predicts that mean times should follow the order $(S/s) < (S/n) < (N/s) \simeq (N/n)$. This is very similar to the order $(S/s) < (S/n) < (N/s) < (N/n)$ predicted by the neural timing model, and generally found by Carterette et al. (1965), Pike et al. (1974), Pike and Dalgleish (1976) and myself (Vickers, 1978), where evidence suggests an appreciable bias towards "signal" responses. However, when bias favours "nonsignal" responses, as in Fig. 65a, then the accumulator model predicts that hits may be slower than correct rejections, as was found by all of the above experimenters where a similar bias appeared to operate. While the relation between correct and incorrect "nonsignal" deserves more attention, both theoretical and experimental, the rank ordering predicted by the accumulator appears to differ substantially from that predicted by the neural timing model, but to correspond well with that found empirically.

## *Conclusions*

So far the proposed model appears to exhibit all the features that we can with some certainty discern in human performance at detecting stimuli. To begin with, the general decision mechanism is especially designed to operate on a distribution of stimulus differences, and lends itself naturally to the hypothesis that signal detection involves the discrimination between a focal and a background stimulus. The regular variation in the mixture of positive and negative stimulus differences, which follows alterations in signal detectability, can account for the form of the psychometric function, while changes in the position and steepness of these functions appear to be determined jointly by the levels of the three criteria, and by their relationships to each other. The latency function relating response time to detectability can be similarly explained as being due to changes in the statistical composition of the inspected stimulus differences and in the criterion levels adopted. The experimentally established variation in both errors and response times as a function of signals varying randomly in detectability is implied by the optional-stopping character of the proposed process, while the information upon which each eventual decision is based is integrated over successive observations, as also seems to be the case empirically.

Besides these basic qualifications, the accumulator model avoids the postulation of a neural clock (which seems in any case to be implausible in other contexts), and dispenses also with the unwieldy assumption of an interval of uncertainty with sensory as well as response criteria. The accumulator provides a better account than either the latency function or the interval of uncertainty model of the relations between the times for correct and incorrect responses. Similarly, a comparison of the times for "signal" and "nonsignal" responses shows the proposed model to be superior to the counter-and-clock process. Meanwhile, both the rank order of response times and the relative times on signal and nonsignal trials lead us to prefer the accumulator to the neural timing model. Finally, unlike a memory-less optional-stopping process or a simple two-counter model, the accumulator can also account for both two and three-category discrimination and for judgments of sameness and difference, without any substantial modification. In effect, on the present approach, signal detection constitutes only one specialized application of a general-purpose decision mechanism.

In contrast to a digital computer, in which a wide variety of operations are performed on information which is stored in one basic form, the last four chapters have thus shown there to be good grounds for suggesting that the elementary quantitative analysis of sensory information by human beings may be performed by a single type of general-purpose decision mechanism,

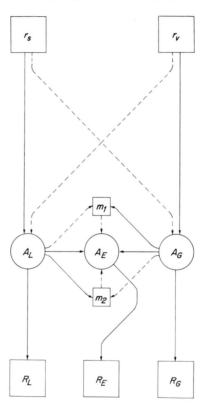

Fig. 67. Hypothetical realization in neurophysiological terms of the general decision module. Receptors for the standard and the variable stimulus are represented by $r_s$ and $r_v$. The accumulative processes $A_L$, $A_E$ and $A_G$ control the response processes $R_L$, $R_E$ and $R_G$ respectively. Solid lines denote excitatory and broken lines inhibitory signals. The processes $m_1$ and $m_2$ represent one way of calculating the modulus $|t_g - t_l|$ of the excitation in $A_L$ and $A_G$ and transforming it into one of two alternative inhibitory signals. The diagram constitutes a more schematic elaboration of the principles illustrated in Fig. 38.

in which qualitatively (or topographically) classified information is sampled until some criterion amount is accumulated. Besides accounting for the empirical patterns of response frequency and time observed in a number of different tasks, this proposed mechanism is conceptually simple and its behaviour is not difficult to simulate. As was suggested in Chapter 3, it is also possible to give the model a neurophysiological realization, embodying only the well-established properties of excitation, inhibition, temporal summation and threshold discharge, and the outlines of a version for the general mechanism are illustrated in Fig. 67. These conclusions, it would seem, are all consistent with the underlying expectation, expressed in the introductory chapter, that the processing of sensory information by the human nervous system reflects the operation of a few simple principles of discrimination and identification, which must have been operative in the most primitive of the early living systems, and which have been preserved by the evolved organism in essentially the same form.

It would, of course, be possible to generate more detailed predictions concerning the effects of bias, caution and discriminability on the precise shapes of the response time distributions. However, there is an almost complete absence of empirical data against which to test them. In any case, as was suggested at the close of the Chapter 1, it may be preferable to evolve our theorizing from a wider variety of constraints than to develop ever more accurate hypotheses concerning a limited number of features of the data. As Wilding (1974) remarks, the data for these simple judgments already have an "appealing regularity", and it is likely that a more fruitful approach would be to consider ways in which the general mechanism outlined so far might account for the behaviour of other dependent variables besides response time and frequency, or for the effects of other independent variables besides bias, caution and discriminability. These, at any rate, are the general aims of the next chapters, which together make up Part II.

# II

# Confidence and Adaptation

# 6

## Confidence

*Every item in the cognitive field, every constituent in whatever object
. . . is perceived or thought of, comes into being by a continuous
emergence out of utter obscurity up to some degree of clearness; and as
this description implies, the emerging occupies some duration of time.*
C. Spearman, "The Abilities of Man" (1927, p. 244.)

Besides the frequency with which alternative responses occur in simple
judgmental tasks, and the times taken to make them, a further important
variable for our eclectic strategy of theory development is the confidence
reported by an observer after making a particular judgment. Although
Watson's behaviourist reaction to a question from Trow on the subject was
that he had "come to the wrong market" (Trow, 1923, p. 4), the feelings of
confidence experienced in the correctness of one's judgments have long
been regarded by many other psychologists, such as Lund, as a "common
factor of our most fundamental experiences" (1926, p. 372). As Audley
(1964) concludes, observers do not appear to have much difficulty in
making reports of confidence, either in terms of a percentage scale from
zero (indicating no confidence whatsoever) up to 100 (signifying complete
certainty), by means of a set of categories (such as the letters a to e), or a set
of terms (such as "suppose", "think", "sure", "certain", "positive"), or
in terms of an estimate that their response will be correct (c.f. Foley, 1959;
Adams and Adams, 1961). In turn, while the function of the experience itself
remains obscure, measures of confidence obtained in these ways have
generally turned out to be quite robust. Indeed, the predictability of the
measures may even have led to a certain disaffection with the topic. In a
recent study by Audley and Mercer, for example, confidence ratings were
obtained from only 5 of their 10 observers, and these results were not
reported since they contained "nothing of special interest" (1968, p. 187).
 In a similar vein, although confidence measures are routinely employed
and play a crucial role in the interpretation of much experimental data (such

as that obtained by rating scale procedures and analysed in terms of signal detection theory), there have been few attempts to develop a theoretical mechanism to explain how they arise. The need for a complete theory has already been amply illustrated in the case of the classical psychophysical model, and the present chapter is intended as a step in this direction. Beginning with the established features of confidence measures, we shall look at two of the simpler hypotheses suggested by them. We shall then examine an alternative *balance of evidence* hypothesis, in which confidence is explained in terms of the accumulator model for two-category discrimination, which was outlined in Chapter 3. Finally, we shall consider how this account can be extended to the more general accumulator mechanism which evolved in Chapters 4 and 5, and how it can be applied to confidence in the other simple judgments discussed in Part I.

## Confidence and Discriminability

One of the earliest studies of the confidence with which an observer makes responses in a discrimination task was that of Garrett (1922). In an experiment on the discrimination of pairs of lifted weights, Garrett found that confidence, expressed as a percentage, appeared to be a monotonic function of stimulus difference, though the degree of confidence expressed by an observer was "not a very reliable index of objective accuracy" (p. 68), and seemed to remain unaffected by changes in the rate of presentation of the stimuli, though these did affect the observer's accuracy. In a later study of judgments of the lengths of two lines, Johnson (1939) obtained similar results, finding that changes in the emphasis of instructions designated as "speed", "usual", or "accuracy", led to large, orderly variations in response time, but had no significant effect on confidence. Similar results were again obtained by Festinger (1943a), who also employed a two-category task, using the method of constant stimuli, in which each of five observers was required to indicate whether a vertical line of variable length was shorter or longer than a standard. As in Johnson's experiment, observers were given "usual" instructions which placed no particular emphasis on speed or accuracy, "accuracy" instructions in which they were exhorted to avoid errors and "speed" instructions in which they were encouraged to respond as quickly as possible. After each judgment observers were asked to express their confidence in its correctness by "constructing a mental scale of confidence" with 0 meaning no confidence whatsoever, 50 representing medium or average confidence and 100 signifying complete certainty, admitting no possibility of error.

When the mean confidence rating (presumably for correct responses only) was plotted against objective stimulus difference $(v-s)$, the confidence

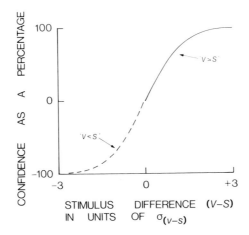

Fig. 68. Idealized confidence function plotted against subjective stimulus difference. The solid line represents values for responses of the form "$V > S$", and the broken line shows (negative) values for responses of the form "$V < S$".

functions obtained by Festinger bore some resemblance to a normal ogive, as illustrated in Fig. 68. As in previous experiments, confidence functions resembled psychometric curves, except that they were shallower. Another difference is that psychometric curves represent the frequency with which one particular response is made as a function of stimulus difference. However, the negative values, comprising the left half of the confidence function, represent mean confidence in correct judgments of "lesser", while the positive values to the right represent mean confidence in correct judgments of "greater".

As in the experiments of Garrett (1922) and Johnson (1939), no consistent change in the standard deviation of the fitted ogives was found from one set of instructions to another, although some deviations from the ogival form were noted. Further confirmation of these results was obtained in a later study of lifted weights by Pierrel and Murray (1963). These authors found that confidence was monotonically related to discriminability, that there was little evidence of a relation between confidence and overall accuracy, and that discrepancies between the patterns of response times for individual observers were not reflected by variations in the curves of their confidence ratings when plotted against stimulus difference.

Agreement among these findings is remarkably good and seems to show that confidence judgments are invariant functions of stimulus difference, independent of the degree of caution exercised by an observer or of his overall accuracy, with the general slope of the relation between stimulus difference and confidence in correct judgments resembling an ogive, but showing characteristic deviations for individual observers. Of these features the relation between discriminability and confidence is the most striking, and the first attempt to integrate judgments of confidence into a theoretical model seems to have been a suggestion by Cartwright and Festinger (1943) that the confidence with which an observer makes a judgment was a linear function of the difference in "potency" between the value of the nearest sensory cutoff $x_c$ and the magnitude of the stimulus difference which elicited a response. Over a series of trials where $x_c$ is held constant, this view implies that confidence should be a direct function of the mean difference between the two stimuli being discriminated. As Irwin *et al.* (1956) point out, this hypothesis would make judgments of zero confidence highly improbable (or strictly impossible if an observation must exceed $x_c$ in order to elicit a response), and Cartwright and Festinger accordingly assume that judgments of zero confidence reflect "the average potency for the duration of a decision" (1943, p. 611, note). With this minor qualification, their hypothesis implies that confidence should be independent of the time taken to reach a decision, since fluctuations in stimulus difference are supposed to occur randomly in time and no temporally cumulative effects are introduced.

Unfortunately, this prediction is directly contrary to the results of several experiments. For example, Henmon (1911) carried out an experiment in which three observers were required to indicate on each of 1000 trials which of two horizontal lines was the longer or shorter, following each judgment with a rating of confidence ranging from "a" for "perfectly confident" down to "d" for "doubtful". Henmon found that there was an inverse relation for all three observers between the time taken and the degree of confidence expressed in a judgment. Similar results were obtained by Johnson (1939) and by Pierrel and Murray (1963), though their findings are less clear because judgments at several degrees of discriminability have been considered together. Finally, Audley (1964) has also reported that for any given level of discriminability, observers were less confident when they took a longer time to reach a decision concerning the relative frequency of red and green light flashes.

## *Confidence and Response Time*

As was mentioned in Chapter 3, Edwards (1965) has shown that for the random walk model, the achievement of a critical difference $k$ between the two totals is tantamount to the attainment of a fixed likelihood ratio. If discrimination were mediated by such a mechanism, therefore, we might expect that all judgments should be made with an equal degree of confidence. However, the fact that both response frequency and confidence appear to be monotonic functions of discriminability seems inconsistent with any model which suggests that an observer responds when he has reached a fixed degree of certainty that the stimuli call for one response rather than another. A second finding, which also conflicts with this view, is that if confidence is interpreted as a subjective estimate of the probability that a given response is correct, then observers seem consistently to underestimate the accuracy of their performance (Pierce and Jastrow, 1885; Fullerton and Cattell, 1892; Henmon, 1911; Johnson, 1939; Festinger, 1943b; Adams, 1957). Figure 69, for example, shows data for the "greater" judgments of one of Festinger's observers (1943b), plotted against percentage confidence obtained at different degrees of discriminability.

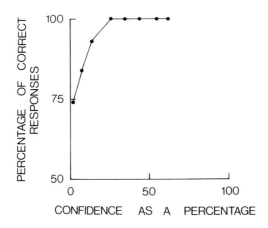

Fig. 69. Results obtained by Festinger (observer J.B. under "speed" instructions), showing percentage accuracy against confidence reported as a percentage (redrawn from Festinger, 1943b, p. 416, Fig. 2c).

These results suggest that observers may base their confidence ratings not on their estimates of the general discriminability of the stimuli, nor on some predetermined likelihood of their being right, but on some *post hoc* feature such as the length of time they have taken to reach a decision. For example, Volkmann (1934) suggested that confidence was simply an inverse linear function of response time. A similar relation was also suggested by Reed (1951), who proposed that confidence $c$ was related to response time $t$ by the equation $c = a/t + b$, where $a$ is a constant and $b$ represents an estimate of response time for an infinitely large stimulus difference.

More recently, Audley (1960) has suggested that confidence may be based on the number of observations made by an observer before reaching a decision, and, as such, should be described by some reciprocal function of response time. Such a view could be accommodated by all four of the main models of discrimination considered in Chapter 3. Moreover, this hypothesis would not only be consistent with the relation between response time and confidence, but also, given the form of the speed–accuracy trade-off function shown in Fig. 34, with the relation between confidence and accuracy. Meanwhile, the apparent dependence of confidence upon discriminability could be explained as being due to the fact that judgments of smaller differences take longer, and hence are made with less confidence.

While it seems necessary on the runs and random walk models to make such a proposal, since there is no other feature of these processes that can be used as a basis for confidence, a more detailed scrutiny of the data reveals some difficulty for this hypothesis. In the first place, a difficulty arises when this hypothesis is used to extend the random walk model. Since this model predicts that the times for incorrect responses should be identical to those for correct, then judgments of confidence should also be the same, irrespective of whether the response is correct or incorrect. However, Pierrel and Murray (1963) found that confidence was lower, while mean response time was higher, for incorrect rather than for correct responses.

Although this last finding may seem, it anything, only to provide some confirmation of the hypothesis as used in conjuction with one of the other models, one further set of results seems to present a more serious difficulty for any attempt to regard confidence as a simple function of response time or of the number of observations taken. In an experiment previously encountered in Chapter 2, Irwin et al. (1956) presented observers with cards on which positive and negative numbers were printed and asked them to judge, after each card, whether the mean of the whole pack of 500 was greater or less than zero, and to express their confidence in this judgment by a number between 0 and 100. As mentioned in Chapter 2, it was found that mean confidence was greater after 20 cards had been inspected than when only 10 had been inspected.

## Confidence as the Balance of Evidence

As Audley (1964) has pointed out, since no final judgment is required from him, this last experiment does not allow the observer to apply a true optional-stopping criterion. In fact, in a later experiment of the same type, Irwin and Smith (1956) did instruct the observer to continue taking observations until he had reached a decision, but no statements about confidence were included in this second study. This is unfortunate, since it might have highlighted the difference between the two situations if, as seems likely, the second study had revealed apparently conflicting results, which were more in line with those of Henmon (1911), Johnson (1939), Pierrel and Murray (1963) and Audley (1964) than with those of the previous study by Irwin et al. (1956).

In any case, it does not seem possible to extend the hypothesis that confidence is an inverse function of the number of observations taken so as to deal with the results of Irwin et al., in which confidence appears to be a direct function of the number of observations. This means that neither the runs nor the random walk models seem capable of accounting for confidence judgments without considerable extension, since no features of these models remain which might serve as a basis. However, a resolution of these difficulties does suggest itself if we consider the way in which an accumulator process might apply both to the optional-stopping situation of Irwin and Smith and to the time-limited sampling experiment of Irwin et al.

The simplest and most plausible application of the accumulator model to the optional-stopping situation of Irwin and Smith is to suppose that the observer accumulates differences between the number on each card and a noise-free standard of zero, until the total of positive or of negative "differences" reaches some critical value $k$, whereupon the response "the mean is greater than zero" or its converse is made. When no final decision is required, as in the experiment of Irwin et al., then we may simply suppose the observer to continue accumulating positive and negative differences until the experimenter tells him to stop. (The application of the recruitment model is similar, except that only the occurrence of positive and negative differences is registered, and their magnitude is ignored. However, in view of the difficulties confronted by this model in accounting for the shapes of the distributions of response times, and the relation between times for correct and incorrect responses, there seems no need to pursue it further.)

If we are to find a consistent basis for confidence, then it seems we must look for some feature which decreases with the number of observations required for a decision in an optional-stopping situation, but increases with the number of observations made in the case of time-limited sampling. This, in turn, depends upon a somewhat more detailed representation of the sequence of events which can be presumed to take place in each situation. For example, if we assume the two criteria to remain equal (with $k = k_g = k_l$), then Fig. 70 illustrates in a schematic way the pattern of change which can be expected in the totals $t_g$ and $t_l$ as observations are accumulated from a normal distribution of stimulus differences with a mean $(V-S) = m$, and a standard deviation $\sigma_{(V-S)} = 1$. Since the values of $t_g$ and $t_l$ will on average be linearly related to the number of observations, the increases in $t_g$ and $t_l$ are represented as straight lines, each of which intersects the level of $k$ at a single point. Of course, since the inspected differences vary randomly, the rate of accumulation in $t_g$ and $t_l$ would not be perfectly regular in practice, and their values would not invariably reach $k$ after a fixed number of observations. However, the simple descriptions presented in Fig. 70 are clearer for present purposes, without being misleading in any important aspect.

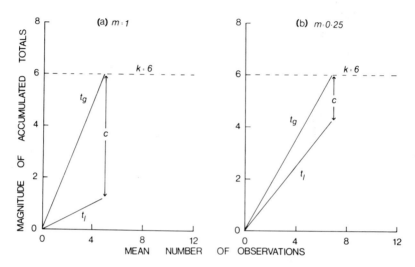

Fig. 70. Representation of the states of the accumulators in the optional-stopping case. Figure 70a shows the states of the totals $t_g$ and $t_l$ accumulated when the observer is presented with a series of observations with a high discriminability $m =$ $(V-S) = 1\sigma_{(V-S)}$. Figure 70b shows the states of $t_g$ and $t_l$ when the series has a small mean $m = 0.25\sigma_{(V-S)}$.

Figure 70 thus illustrates the average values of the totals $t_g$ and $t_l$ when the accumulator process is presented with (a) a highly discriminable series normally distributed stimulus differences, with $m = 1$, and (b) a series of low discriminability, with $m = 0.25$. Since a reduction in $m$ means that the average value of the positive differences is reduced, while that of the negative is increased, then, as can be seen from Fig. 70b, the rates of accumulation in the two totals become more similar as discriminability is diminished. As a result, when the terminating factor is a critical amount of evidence $k$, then a decision (such as "$V > S$") will be reached after fewer observations when $m$ is high than when it is low. At the same time, the difference $c$ between the totals *at the moment a decision is reached* is greater when $m$ is high. In other words, as the number of observations required to reach a decision is increased, following a reduction in discriminability, so the difference between the totals at the moment of decision is diminished.

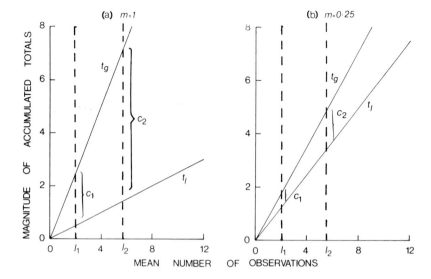

Fig. 71. Representation of the states of the accumulators in the case of time-limited sampling. Figure 70a shows the case when the series of observations has a high discriminability $m = 1\sigma_{(V-S)}$, while Fig. 70b shows the case when $m$ is a low $0.25\sigma_{(V-S)}$. In both cases the difference $c$ between the totals $t_g$ and $t_l$ is greater for a longer time limit $l_2$ than for a shorter limit $l_1$.

By comparison, Fig. 71 illustrates the states of the totals $t_g$ and $t_l$ in a situation where positive and negative stimulus differences are likewise accumulated from distributions with the same means as in Fig. 70, but where the taking of observations is terminated solely and directly by some arbitrary time limit $l$. As can be seen from both Figs 71a and 71b, the difference $c$ between the totals grows larger as the limit is increased from $l_1$ to $l_2$ (with the value of $m$ held constant). In this time-limited situation, therefore, when discriminability is held constant and the number of observations is varied by manipulating the value of $l$, then the difference between the totals increases as the limit on the number of observations taken is increased.

As is perhaps now evident, the crucial difference between the two situations is simply that in the optional-stopping paradigm (illustrated in Fig. 70) the number of observations taken varies as a function of stimulus discriminability, while in the time-limited paradigm illustrated in Fig. 71, the number of observations required is fixed solely and directly by the time limit itself. In the first case, the difference $c$ decreases as a function of the number of observations required to achieve a fixed criterion $k$, while in the second, the value of $c$ increases as a function of the number of observations elapsing before a fixed time limit $l$. Meanwhile, the accumulation process remains the same in both situations; it is only the conditions for terminating it which differ. If the first case is accepted as an adequate representation of the optional-stopping paradigm used by Henmon (1911), Johnson (1939), Pierrel and Murray (1963) and Audley (1964), and if the second is taken as representing the time-limited design employed by Irwin *et al.* (1956), then an obvious theoretical counterpart for confidence suggests itself, and one which provides a neat resolution of the apparent conflict between the two sets of results.

As I have suggested (Vickers, 1972a), the obvious candidate as a basis for confidence would seem to be the difference $c$ between the quantities accumulated at the moment a decision is reached (in the optional-stopping situation), or a judgment of confidence is requested by the experimenter (where the taking of observations is terminated by a time limit). In the former case, the fastest responses of an observer will be those where he has observed only positive or only negative differences, so that the difference between the totals accumulated approaches a maximum value of $k$. Whenever he encounters a mixture of positive and negative differences, the rate of accumulation in the "successful" accumulator will be less, more observations will be required and the difference between the accumulators at the moment of a decision will be less. In contrast, in the latter case the accumulators gradually show a greater difference as the limit to the number of observations is increased. The apparent discrepancy between the two situations is resolved when we recognize that the occurrence of very short times in the optional-stopping case is an indication that a series of observations has a particular statistical composition (e.g. an almost unbroken run of differences of one sign), whereas differing numbers of observations in the time-limited case imply no differences or constraints in the sequence of observations made.

## Confidence in Two-category Discrimination

The hypothesis that a basis for subjective confidence is to be found in the difference between the amounts of evidence accumulated in favour of the two alternatives seems to harmonize well with the conclusion by Adams and Adams that "the explanatory mechanism that seems most plausible . . . is some kind of differentiation and discrimination of internal cues—'feelings of doubt'—aroused by an external situation" (1961, p. 43). In addition, the hypothesis has a number of interesting implications, many of which are intuitively obvious. Some, however, have emerged from a number of computer simulations of the accumulator model for two-category discrimination, which was outlined in Chapter 3.

In these simulations, the confidence with which a response is made is interpreted as the difference between the totals $t_g$ and $t_l$ at the moment a criterion amount of positive or negative stimulus difference is attained in either. That is, confidence in a response of the form "$V > S$" is taken as the difference $(t_g - t_l)$ at the moment that $t_g$ reaches the same value as the criterion $k_g$ (with $t_l$, of course, being less than $k_l$). Conversely, confidence in the alternative form "$V < S$" is reckoned as the difference $(t_l - t_g)$ at the moment that $t_l$ reaches the criterion $k_l$ (with $t_g < k_g$). In all other respects, the simulations resemble those discussed in Chapter 3. Following the sequence of the earlier part of the present chapter, the results which immediately concern us are those relating the theoretical counterpart of reported confidence to discriminability, to accuracy and to response time. I shall deal with each of these in turn.

## Predicted Relations between Confidence and Discriminability

In the first place, for a particular value of $k$ it is intuitively obvious that confidence will be a monotonic function of the mean stimulus difference $\overline{(V-S)}$, since large $\overline{(V-S)}$ differences will tend to fill up one accumulator to the exclusion of the other, while small differences will result in the totals accumulated being more similar. The exact shape of the function, however, will depend on how the observer uses the confidence rating scale. The reason for this can be seen in Fig. 72, which shows, for several different degrees of discriminability, the mean difference obtained in the simulations between the value of $k$ (i.e. the total accumulated for the response that is triggered) and the amount present in the other accumulator at that moment. Although this difference approaches $k$ for very easy discriminations, it does not fall to zero when there is no difference between the stimuli. Therefore, while an observer who operates in the same way as the simulated process may naturally equate a difference of $k$ between the two accumulators with a confidence rating of 100%, he will be in something of a quandary when dealing with the minimum difference.

In order to resolve this difficulty, he may, for example, reserve the rating of 0% for a (theoretically unattainable) difference of zero between the accumulators. In this case his confidence rating for judgments of identical stimuli will be quite high (around 50% for $k = 7$). However, he will also be contravening the usual experimental instructions to use the complete scale. If he does so nevertheless, his confidence curve will assume a shape similar to that shown as scaling strategy A in Fig. 73a.

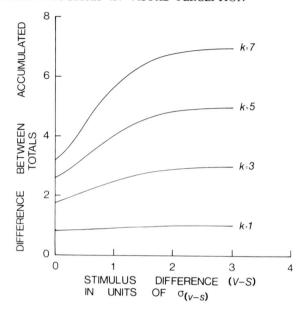

Fig. 72. The mean difference $c$ between the amounts accumulated in the two stores $t_g$ and $t_l$ for various values of $k_g = k_l$ at the moment a critical amount $k_g$ is accumulated and a response of the form "$V > S$" initiated.

On the other hand, of course, he may succeed in following experimental instructions to use the complete scale, and assign a rating of 0% to the smallest difference he encounters between the accumulators (e.g. where he makes an error on a very large stimulus difference). Such a strategy, however, would appear to be somewhat difficult to follow in practice, and Fig. 73b shows instead the pattern obtained for simulated confidence measures for correct responses under a slightly different compromise strategy (B). According to this convention, a rating of zero was assigned to the mean difference between the accumulators when the stimuli were identical, as well as to any occasion on which the difference between the accumulators fell below this.

Although these functions are more complex than the normal ogive, they do not lead us to expect any startling departures from the ogive in empirical data. Indeed, given the usual variability of experimental results, it might be thought unlikely that any deviations of this kind could be detected. Improbable though it may seem, however, deviations of this kind have been noted by Festinger (1943a). Of his five observers, for example, data for one were singled out as rising slightly later than the ogive, then more sharply and then levelling out more rapidly. These data are shown in Fig. 74a and

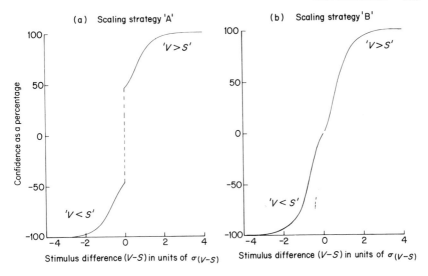

Fig. 73. The shape of the confidence curves produced when different scaling strategies are applied to the hypothetical basis for confidence in the two-category accumulator model. Figure 73a shows the shape of the curve produced when the process represents a maximum difference of $k$ between the totals $t_g$ and $t_l$ by a rating of 100%, and a difference of zero *between the totals* by 0%, with a linear scaling between these limits. Figure 73b shows a typical curve produced when the process follows the same convention for a difference of $k$ between the totals, but represents confidence when the *stimulus difference* is zero by 0%, with a linear scaling between these limits.

resemble the curve in Fig. 73a (though there is also some indication that this observer's scaling may have been different for "lesser" and "greater" responses).

Of the remainder, three observers produced curves resembling Fig. 73b, in which there was "a more rapid initial rise than the ogive, a slight levelling off at the point of subjective equality, and then again a rise more rapid that that of the ogive" (1943a, p. 295). Festinger suggested that these differences seemed to result from variation in the use of the confidence scale, since the first observer concentrated his ratings between 50 and 100%, while the other three concentrated theirs towards zero. Figure 74b shows data for the observer in whom this latter tendency was most pronounced. These data clearly resemble the theoretical curve shown in Fig. 73b, and suggest that one—if not *the*—important difference between confidence functions for different observers lies in their varying employment of the full range of the rating scale. Thus, the proposed model not only accounts well for these features of the data, but also gains some intuitive support from complaints by some observers that they could not give a rating of zero confidence in a judgment since they had after all somehow reached a decision in favour of one rather than the other alternative.

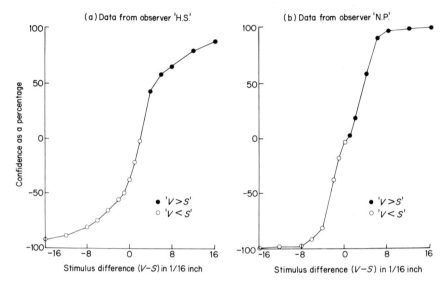

Fig. 74. Empirical confidence functions obtained by Festinger (1943a). Figure 74a shows data for observer H.S. under "speed" instructions, while Fig. 74b shows data for observer N.P. under "accuracy" instructions respectively. Filled circles represent data for responses of the form "$V > S$" and empty circles those of the form "$V < S$" respectively.

The model also explains why confidence functions do not appear to be sensitive to changes in the compromise between speed and accuracy adopted by an observer. Figure 75 shows the obtained measures of simulated confidence for three values of $k$ ranging from 1 up to 5, plotted against the corresponding values for the same stimulus differences when $k = 7$. It is clear that the functions have a nearly linear relation to each other. Given that an observer will follow experimental instructions and assign a rating of 100 to the largest confidence value encountered in a particular experimental condition, and a value of 0 according to one of the strategies outlined above, then these scaled confidence functions will retain more or less the same shape, irrespective of the value of $k$. According to this view, then, an observer does make more confident decisions when he adopts a greater degree of caution. However, the use of a rating response, together with the usual experimental instructions to utilize the complete scale, encourages him to make judgments of confidence that are relative to other judgments made within the same condition, rather than estimates that can be interpreted in absolute terms.

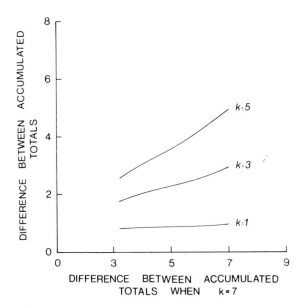

Fig. 75. The difference $(t_g-t_l)$ between the totals in the two-category accumulator process at the moment a critical amount $k_g$ is reached and a response of the form "$V > S$" initiated. The differences for various values of $k_g = k_l$ are plotted not against $(V-S)$, but against the difference $(t_g-t_l)$ observed at each particular value of $(V-S)$ when the value of $k_g = k_l = 7$. The functions are practically linear.

## The Predicted Relations between Confidence and Accuracy

The relations between confidence and discriminability outlined above explain why confidence and accuracy should be directly related for an individual observer within one experimental condition, since confidence is higher for larger stimulus differences and these in turn are discriminated with fewer errors. Conversely, the invariance in the shape of the predicted confidence function with changes in caution ($k$) explains why overall confidence measures do not correlate over different observers with measures of overall accuracy.

Meanwhile, a further feature noted above was that observers seemed consistently to underestimate the accuracy of their performance. Figure 76a shows the percentage of correct responses produced by the simulated accumulator process, plotted as a function of the difference between the accumulators at the moment of a decision (i.e. the hypothetical basis for confidence). Figure 76b, which shows percentage accuracy plotted against confidence values, but scaled in the same way as those of Fig. 73b, illustrates the underestimation of performance that would be predicted by an accumulator model.

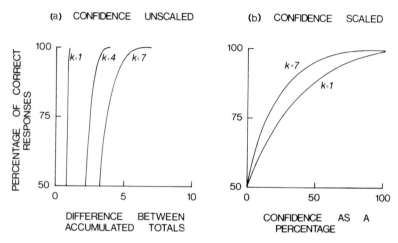

Fig. 76. The general form of the relations between accuracy and the basis for confidence obtained in computer simulation of the two-category accumulator process. Each curve in Fig. 76a shows how the obtained percentage of correct responses, for a particular value of $k_g = k_l$, rises as the difference between the totals increases with larger stimulus differences. The curves in Fig. 76b show how the corresponding curves in Fig. 76a appear when the difference between the totals is scaled according to the scaling strategy "B", illustrated in Fig. 73b.

Also within the context of errors, Fig. 77 shows the unscaled confidence values for incorrect judgments produced by the simulated process at different values of $k$. Although a particular scaling strategy might obscure this for very small stimulus differences, we should in general expect from this that confidence ratings for errors would be lower than those for correct responses, as was indeed found by Pierrel and Murray (1963).

## Predicted Relations between Confidence and Response Time

The relations between confidence and response time predicted by an accumulator process are detailed and interesting. In the first place, when mean stimulus difference is held constant, confidence will be an inverse

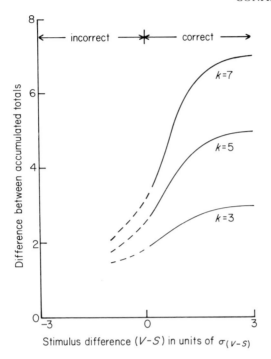

Fig. 77. The form of the relation between the difference $(t_g-t_l)$ and stimulus difference obtained in computer simulation of the two-category accumulator process at the moment a critical amount $k_g$ is accumulated, and a response of the form "$V > S$" initiated. The curves shown are for responses of the form "$V > S$", when $k_g = k_l$, with correct responses shown as solid and incorrect as broken lines.

function of time, since observations varying randomly with a constant distribution are taken at a steady rate, and it is this which determines the difference between the full and the partly-filled accumulators at the moment of a decision. In particular, the determining fact is the relative rate at which the "successful" and the "unsuccessful" accumulators fill up. For example, as the mean stimulus difference $(V–S)$ is reduced, a series of smaller positive differences between stimuli will lead to a lower rate of filling of the successful accumulator, while the generally larger negative differences which result will give rise to a higher rate of filling of the unsuccessful accumulator. In consequence, the eventual response will take longer and the confidence (or difference between the totals accumulated) will be lower.

Figure 78 shows how the difference between the totals varies as a function of the mean number of observations taken by the simulated process at various mean stimulus differences. It will be noticed that the functions for

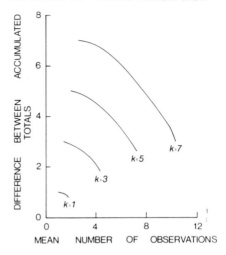

Fig. 78. Unscaled difference $(t_g-t_l)$ between the totals obtained in computer simulation of the two-category accumulator process as a function of the mean number of observations taken at different levels of discriminability.

different values of $k$ are quite separate. Thus, it is clear that the model predicts that the function relating confidence to response time varies with the degree of caution. No experimental data are known which bear upon this question, however, though it does not seem to be too difficult to test.

In this connection, it might be thought that, since the unsuccessful accumulator fills up more slowly when the observer is dealing with an easy judgment involving a clear stimulus difference, then the rate at which confidence diminishes with time should be slower for an easy than for a difficult discrimination. However, although the decrease is slower, the point at which it begins is earlier, since the larger differences falling into the successful accumulator fill it up sooner. This "backdating" seems to cancel out any slowing in the unsuccessful accumulator. As a result, confidence seems to diminish as a similar function of time, irrespective of the discriminability of the stimuli.

A tentative curve, based on a brief simulation of the proposed process, is shown in Fig. 79a. Meanwhile, some empirical support for this prediction is shown in Fig. 79b, which presents the results of an unpublished pilot experiment I have carried out, similar to that of Irwin and Smith (1956), in which one observer inspected numbered cards one at a time until she decided whether the mean for the whole pack was positive or negative, whereupon she expressed her confidence in the judgment. Data for the pack with the larger mean appear to fall on the same curve as those for the pack

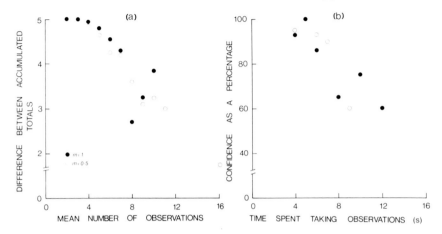

Fig. 79. Figure 79a shows unscaled difference $(t_g-t_l)$ between the totals, obtained in computer simulation of the two-category accumulator process, as a function of variations in the number of observations due to fluctuations in the "statistical quality" of the observations. Filled circles represent data where the mean stimulus difference was high ($m = 1$) and empty circles represent data when $m$ was low (0·5). Figure 79b shows confidence ratings from an unpublished study which I carried out, obtained after varying amounts of time spent taking observations in an optional-stopping task. Filled circles represent results for an easier discrimination (with a large mean difference between the stimuli) and empty circles those for a more difficult discrimination. Results are for one observer only.

with the smaller mean. (It should be noted that these results are not directly comparable with those of Johnson (1939) and Pierrel and Murray (1963), since these experimenters have analysed their results in a different way by averaging times for all responses made with a certain level of confidence, rather than keeping the times and ratings distinct for each degree of discriminability.)

## Predicted Relation between Confidence and Response Bias

Some idea can be gained from the pattern of response times, predicted by the runs, random walk and recruitment models for biassed values of $k$, of the pattern of confidence measures that might be expected on the supplementary hypothesis that confidence is an inverse function of response time. However, since these models do not give a good account of response time, and since the supplementary hypothesis does not yield a satisfactory description of confidence, it does not seem worthwhile to develop this approach in more detail, particularly in view of the extreme scarcity of relevant data.

As far as the accumulator model is concerned, there seems to be a satisfactory basis for confidence, when the observer adopts an unbiassed attitude towards the two alternatives, in the hypothesis that confidence is a direct linear function of the difference between the magnitudes accumulated in the two counters at the moment a decision is reached. However, it is clear that, where severe bias exists, then this account of confidence would lead us to predict that cases will arise where an observer will make a judgment in favour of one alternative, but express afterwards a certain degree of conviction that the other response would have been correct. For example, where $k_g = 2$ and $k_l = 5$, then a decision may be reached when the first accumulator reaches a critical value of 2, although the second has a higher value of 3 (which is nevertheless well below its critical value of 5). In this case, the difference between the amounts ("successful" minus "unsuccessful") will be negative, and should indicate a certain degree of confidence that the response controlled by the second accumulator would in fact have been more appropriate.

In the complete absence of experimental data relevant to this issue, there seem to be two theoretical alternatives left open. The less satisfactory approach is to modify slightly our hypothesis concerning confidence and redefine it as the amount by which the accumulated magnitude in the "unsuccessful" accumulator falls short of the critical value for that accumulator. This would leave the basis for confidence unchanged where values of $k$ for the two alternative responses were equal, and would avoid cases of "paradoxical confidence" such as the one just outlined: on this basis, the observer would never feel sure that he had made a mistake. However, this seems to be unsatisfactory for two main reasons. Firstly, observers frequently report that they have made an incorrect response and attempt to correct it if given the opportunity (Rabbitt, 1966). Secondly, this would enable an observer to boost his confidence artificially by adopting strongly biassed values of $k$, since the higher the value of $k$ for the unsuccessful alternative, the greater would be his confidence in the successful one.

The second, and more satisfactory alternative is to leave the hypothesis concerning the basis of confidence unchanged. Using this approach, the observer who employs a marked bias in favour of one alternative will frequently report afterwards, with a certain degree of confidence, that the other alternative was the correct one. However, he will do this only when it was likely that he had in fact made an error. When his response is correct, the amount accumulated in the successful accumulator will, on average, be greater than that accumulated in the unsuccessful one, however large the disparity in values of $k$. Such a view would imply that observers are capable of noticing (though not always correctly) when they have made an incorrect response due to bias, even in the absence of any feedback from the experimental situation. This feature, in turn, suggests a useful means whereby an observer might adjust response bias in order to adapt to changes in the statistical composition of the sequence of stimuli with which he has to deal. A more detailed examination of this possibility will be made in Chapter 7. Before embarking on this, however, I shall conclude the present chapter by looking at the extent to which the "balance of evidence" hypothesis can be generalized to account for the other types of simple decision that appear to be mediated by an accumulator process.

## Confidence in Three-category Tasks

We have seen so far that the most viable basis for reports of confidence in two-category discrimination appears to lie in the difference between the amounts of evidence collected in the two relevant accumulators at the moment a decision is reached. This hypothesis seems to be consistent with all the known features of confidence judgments and moreover, appears to offer a means whereby an observer might register the fact that he had made a wrong decision.

If we are to extend the same hypothesis to the three-category judgment, however, we must expect some inevitable complication. This arises because an observer's assessment of confidence in his responses appears to be relative. For example, an observer in a three-category task may be highly confident that his response should have been "greater" rather than "lesser", but much less confident that it should have been "greater" rather than "equal". Similarly, an observer may be more confident that his response should have been "greater" rather than "lesser" than he would be if asked how confident he was that it should have been "greater" rather than either "lesser" or "equal".

For this reason the analysis of confidence in the three-category case becomes somewhat more complex. Indeed, it is possible in the three-category case to distinguish no less than 12 possible comparisons that might logically be made by an observer. These are listed below, classified into simple and compound comparisons. (An expression of the form $C(G/L)$ denotes the confidence that a given response should have been "greater" rather than "lesser", and an expression of the form $C(G/E.L)$ denotes the confidence that a given response should have been "greater" rather than either "equal" or "lesser".)

| Simple | | Compound | |
|---|---|---|---|
| (i) $C(G/L)$ | (iv) $C(E/L)$ | (vii) $C(G/E.L)$ | (x) $C(E.L/G)$ |
| (ii) $C(L/G)$ | (v) $C(L/E)$ | (viii) $C(L/E.G)$ | (xi) $C(E.G/L)$ |
| (iii) $C(E/G)$ | (vi) $C(G/E)$ | (ix) $C(E/G.L)$ | (xii) $C(G.L/E)$ |

### Simple Comparisons

It is convenient to discuss the two main classifications in turn. Of the six simple comparisons, (i) and (ii) are clearly appropriate to situations resembling two-category discrimination where the intermediate response is inactive, or has been suppressed. In all six, however, the application of the "balance of evidence" hypothesis is similar. If confidence in a particular response is determined by the total weight of evidence for that response minus the weight of evidence in favour of the alternative, then the expressions for confidence in each of the simple comparisons are quite straightforward. Where the evidence totals for the "greater", "lesser" and "equal" responses are $t_g$, $t_l$ and $(t_g + t_l) - |t_g - t_l|$ respectively, then the expressions for confidence are as follows:

| | | | | |
|---|---|---|---|---|
| (i) $C(G/L) = t_g - t_l$ | … (1a); | (iv) $C(E/L) = t_g - |t_g - t_l|$ | … (2b); |
| (ii) $C(L/G) = t_l - t_g$ | … (1b); | (v) $C(G/E) = |t_g - t_l| - t_l$ | … (3a); |
| (iii) $C(E/G) = t_l - |t_g - t_l|$ | … (2a); | (vi) $C(L/E) = |t_g - t_l| - t_g$ | … (3b); |

If, for the sake of simplicity, $k_g$ is supposed to be equal to $k_l$ and both are represented by $k$, then a general idea of the appropriateness of these formulations can be obtained by considering the values taken by Eqs (1a) to (3b) when $t_g$ and $t_l$ fulfil certain limiting conditions (e.g. when $t_g$ is zero and when $t_l$ is equal to the criterion amount $k$, so that all of the evidence favours a "lesser" response). As set out in Table IV, these values show that the general pattern of the hypothesized basis for confidence seems to be eminently reasonable. For example, confidence in the "greater" rather than the "lesser" response (i.e. $C(G/L)$) is at a minimum of $-k$ when $t_g = 0$, and $t_l = k$, so that all the evidence favours the "lesser" response. When $t_g = t_l$, so that the evidence is exactly balanced, then $C(G/L)$ is zero. Finally, when $t_l = 0$ and $t_g = k$, so that all the evidence favours the "greater" response, then confidence in that response rather than the "lesser" reaches a maximum of $k$.

Similarly, if we hold the evidence totals constant and work down the table comparing the evaluations for different comparisons, then again the

Table IV. Evaluations of the basis for confidence for the six simple comparisons under three sets of limiting conditions.

| Confidence Expression | $t_g = 0$ $t_l = k$ | $t_l = t_g = k$ | $t_l = 0$ $t_g = k$ |
|---|---|---|---|
| 1a. $C(G/L)$ | $-k$ | $0$ | $k$ |
| 1b. $C(L/G)$ | $k$ | $0$ | $-k$ |
| 2a. $C(E/G)$ | $0$ | $k$ | $-k$ |
| 2b. $C(E/L)$ | $-k$ | $k$ | $0$ |
| 3a. $C(G/E)$ | $0$ | $-k$ | $k$ |
| 3b. $C(L/E)$ | $k$ | $-k$ | $0$ |

results accord well with what we should intuitively expect. For example, when no evidence has been collected in the "greater" accumulator (so that $t_g = 0$), but that in the "lesser" is equal to the maximum of $k$, then $C(G/L)$ reaches a minimum $-k$, while $C(L/G)$ and $C(L/E)$ both reach the maximum of $k$. Conversely, when there is no evidence in the "lesser" ($t_l = 0$) and a maximum of $k$ in the "greater", then both $G(G/L)$ and $C(G/E)$ reach the maximum of $k$, while $C(L/G)$ reaches the minimum of $-k$. Similarly, when $t_l = t_g = k$, then $C(E/G)$ and $C(E/L)$ reach the maximum of $k$, while both $C(G/E)$ and $C(L/E)$ reach the minimum of $-k$.

## Compound Comparisons

Although confidence ratings embodying comparisons between specific response alternatives can rarely—if ever—have been obtained in a three-category task, there appears to be no reason in principle why this should not be done. Of more immediate relevance in the present context, it is useful to consider the pattern of these simple measures, since they allow us to evaluate the compound judgments of confidence. In particular, if we regard these simple comparisons as components of the compound judgments, then we can arrive at expressions for comparisons (vii) to (xii).

When compound comparisons are made, the simplest and most plausible assumption seems to be that these are made up of two simpler comparisons, and that the confidence in a compound comparison is determined by the arithmetic mean of the separate confidence values for the two simpler comparisons. In other words, the basis for confidence in the six compound comparisons can be expressed as follows:

(vii)  $C(G/E.L) = \frac{1}{2}\{C(G/E) + C(G/L)\};$
(viii) $C(L/E.G) = \frac{1}{2}\{C(L/E) + C(L/G)\};$
(ix)  $C(E/G.L) = \frac{1}{2}\{C(E/G) + C(E/L)\};$
(x)  $C(E.L/G) = \frac{1}{2}\{C(E/G) + C(L/G)\};$
(xi)  $C(E.G/L) = \frac{1}{2}\{C(E/L) + C(G/L)\};$
(xii)  $C(G.L/E) = \frac{1}{2}\{C(G/E) + C(L/E)\}.$

After substituting the appropriate evaluations from Eqs (1a) to (3b) and simplifying where appropriate, these expressions then become:

(vii)  $C(G/E.L) = \frac{1}{2}\{|t_g - t_l| + (t_g - 2t_l)\}$   ... (4a);
(viii) $C(L/E.G) = \frac{1}{2}\{|t_g - t_l| + (t_l - 2t_g)\}$   ... (4b);
(ix)  $C(E/G.L( = \frac{1}{2}\{(t_g + t_l) - 2|t_g - t_l|\}$   ... (5a);
(x)  $C(E.L/G) = \frac{1}{2}\{(2t_l - t_g) - |t_g - t_l|\}$   ... (5b);
(xi)  $C(E.G/L) = \frac{1}{2}\{(2t_g - t_l) - |t_g - t_l|\}$   ... (6a);
(xii)  $C(G.L/E) = \frac{1}{2}\{2|t_g - t_l| - \frac{1}{2}(t_g + t_l)\}$   ... (6b).

As with the simple comparisons, a general evaluation of the basis for confidence in the compound comparisons can be gained by examining the values taken by expressions (4a) to (6b) under certain limiting conditions of $t_g$ and $t_l$. These are shown in Table V and, once again, the general pattern of values seems completely reasonable. For example, the value of $C(G/E.L)$ is at a maximum of $k$ when the evidence for the "greater" response is at a maximum (i.e. when $t_g = k$), and that for either the "lesser" or the "equals" response is at a minimum (i.e. when $t_l = 0$, and when, consequently, the evidence for the "equals" response $(t_g + t_l) - |t_g - t_l|$ is also equal to zero). When $t_g = t_l = k$, then confidence in the "greater" rather than in either the "lesser" or the "equal" responses assumes a minimum of $-\frac{1}{2}k$, as it also does when all the evidence favours the "lesser" alternative (i.e. when $t_l = k$ and $t_g = 0$).

As with the simple comparisons, if we hold the evidence totals constant and work down each column of the table, then again the pattern is entirely plausible. For example, when $t_g = 0$, and $t_l = k$, then both $C(G/E.L)$ and $C(E/G.L)$ assume the minimum of $-\frac{1}{2}k$, while $C(L/E.G)$ reaches the maximum of $k$. The converse pattern can be seen in the third column where $t_l = 0$ and $t_g = k$. Meanwhile, when $t_g = t_l = k$, as in the middle column, then confidence is at a maximum of $k$ for the "equals" response (i.e. $C(E/G.L)$) and reaches a minimum of $-\frac{1}{2}k$ in the case of each of the two alternatives (i.e. $C(G/E.L)$ and $C(L/E.G)$).

Table V. Evaluations of the basis for confidence for the six compound comparisons under three sets of limiting conditions.

| Confidence Expression | $t_g = 0$ $t_l = k$ | $t_g = t_l = k$ | $t_l = 0$ $t_g = k$ |
|---|---|---|---|
| (vii) $C(G/E.L)$ | $-\frac{1}{2}k$ | $-\frac{1}{2}k$ | $k$ |
| (viii) $C(L/E.G)$ | $k$ | $-\frac{1}{2}k$ | $-\frac{1}{2}k$ |
| (ix) $C(E/G.L)$ | $-\frac{1}{2}k$ | $k$ | $-\frac{1}{2}k$ |
| (x) $C(E.G/L)$ | $-k$ | $\frac{1}{2}k$ | $\frac{1}{2}k$ |
| (xi) $C(E.L/G)$ | $\frac{1}{2}k$ | $\frac{1}{2}k$ | $-k$ |
| (xii) $C(G.L/E)$ | $\frac{1}{2}k$ | $-k$ | $\frac{1}{2}k$ |

## *Confidence in Three-category Decisions*

Of these various compound comparisons, those for the three which are concerned with confidence in a single response as opposed to either of the other two alternatives would seem to be most readily applicable to the usual three-category paradigm (i.e. (vii), (viii) and (ix)). Although any of the other compound comparisons would be possible in principle, it seems likely that, in practice, most observers in a three-category situation would be naturally inclined to make an assessment of confidence solely with respect to the single decision just reached by them. On the other hand, in making judgments of sameness and difference, the response "different" can be elicited by either of the "greater" or the "lesser" decision outcomes. The basis for reported confidence in "same" and in "different" responses, therefore, would seem to be most appropriately sought in expressions (5a) and (6b) respectively. Similarly, if we suppose that the response "signal" is triggered by a decision outcome of the form "$V > S$", and the response "nonsignal" by either of the outcomes "$V = S$" or "$V < S$", then the appropriate basis for reported confidence would seem to be given by expressions (4a) and (5b) respectively. Conversely, in cases where the signal to be detected is a decrement, rather than an increment, the respective expressions for "signal" and "nonsignal" would be (4b) and (6a).

The pattern of confidence measures generated by the accumulator model as it applies to signal detection and to judgments of sameness and difference will be briefly considered in the following sections. For the present our concern lies with the behaviour of the hypothesized basis for confidence within the three-category situation. As in the case of response frequencies and times, the pattern of hypothetical confidence measures has been examined by means of computer simulation. In fact, the hypothetical measures shown in Fig. 80 are based on an application of expressions (4a), (4b) and (5a) at the conclusion of each trial of the same simulation from which the patterns of response frequencies and times, shown in Figs 47 and 50, were drawn.

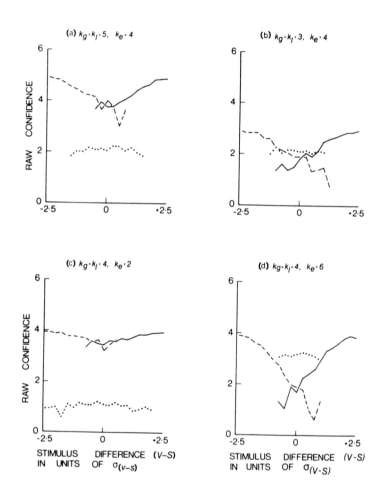

Fig. 80. Measures of "raw" (i.e. unscaled) confidence obtained in computer simulation of the accumulator model for three-category discrimination, for various combinations of values of the criteria $k_g$, $k_l$ and $k_e$. Measures of the basis for confidence in responses of the form "$V > S$" are shown as solid lines, those for responses of the form "$V < S$" as broken lines and those for responses of the form "$V = S$" as dotted lines, respectively.

Figure 80 thus shows the pattern of unscaled hypothetical confidence measures for both intermediate and extreme responses, as made by the simulated three-category accumulator model, operating with the same combinations of criterion values that were used to generate the patterns of response frequencies and times shown in Figs 47 and 50. As can be seen from Fig. 80, the confidence functions for the extreme responses resemble the sigmoid curves found empirically in two-category discrimination and predicted by the two-category version of the accumulator mechanism. Meanwhile, the function for the intermediate response resembles a very slightly bow-shaped curve.

As in Figs 80a and 80b, when the criterion $k_e$ for the intermediate remains constant and those for the extreme responses are reduced, confidence in the latter responses declines, while confidence in the former response remains virtually unchanged. Conversely, when criteria for the extreme responses are held constant, but that for the intermediate is increased, as in Figs 80c and 80d, then confidence in the former is little changed, except for stimulus differences close to zero, while that for the intermediate responses is increased. Although such increases or decreases could be obscured by the application of various scaling strategies, as was discussed earlier (pp. 181–185), it remains the case that the hypothetical basis for confidence in a response is dependent upon the caution with which it is made. So far as its internal working is concerned, therefore, the accumulator model of three-category judgment would appear, in the words of Epictetus, to have "the confidence of its caution".

Although no relevant data are known concerning empirical confidence measures in three-category tasks, the behaviour of the hypothetical measures in Fig. 80 seems to be quite plausible. In addition, a comparison of Figs 80 and 50 shows that, in the three-category case at least, the hypothetical confidence measures are not simple inverse functions of response times generated by the simulated process. In particular, as the bias towards an intermediate response is varied, the changes in the relationship between the times for extreme and those for intermediate responses are not echoed by exactly converse changes in the relationship between the hypothetical confidence measures for these two categories of response. For example, when $k_g = k_l = 5$, $k_e = 4$ and $(\overline{V-S}) = 0$, as in Fig. 50a, then response times for both intermediate and extreme responses are closely similar. However, as can be seen from Fig. 80a, the same relationship does not hold for the pattern of hypothetical confidence measures, although the parameters $k_g$, $k_l$ and $k_e$ have the same values as those in Fig. 50a. If empirical measures of confidence could also be shown to be at least partly determined by which response was made, as well as by the time taken to make it, then the "balance of evidence" hypothesis would gain some support, while the view that confidence is simply an inverse function of response time would be further discredited. Due to the ease with which the bias towards an intermediate response can be manipulated, the three-category task would seem to provide a useful paradigm within which questions of this kind might be investigated.

## Confidence in Same-Different Judgments

Since no empirical data are known concerning confidence ratings in judgments of sameness and difference, it is perhaps sufficient at this stage simply to present the results obtained when expressions (5a) and (6b) were applied to the totals in the "greater" and "lesser" accumulators at the conclusion of each trial of the same simulation as that on which Figs 54 and 55 are based. The pattern of confidence measures thus generated is shown in Fig. 81, and is largely predictable from that for the three-category simulation. In the absence of any relevant experimental data, the main point of these results is to demonstrate that the constraint of commensurability, which was invoked in Chapter 4 to help determine the criterion for the intermediate response, is clearly beginning to pay dividends. Because the totals which are tested against the respective criteria for each of the three possible decision outcomes are all commensurable, post-decisional comparisons can be made between any one total (or combination of totals) and any other total (or combination of totals). As a result, it is a simple matter to derive expressions for the hypothesized basis of confidence in any of the twelve comparisons distinguished above.

## Confidence in Signal Detection

The advantage of commensurability extends, of course, to the post-decisional comparisons which form the hypothesized basis for confidence in "signal" and "nonsignal" responses. As with the other judgments, the pattern of the hypothetical measures has been examined by means of the same computer simulation as was used to generate the response frequencies and times presented in Figs 63 and 65. In this case, the criterion for the "lesser" outcome was assigned a very high value, so that "nonsignal" responses were virtually never elicited by it. Accordingly the expressions used for evaluating the hypothetical confidence measure for "signal" and "nonsignal" responses were those of (4a) and (5b), respectively. As in the case of three-category decisions and judgments of sameness and difference, there appear to be no experimental data with which the hypothetical patterns might be compared. However, within each combination of criterion values at least, the patterns shown in Fig. 82 exhibit no surprises.

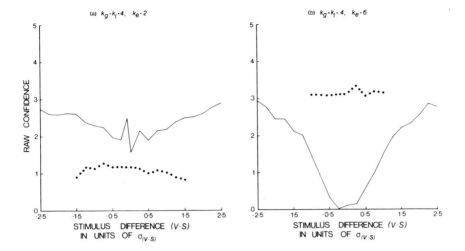

Fig. 81. The pattern of raw (unscaled) confidence measures obtained in computer simulation of an accumulator model of same–different judgment for the same combinations of the values of the criteria $k_g$, $k_l$ and $k_e$ as were employed in Figs 54 and 55. "Different" responses are denoted by solid and "same" responses by dotted curves.

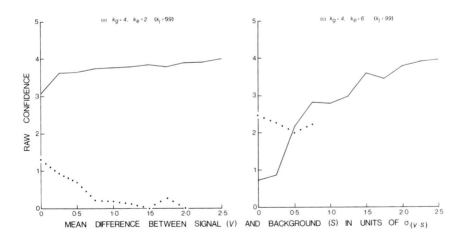

Fig. 82. The pattern of raw (unscaled) confidence measures obtained in computer simulation of an accumulator model of signal detection for similar combinations of criterion values to those employed in Figs 63 and 65. "Signal" responses are represented by solid and "nonsignal" by dotted durves.

It thus seems reasonable to conclude that the extension of the balance of evidence hypothesis to signal detection, same–different judgments and to three-category tasks has confirmed the usefulness of the constraint that the evidence totals accumulated for each of the various alternatives should all be commensurable. Meanwhile, the explanatory potential of the general accumulator process is considerably enhanced by the naturalness with which it accounts for a wide variety of experimental findings concerning a further dependent variable besides that of response frequency and time. Some of the more puzzling features of this variable, such as its insensitivity to changes in caution, can be explained by the hypothesis in terms of the relation between the scaling strategy adopted and the hypothesized basis for confidence. Others, such as the apparent underestimation by observers of the accuracy of their own performance, are neatly paralleled by the behaviour of the theoretical model. Of possibly even greater importance, however, is the fact that the proposed hypothesis provides the observer with a veridical source of information concerning the accuracy of his own performance. It is the possible significance of what Titchener (1909) called this "feeling of reality" which constitutes the main topic of the next chapter.

# 7

# Adaptation

*Socrates: "My thesis then is this: when the 'harmony' in an organism is disturbed, there is at once a dissolution of the normal condition and simultaneously an origination of pain . . . On the other hand, when it is reconstituted and reverts to its normal condition, pleasure is originated."*
Plato, "Philebus" (trans. A. E. Taylor, 1956, 31D).

## The Problem of Adaptation

The general decision model which we have developed in the preceding chapters appears to have considered flexibility, scope and economy. As it stands, however, it suffers from one major disadvantage: it remains impossible for the process to exploit the presence of constraints in the sequence of stimuli encountered by it, or to adapt to changes in the general quality of the sensory information upon which it operates, without making additional assumptions, which, though plausible, must remain *ad hoc*. For example, in an experiment already encountered in Chapter 2, Irwin and Smith (1956) instructed observers to continue inspecting a sequence of positive and negative numbers, printed on cards and drawn one at a time from a pack of 500, until they had decided whether the average of the whole pack was greater or less than zero. Both the mean and standard deviation of the packs were varied and it was found that when the standard deviation was high, observers required more cards to reach a decision than when it was low, irrespective of the mean value of the pack. Irwin and Smith interpreted these results as evidence against the discrimination model proposed by Cartwright and Festinger (1943), since, according to this model, any increase in the variability of the subjective $(V–S)$ differences should give rise to shorter decision times, because a greater proportion of the distribution would fall outside the region of no-decision, and large positive and negative differences would occur more frequently.

At first sight, these results would seem to have a disturbing relevance also to the accumulator model of two-category discrimination, which would make the same prediction in this situation as the model of Cartwright and Festinger. As has already been argued in Chapter 2, however, Irwin and Smith's interpretation is open to question because it is unlikely that observers maintained the same values of $k$ (however the criterion is defined) for the packs with higher variance as for those with the lower. Each card was shown for approximately 2·5 s, and between 20 and 40 cards were inspected on average before a decision was reached. Observers had ample opportunity, therefore, to vary the values of $k$, even during the process of reaching a decision. Moreover, since the high standard deviation of 7·5 was almost four times greater than the lower one of 2·0, it seems almost certain that observers would have noticed the marked changes in the statistical quality of the observations made available to them, and that they compensated accordingly.

At the same time, it must be admitted that such "explanations" lack both generality and predictive power. Indeed, as it stands, the general decision model developed so far remains unable to account for a wide range of phenomena, which may be loosely described as "adaptive", without supposing that the observer manipulates the values of $k_g$, $k_l$ and $k_e$ according to some plausible, but *ad hoc* hypothesis. Such features of judgmental behaviour include the effects of changes in the range, distribution, or sequence of stimulus differences, and are—to a great extent—of the same kind as those to which Helson (1964, 1971) has so eloquently drawn attention in terms of adaptation-level theory.

As Treisman points out, however, despite their emphasis on adaptive phenomena, Helson and his co-workers have been largely concerned with finding a satisfactory empirical formula for relating features of judgmental behaviour to certain previously neglected variables, such as contextual stimuli, rather than with the attempt to specify some "underlying mechanisms whose operations might explain the relationships summarized by adaption-level theory formulae" (1973, p. 569). Accordingly, while the interest of the present chapter focusses upon comparative decisions, rather than upon the absolute judgments which are Helson's main concern, its purpose is in effect to try to arrive at an explanatory mechanism of the kind advocated by Treisman. To this end, therefore, this chapter begins by considering the implications of a mechanism using externally supplied information about errors, before going on to develop an adaptive model for two-category discrimination, based on negative, rather than positive, feedback. After describing some of the general properties of the proposed model, I will then conclude by considering how this adaptive principle might be extended to the more general decision mechanism outlined in Chapters 4, 5 and 6.

## An Adaptive Mechanism Based on Positive Feedback

If a stimulus difference of size $m$ were embedded within a series of very small differences, we should normally expect an observer to make a slower, more careful judgment of $m$ than if it were embedded in a series of very large differences, and we should "explain" this by arguing that the observer would be inclined to adopt higher values of $k$ when the task was generally more difficult. However, a more complete explanation for such changes would relate any increase or decrease in $k$ to some specific feature of the experimental situation. For example, it might be surmised that the observer had access to some external feedback about his accuracy, and that he raised or lowered the appropriate criterion values accordingly. More specifically, if discrimination is assumed to be mediated by an accumulator process, then it might be supposed that, in the two-category situation, the levels of $k_g$ and $k_l$ would be reduced by a small amount every time the responses "$V > S$" or "$V < S$" respectively, were made correctly and increased by the same amount if they turned out to be incorrect. Where the results of responses have such a direct effect on the making of subsequent responses, the situation can be classified as one of *positive feedback* (Kalmus, 1966; Milsum, 1966; McFarland, 1971; Jones, 1973).

As soon as we begin to examine such a mechanism in detail, however, then the importance of certain general properties quickly emerges. For example, Fig. 83 depicts the behaviour of the criterion levels in a computer simulation of a two-category accumulator process, in which the levels of $k_g$ and $k_l$ were reduced by a small amount $(0.25\sigma_{(V-S)})$ every time the responses "$V > S$" or "$V < S$" respectively, were made correctly and were increased by the same amount whenever the corresponding response was incorrect. The results shown here are based on a single simulation, in which $k_g$ and $k_l$ were initially set to $5\sigma_{(V-S)}$ and a series of stimulus differences, ranging in mean value from $-1.6$ up to $1.6$, in steps of $0.2\sigma_{(V-S)}$, were presented in random order, following the method of constant stimuli.

As can be seen from Fig. 83, the criterion levels in this situation steadily diminish as the trials proceed, with one level (that of $k_l$) diminishing at a faster rate and decreasing to zero by the fortieth trial. The model is clearly not successful as an adaptive process, and it is instructive to consider why it behaves as it does. In the first place, the steady decrease in both criteria is due to the fact that, provided the levels of $k$ are not too dissimilar and remain above zero, the chances of a correct response are higher than those of

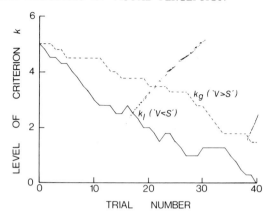

Fig. 83. The behaviour of the criterion levels $k_g$ and $k_l$ in a simulation of a two-category accumulator process in which the criterion is increased by $0.25\sigma_{(V-S)}$ whenever an incorrect response is triggered by reaching that criterion, and decreased by $0.25\sigma_{(V-S)}$ following a correct response.

an incorrect one: as a result, the chance of a reduction in $k_g$ or $k_l$ is higher than the chance of an increase. In the second place, the faster reduction of $k_l$ is simply due to the fact that this was the first criterion level to be attained, and consequently trigger a response (together with the likely consequence of a reduction in its associated criterion level). With each further reduction the accumulator in question becomes even more likely to be triggered, so setting up a "vicious circle" or positive feedback loop.

As a control system this model is clearly unsatisfactory. It cannot be improved, for example, by making adjustments every three or four trials, rather than every trial, since this merely slows down the rate at which the criterion levels sink. Nor can it be improved by making upward adjustments of greater magnitude than the downward, since any temporary bias between the two criterion levels will send the adjustments irretrievably off in one direction or the other. In effect, the model resembles a solid object in a position of unstable equilibrium, where the slightest force in one direction rather than the other will send it toppling out of control.

## An Adaptive Mechanism for Two-category Discrimination Based on Negative Feedback

In order to preserve the stability of the process, it seems we must suppose that there is some internal level, standard, or reference variable, which the mechanism is designed to maintain. This level cannot be simply the values of $k_g$ and $k_l$, since such a process would remain unadaptive. As we have also seen in Chapter 2, experimental evidence suggests strongly that an observer does not try to keep constant either the proportion of correct responses or the time taken to make them. Besides, a moment's reflection is sufficient to show that such a process would also be maladaptive.

The only remaining element in the accumulator process is the basis for the confidence with which a response is made, and it is this last alternative which appears to be the most plausible. While individual responses may not be made to a pre-determined level of confidence, as suggested by models employing a likelihood ratio criterion, it is still possible that the observer may try to make judgments on the average with a certain level of confidence, although he cannot guarantee this in the case of any particular judgment. It has already been shown in Chapter 6 that the confidence with which an observer reaches a decision can provide a useful link with the objective world, capable of alerting him to the fact that he has made an error. The essential ingredients for a *negative feedback* mechanism could therefore be provided by supposing that, whenever an observer's actual confidence in a response exceeded, or fell below, a certain "target" level, the criterion level controlling that response was adjusted downwards or upwards respectively. The necessary "mismatch" signal could be generated simply by subtracting the target level of confidence from the actual level each time a response was made, with positive discrepancies giving rise to a reduction in criterion level and negative discrepancies giving rise to an increase. This hypothesis, that confidence functions as a reference variable for the correction and control of performance, seems closely analogous to the view that a major factor governing the behaviour and development of higher animals is the achievement and maintenance of a certain level of competence in their interactions with the environment (White, 1959; Conolly and Bruner, 1974). In the remainder of this section we shall develop certain aspects of this hypothesis in more detail.

## Intermittency in Control

In the first place, it would be possible to envisage such a system making corrections to $k_g$ and $k_l$ after every single response. However, this seems implausible since each amount of over-confidence or under-confidence could be merely the product of chance variations in the sequence of stimulus differences. Instead, it seems more reasonable to suppose that chance deviations from the target level would be relatively ineffective, and that only established trends in the stimulus sequence should reliably provoke a corrective adjustment. One way of damping the system to achieve this would be to allow corrective adjustments to $k_g$ or $k_l$ to be made only after every $n$ responses. However, this would embody the notion of a fixed sample statistical decision process, which we have already seen in Chapter 2 to be at odds with experimental evidence. A more satisfactory (and economical) alternative, therefore, is to suppose that the amounts of over-confidence and under-confidence are accumulated in exactly the same way as the original positive and negative stimulus differences, that is, until a preset criterion amount $K$ of over- or under-confidence has been accumulated. For the present, there seems to be no reason to postulate different values of $K$ for over- and under-confidence, nor to suppose that $K$ is variable (although different observers may operate with different values of $K$). The main effect of $K$ is to govern the average frequency of adjustments by specifying the amount of evidence required.

## Proportionality of Adjustments

A further detail concerns the amounts by which the values of $k_g$ and $k_l$ should be adjusted. The model depicted in Fig. 83 is based on making a constant increment or decrement at each adjustment. Again, however, this appears implausible, since we should expect observers to have some awareness of the abruptness of a change in the sequence of stimulus differences and to react accordingly. For example, if a long series of very small differences were suddenly followed by a series of very large differences, we should expect an observer to drop his criterion levels more quickly than if the second series were only marginally larger than the first. The simplest way of achieving this seems to be to use a measure of the "confidence in the adjustment" to determine the amount of the adjustment, that is, to add or subtract an amount proportional to the difference between the amounts accumulated in the "control" accumulators at the moment a critical level $K$ is reached in one. Like $K$, the coefficient $x$, which determines the actual proportionality of the adjustments, may be supposed to remain quite stable, although varying from one observer to another. The main effects of variation in this coefficient of adjustment can be regarded as analogous to those following a change in the gearing of a physical control system.

---

Fig. 84. Flow diagram of an adaptive accumulator model of two-category discrimination. The primary decision process situated above the broken line corresponds to that shown in Fig. 31. Whenever a primary decision is reached, its associated confidence (($t_g-t_l$) or ($t_l-t_g$)) is compared with the corresponding target level $C_G$ or $C_L$. For each primary response, positive and negative discrepancies from target are then accumulated separately until a criterion amount of over- or under-confidence is reached, whereupon the primary criterion levels are reduced or increased respectively.

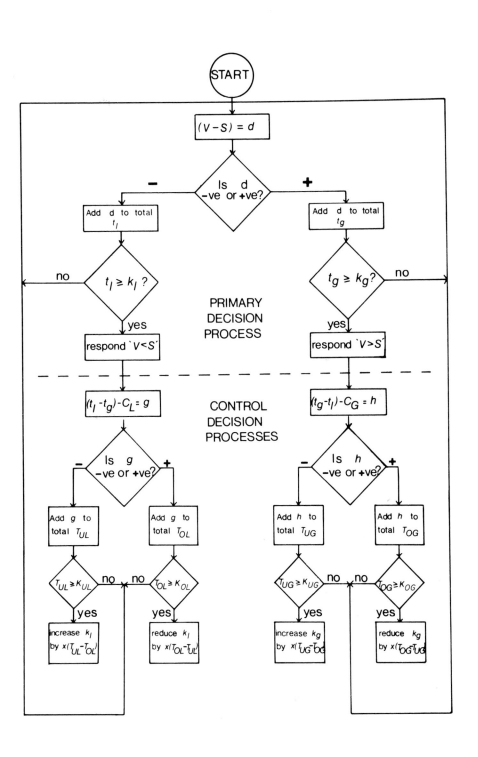

## The Operation of the Adaptive Mechanism

Figure 84 shows a simple way of embodying these considerations in a control mechanism capable of regulating the behaviour of an accumulator process for two-category discrimination. It consists of an additional two-category accumulator process, attached to each of the possible responses by the primary decision process. When a response (such as "$V > S$") is made, the basis for confidence $(t_g - t_l)$ is measured and compared with the target level $C_G$ (or $C_L$ if the converse response is made). If the difference $v = (t_g - t_l) - C_G$ is positive, the amount $v$ is added to a total $T_{OG}$. Conversely, if it is negative, it is added to a different total $T_{UG}$. As soon as $T_{OG}$ or $T_{UG}$ reach or exceed a predetermined level ($K_{OG}$ or $K_{UG}$) of over- or under-confidence respectively, a reduction or an increase to $k_g$ is made; the totals $T_{OG}$ and $T_{UG}$ are then reset to zero. If $T_{OG}$ first reaches $K_{OG}$, then the value of $k_g$ is decreased by an amount $x(T_{OG}-T_{UG})$ which is directly proportional to the difference $(T_{OG}-T_{UG})$. Conversely, if $T_{UG}$ first reaches $K_{UG}$, then the value of $k_g$ is increased by an amount $x(T_{UG}-T_{OG})$ directly proportional to the difference $(T_{UG}-T_{OG})$.

Corrections are also made to $k_l$, depending upon the outcomes of a second controlling accumulator process, attached to the response ("$V > S$") and operating independently, but in exactly the same way. The critical values of $K_{OG}$ and $K_{OL}$ for over-confidence, and of $K_{UG}$ and $K_{UL}$ for under-confidence in the "greater" and "lesser" responses respectively, would usually be supposed to be equal. However, appropriate instructions, or exposure to particular stimulus sequences, could perhaps be supposed to influence the relative values of $K_{OG} = K_{UG}$ on the one hand, and of $K_{OL} = K_{UL}$ on the other.

To keep the control decision process of the same kind as the primary process, the same conventions for clearing the control accumulators have been observed. That is, only the two control accumulators associated with one primary response are cleared when one of them reaches $K$ and triggers an adjustment. This means that there will usually be an appreciable lag between successive revisions of the same primary criterion ($k_g$ or $k_l$), although revisions of different criteria may follow each other in relatively quick succession. As an alternative, it would be possible to clear all the control accumulators whenever any adjustment was triggered. However, this again seems counter-intuitive. For example, it would produce an inefficient delay in the downward revision of the second of two primary criteria, even when the accumulated evidence for this second adjustment was almost as strong as that for the downward revision of the first.

# General Properties of the Two-category Adaptive Accumulator Model

The system outlined in Fig. 84 has several general advantages. In the first place, it is simple and economical. Secondly, like the original accumulator model it can easily be translated into a neurophysiological version, embodying the same processes of excitation, inhibition, storage and threshold discharge. In the third place, since the quantities transmitted between any two nodes are commensurable, the system has a flexibility which recommends it from an evolutionary point of view. Meanwhile, extensive computer simulations of this adaptive accumulator model show it to be a stable system, capable of responding appropriately to a wide variety of constraints in the stimulus sequence and of simulating behaviour in a number of different tasks.

At the same time, it is perhaps as well to emphasize that the adaptive model is really no more complicated than the static version. Performance measures based on response frequency, time and confidence remain primarily a function of bias (now interpreted as the relation between the target levels of confidence set for each response), caution (i.e. whether the target levels of confidence are set high or low) and stimulus difference. Target levels of confidence are thus analogous to criterion levels in the simpler, static model and may likewise be thought of as susceptible to change by experimental instructions, by manipulation of some payoff matrix, by other motivational determinants, or perhaps by other control processes. The main development is that under the heading of "stimulus difference" must now be included a much wider variety of factors, besides that of magnitude, such as the range of stimulus differences, the distribution of differences and the sequence in which they are presented.

As in the case of the static version, the behaviour of the adaptive accumulator model has been investigated by means of extensive computer simulation. In examining the properties of the model, however, we encounter a somewhat ironic consequence of its dramatic expansion in theoretical power: it becomes possible to deal with such a rich variety of different situations that it would be tedious to deal with them all systematically. Therefore, in order to try to communicate a general characterization of the model, we shall focus attention on only a few key features of its behaviour. These include the effects on the performance of the process of presenting a random sequence of objective stimulus differences, effects of variations in the distribution of differences and effects of a particular (non-random) sequence of stimulus differences.

## Effects of a Random Sequence of Stimulus Differences

Of the three psychophysical methods distinguished at the beginning of Chapter 2, the most widely accepted is the method of constant stimuli, in which each of several values of the variable is presented for comparison with the standard, so as to constitute a random sequence of objective stimulus differences. In the first set of simulations to be discussed, this procedure was followed over a series of 2000 trials for each combination of the values of the parameters $C_G$, $C_L$, $K$ and $x$. At each trial, the hypothesized process was presented with one out of a random series of 21 distributions of stimulus differences, with means varying from $-1.9$ up to $1.9$ in steps of $0.2\sigma_{(V-S)}$ and a constant standard deviation $\sigma_{(V-S)} = 1$. Values of $C_G$ and $C_L$ were held equal throughout and are simply represented as values of $C$. Similarly, the criterion values adopted for the control accumulators ($K_{OG}$, $K_{UG}$, $K_{OL}$ and $K_{UL}$) are all assumed to be equal, and are represented by $K$, while the coefficient of adjustment $x$ is assumed to be the same, irrespective of which adjustment is made, or which response criterion is adjusted. The results to be considered are concerned with the pattern of response frequencies and that of response times.

### Response Frequency

The first point to emerge from this study is the reassuring one that the curve relating response frequency to stimulus difference does not appear to differ from the sigmoid psychometric function found experimentally and predicted by the static version of the accumulator model. However, in the dynamic version the precision of this curve depends not only upon the values of the target confidence $C$, but also upon the criterion $K$ adopted for the control accumulators and upon the coefficient of adjustment $x$. For example, Fig. 85 shows how for two values of $K$ and five values of $x$, the standard deviation $\sigma$ of the psychometric function for responses of the form "$V > S$" decreases as the value of $C$ is increased. The decrease in $\sigma$ with higher values of $C$ corresponds to the increase in precision with higher values of $k$ predicted by the static model, and can be regarded as a more fundamental interpretation of the empirical speed–accuracy trade-off discussed in Chapter 2. Meanwhile, the dependence of $\sigma$ on $x$ and on $K$ implies that the coarser the control exerted by the model and the more intermittently it is applied, the poorer will be the discriminative capacity of the dynamic process. Within the present situation at least, where there are no constraints in the stimulus sequence, it appears that the finer the corrections made by the model, and the more frequently they are made, the more stable will be its behaviour, and the higher its discriminative power.

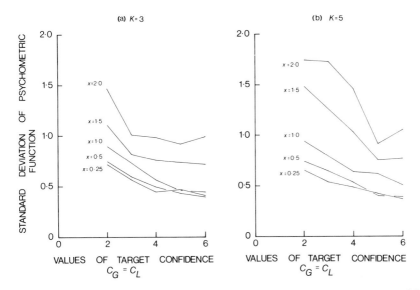

Fig. 85. The pattern of changes in the relation between the standard deviation of the psychometric function for responses of the form "$V > S$" and the target levels of confidence ($C_G = C_L$) set for the proposed adaptive process. Figure 85a shows the pattern when the control criteria $K_{UL} = K_{OL} = K_{UG} = K_{OG} = 3$ and Fig. 85b the pattern when the value is 5. Each curve is based on a computer simulation of 2000 trials for each value of $K$ and each value of the coefficient of adjustment $x$, at each of 5 levels of $C$.

While the proposed model can exploit the presence of any constraint in a sequence of stimuli, therefore, the adaptive mechanism can evidently be at a disadvantage in dealing with an unconstrained situation, such as that specified by the method of constant stimuli, in which the sequence of stimuli is quite random. Under these circumstances, temporary inequalities in the primary criterion levels $k_g$ and $k_l$ can sometimes lead to runs of responses which are longer than the chance median length which we should expect. Figure 86, for example, presents the results of some simulations, which show that the median run length for responses emitted by the adaptive process tends to increase as target confidence $C$ is increased, as the adjustment $x$ becomes coarser and as corrections become more intermittent (i.e. as $K$ increases). It seems to be this tendency to develop temporary, fluctuating biasses in favour of one response or the other which is responsible for the apparent loss in discriminative power as adjustments become coarser and control more intermittent. Such a situation might arise, for example, where external feedback was presented. If this had the effect of enhancing the existing internal feedback, then adaptive corrections to a random sequence of stimuli would become exaggerated and discriminative capacity reduced. This would explain, for instance, the otherwise surprising finding by McNicol (1975) that, whenever external feedback was provided, detectability measures (calculated from absolute judgments of loudness) were reduced.

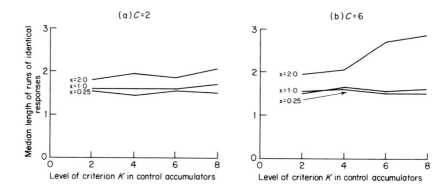

Fig. 86. Median length of a run of identical responses made by the proposed adaptive decision model as a function of the level of the criterion $K$ in the control accumulators (assuming $K_{UL} = K_{OL} = K_{UG} = K_{OG}$). Figure 86a shows the pattern for a low target confidence ($C_G = C_L = 2$) and Fig. 86b the pattern for a high value. Each curve is based on a computer simulation of 2000 trials for each value of $C$ and each value of the coefficient of adjustment $x$, at each of 4 values of $K$.

## Response Time

As in the case of the static model, the results of simulation show that the time to make correct responses is an inverse function of the magnitude of stimulus difference, irrespective of the values of the $C$, $K$, or $x$. As also in the case of the static model, a general increase in caution following an increase in $C_G$ and $C_L$ results in longer response times with fewer errors and an increase in the steepness of the function relating times for correct responses to magnitude of stimulus difference. Again as with the static model, there is a change in the symmetry of the functions relating time taken to discriminability. However, whereas these functions for the static model changed from roughly symmetrical to markedly assymetrical as $k$ was increased, the changes for the adaptive version are a function of both the target confidence $C$ and the control criterion $K$, as well as the coefficient of adjustment $x$, and are correspondingly a little more complex.

Figure 87 illustrates the pattern of changes obtained in response time

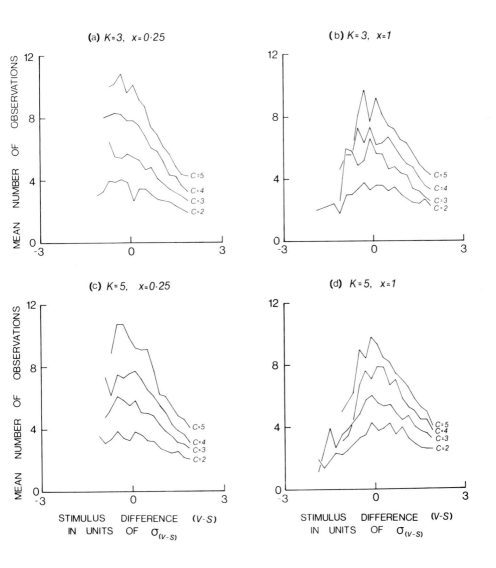

Fig. 87. Mean number of observations taken by the proposed adaptive discrimination process to reach a decision of the form "$V > S$", plotted as a function of stimulus difference ($V$–$S$), for 2 different values of $K$, 2 values of $x$ and 4 values of $C$. Each curve is based on data from a computer simulation of 2000 trials for each value of $C$, $K$ and $x$. During each series of 2000 trials, the model was presented with a random series of noisy stimulus differences, with means varying from $-1.9$ up to $+1.9$ in steps of $0.2\sigma_{(V-S)}$, and a standard deviation $\sigma_{(V-S)}$, according to the method of constant stimuli.

functions for the simulated adaptive process as these three parameters of the adaptive model were varied. The functions exhibit several interesting features. In the first place, when $C$ and $x$ are held constant, there is a very slight tendency for times for correct responses to be lengthened as $K$ is increased, while times for incorrect responses become noticeably shorter. This tendency is particularly marked with higher values of $C$ and $x$ than those shown here, when times for correct responses become dramatically longer than those for incorrect. A similar effect follows an increase in the value of $x$ and is particularly marked with high values of $C$ and $K$. Both effects are presumably due to an increasing disparity in the values of $k$ for which response times are obtained, which in turn is due to the greater violence of the corrections as $K$ and $x$ are increased. The further upward the values of $k$ are jolted by any correction, the longer will be the times for correct responses and the smaller will be the number of errors. Conversely, when values of $k$ are allowed to descend, many more errors will be made and these will be made in a relatively short time. The net result is that, when times are averaged over a range of values of $k$ (as happens when the system makes a series of adjustments during a run) mean times for incorrect responses may turn out to be longer, the same as, or even shorter than those for correct, with the last tendency being more marked the greater the range of values of $k$ adopted.

As argued in Chapter 3, data from a large number of discrimination experiments suggest that the times for incorrect responses are similar to those for correct when the degree of caution is low, but become relatively longer as caution is increased (e.g. Henmon, 1911; Kellogg, 1931; La Berge, 1961; Cross and Lane, 1962; Pierrel and Murray, 1963; Wollen, 1963; Pickett, 1967, 1968; Audley and Mercer, 1968; Laming, 1968; Pike, 1968, 1971; Vickers, 1970; Vickers et al. 1971; Wilding, 1971, 1974). Along with some unpublished data (Hornsby; Vickers and Domac; Vickers and Willson), these results are consistent with the trend produced by the simulated adaptive accumulator model and presented in Fig. 87. In addition, however, Fig. 87 suggests that, when corrective adaptations give rise to marked temporary biasses in criterion values, then cases will arise where times for incorrect responses are distinguishably lower than those for correct.

Consistent with this expectation, a number of simple choice experiments have indeed reported that times for errors were shorter than those for correct responses (e.g. Weaver, 1942; Hale, 1968, 1969; Laming, 1968; Swensson, 1972). Although their interpretation must remain somewhat clouded by the fact that none of the studies employed a two-choice discrimination task in which both stimuli were presented simultaneously for comparison, all of them provide grounds for inferring that some fluctuation or temporary biassing in criterion values occurred. For example, in the early study by Weaver (1942) one hundred observers were required to press one of four keys "at top speed" in response to a series of over 1000 "unmistakeably different" green, blue, red and yellow stimuli. As soon as the correct key was pressed, the stimulus was changed in an order that was "random", except that no stimuli were immediately repeated, and an orderly sequence from left to right or vice versa was excluded. Weaver found that the mean times for incorrect responses were significantly lower (by about 22 ms) than those for correct responses. At the same time, the likelihood that errors in this experiment mainly arose from short periods during which some criterion values were temporarily lowered is strengthened both by the presence of constraints in the stimulus sequence, and by Weaver's finding that the times for the two correct responses immediately preceding an error were shorter than the mean times for all correct responses, irrespective of where they occurred.

A similar interpretation would seem to apply to the results of Hale (1968, 1969), Laming (1968) and Swensson (1972). For example, in two similar choice-reaction studies, Hale (1968, 1969) found that there was evidence of strong sequential effects in the form of a decrease in the time for correct responses which followed runs of identical stimuli. Again, Laming (1968) reported evidence of sequential effects in all four of his two-choice experiments in which the *a priori* probability of making the alternative responses was varied. Finally, in one further experiment in which observers had to identify one of two orientations of a rectangle, Swensson (1972) studied the effect on response times and errors of varying the monetary rewards for fast—relative to accurate—responding. Swensson found that mean times for incorrect responses (other than "guesses") were shorter than those for correct responses when the observer was rewarded for speed, but became equal to, or longer than, correct responses when the observer performed more slowly and accurately. Although no sequential analysis was carried out, it seems likely, in view of the resemblance of Swensson's experiments to the others cited here, that, at least at fast speeds, Swensson's highly practised observers responded to sequential relations in the stimulus sequence. Indeed, Swensson himself recognizes that some fluctuation or temporary bias in values of $k$ could account for his results.

All the experiments discussed above encouraged the adoption of a set for speed, all used highly discriminable stimuli and all used tasks in which stimuli had to be identified by comparison with some remembered standard. Each of these factors seems likely to favour the occurrence of sequential effects and some, such as intertrial interval, have been shown to be important in this connection (e.g. Laming, 1968). Effects of fluctuation and bias in $k$ seem likely to be most evident in experiments like these where the need to process the actual stimulus is at a minimum, and where the observer is under pressure to make use of any information he can glean, either from the stimuli themselves, or from the stimulus sequence, in order to achieve and maintain a high rate of continuous responding.

## Effects of Variations in the Distribution of Stimulus Differences

The properties of the two-category version just considered are characteristic of the behaviour of the adaptive model under stable conditions, where the sequence of objective stimulus differences is random, where the range of objective differences above and below zero is identical, where the intervals between differences are equal and where each difference has the same probability of occurring. Although these represent the conditions most frequently encountered in studies employing the method of constant stimuli, its defining constraint of a random sequence of objective stimulus differences occurring with stable probabilities still permits a wide variation in the actual distribution of the differences. The most obvious modifications of this kind take the form of variations in the proportions of positive and negative differences (and hence in *a priori* response probabilities), shifts in the range of differences, or inequalities in the distribution of differences within a given range. While the static model remains insensitive to such changes, the adaptive version shows clear differences in its response. In this section I shall deal briefly with each of these three types of effect.

### Effects of Changes in *A Priori* Response Probabilities

As with other aspects of the behaviour of the adaptive model, its responses to variations in the distribution of objective stimulus differences have been investigated by means of computer simulation. Some typical results are presented in Figs 88a and 88b, which show effects of varying the *a priori* response probability on the probability of making a "greater" response and on the time taken by the hypothetical process to make it. The results given in Fig. 88 are based on two separate simulations of 2000 trials each of the adaptive model. In each trial, one out of a range of 20 distributions of $(V–S)$ differences, each with a standard deviation $\sigma_{(V-S)} = 1$, and with means varying from $-1{\cdot}9$ up to $1{\cdot}9$ in steps of $0{\cdot}2\sigma_{(V-S)}$, was presented to the hypothetical process. In both simulations, the model operated with a value of 4 for the control criterion $K$, a value of $1{\cdot}0$ for the coefficient of adjustment $x$, and with a value of 3 for each of the target levels of confidence $C_G$ and $C_L$. In both cases also the sequence of $\overline{(V–S)}$ differences was random, the only difference being that, in one case, the probability of a positive value of $\overline{(V–S)}$ was set at $0{\cdot}2$, while in the other this was increased to $0{\cdot}8$.

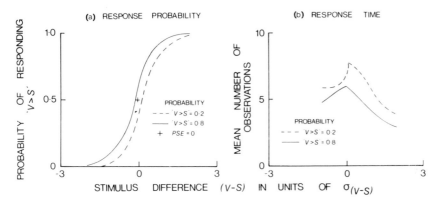

Fig. 88. Effects obtained in simulation of the adaptive model on (a) response probability and (b) response time as a result of varying the *a priori* probability of a response of the form "$V > S$".

As can be seen from Fig. 88a, one effect of increasing the *a priori* probability of a "greater" response from 0·2 up to 0·8 is to shift the 50% threshold, or *PSE*, downwards. The reason for this is that such an increase reduces the proportion of trials on which the "greater" response is made incorrectly—and hence with very low confidence. As a result, the adaptive model can "afford" to lower $k_g$ and still maintain on average the same target level of confidence $C_G$. At the same time, increasing the *a priori* probability of the "greater" response means that there will be a higher proportion of trials on which the "lesser" response will be made incorrectly. Consequently, the model must raise the value of $k_l$ in order to preserve, on average, the target level of confidence $C_L$. As evident in Fig. 88a, these adaptations have the effect of shifting the *PSE* from above to below zero, indicating a bias towards the "greater" response.

Meanwhile, as can be seen in Fig. 88b, the pattern of times for the "greater" response is lowered. This effect coincides with the finding by Hyman (1953) and Laming (1969) that the response with the higher *a priori* probability was made in a shorter time, while, conversely, the response with lower *a priori* probability took a longer time—both relative to each other, and to the case where both responses were equiprobable. The behaviour of the adaptive model is also confirmed by Laming's finding that there was an increased likelihood of making the alternative response as the *a priori* probability of a given response was reduced.

## Effects of Shifting the Range of Stimulus Differences

The response of the adaptive model to a change in the *a priori* response probabilities yields some insight into the effects of a shift in the range of objective stimulus differences. Figure 89, for example, shows some typical effects obtained when the range of objective differences was shifted. The data in Fig. 89 are based on two simulations of 2000 trials each. In one set of trials, the range of 20 equally likely objective differences extended from $-3\cdot1$ up to $0\cdot7$ in steps of $0\cdot2\sigma_{(V-S)}$, while in the other, the range extended from $-0\cdot7$ up to $3\cdot1$. In both sets of trials, the sequence was random and the same values of $K$, $x$, $C_G$ and $C_L$ were employed as in the previous simulation.

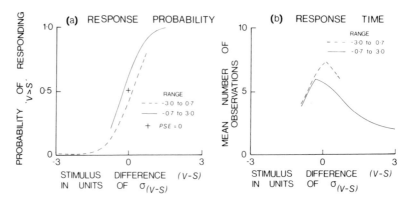

Fig. 89. Effects obtained in simulation of the adaptive model on (a) response probability and (b) response time, as a result of shifting the range of stimulus differences.

Figure 89a shows the effect of shifting the range upwards or downwards on the probability of a "greater" response by the hypothetical process: for a range displaced towards the negative, the *PSE* is shifted upwards, while for a range displaced towards the positive, the *PSE* is shifted downwards. As when the *a priori* probability of a "greater" response is reduced, so a "lesser" response becomes appropriate on a higher proportion of all trials when the range is shifted towards the negative. As a result, the criterion $k_l$ is lowered while the value of $k_g$ is raised. Exactly converse effects occur if the range is shifted so that the objective stimulus difference of zero falls below the midpoint of the range.

Figure 89b shows the effects of shifting the range on the pattern of times taken by the hypothetical process to make a "greater" response. When the range of differences is displaced upwards, the mechanism adapts to the increased chances of making a "greater" response correctly by lowering the value of $k_g$ (and raising that of $k_l$), thereby producing faster times for the "greater" response and slower times for the "lesser". Conversely, when the range of differences is displaced downwards, the mechanism will produce faster times for "lesser" responses and slower times for "greater". Clearly, it is also possible that there may be some interaction between the magnitude of the objective stimulus differences and the probability of their occurrence. For example, shifting the range upwards or downwards will not produce the same effects if the overall *a priori* probabilities of making a "greater" or a "lesser" response are held constant.

## Effects of Extending the Range of Stimulus Differences

In the adaptive accumulator process it is obvious that, when the values of $C$ for the two alternative responses are equal, then the values of $k_g$ and $k_l$ will reach a maximum at a stimulus difference of zero. If a substantial block of trials (e.g. more than 10) consisting of objective stimulus differences close to zero is followed by a block composed of clearly discriminable stimulus differences, then values of $k$ for this second block should be lowered and responses should speed up (though this effect may be hard to distinguish from the normal expectation that, with $k$ held constant, response time will be lower when discriminability is greater). However, the adaptive model predicts that the addition of any clearly discriminable stimulus difference to a series will tend to elicit faster responses not only to that difference but also to all other smaller stimulus differences.

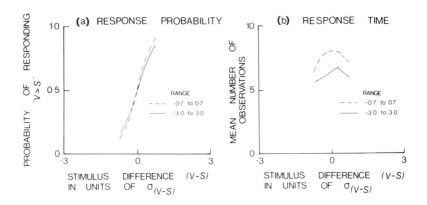

Fig. 90. Effects obtained in simulation of the adaptive model on (a) response probability and (b) response time, as a result of extending the range of stimulus differences.

Figure 90, for example, shows typical effects of adding a highly discriminable stimulus on the pattern of response frequencies and times taken by the hypothetical process to respond to a narrow range of small stimulus differences. As with the other simulations, 2000 trials were run under each of two conditions. In each trial of the first condition, one of eight objective stimulus differences, ranging from $-0\cdot7$ up to $0\cdot7$ in steps of $0\cdot2\sigma_{(V-S)}$ and arranged in random sequence, was presented to the hypothetical process, which operated with the same values of $C_G$, $C_L$, $x$ and $K$ as in the two immediately previous simulations. In the second, the same eight differences were presented with the addition of one large difference, which was either $\pm3\sigma_{(V-S)}$. In both conditions all the differences were equiprobable. As is evident from Fig. 90, the behaviour of the model conforms to what we should intuitively expect, if values of $k_g$ and $k_l$ were lowered in response to the increase in the overall discriminability of the stimulus sequence.

Similar effects were obtained in other simulations when the distribution of stimulus differences was altered so that the largest difference was presented more frequently than the other differences. Converse effects occur, of course, when a range of stimulus differences is compressed around zero, or when a relatively small difference is presented more often than the others. The size of the interval between stimulus differences also affects performance. However, this does not seem to be a very interesting variable within the context of the method of constant stimuli. It has more importance, perhaps, for the method of limits and is discussed immediately below in that connection. For the present, it is sufficient to note that, in principle, the model is sensitive to any change in the range and distribution of stimulus differences, although some changes may be relatively ineffective in practice.

## Effects of a Progressive Sequence of Stimulus Differences

While adaptive effects of the above kinds may arise in response to a random series of stimuli, particular sequences of stimuli may also give rise to effects that are important and interesting. According to the usual method of constant stimuli, the sequence of stimulus differences is random, and the result is that levels of $k$ settle down to some average value and fluctuate about it with no systematic variation. In the method of limits, however, the sequence consists of a regular progression from (say) a large negative difference up, through zero, to a large positive difference (or vice versa). The use of the method of limits in psychophysics thus resembles the feeding of a ramp input into a control system, and is one of a variety of techniques designed to reveal instability, or a tendency to overshoot or undershoot on the part of the system. Thus, whereas the method of constant stimuli is appropriate for a study of the features of an adaptive system in a steady state, the method of limits may be expected to reveal more about the dynamic characteristics of the hypothesized decision process.

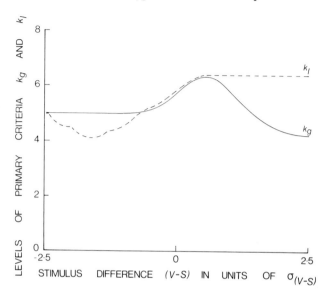

Fig. 91. Mean values of the primary response criteria $k_g$ and $k_l$ taken by a simulation of the proposed adaptive process on successive trials under testing with an ascending series of stimulus differences according to the method of limits. The pattern shown is based on a computer simulation in which the coefficient of adjustment $x = 0.25$, $K = 2$ and $C_G = C_L = 4$.

## The General Pattern of Response

Some idea of the potential complexity of judgmental behaviour exhibited by the model under testing with the method of limits can be gained from the pattern of changes in the levels of $k_g$ and $k_l$ in the adaptive model as stimulus difference is gradually increased from a clear negative value up to a clear positive value. A typical pattern is shown in Fig. 91, where the stimulus difference is increased from $\overline{(V-S)} = -2.5$ up to $\overline{(V-S)} = 2.5$ in steps of $0.1\sigma_{(V-S)}$. At the start of the simulated run when the mean stimulus difference of $-2.5$ is presented, it is assumed that the levels of $k_g$ and $k_l$ are equal (in this case both were set at 5). Since $V$ is clearly less than $S$ for the first few trials, the immediate response by the adaptive model is to lower the value of $k_l$, which reaches a minimum of about 4 when $\overline{(V-S)}$ takes a value of about $-1\cdot5$. Thereafter, the steady decrease in stimulus difference as the run approaches zero causes $k_l$ to be adjusted upwards again. This upwards revision continues past a stimulus difference of zero, since the presented stimulus differences, although now increasing, are taking steadily greater positive values—all of which call for the alternative response (i.e. "$V > S$"). The value of $k_l$ reaches a maximum of about $6\cdot5$ when $\overline{(V-S)}$ takes a value of about $0\cdot5$. From then on the value of $k_l$ remains unchanged, presumably because no more "lesser" responses are made and hence no further increments of over-confidence or under-confidence accumulate to trigger an adjustment.

For the same reason the initial value of $k_g$ remains stable at 5 until $\overline{(V-S)}$ approaches a value of about $-0\cdot5$. At this point the stimulus difference, while negative, is small. As a result a few "greater" responses are made (incorrectly) and the value of $k_g$ is accordingly increased. This increase reaches a maximum of about $6\cdot5$ after the point of zero stimulus difference has been passed. Thereafter, the level of $k_g$ approaches a minimum of 4 as $\overline{(V-S)}$ approaches a value of $2\cdot5$ or more. This minimum value, of course, is dictated by the fact that the target level of confidence chosen for this simulation was $4\cdot0$. The approach of $k_g$ to the target level means that, when $\overline{(V-S)}$ approaches $2\cdot5$ or more, virtually all of the evidence is accumulating in one accumulator, as we should indeed expect.

## The Effect of Step Size

It seems likely that this dynamic process would be sensitive to a number of factors, such as the starting point of the series, the step size and the intermittency and extent of the corrections to $k_g$ and $k_l$. In studying these effects, however, a slightly different procedure was adopted from that usually followed in the method of limits. As Brown and Cane (1959) have shown, the probability $P$ that the $r$th trial in an ascending (or descending) series will terminate at the $r$th value of the objective stimulus difference $d$, is different from the underlying probability $p$ that, when presented with a particular stimulus difference $d_r$, the observer will make the alternative response. Since it is assumed in the latter case that the difference is presented for judgment, the probability $p$ is an unconditional one. In contrast, the former measure $P$ depends both upon the underlying probability $p$ and on whether the run is still progressing or has already been terminated. As Brown and Cane demonstrate, the probability $P$ is therefore a compound probability, which depends both upon the starting point chosen for the series of values of $d$, and also upon the size of the intervals separating successive values of $d$. In straightforward terms, the more opportunity an observer is given to change his response from "$V < S$" to "$V = S$" or

"$V > S$", the higher the probability that he will do so at some point earlier in the sequence.

In studying the effect of step size on the behaviour of the simulated adaptive model, therefore, a slightly different procedure was followed, in which each run was started at a fixed value of $V$ (considerably less than $S$) and continued in regular steps until a second fixed value of $V$ (considerably greater than $S$) was reached, *irrespective of whether or not the response changed*. In this way, the proportion of responses of each type ("$V < S$" or "$V > S$") at each stimulus difference was given directly, and a value of $V$ could be calculated at which 50% of each type of response might be expected and which was logically independent of starting point or step size.

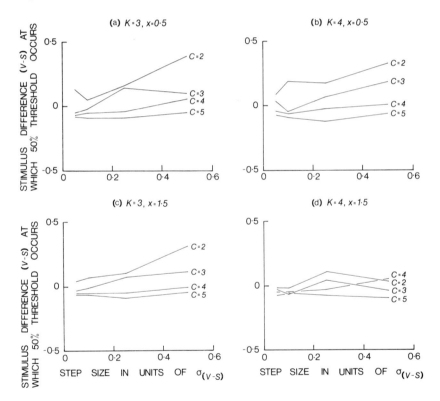

Fig. 92. Mean stimulus difference at which the 50% differential threshold occurred when the simulated adaptive process was tested, according to the method of limits, with an ascending series, in which the mean difference between two stimuli $V$ and $S$, with $\sigma_{(V-S)} = 1$, was increased from $-2 \cdot 5$ up to $2 \cdot 5\sigma_{(V-S)}$. Each curve is based on a computer simulation of 2000 trials at each of 4 values of the step size, and at each of the specified values of $K$, $x$ and of the target confidences $C_G = C_L$.

These 50% thresholds were calculated by fitting normal ogives to the curve relating responses of the type "$V > S$" to stimulus difference $\overline{(V-S)}$ and calculating their means.

Figure 92 summarizes some typical results yielded by a programme of simulations of the proposed adaptive model, tested on the method of limits by the above procedure. As is clear from all four sets of graphs, the smaller the step size, the more the threshold regresses towards the starting point with the rate of regression being steep for runs with low target confidence (e.g. $C = 2$), and decreasing to about zero when $C$ adopts a high value of around 5. Comparing Figs 92a with 92c, and 92b with 92d, it can be seen that this rate of regression is also reduced as the coefficient of adjustment $x$ becomes greater. Comparing Figs 92a with 92b, and 92c with 92d, it also appears to be the case that the rate is reduced as the value of $K$ is increased. Thus, the effect of step size seems to be most marked when the process operates with low target confidence and makes fine adjustments to $k$ at frequent intervals. Conversely, the effect seems least pronounced when the level of target confidence is high and the process makes large adjustments to $k$ at infrequent intervals. Put crudely, the effect of step size seems most important when responses are primarily determined by the momentarily perceived values of $V$ and $S$ in a process that exhibits a continuous but gradual adaptation, while the effect seems least influential when responses are based on a careful statistical evaluation of the perceived values of $V$ and $S$ by a process which then makes a more dramatic adaptation to a sequence of stimuli.

## Starting-point

The sequence of stimulus values presented to the model were given a common starting-point at a considerable distance from the threshold, so that the model would have "settled down" long before the threshold was reached, and so that the effect of starting-point would be minimized. In principle, some idea could also be gained of the effect of various starting-points on the behaviour of the model. However, while it is clear that there would be some effect (at least where the starting-point approached the limiting cases of a stimulus difference of $-\infty$ or 0), what effect there is would depend partly upon the original, unadapted state of the model. Since it would be difficult (or impossible) to make an estimate of the unadapted state of a human observer in a similar situation, it was felt that the chances of obtaining useful empirical data on this question were negligible, and so this aspect of the model has been left unexplored for the present.

## Effects of Biassing $C_G$ and $C_L$.

Of greater importance experimentally, is the question of the possible effects of setting up some bias in favour of one response (or against the other). A clear example of such effects is shown in a series of experiments by Holland (1961) on critical flicker-fusion frequency and on the duration of the spiral after-effect. In one experiment, following the method of limits, Holland presented observers with an alternating series of descending and ascending trials, on which flash frequency was decreased or increased. Observers were required to report the appearance of flicker or fusion respectively. In the "normal" condition, observers were given neutral instructions to indicate on descending trials when the stimulus appeared to flicker and, on ascending trials, when it appeared continuous. In the "low criterion" condition, instructions stressed that observers should report immediately the very first appearance of flicker or of fusion, while, in the "high criterion" condition, observers were instructed to report only when they were quite certain that the stimulus appeared flickering or that it was completely fused.

Holland found that, under normal conditions, there was only a very small discrepancy of about 0·1 flashes per second between the flicker (descending) and the fusion (ascending) thresholds. However, in the low criterion condition this discrepancy was increased to 1·81 with a higher flicker threshold and a lower fusion threshold, so that the descending and ascending runs failed to meet. In contrast, the high criterion condition produced results in which the descending and ascending runs overlapped, with a discrepancy between them of 2·98 flashes per second. Analogous effects of similar instructions were also found in a further experiment on the perceived duration of the after-effect of viewing an Archimedes Spiral.

We have already seen that comparable errors of anticipation or habituation can be observed in the proposed adaptive model, depending on the fineness and intermittency of the adjustments and on the target level of confidence. However, the situation studied by Holland implies that the judgmental process on descending runs is biassed either in favour of a flicker response or against it, and that a complementary bias exists on ascending runs. Such a bias can be set up by making the target confidences $C_G$ and $C_L$ for the two alternative responses unequal. For example, we may consider an ascending series of trials, in which the value of a variable $V$ is being gradually increased from less than the standard $S$ up to a value greater than $S$, and the model is set to respond either "$V < S$" or "$V > S$". Under "normal" conditions we should expect the target levels of confidence to be unbiassed, i.e. $C_G = C_L$. However, when we want to examine the effects of a "low criterion" and make sure that the process will change from a "lesser" to a "greater" response at the first indication that $V$ is approaching $S$ in magnitude, then the appropriate procedure is to bias the process by setting $C_G < C_L$. When this is done we should expect that the sequence of responses on an ascending run would change sooner from "$V < S$" to "$V > S$". Conversely, on descending runs, a "low criterion" condition would correspond to the opposite bias, i.e. $C_L < C_G$. Thresholds measured under these conditions should show the same kind of discrepancy as found by Holland, where the threshold on descending trials is markedly higher than the threshold found for ascending trials. Similarly a "high criterion" would correspond to the converse bias, with $C_G > C_L$ on ascending runs and $C_L > C_G$ on the descending series, and in this case we should expect the threshold on descending trials to be lower than the threshold for ascending trials.

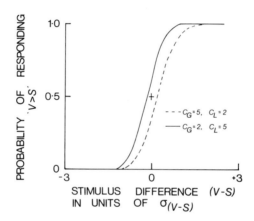

Fig. 93. The probability of responding "$V > S$" at each stimulus difference when the simulated adaptive discrimination process was tested, according to the method of limits, with an ascending series in which the mean difference between two noisy stimuli, with $\sigma_{(V-S)} = 1$, was increased from $-2.5$ up to $2.5$ in steps of $0.25\sigma_{(V-S)}$. Each curve is based on a simulation of 2000 trials for each of the two specified combinations of the target confidences $C_G$ and $C_L$, with $K = 3$ and $x = 1.0$. The intersection between the $0.5$ response probability level and the point of zero stimulus difference is indicated by a cross.

As expected, the behaviour of the adaptive model conforms to this pattern. Figure 93 shows how the frequency of "greater" responses changes on ascending runs for bias corresponding to a "low criterion" ($C_G < C_L$) or to a "high criterion" ($C_L < C_G$). While the discrepancy between the two thresholds may be reduced or increased by choosing suitable combinations of values of the step size, coefficient of adjustment, or the control criterion

$K$, it seems reasonable to conclude that the bias for or against a change in response is an important, though not the sole, determinant of the traditional errors of anticipation and habituation observed in the method of limits.

## The General Adaptive Model

Enough evidence has been presented, perhaps, to show that the adaptive version of the two-category accumulator process constitutes an explanatory mechanism of considerable power. When presented with a series of randomly varying objective stimulus differences, the process gives a good account of the relations between bias, caution and discriminability, on the one hand, and the dependent variables of response frequency and time on the other. In addition to accounting for the results reviewed in Chapters 2 and 3, the model is consistent with the finding that, under certain circumstances, times for incorrect responses may be shorter than those for correct. As is to be expected from an adaptive process, the model is also sensitive to a number of manipulations of the stimulus input to which the static version does not respond. Many of the predictions, it is true, are so simple as to appear only common sense. However, the prediction of behaviour of this kind has in the past usually involved the supposed manipulation by an observer of primary criterion values according to some plausible, but strictly *post hoc* principle. At the very least, the proposed dynamic mechanism represents a more satisfactory approach than the invocation of an intelligent homunculus to drive an otherwise static model.

At the same time, the discussion so far has been restricted to the adaptive version of a two-category accumulator process, and the question naturally arises as to whether the more general three-category process could be endowed with a similar adaptability. In the concluding section of the present chapter, therefore, I shall look briefly at how this may be achieved and at one of the more obvious applications of the general adaptive mechanism.

### The Operation of the General Version

The operation of the general model is similar in all important respects to that of the two-category version. In the case of three-category judgments, for example, the basis for confidence in each of the outcomes "$V > S$", "$V < S$", or "$V = S$" is compared with a corresponding target level $C_G$, $C_L$, or $C_E$ respectively, with amounts of over- and under-confidence being accumulated in three sets of control accumulators (one set for each outcome by the primary decision process). The only major difference in the three-category case is that a third pair of control accumulators needs to be added to cope with the "equals" outcome, together with an associated target level of confidence $C_E$. As in the two-category version, amounts of over- and under-confidence are accumulated in each pair of control accumulators until a critical amount is reached in one member of the pair, whereupon a corrective adjustment is made to the appropriate primary criterion level, and the quantities collected in that pair of control accumulators are returned to zero.

Figure 94 presents a flow diagram of the adaptive process envisaged for three-category tasks. Apart from the additional pair of control accumulators, the only (minor) difference from the two-category model is that the expressions for confidence in each outcome are those appropriate to three-category decisions, namely: expressions (vii), (viii) and (ix), as evaluated by Eqs (4a), (4b) and (5a) in Chapter 6 (p. 194). Otherwise the modular structure of the theoretical mechanism ensures that simple configurations, such as those outlined in Figs 84 and 94, will continue to function whether or not particular units are added or subtracted.

One further distinction emerges when the application of the model to judgments of sameness and difference and to signal detection is considered. In the case of the former judgment, it seems clear that the most appropriate basis for reported expressions of confidence in the judgments reached by the process would be given by Eqs (5a) and (6b) on p. 194 (i.e. $C(E/G.L)$ and $C(G.L/E)$), since these correspond to the definitions of the response forms "same" and "different" respectively. At the same time, it is highly probable that a human observer would notice if all the "different" stimuli were instances in which $V$ was greater than $S$, rather than an equal mixture of "greater" and "lesser" cases. For this reason, it seems preferable to leave the operation of the general adaptive model exactly as it is for three-category judgments, i.e. the criterion values are adjusted by comparing expressions (vii), (viii) and (ix) with their respective target levels of confidence. By employing these as the basis for internal adjustments, the process retains the capacity for making finer discriminations than may in fact be required from it.

Similarly, in the case of signal detection the underlying three-category mechanism may be assumed to operate in exactly the same way as for three-category decisions or judgments of sameness and difference. Only the attachment of overt responses to decision outcomes and the evaluation of evidence for the purpose of expressing confidence in the overt responses need be assumed to vary. Specifically, this means that, when "signal" stimuli involve only increments, rather than a mixture of increments and decrements, then expressions (vii) and (ix) (i.e. $C(G/E.L)$ and $C(E/G.L)$) provide the basis for evaluating confidence in the two overt response alternatives, whereas expressions (vii), (viii) and (ix) are used for the

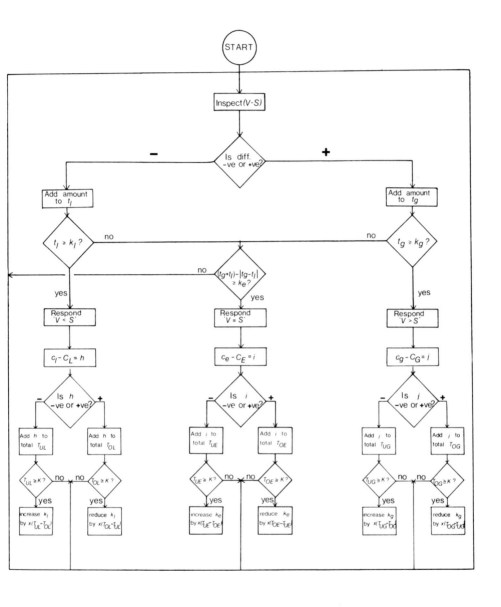

Fig. 94. The sequence of operations envisaged in the adaptive model of three-category judgment. The values of $c_l$, $c_e$ and $c_g$ are given by Eqs (4a), (4b) and (5a) respectively (see Chapter 6).

purposes of internal assessment and adjustment.

The general adaptive model may thus be supposed to operate in exactly the same way whether the experiment is a two-category discrimination, a three-category one, a judgment of sameness and difference, or a signal detection task. Only the attachment of overt response labels and the evaluation of accumulated evidence for the assessment of these overt response alternatives need be supposed to vary. The fact that the mechanism retains the capacity to perform more intelligently in some instances than the constraints of a particular design may allow would seem at least to do a certain ironic justice to the problem of investigating the infinitely adaptable behaviour of human beings by means of a rigorous experimental method.

As it stands, then, the general adaptive model is clearly capable of an immense variety of applications, most of which at present far outrun the experimental data needed to evaluate them. For example, some preliminary simulations show the model to be capable of simulating at least the gross features of human judgmental behaviour in the third of the traditional psychophysical procedures, the method of adjustment. However, in the absence of relevant empirical studies, the systematic exposition of the various detailed properties of the model seems a somewhat academic exercise at present. Since some of the more important properties will in any case be encountered later, I shall conclude this section with a single illustration of one of the more obvious applications of the model, namely, the problem of vigilance.

## The Traditional Vigilance Problem

One of the simplest situations in which some form of adaptation appears to occur is in the area of research into vigilance, i.e. into the changes in performance which occur when human observers are required to monitor a display for the appearance of a faint signal, which occurs only infrequently and after unpredictable intervals. Useful reviews of theoretical and experimental work on vigilance have been given by Davies and Tune (1970) and Jerison (1977).

In one particular approach, reviewed by Swets (1977), researchers over the last fifteen years have followed the suggestions of Howland (1958) and Egan et al. (1961), and have attempted to apply the concepts and procedures of the theory of signal detection to an analysis of the decrease in the percentage of signals correctly detected as the vigilance session proceeds. Although the decrement may sometimes be at least partly due to a reduction in his sensitivity, it appears from this work that the major effect arises from a progressive increase in the strictness of the decision criterion employed by the observer (Loeb and Binford, 1964; Colquhoun and Baddeley, 1964, 1967; Broadbent and Gregory, 1965; Jerison *et al.*, 1965; Mackworth, 1965; Taylor, 1965; Binford and Loeb, 1966; Colquhoun, 1966, 1969; Levine, 1966; Baddeley and Colquhoun, 1969; Williges, 1969). A second effect, which accompanies this decrement, is a certain systematic variation in the pattern of response times (Buck, 1966; Davies and Tune, 1970).

Clearly, the adaptive form of the proposed general decision module would be most satisfactory on both these counts. As outlined in the last section, the general module can be made adaptive in exactly the same way as for three-category judgment. In order for it to function as an adaptive model for signal detection, the only modification required is the attachment of the response "signal" to the "$V > S$" outcome, and the response "nonsignal" to each of the "$V = S$" and the "$V < S$" outcomes. In any situation where the objective probability of a signal is changed from practice to test trials, this adaptive model would predict some variation in both response frequency and response time. In particular, when signal probability is reduced, as in most vigilance experiments, then a lower proportion of non-signal responses will be made incorrectly (and hence with lower confidence). As a result, the adaptive model can afford to lower the criteria (mainly $k_e$) controlling the nonsignal response. Precisely converse effects will occur for the signal criterion $k_g$, which must be adjusted upwards in order to preserve, on average, the target level of confidence.

Figure 95 shows the results of a computer simulation of 40 sessions, in which the adaptive model operated in signal detection mode on a series of 1000 (focal-background) stimulus differences, with means of 0 or $0\cdot5\sigma_{(V-S)}$ and with $\sigma_{(V-S)} = 1$. In each session, the first 100 trials consisted of 50 nonsignal stimuli (with $\overline{V-S} = 0$) and 50 signals (with $\overline{V-S} = 0\cdot5$), presented in random order. The remaining trials consisted of nine consecutive blocks of 100, in each of which only two signals were presented, thereby reducing the objective signal probability from $0\cdot5$ to $0\cdot02$. As can be seen from Fig. 95a, the proportions of "hits" and "false alarms" both decline after the first "practice" block of 100 trials. Meanwhile, as is evident in Fig. 95b, the times taken to make these responses increase over the subsequent "test" sessions.

The decline in the proportion of signals correctly detected, and in the proportion of "false alarms" corresponds to the classic findings of vigilance experiments. In addition, the increase in the time for "hits" is confirmed by the results of several experiments reviewed by Buck (1966). More tellingly, perhaps, the predicted apparent slight decrease in the time for "correct rejections" has been corroborated in unpublished experiments by Davies, Taylor and Tune (Davies and Tune, 1970, p. 17). As it stands, therefore, the general adaptive model would seem to bid fair to being the first precisely

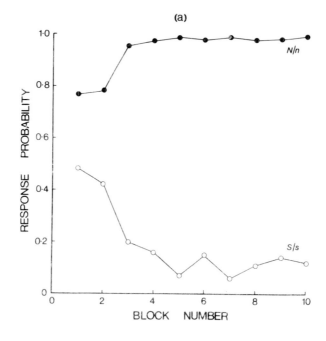

(a)

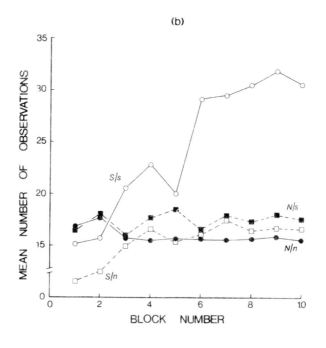

(b)

specified mechanism to account successfully for the adaptive changes which take place in performance during traditional vigilance tasks (at least in those instances where changes in arousal do not appear to function as an additional complicating factor).

## *The Significance of a General Adaptive Module—Some General Conclusions*

Taken as a whole, the proposed adaptive model appears to represent a useful step forward in our theoretical understanding of human perceptual judgment. Indeed, while alternative formulations may improve on the detail and accuracy of the predictions made by the model, it is difficult to conceive of one that does not have several features in common with the present process. For example, it appears necessary for any alternative to depend on negative feedback as an input to the controlling system, and therefore to presuppose some pre-set target level which the system is trying to maintain. Again, it seems inevitable that any alternative process would be expected to allow for some variability in the size of the corrective adjustments made by it, and in the frequency with which they were made. At present, the process outlined in this chapter would appear to be one of the simplest possible embodiments of these features.

As a mechanism for discrimination and identification, the suggested adaptive model is clearly more complete than the static version. At the beginning of this chapter, for example, it was mentioned that the decrease in response time predicted by the static version following an increase in the variance of the observations was contradicted by results obtained in the expanded judgment task of Irwin and Smith (1956). In order to reconcile the static version with the data it whould be necessary to suppose that the observer made appropriate adjustments to the criterion levels. While this supposition seems reasonable, the disadvantageous behaviour, which would otherwise be exhibited by the static model in this situation, could also be viewed as a veritable stress for evolution in the direction embodied by the proposed configuration of elementary accumulator processes into a self-contained adaptive system. Besides accounting for a much wider array of phenomena than the static version, the resulting adaptive mechanism has the advantage of suggesting a function for the experience of confidence,

---

Fig. 95. The pattern of (a) response probabilities and (b) response times obtained in simulation of the adaptive module in signal detection mode, with $K = 5$, $C_G = C_E = 5$, $x = 2$ and $k_l$ being made inoperative by setting $C_L$ to 99. Solid lines represent correct and broken lines incorrect responses. Open symbols denote signal responses and filled symbols denote nonsignal responses.

rather than regarding it as a convenient, but mysterious, epiphenomenon.

Of equal significance is the fact that the general adaptive mechanism embodies the simple principles of discrimination, identification and self-regulation, which, it was argued in Chapter 1, would be a prerequisite to the survival and evolution of the most primitive of the first mobile organisms. The neurophysiological embodiment of even a single adaptive accumulator process, operating on the outputs from a pair of photoreceptors, would endow an organism with some capacity for responding in an advantageous and flexible way to differences in illumination. The full significance of the general adaptive mechanism, however, lies in Goodson's corollary (1973), quoted in Chapter 1, that "all living organisms, from the simplest to the most complex, reflect more or less elaborate versions of these simple principles".

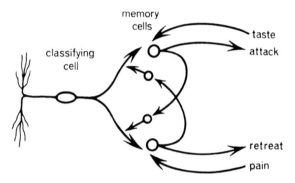

Fig. 96. Representation of a mnemon. The classifying cell gives rise to two alternative responses. Positive or negative effects reinforce the response made or increase the likelihood of making the alternative response. The unused pathway is then closed by means of inhibition from the small memory cells. (Reproduced, with permission, from Young, 1965).

As was also argued in Chapter 1, if the evolution of a more complex nervous system is borne in view then, at each stage, the evolving system must be capable of functioning as a complete, self-contained process. With this constraint in mind, and following the powerful example of cellular aggregation in the natural world, it seems almost certain that the significance of an adaptive mechanism of the kind proposed in this chapter, is that it is capable of functioning as an independent, self-contained module within other configurations of similar modules. In other words, the adaptive accumulator module may be capable of serving as a fundamental functional unit in higher cognitive activity.

Besides the considerations already encountered in this book, there are some other grounds for believing that the proposed process is capable of fulfilling such a role. For example, the adaptive accumulator mechanism has much in common with the notion of a "mnemon", or fundamental memorising unit, proposed by Young (1965) and represented in Fig. 96. The main differences are that the mnemon lacks the capacity to make identifications, and that the memory cells (or accumulative processes) are modified by the consequences of external responses rather than through an appraisal by the system of its own internal states following a response. The similarity is perhaps more clearly borne out in von Foerster's representation of a mnemon (1968) (Fig. 97) in terms which illustrate its embodiment of the essential features of a "cognitive tile" or fundamental computational unit of cognitive activity. The close resemblance between this representation and the adaptive decision module is immediately clear from the similar information-flow diagram of the latter in Fig. 98. In addition to the differences already mentioned, there is one minor one, namely, that feedback in von Foerster's system affects both response processes in a

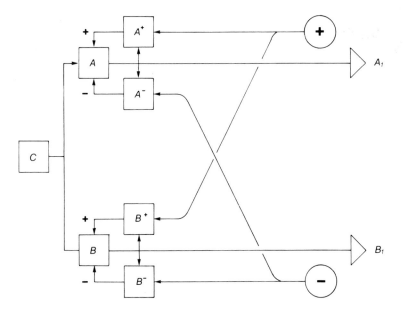

Fig. 97. Information flow diagram of a mnemon, showing the classifying cell ($C$), response initiating neurons $A$ and $B$ and two memory cell complexes which alter the behaviour of $A$ and $B$ depending upon the positive or negative results of previous responses $A_1$ and $B_1$. (Redrawn, with permission, from von Foerster, 1968).

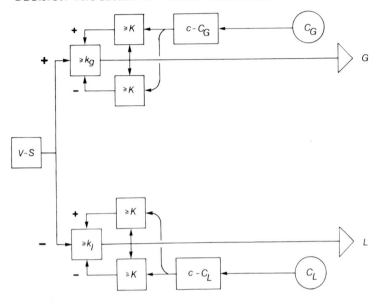

Fig. 98. Representation of the adaptive two–category decision process in the same information-flow terms as employed by von Foerster (Fig. 97). The diagram shows the relation between the primary decision processes $k_g$ and $k_l$, the control processes (uniformly symbolized by $K$), the basis for confidence $c$ and the target levels $C_G$ and $C_L$. Observation of a series of $(V-S)$ differences leads to the production of a "greater" or a "lesser" response, $G$ or $L$.

complementary way, whereas feedback in the adaptive decision module is linked to a single response system. However, this distinction seems to be a difference in detail, rather than one of principle.

The adaptive decision module also shares with von Foerster's cognitive tile one other important property. Since the quantities transmitted between any two nodes in the module are commensurable, this means that information from any part of the module can be transmitted to any part of any other. Thus the behaviour of one module can modify that of another in a large number of ways. As von Foester argues, this means that a rich variety of tessellations or configurations of these units is possible. The net result is that the adaptive decision module would seem to possess a flexibility and versatility that endow it with considerable evolutionary potential.

The conclusions which have emerged from the first two parts of this book would seem, therefore, to have implications which extend far beyond the concerns of traditional psychophysics. They suggest a view of the functioning of the brain in which an adaptive decision function is the smallest useful element of organization. They imply also that more molar aspects of human cognitive activity may be understood as the surface representations of the internal interactions of these basic functions. The first Chapter of Part III is accordingly devoted to a detailed examination of how a more complex cognitive task might be explained in these terms. Following this, Chapter 9 looks at the way in which this approach might be extended to the larger problem of perceptual organization. Finally, the concluding chapter considers some further implications, both general and specific, of this view of perception.

# III

## Complex Decision Processes

# 8

# The Identification of Stimuli

*There is no perfect similarity anywhere.*
G. W. Leibniz, "Acta eruditorum", September 1698
(*in*: L. E. Loemker, 1956)

In addition to the ubiquitous dependent variable of response frequency, many of the fundamental properties of the adaptive decision module developed in Parts I and II are expressed in terms of the time required to reach a certain state (usually that of some decision outcome). An important constraint, therefore, in selecting a more complex cognitive activity in which to explore the applicability of this modular approach, is that there should be sufficient empirical data on response times associated with it. Fortunately, the study of stimulus identification, or choice reaction, has been accompanied by a long history of response time measurement, which extends as far as the early attempts in 1868 by the Dutch physiologist, Donders, to measure "the shortest possible time for a simple thought" (1969a, p. 432).

In the present chapter, therefore, I shall begin by considering one of the most characteristic phenomena associated with stimulus identification, and one of the earliest (and most widely supported) hypotheses concerning the underlying mechanism, namely, the *serial elimination* model developed by Hick (1952b) and Welford (1960, 1968). In view of the problems encountered by a hypothesis of this kind, a second main class of *parallel elimination* model is then considered, in which alternative identifications are eliminated simultaneously, rather than in succession. Since an eliminative procedure leads to difficulties in accounting for adaptation, however, the next alternative examined is a *parallel eventuation* process, in which several decision modules compete for identification of the presented variable with the remembered standard linked to each module. Like the individual module, such a process, it turns out, appears to embody a "stress for adaptation", and the main properties of an adaptive version are therefore presented in some detail, along with the relevant empirical evidence. Finally, some unexpected properties of an adaptive parallel eventuation process are described and proposed as an explanation for a set of phenomena—the so-called "Yerkes–Dodson" effects—which have so far resisted a detailed theoretical analysis.

## Hick's Serial Elimination Model and the Relation between Choice Reaction Time and the Number of Stimulus-Response Alternatives

In his studies, Donders (1868, 1969b) distinguished between three different types of reaction-time experiment: the "$a$-reaction", in which one and only one response has to be made upon the presentation of one and only one stimulus; the "$b$-reaction", where one out of any number $n$ of possible stimuli might be presented, to each of which a different one out of $n$ possible responses is required; and the "$c$-reaction", where any one out of $n$ possible stimuli might occur, but where a single response is required to only one stimulus. In terms of Donders' analysis, the present chapter is concerned with the $b$-reaction and I shall begin by considering one of the most widely known of its properties.

### Choice Reaction Time and the Number of Stimulus-Response Alternatives

Donders went on to measure the response times for the $a$-, $b$- and $c$-reactions for various values of $n$ and found that, for a given value of $n$, times for the $b$-reaction were longest, followed by those for the $c$-reaction, with those for the $a$-reaction being shortest. The difference $(RT_c - RT_a)$ between reaction times for the $c$-reaction and the $a$-reaction he interpreted as a measure of the time taken to identify one out of $n$ stimuli, and suggested that the additional time required in the $b$-reaction to select one out of $n$ responses could be calculated from the difference $(RT_b - RT_c)$.

While various aspects of Donders' subtractive method have been questioned (e.g. Woodworth and Schlosberg, 1954; Sternberg, 1969; Rabbitt, 1971), his basic conceptualization of the process of choice as involving a sequence of non-overlapping sub-processes comprising stimulus identification followed by response selection, has had a long-lasting and widespread influence (cf. Welford, 1960, 1968; Smith, 1968). In the case of the $b$-reaction, these assumptions have been applied primarily to the finding that, at least in relatively unpractised tasks, there appears to be a direct, monotonic relationship between the time taken to identify (and respond to) a stimulus and the number $n$ of possible stimuli that might be presented within a clearly defined series of trials.

For example, in the first systematic investigation of choice-reaction time carried out in 1885, Merkel presented observers with the Arabic numerals 1 to 5, which were to be responded to by the fingers of the left hand, and the Roman numerals I to V, which were similarly assigned to fingers of the right hand. In any series of trials, one out of a given number of these stimuli was presented and each of the same number of corresponding responses was timed. When the choice-reaction times obtained by Merkel were plotted against the logarithm of the number of alternative stimuli $n$, the points were reasonably well fitted by a straight line (Hick, 1952b). Similar results were obtained by Hick, using a roughly circular array of $n$ lamps, any one of which could be lit as a stimulus, and by Crossman (1953), who required observers to sort packs of well-shuffled playing cards into varying numbers of categories, such as red and black, or hearts, clubs, spades and diamonds.

## The Serial Elimination Model

Of the several mechanisms suggested by Hick to explain this relation, the most familiar is one which involves a process of serial dichotomization and elimination of the stimulus alternatives. According to Welford's succinct version of this model, the observer identifies the stimulus by "making a series of sub-decisions, each taking approximately the same time. With the first he identifies the signal and the response to it as lying within one half of the total probabilities; with the second as lying within one half of this half, and so on until the specific signal and response have been found. He is not able to make his divisions into exact halves unless $n$ is an exact power of 2, but can do so approximately in other cases. In any case, the model would still give approximately the correct result so long as the observer started by rejecting broad classes of possibility and then went on to reject finer classes within a broad class chosen" (1968, p. 71).

On this model, the larger the number of alternative stimuli, the greater the number of dichotomizing sub-decisions required to eliminate all but the correct stimulus, and the longer on average will be the time taken to respond. For example, on a strict dichotomizing strategy, where the observer concludes without further test that the last remaining alternative is the correct one, then one test would be sufficient to identify one out of two alternatives, two tests would be needed for four alternatives, three for eight, and so on. If each test is assumed to take approximately the same time, and subsequent tests are independent and do not overlap, then the predicted relationship between mean reaction time over all responses and the number of alternative stimuli should indeed be logarithmic (Welford, 1960).

## Difficulties with the Serial Elimination Model

While this last prediction is an attractive feature of the model, the apparent simplicity of the hypothesized process is deceptive and some of the underlying assumptions are questionable. In particular, problems arise concerning the nature of the sub-decisions and the embodiment of subjective expectancies. In addition, the apparent effects of practice pose a severe difficulty for any process of this kind. We shall consider each of these aspects in turn.

### The Nature of the Sub-decisions

The first difficulty concerns the nature of the mechanisms which, it must be assumed, underly each sub-decision. It is supposed, for example, that the times for each sub-decision are approximately equal, although the work on discrimination reviewed in Chapters 2 and 3 could be taken to suggest that sub-decisions between finer classes should take longer than those between broad classes. This possibility highlights the need to specify the nature of the sub-decisions. We need to know, for example, whether a sub-decision which eliminates a range of alternatives is of the same kind, and takes the same time, as a sub-decision which confirms the existence of a signal.

In an attempt to make this aspect of the model more explicit, Welford (1968) suggests that the process underlying each sub-decision may be analogous to the random walk or accumulator processes discussed in Chapter 3. According to such a model, the identification of (say) one of a horizontally linear array of stimuli could be effected by a series of sub-decisions as to whether the presented stimulus occurred to the left or the right of a sequence of reference points. As Fitts (1966) suggests, the trade-off between speed and accuracy observed in choice-reaction experiments could be accounted for by supposing that the criteria employed in each sub-decision might be raised or lowered, while bias in favour of particular responses could be explained by supposing that the two criterion levels for each sub-decision might differ.

As Welford comments, such an approach would be extremely flexible, but there are a number of disadvantages in its application even to a simple situation, such as the identification of stimuli arrayed on a single dimension. For example, when there are three or more stimuli, requiring two or more sub-decisions, it is not certain that lowering the criteria for each sub-decision will produce shorter average times for incorrect responses, though this should increase the number of errors. The reason is that an error early in the sequence of sub-decisions will render all subsequent tests inappropriate. The later sub-decisions will then be between indiscriminable (or equally inappropriate) alternatives, and would be expected to be more difficult and to take longer.

## Expectancy

It is perhaps possible that, by making particular assumptions, a process of this kind might still perform appropriately. However, the generation and testing of clear predictions on this issue would represent a formidable task. In any case, a second complication follows from the consideration that, if the pattern of subjective expectancies is thought of as being embodied in the pattern of criterion levels for each sub-decision, then it seems necessary to assume that each sub-test is unique to a particular stage in the dichotomization process. Another possibility is to suppose that alternative responses are eliminated by a common sub-test, but in a sequence which may reflect the pattern of subjective expectancies. While these strategies appear equally practicable, both involve an additional memory load together with a number of unspoken assumptions concerning the memorizing (and forgetting) process.

## Effects of Practice

These disadvantages are not decisive and might perhaps be overcome in an attempt to translate the model into a more detailed form. Unfortunately there exists a growing body of evidence which appears to call into question the very *raison d'être* of a serial model. In a recent review, Teichner and Krebs (1974) examined data from 59 studies of choice-reaction and showed that the slopes of the equations relating choice-reaction time and the number of stimulus alternatives decreased steadily as a function of practice, and approached zero with very large amounts of practice. While some of this reduction may be due to a decreased involvement of the process of translating between stimuli and responses, as suggested by Welford (1968), the possibility that the slope relating choice-reaction time to number of stimulus alternatives may decrease to zero appears to rule out the operation of a serial dichotomization process.

Among the other studies which reinforce this view, Teichner (1954) has shown, for example, that simple reaction time is not much affected by practice, while we (Vickers *et al.*, 1972) have found that times taken to discriminate between two highly discriminable alternatives remain quite high (around 500 ms), even when the need to respond quickly is strongly emphasized. These results suggest that the time required for an individual inspection is very little affected by practice, and that the time required for a minimal number of inspections of the sensory input is substantial. Even if successive sub-decisions in a multi-choice task were each made on the basis of a single observation, therefore, we should expect that there would still be an appreciable rise in response time as the number of alternative stimuli (and hence the number of necessary sub-decisions) is increased. However, recent results by Smith (1977), using a highly compatible task, showed that differences between times for eight and four choices were not significant, while those between times for four and two choices were barely significant, and in any case were very small (13–19 ms), even though the amount of practice was only moderate. Findings such as these indicate that practised observers do not employ a serial process, and lead us to look for an alternative model in which the relation between response time and the number of stimulus-response alternatives can be realistically supposed to change with practice or familiarity.

## Serial Position Effects and a Parallel Elimination Process

One obvious way of modifying the serial elimination model so as to allow choice time to become less directly dependent upon the number of stimulus-response alternatives would be to suppose that the various sub-decisions are made simultaneously, rather than in sequence, as in the kind of model considered by Hick (1952b), Christie and Luce (1956), Rapoport (1959) and Laming (1966). On this approach, the reaction time to one of $n$ stimuli is determined by the longest of $n$ elementary decision processes, all operating independently and in parallel. In such a model, the addition of further elementary decision processes makes it more likely that, for a given variable, one (or more) processes will take a long time. Indeed, it can be shown that the mean time taken to respond should be an approximately logarithmic function of $n$ (Rapoport, 1959; Laming, 1966). Before embarking upon a consideration of the properties of such a model, however, we must follow out the implications of a particular class of phenomena—the so-called serial position effects—for the representation of stimuli in a process of this kind.

### Serial Position Effects

One complication for a parallel elimination process is that when the distributions for the elementary processes are assumed to be the same, then mean response times should also be the same for all stimulus alternatives, provided that they are presented randomly and with equal probability. However, a number of studies have shown that relations between stimuli, such as discriminability or position in a linear array, have marked effects on the observed pattern of response times and errors. For example, in an experiment in which observers were required to sort a pack of cards into two, three, four, or five piles of cards, each showing different numbers of spots, Crossman (1955) found that the time taken to complete a sorting increased as a function of a measure $C$ of the confusability of the numbers of spots. When sorting times were plotted against $C$, irrespective of the degree of choice, the data were quite well fitted by a straight line. This finding suggests that discriminability, rather than degree of choice *per se*, may be a basic determining factor in multi-choice experiments, at least when stimuli are arrayed on a single dimension. In agreement with this conclusion, Docherty (1968) found that discriminability between alternatives did affect response time, although, within the range of discriminability studied in his experiments, differences in discriminability as measured by the $C$ function could not alone account for the relationship between information transmitted and response time.

To account for his results, Crossman (1955) surmised that each stimulus in a linear sequence may be confused with every other and argued that the likelihood of confusing one stimulus with another should increase as a function of $n$, with stimuli at the beginning and the ends of an array being less subject to confusion than those in the middle. In a later paper, Murdock (1960) proposed a similar, though converse, measure, in which the distinctiveness of a given stimulus is a function of the difference between it and all other stimuli in the array, considered as a proportion of the total distinctiveness of all the stimuli in the array. An outstanding feature of this measure is the U-shaped curve of distinctiveness associated with the successive stimuli from a linear array.

It is true that Murdock's measure is intended mainly as a concise empirical description, while the underlying serial mechanism postulated by Crossman (1955) is at best incompletely specified (Hughes, 1964) and was subsequently abandoned in favour of a parallel process (Crossman, 1964). Nevertheless, the implied effects of discriminability and serial position appear to be borne out experimentally. For example, in a set of three experiments on absolute judgment, Murdock (1960) found that the percentage of times each of nine different loudnesses was correctly identified by a number from 1 to 9 was closely matched by the percentage distinctiveness calculated for each stimulus.

A similar correspondence was found by Murdock on reanalysing the results of three other experiments on absolute judgment by Garner (1953), Eriksen and Hake (1955) and Alluisi and Sidorsky (1958). Murdock likened the form of these results to the serial position effect found in studies of verbal learning (Bugelski, 1950; McCrary and Hunter, 1953; Braun and Heymann, 1958), as well as to serial effects observed in maze learning (Hull, 1948). What appears to be an analogous serial position effect in the case of response times was also noted by John (1969) in a choice-reaction experiment in which, for one observer, each of a linear array of ten stimulus lights was assigned from left to right a number 1, 2, . . ., 10. More recently, Welford (1971), Nettelbeck and Brewer (1976) and Smith (1977) have all published data from choice-reaction tasks which show that response times to stimuli at the ends of an array are shorter than those to stimuli in intermediate positions. As Welford (1971) points out, such results are inconsistent with the notion of a parallel set of identical processes, all operating independently.

## A Parallel Elimination Process with a Finite Representational Space

One possible solution to this problem is to postulate a set of parallel, independent decision processes, which continue to operate in exactly the same way, but which depend upon an input which itself reflects the relative discriminability of the alternative stimuli. Figure 99 gives a flow diagram of such a model, so designed as to embody as a basic module the two–category accumulator process outlined in Chapter 3. According to this approach, the observer can be thought of as storing subjective standards $S_1$, $S_2$, . . . $S_n$, corresponding to each of the alternative stimuli $V_1$, $V_2$, . . . $V_n$, with each standard varying randomly about a mean $\bar{S}$, with a certain standard deviation $\sigma_S$. Any stimulus $V$ presented to the observer would also be supposed to be subject to some random disturbance in its neural representation, and to be capable of being similarly described by a mean $\bar{V}$, and a standard deviation $\sigma_V$. For the sake of simplicity, the distributions of $V$ and $S$ are assumed to be normal and uncorrelated, though these assumptions are not crucial.

Whenever a given value of $V$ is presented for identification, the observer is thought of as comparing this simultaneously with each of the possible standards $S_1$, $S_2$, . . . $S_n$. For each standard, the results of successive comparisons with the variable are added to the appropriate total of a separate two-category accumulator process. The main difference between the operation of each accumulator module and the process outlined in Chapter 3 is that whenever a critical value of the criterion $k$ is reached, one further test is made. If this accumulator module is not the last to reach a criterion, then a response of the form "$V > S$" or "$V < S$" is made. However, unlike the simple two-category situation, these responses are assumed to be covert, rather than observable, and to have the primary function of eliminating the possibility of identifying the variable with the standard associated with that module. On the other hand, if this module is the last to reach criterion, then the response is changed from a covert "greater" or "lesser" form into an overt response, in which the variable is

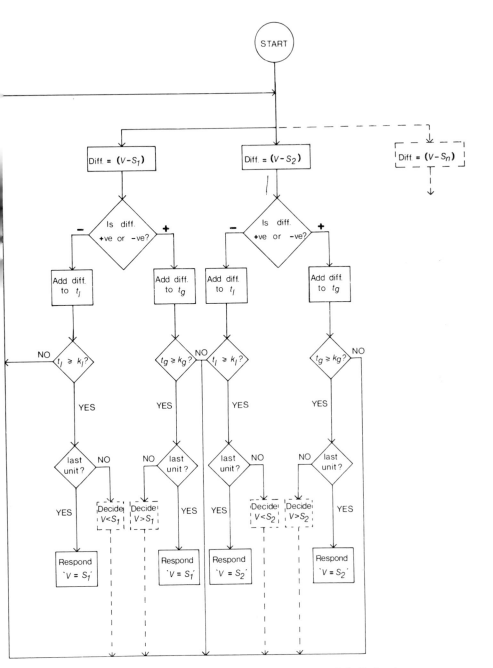

Fig. 99. Flow diagram of the operations envisaged in a parallel elimination process embodying an array of two-category decision processes. The broken lines in the lower section indicate covert decisions, which do not give rise to an observable identification response.

identified with the standard corresponding to the accumulator process in question. Any increase in the number of stimulus alternatives can be accommodated simply by postulating further standards, with corresponding modules added in parallel.

To investigate the behaviour of a model of this kind, a computer simulation was carried out in which the process outlined in Fig. 99 was presented with each of 3, 4 and 10 levels of choice. On any one level, the process was presented at each trial with a distribution of magnitudes, with a mean $\bar{V}$, and a standard deviation $\sigma_V$. Successive random observations from this distribution were then simultaneously compared by the process with observations drawn randomly from each of a set of $n$ distributions, with means $S_1, S_2, \ldots, S_n$, and a common standard deviation $\sigma_S$. The $n$ streams of positive and negative differences generated by each of the $n$ sets of comparisons were then separately accumulated in each of $n$ two-category accumulator processes, one for each value of $\bar{S}$. This procedure was continued until all accumulator processes had reached a decision, with the value of $V$ being identified with the standard associated with the last accumulator process to reach a criterion amount $k_g$ or $k_l$ of positive or negative $(V-S)$ difference. In the case of the last process reaching the criterion simultaneously with one or more others, a random selection was made among them.

In order to accommodate the effects of serial position, the simulation was also based on Crossman's suggestion (1955) that for any one dimension, there may be a finite space in which to represent all possible values of the stored standards (or the presented variables). Accordingly, for the three-choice situation both variables and standards had means of 10, 15, and 20 $\sigma_{(V-S)}$ units; for the 4-choice, the means were 10, 13·33, 16·67 and 20; and for the 10-choice the means ranged from 10 up to 20, in steps of 1·11. There was thus an increasing overlap between standards as more were added to the ensemble, with most overlap occurring in the middle of the array and least at the two extremes. Meanwhile, the mean value of the presented variable varied randomly from trial to trial, with each of the $n$ values being equally probable. A standard deviation of 2 was assigned to both variables and standards, and the criteria $k_g$ and $k_l$ associated with each of the $n$ two-category processes were in all cases set to 7. A total of 2000 trials was simulated at each of the three values of $n$.

## Serial Position Curves

The results are shown in Fig. 100. As can be seen from Fig. 100a, the model predicts that when stimuli are ordered along a single dimension and responses are compatible, then the proportion of correct responses falls on a

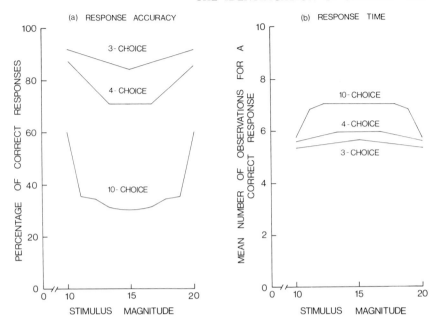

Fig. 100. The pattern of (a) response accuracy and (b) response time obtained in computer simulation of the parallel elimination process. The individual curves present data for different degrees of choice, with the values of variables and standards extending in all cases from 10 up to $20\sigma_{(V-S)}$ units and separated by equal intervals.

U-shaped curve, with responses at the ends being appreciably more accurate than those in the middle. Meanwhile, Fig. 100b shows that the times for correct responses fall on a similar, but inverted, curve, with times for the end stimuli being appreciably faster than those for stimuli in intermediate positions. As suggested by the formulations of Crossman (1955) and Murdock (1960), both effects are due to the fact that any value of the presented variable will be at a different distance from various standards, with values of the variable corresponding to extreme positions being more distinguishable on average than those in intermediate positions.

## Number of Stimulus-Response Alternatives

Further effects of discriminability follow from the fact that the present model, unlike that considered by Hick (1952b), Christie and Luce (1956), Rapoport (1959) and Laming (1966), depends upon certain assumptions concerning the representation of both variables and standards. For example, the assumption that an increase in $n$ should be represented by a simple increase in the mean value(s) of the associated standard(s) has been found in other simulation work to result in only a slight slowing in the average time for correct identifications as *n* is increased. In contrast, the simulation results presented in Fig. 101 show that for the pure elimination model under discussion there is a negatively accelerated rise in the mean number of observations elapsing before a final identification is (correctly) made when this is plotted against *n*. The assumption of a fixed representational space adopted here means that there is an increasing overlap as more standards are added and the resulting increase in confusability takes more time to resolve. Although the slopes of the functions in Fig. 101 are very gradual, the rise in response time becomes slightly steeper as the degree of caution is increased for all alternatives.

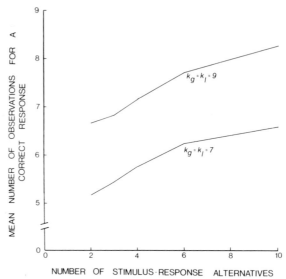

Fig. 101. Pooled estimates of the number of observations required for a correct response in simulation of the parallel elimination model, plotted against the number of stimulus-response alternatives. As in Fig. 100, the value of $\sigma_V = \sigma_S = 2$, both variables and standards take values between 10 and $20\sigma_{(V-S)}$ and are separated by equal intervals.

## The Problem of Adaptation

While the general performance of the parallel elimination process seems to be appropriate, one aspect of its behaviour has so far passed unremarked. In simulating the model criterion values of $k_g = k_l = 7$ were chosen so as to make its behaviour comparable to some extent with that of the single two-category process outlined in Chapter 3. However, as the attentive reader may have noticed, the proportions of errors shown in Fig. 100a are unusually high. Clearly, criterion values would have to be set much higher than 7 if the behaviour of the model were to be representative of empirically observed proportions. In the case of the adaptive two-category process introduced in Chapter 7, such adjustments occur automatically as the theoretical counterpart of subjective confidence departs from its target level. It would greatly increase the scope of the multi-choice model if some way could be found of making it adaptive as well.

## Independent Adaptation within each Module

At this point, we begin to run into difficulties. One possible strategy in the design of an adaptive version would be to employ a set of two-category discrimination processes, each capable of adapting independently in exactly the same way as the adaptive model of two-category judgment proposed in Chapter 7. On this approach, the confidence in any sub-decision would be assessed with reference only to the one other alternative sub-decision possible within the same module. Unfortunately, this assumption leads to some undesirable consequences. For example, preliminary simulation work suggests that when one alternative becomes more probable than the other, then the overall time to make the final identification may be shortened, provided that the alternative standards are similar in value, so that there is scope for the criteria dealing with them to be decreased. However, when the alternative standards are very different from the correct, highly probable one, then these alternatives will already be eliminated with maximum confidence and their associated criteria cannot be lowered further. On the other hand, when the variable is equal to the standard in question, then the final discriminative outcome is strictly inappropriate and the predominant effect of an increase in the probability of that value of the variable is likely to be an increase in the criteria associated with the correct standard. In turn, the result of this adaptation will be an increase in response time to the more probable alternative, which is contrary to empirical findings (and also to common sense).

## Adaptation Relative to Other Modules

It might be argued that a better approach would be to make the adjustments within each module less independent, so as to reflect better the confidence with which a final identification is made relative to that with which the other alternatives might have been so identified (but were not). However, in the case of the present parallel elimination process, this approach meets with what appears to be a basic difficulty. The problem is that the elimination of a module means that no more evidence is accumulated by it, so that the evidence accumulated in the module which triggers the final identification can be compared only with evidence in other modules which is now "out-of-date". In order to make an unbiassed comparison of the evidence for various alternatives, some additional system for up-dating the evidence in the eliminated modules would have to be devised, and this inevitably makes the model too complex to be useful. Viewed in an evolutionary light, the parallel elimination model would seem to be a process which, though viable within a limited extent, is incapable of adaptation and is likely, therefore, to represent a dead end in development.

## A Parallel Eventuation Model

The difficulties encountered in attempts to make the parallel elimination model adaptive appear to stem from the eliminative characteristics of the process. Besides these difficulties, some other aspects of the logic of an elimination process give grounds for discomfiture. In the first place, we must assume that the system somehow keeps track of the number of alternatives eliminated in order to interpret the final sub-decision as an identification rather than an elimination. Again, the system is bound irrevocably to the stimulus response relations established for it. For example, it would be possible for an experimenter to familiarize a human observer with standards of 100 grams and 200 grams, to instruct him to identify each of a sequence of presentations of these weights as "one" or "two" and then to insert a 500 gram weight somewhere in the series. At this point a human observer would probably follow the instructions and respond "two", but remark that the weight in question felt much heavier than the other "twos". In contrast, the parallel elimination model has no capacity for modifying its responses, and has no option but to classify as "two" any weights heavier than the upper standard.

Besides its lack of adaptability, the parallel elimination model appears to be a peculiarly indirect process, and instances of the natural occurrence of this kind of system are hard to think of. The present section, accordingly, examines a more direct alternative—a parallel eventuation process, which has several counterparts in more molar contexts. After demonstrating some of the difficulties which confront a static version of the process, the section closes by describing an adaptive version, which appears to have considerable plausibility.

## A Static Parallel Eventuation Process

Since the basic task for an observer is to identify the presented variable with one of a set of remembered standards, a more direct approach would seem to be to look for a parallel system in which the various sub-processes competed directly to achieve a true identifying response. One such sub-process is of course embodied in the accumulator model of three-category judgment outlined in Chapter 4. If the two-category modules of the parallel elimination process are replaced by three-category modules, then we have the basis for a system in which a given variable may be directly identified with a stored standard. All that is necessary is to allow only an outcome of the form "$V = S_n$" to give rise to an *overt* response. Decision outcomes of the form "$V < S_n$" or "$V > S_n$" may still occur, but must be assumed to remain *covert* and, unlike the original three-category situation, cannot be allowed to interrupt the build-up of evidence in the associated "equals" accumulator.

A flow diagram of this model is shown in Fig. 102. As in the parallel elimination process, it is assumed that standards $S_1, S_2, \ldots S_n$ are stored corresponding to each of the alternative stimuli $V_1, V_2, \ldots V_n$, and that each standard and each variable varies randomly about a mean $\bar{S}$ or $\bar{V}$, with standard deviations $\sigma_s$ and $\sigma_v$ respectively. Similarly, the distributions of $V$ and $S$ are assumed to be normal and uncorrelated. Again, as in the parallel elimination process, the momentary value of the presented variable $V$ is compared simultaneously with the momentary values of each of the stored standards. The results of each comparison are totalled in the "greater", "lesser" and "equal" stores of the associated three-category module. Comparisons are continued at a steady rate, each comparison taking the same time, until the value in the intermediate store of any module reaches its criterion level, whereupon an overt identification response of the form "$V = S$" is triggered and the process is complete.

If, by chance, two or more modules happen to reach their criterion levels at the same time, then an identification response is chosen at random from among these modules. Whenever any module emits an identification response, all intermediate stores are cleared and the system is ready to be presented with a new variable. Should the criterion for a "greater" or "lesser" covert response be reached before that for an overt "equals" response, then the totals in the "greater" and "lesser' stores for that module are cleared. However, the total in the associated intermediate store is left untouched, so that accumulation of evidence for the identification response continues uninterrupted by any "asides" on the part of the system.

It would be possible to streamline the model by omitting the "greater" and "lesser" stores altogether and depriving the model of the capacity for making covert responses. Against this, it was felt that the ability to make asides was a useful property, which meant that the model need not be limited to the response repertoire originally assigned to it. For example, where an overt identification response has been preceded by one (or more)

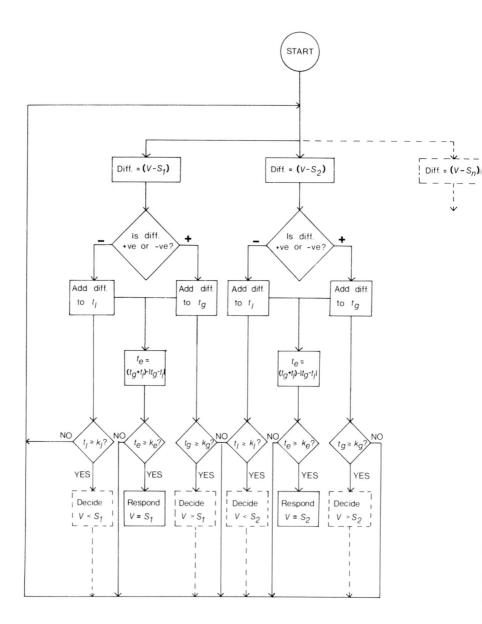

Fig. 102. Flow diagram of a non-adaptive parallel eventuation process, embodying an array of three-category decision modules. The broken lines in the lower section indicate covert decisions, which do not give rise to an observable identification response.

"greater" or "lesser" covert responses, it would be possible for the system to adjust the value of the identified standard in the direction indicated by the covert response(s). Thus, in principle, the model could be endowed with a set of initial standards, which it might then use to rate a new set of stimuli falling within an entirely different range. At the cost of not simplifying the statement of the model, it seemed worthwhile to preserve this useful potential for development.

The proposed parallel "eventuation" model contrasts with a parallel elimination or death process, in which the variable of interest can be thought of as analogous to the average time for a population of individuals with varying lifetimes to die out completely (cf. Feller, 1950). Analogies for the proposed model might be sought in certain birth processes, or, alternatively, the system could be viewed as a race between $n$ parallel and independent identification sub-processes. However, because it is not necessary that all the sub-processes should be racing towards the same finishing line (i.e. criterion), the label "eventuation" has been chosen. The term contrasts with the literal sense of "elimination", and is intended to characterize a parallel set of independent sub-processes which continue to build up in an uninterrupted manner until some threshold is exceeded in one of them, whereupon a simple identification response "eventuates".

## Difficulties with the Static Version of a Parallel Eventuation Process

One ironic consequence of postulating an eventuation rather than an elimination process is that it becomes necessary, rather than simply desirable, to endow the system with adaptive properties. The reason emerges when we consider the effects of increasing the number of stimulus alternatives presented within a given range.

These effects have been studied by means of a computer simulation of the eventuation process outlined in Fig. 102. Three levels of choice were examined, namely $n = 3$, 4 and 10, with mean values of variables and standards being arranged in equal steps between 5 and 9 units. The standard deviation assigned to both variables and standards was 1·5, and the criteria $k_g$, $k_l$ and $k_e$ associated with each of the $n$ three-category modules were in all cases set to 5. A total of 2000 trials was conducted at each of the three values of $n$. The main results are presented in Fig. 103.

Figures 103a and 103b show effects on the pattern of errors and response times of increasing the number of alternatives within a given range of stimulus values from 3, through 4, up to 8 choices. As evident in Fig. 103a, when the number of choices goes up, so does the number of errors at each

## (a) RESPONSE ACCURACY

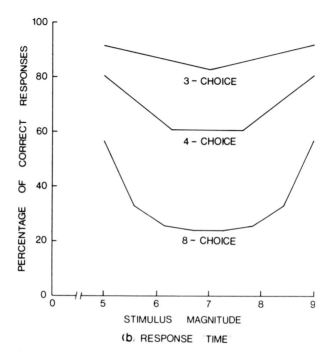

## (b) RESPONSE TIME

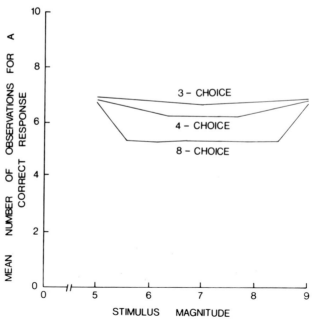

point in the serial position curve. However, when we turn to look at the pattern of response times in Fig. 103b we make two disconcerting discoveries. In the first place, we find that times for the intermediate positions are actually shorter than those for the two ends, which is the direct opposite of the empirical findings of Murdock (1960), John (1969), Welford (1971) and Smith (1977). In the second place, and even more alarming, we find that the times for 8 choices are faster than those for 4, which in turn are faster than those for 3. Again, this appears to be in direct conflict with all the known experimental findings in the area. "How", we might ask, "could we have gone so wrong?"

The reason for this strange behaviour is perhaps most easily conveyed by an analogy. If we consider each sub-process or module as a runner in a race, then we can regard the rate of accumulation of evidence as analogous to the speed of running, and the attainment of a criterion amount of evidence as equivalent to crossing the finishing line. (For the sake of simplicity we may suppose that criterion levels are the same for all modules). Given the usual random fluctuation in the quality of the evidence collected, then, we should expect that on some occasions a particular module will run a little faster than on others, and sometimes a little slower. In general, however, the theoretically correct module will usually be the one which is accumulating most evidence, and this is analogous to the fastest runner or "favourite".

Now, if the favourite is pitted against poor competition he will tend to win the race even when his performance is quite slow. On the other hand, if he is run against stiff competition, then he will be likely to win fewer races and to win those only when his performance is very fast. Therefore, if we were to calculate the average time taken by the favourite to win on occasions when the competition has been poor we should expect this to be lower than when the competition was fierce.

The situation is exactly analogous for the "correct" module in the parallel eventuation process if we consider "poor competition" as designating rival alternatives which are quite different from the standard associated with the correct module, and so generate evidence at a slower rate, while "close competition" denotes a situation in which the possible alternatives are similar to the correct standard, and hence generate evidence at similar rates. As more stimulus alternatives are added within a fixed range, adjacent alternatives are packed more closely together, and competition against the

Fig. 103. The pattern of (a) response accuracy and (b) response time obtained in computer simulation of the non-adaptive parallel eventuation process. The individual curves present data for different degrees of choice, with the values of the variables and the standards extending in all cases from 5 up to $9\sigma_{(V-S)}$ units and separated by equal intervals.

correct module is intensified. When the degree of choice is increased, therefore, we should expect the correct module to win less often but in a faster time on average.

Similar effects would be expected in other situations where the relative discriminability of the correct module is reduced, as happens, for example, near the middle of a series. The effects appear to be a necessary property of any simple system of parallel sub-processes which are all racing towards some finishing line, with "victory" being accorded to the first sub-process to cross it. On the face of it, these characteristics would seem to rule out the possibility that the mechanism underlying choice-reaction or absolute judgment might take the form of a simple, parallel eventuation process.

## An Adaptive Parallel Eventuation Process

One possible remedy, which is followed by Smith (1977), is to suppose that the sub-processes do not proceed strictly in parallel, but are inched along by a translation process which considers each stimulus possibility in turn, taking a longer time to convert into a suitable form for response those with higher amounts of excitation. A similar set of assumptions could also be grafted onto the present eventuation model. However, the impressive economy of a model constituted solely from a modular mechanism of simple judgment would be destroyed by the addition of a monitoring or translating system, with its associated assumptions concerning the order of servicing sub-processes, the time required for servicing, the nature of the transfer function governing the translation from stimulus to response, together with possible temporal changes over a series of iterations. Besides this, the assumption that high levels of stimulus excitation take longer to convert into a form suitable for triggering a response seems counter-intuitive, if not biologically hazardous. Further, in attempting to make the process adaptive, it would seem more natural to concentrate on the flexible iteration process rather than on the relatively autonomous sub-processes. However, by discarding the modular approach prefigured in Chapters 5 and 7, the parallel eventuation model would lose any integrity it might otherwise claim to possess.

Suppose, for the moment, that we ignore the embarrassing propensities of the parallel eventuation model as it stands and consider the problem of making it adaptive. In the interests of parsimony we should expect it to operate in a similar way to the simple adaptive processes outlined in Chapter 7, and to seek to maintain a certain target level of confidence in each response. It is obvious that, as in the adaptive three-category model, the evidence for each of the possible identification responses is given directly by the quantities registered in each of the corresponding intermediate accumulators. It seems equally clear, however, that the relevant measure of confidence in a given identification response cannot be provided by a comparison of the evidence total for the overt response with those for any covert "greater" or "lesser" response, but should be determined by some difference between the total for the overt response in question and the total(s) for the other overt response alternative(s). In other words, we are concerned with assessing the evidence for the chosen response relative to that for some (or all) of the other permissible alternatives, rather than with the question of whether some other form of response, not currently allowed, might have been more appropriate.

There are a number of ways of assessing the confidence in one out of a number of responses (greater than two). For example, we could suppose, by analogy with Crossman's (1955) and Murdock's (1960) expressions for discriminability, that confidence might be determined by the average of all the differences between the evidence total for the chosen response and the totals for each of the other possible responses. An alternative approach, also adumbrated by Crossman, is to suppose that confidence is determined by the average difference between the evidence total for the chosen response and those of its two nearest neighbours in the array of standards. In the development of the model which follows, this second approach was chosen, partly because it is arithmetically simple, partly because it involves the same kind of calculation as for the original three-category process and partly because it is more sensitive to any increase in $n$ than a simple arithmetic mean of all the differences.

On the assumption that the system is geared to maintaining the average difference in evidence between the winning response and that of its two nearest neighbours, we can make the parallel eventuation process adaptive simply by attaching control accumulators to the response outputs of each of the intermediate sub-processes (Fig. 104). These control accumulators operate in exactly the same way as the ones outlined in Chapter 7. For present purposes, the subsidiary parameters governing the intermittency and extent of their adjustments (i.e. the level of the criterion $K$, and the value of the coefficient of adjustment $x$) may be assumed to be fixed at the same values for all modules. Irrespective of the values of these parameters, the general properties of the model survive, provided, of course, that we avoid limiting values, such as $K = 0$, or $x = 0$, where the model ceases entirely to make adaptive corrections.

If we wish, we can also attach control accumulators to each of the covert "greater" and "lesser" responses, so that adjustments may be made to $k_g$ and $k_l$, depending upon an assessment of confidence in one covert response

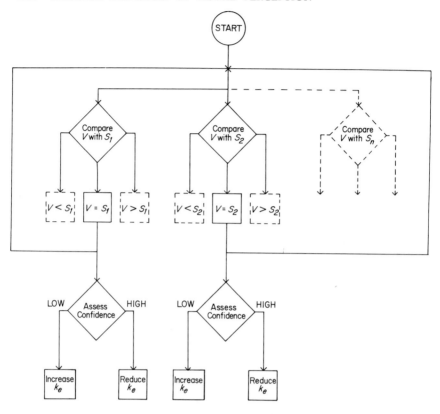

Fig. 104. Flow diagram of the sequence of operations envisaged in an adaptive parallel eventuation process. Primary decisions are taken by an array of three-category modules (represented by lozenge-shaped blocks in the upper half of the figure). Overt responses rising from these primary decisions are then evaluated by secondary two-category accumulator processes responsible for adjusting the intermediate criterion $k_e$ in the corresponding primary module. Decision outcomes of the form "$V > S$" or "$V < S$" are regarded as giving rise to covert responses.

with respect to the other two responses that might be issued by that module, as outlined for the adaptive model of three-category judgment in Chapter 7. All that happens as a result is that the criteria for the extreme (covert) responses within that module tend to keep in line with the criterion for the intermediate (overt) response, and ride up or down with it. Since the overt response remains unaffected by this, no change in the performance of the model is observable. However, the model retains a useful capacity for making internal "asides" with a stable degree of confidence. As pointed out above, this endows the system with the potential to generate a fresh set of standards or rating responses if necessary.

## Some Basic Properties of an Adaptive Parallel Eventuation Process

As with the parallel elimination and the static eventuation models, the main properties of the adaptive parallel eventuation model have been studied by means of computer simulation. The general outlines of each simulation conform to the sequence of operations portrayed in Fig. 104. In all the adaptive simulations discussed in the rest of this chapter the level of $K$ in all control accumulators was set at 4, while the coefficient of adjustment $x$ was set to a moderate figure of $0 \cdot 75$. The parameters of importance are thus the number $n$ of stimulus-response alternatives, the values $\bar{V}_1, \bar{V}_2, \ldots, \bar{V}_n$, and $\bar{S}_1, \bar{S}_2, \ldots, \bar{S}_n$, of the variables and the standards, the standard deviations $\sigma_V$ and $\sigma_S$ associated with the variables and the standards and the target level of confidence $C_E$ set for the intermediate (identification) responses. For the sake of brevity these are given in the legends attached to the figures presenting the results for each of the main effects studied. These were: (1) the effects of varying $n$; (2) the times for correct and incorrect responses; (3) serial position effects; and (4) effects of preparation. I shall deal with each of these in turn.

### Effects of Varying the Number of Stimulus-Response Alternatives

#### Percentage of Errors and $n$

Figure 105a shows that the percentage of errors made by the simulated process (averaged over all stimulus-response alternatives) increases as a negatively accelerated function of the number of alternatives $n$, with the percentage for any given value of $n$ rising as a direct function of the noise $\sigma_S$ associated with the standards. As is only to be expected, Fig. 105b shows that both absolute values and—to a small degree—the rate of increase are reduced when a higher target level of confidence is employed. To this extent, therefore, the behaviour of the adaptive parallel eventuation model resembles that of the non-adaptive version. This behaviour coincides with the general finding that errors increase as a function of degree of choice, and also corresponds to what we should intuitively expect of a human observer.

#### Mean Number of Observations and $n$

When we come to consider the response times taken by the simulated process, it turns out that the imposed requirement of adaptability has

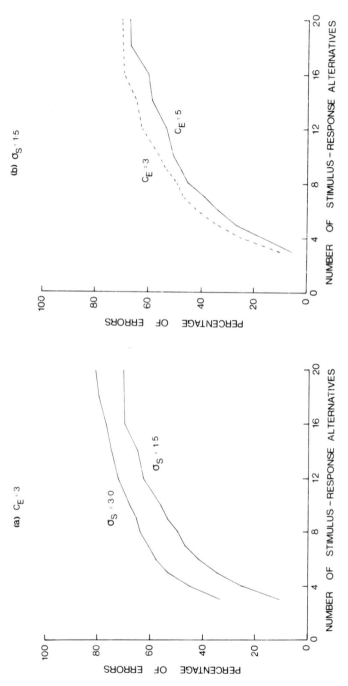

**(a)** $C_E = 3$

NUMBER OF STIMULUS – RESPONSE ALTERNATIVES

PERCENTAGE OF ERRORS

$\sigma_S = 3.0$

$\sigma_S = 1.5$

**(b)** $\sigma_S = 1.5$

NUMBER OF STIMULUS – RESPONSE ALTERNATIVES

PERCENTAGE OF ERRORS

$C_E = 3$

$C_E = 5$

Fig. 105. The percentage of errors made by the simulated adaptive parallel eventuation process for (a) two values of $\sigma_S$ and (b) two values of $C_E$. The value of $\sigma_V$ was in all cases set to 1.

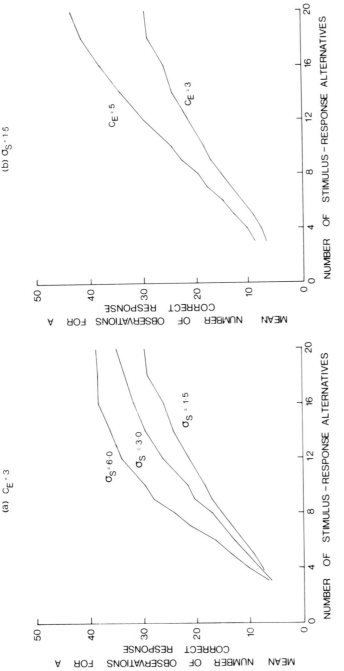

(a) $C_E = 3$

(b) $\sigma_S = 1.5$

Fig. 106. The pattern of response times obtained in simulation of the adaptive parallel eventuation process. Figure 106a shows the functions obtained for different values of $\sigma_S$, when $C_E$ is held constant. Figure 106b shows the functions obtained with different values of $C_E$ when $\sigma_S$ is held constant. As in Fig. 105, the value of $\sigma_V$ was in all cases set to 1 and the coefficient of adjustment was 0·75.

produced a gratifying transformation in the pattern which characterized the non-adaptive version. For example, Fig. 106a shows that the mean number of observations required by the adaptive process to make a correct response now increases as a function of $n$. The function appears slightly S-shaped, particularly when the standards are assigned a low degree of variability. A trace of this remains on the logarithmic plot shown in Fig. 107 and, indeed, also appears to characterize the empirical data of Hick (1952b) and Merkel (1885), as plotted by Laming (1966).

## Effects of Practice and Familiarity

Again in contrast to the non-adaptive version, Fig. 106a shows that the effect of increasing the variability of the stored standards $\sigma_S$ is to increase the mean number of observations required for a correct response. If we suppose that practice and familiarity serve to reduce the variability of the stored standards, then the decreased steepness of the response time curves as $\sigma_S$ is

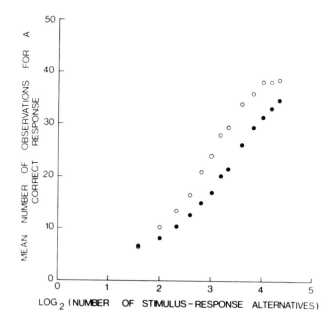

Fig. 107. The pattern of response times obtained in simulation of the adaptive parallel eventuation process, plotted against the logarithm (to the base 2) of the number of stimulus-response alternatives. Open circles denote data when $\sigma_S = 6$ and filled circles those when $\sigma_S = 3$. As in Figs 105 and 106, the value of $\sigma_V$ was in all cases set to 1 and the coefficient of adjustment was 0·75. In the case of both curves the value of $C_E$ was set to 3.

reduced is in line with Teichner and Krebs' generalization (1974) that the rate of rise in time with $n$ is a function of practice. Although it seems unlikely that practice would affect the value of $\sigma_V$, it seems reasonable to suppose that the value of $\sigma_S$ might be sufficiently reduced by practice for the predicted rate of rise in time with $n$ to approach zero. Finally, as we should expect, on the basis of a trade-off function between speed and accuracy, the rate of increase in response time is accelerated with higher target levels of confidence, as illustrated in Fig. 106b.

The differences in behaviour between the adaptive and the non-adaptive models are not difficult to understand. As in the non-adaptive case, when more stimulus alternatives are added within the same range, the distributions of the momentary values of the stored standards overlap to a greater extent and the likelihood of error is increased. As the discriminability of alternative stimuli is decreased thereby, so also is the average confidence with which an identification is made. The adaptive version attempts to counteract this by increasing criterion levels, but, although this slows down the rate of increase in errors, it does not arrest it entirely. In turn, more observations are required to satisfy the heightened criteria. Using this approach, therefore, the increase in response time observed as a function of $n$ represents the results of an adaptation designed to preserve the level of confidence with which responses are made as discriminability is decreased. Thus the adaptive aspect of the process is not an added refinement, but an integral part of its design without which it would continue to discriminate, but with a degree of caution curiously unrelated to the demands of the task.

## Times for Correct and Incorrect Responses

In Chapter 7, a number of experiments were encountered in which times for incorrect responses were shorter than those for correct. It was recognized that such a finding was inconsistent with the non-adaptive version of the accumulator model of two-category judgment, though not with the adaptive version outlined in that chapter. At the same time, some reservations were attached to the interpretation of these experiments. All of them, for example, involved the identification of a presented variable as being one of a number of possible alternatives and are thus more relevant perhaps to the present discussion. While some further strictures were mentioned in Chapter 7, such as the presence of constraints in the stimulus sequence of Weaver (1942), and the evidence of temporary fluctuations and bias in criterion values, these lose their force in the context of the adaptive multi-choice model, in which adaptation is highly likely to produce evidence of some sequential effects.

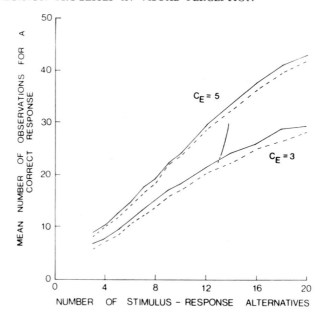

Fig. 108. The pattern of times for correct and incorrect responses obtained in simulation of the adaptive parallel eventuation model, with correct responses denoted by solid and incorrect by broken lines. The value of $\sigma_V$ was set to 1·2, $\sigma_S$ to 1·5 and the coefficient of adjustment to 0·75. The value of $C_E$ for the upper pair of curves was 5, while that for the lower pair was 3.

In agreement with the findings of these experiments, Fig. 108 shows clearly that the mean number of observations taken by the simulated multi-choice model is smaller for incorrect than for correct responses, irrespective of the degree of choice and, as far as can be judged, from the level of target confidence. The behaviour of the model is also echoed by Hale's finding (1968) that times for errors were shorter than those for correct responses irrespective of the degree of choice involved, as well as by his conclusion (1969) that this relation held, whether instructions emphasized speed or accuracy.

Several factors appear to contribute to the predicted (and observed) difference in the relation between times for correct and incorrect responses between the two-category and the multi-choice situations. In the former case, the incorrect accumulator will be less likely to receive an input than the correct, and the magnitude of the input it does receive is likely to be smaller. In addition, the rate of accumulation in the incorrect accumulator will be further slowed by the fact that it receives an input only when the sign of the inspected difference is in its favour. Errors will therefore take longer than correct responses, except when criterion levels for the two alternative responses are so low that only one or two observations are required to reach either level, or when temporary biasses or fluctuations in criterion levels result in most of the errors being made in a short time at low criterion values. Undoubtedly, these last factors may also operate in the case of the adaptive multi-choice model. However, one further important factor in speeding up the relative times for errors would appear to be the fact that, unlike the two-category version, evidence in the multi-choice model continues to accumulate simultaneously in all identifying accumulators, whether correct or incorrect.

## Serial Position Effects

When we turn to look at effects of the serial position of a stimulus we again find a dramatic improvement in the correspondence between the trends in empirical data and the behaviour of the proposed adaptive model. Certain features of the model emerge as important determinants of a subtly inter-dependent pattern of changes in the theoretical counterparts of response time, accuracy and confidence, in which an increase in the number of stimulus-response alternatives may produce quite complex serial position effects. In order to gain some insight into these interactions, it is useful to begin by considering the pattern of confidence measures predicted by the *non-adaptive* version of the model, since it is the interplay between actual and target confidence and the discriminability of the several alternatives which governs the eventual pattern of errors and response times.

### The Pattern of Theoretical Measures

*Confidence.* Figure 109a shows the unscaled confidence measures generated for different numbers of stimulus-response alternatives $(n)$ by a computer simulation of the adaptive multi-choice model in which the coefficient of adjustment $x$ has been set to zero, and where the value of $k_e$ is constant and the same for all alternatives. It can be seen that the pattern changes as the number of alternatives is increased. The simplest patterns are those for three and four alternatives, where correct responses to the two end stimuli are made with high confidence, while those to the middle stimulus achieve only a low level of confidence. These resemble the U-shaped curves predicted for the proportion of correct responses by Crossman (1955) and Murdock (1960). However, it is clear from Fig. 109a that the behaviour of the theoretical process is not restricted to such a simple pattern: increases in $n$ beyond 5 result in the distinct formation of additional minima at the two "penultimate" positions immediately adjacent to either end.

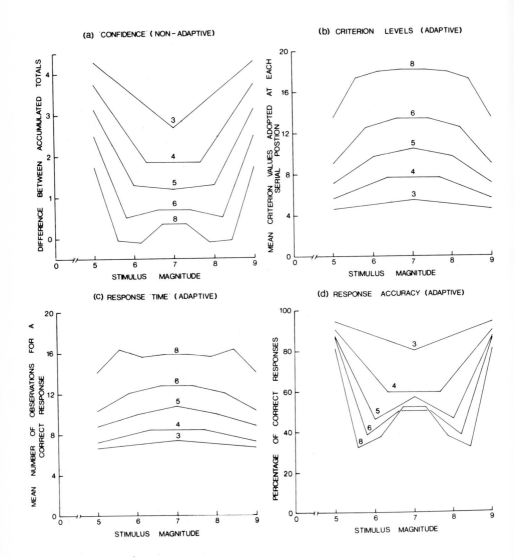

Fig. 109. Serial position effects obtained in simulation of the parallel eventuation process for different degrees of choice, as indicated for individual curves. Figure 109a shows the pattern of confidence measures when the process operates in non-adaptive mode. Figures 109b, 109c and 109d show the values adopted by the identification criteria, the pattern of response times and the percentage of correct responses respectively, when the process operates in adaptive mode. In all cases $\sigma_V = 1\cdot0$, $\sigma_S = 1\cdot5$, $C_E = 3$. In the case of Figs 109b, 109c and 109d, the coefficient of adjustment was $0\cdot75$.

This is an intriguing—and unexpected—result. However, it is not too difficult to understand when we contemplate the favoured niche occupied by the end stimuli. According to the adaptive model, confidence in a correct response to a stimulus at the end of an array will be relatively high, since its second nearest neighbour is (in this case) twice as far as the closest, and the average difference in evidence will be enhanced in consequence. On the other hand, predicted confidence in correct responses to penultimate stimuli can be expected to drop sharply, because the evidence totals in both adjacent modules will, on average, be quite similar. On the non-adaptive model, therefore, the major effect of increasing $n$ is to lower confidence in correct responses to all stimuli, while bringing the two secondary minima into prominence as values for the penultimate stimuli are shifted towards the limits of the array.

The behaviour exhibited by the adaptive process may thus be construed as the resultant effect of an interplay between stimulus discriminability and serial position on the one hand, and on the other, the adaptive shifts in criterion levels made by the model in response to the uneven pattern of confidence measures that these factors tend to generate. Before looking at the empirical evidence, we shall go on to consider each of the other main effects, namely, those on criterion values, on the mean number of observations and on the pattern of response frequencies.

*Criterion values.*    Figure 109b shows the average criterion values set by the *adaptive* process in attempting to maintain a certain target level of confidence in the identification of similar sets of stimuli. Clearly, the lowest values are those for responses which would otherwise be made with greatest confidence, namely, correct identifications of the end stimuli. Conversely, high criterion values are set for those responses which would otherwise be made with relatively low confidence, namely, the penultimate and all intermediate stimuli. A little surprisingly, perhaps, criteria for the penultimate stimuli in Fig. 109b do not appear to be set appreciably higher than those of the middle stimuli. Although much more work remains to be carried out in order to tease out the relations between the target level of confidence adopted, the noise associated with variables and standards, and the number and spacing of stimuli, what does seem clear at this stage is that most of the curves exhibit clear inflexion points at or near the penultimate stimulus positions.

*Mean number of observations.*    Meanwhile, Fig. 109c shows the mean number of observations taken by the simulated adaptive model to correctly identify varying numbers of stimuli ranging from $n = 3$ up to $n = 8$. As can be seen from the figure, an immediate consequence of the low criteria adopted for the end responses is that the correct identification of end stimuli requires fewer observations than that of intermediate stimuli. At least for 3- and 4-choice tasks, it follows that the times taken to identify the middle stimuli correctly are longer. For higher values of $n$, however, no single characterization seems to fit all curves; various combinations of target confidence, noise levels, values of $n$ and stimulus spacings produce three main varieties of curve, namely, inverted U-shaped, M-shaped and even functions with triple peaks.

*Response frequency.*   Although the precise conditions under which these configurations emerge remain unclear, the pattern of response frequencies produced by the simulated model (Fig. 109d) gives strong grounds for exploring the question further. Since the identification criteria for the end modules are low, these responses are made quickly and there is little chance of their being forestalled by a rival response. In contrast, since the penultimate responses have high criterion levels, they require more observations than the end ones and tend to be anticipated (often wrongly) by their faster neighbours. The result, as can be seen in Fig. 109d, is that when $n > 5$, the percentage of penultimate stimuli correctly identified is lower than for any other position in the array. At the same time, when $n > 5$, the disadvantage of close proximity to the very fast end modules diminishes as responses further from the ends are considered, so that the proportion of stimuli correctly identified rises towards the middle. The net result is that for values of $n > 5$, the percentage of stimuli correctly identified is highest at the ends and is followed by those near the middle, while the lowest percentage of correct identifications occurs for stimuli just adjacent to the ends.

## Comparison with Empirical Evidence

*Response frequency.*   While there is not a great wealth of empirical data on serial position effects in identification, what there is offers some support for the proposed adaptive model. For example, the tendency for end stimuli to be correctly identified more often than those in intermediate positions is analogous to the serial position effects in studies of absolute judgement reviewed by Murdock (1960). Of more direct relevance, John (1969) found that, when stimuli arrayed from left to right were identified by numbers from 1 to 10 in order, then the two end stimuli were always identified correctly and errors were associated only with the intermediate stimuli. Even more clearly, in a recent experiment on choice-reaction, in which observers were provided with a reference point in the middle of the stimulus array, Welford (1971) obtained a pattern of correct responses which resembled that of the 8-choice situation depicted in Fig. 109d.

Welford's results are shown in Fig. 110a. Since the middle stimuli were just about as well differentiated from each other in the absence of a centre line as in the presence of one, Welford concluded that a model based on discriminability was not supported. While Welford's conclusion may apply to the non-adaptive version of the present model, however, it appears that the adaptive version gives a good account of his data. Moreover, the model is consistent with Welford's observation that the insertion of external reference points had little effect on the discriminability of the stimuli. The outstanding advantage of the adaptive model is that the superior accuracy of the end response, and the greater accuracy of the middle, relative to the penultimate responses, follow as natural consequences of the mechanism and require no special additional explanation.

*Response times.*    Turning to the pattern of response times, we again find a correspondence between the behaviour of the theoretical process and that of empirical data. For example, Fig. 110b shows data obtained by Welford (1971) in an 8-choice experiment. The shortest response times are those to the end stimuli, as generally predicted by the model when the variability associated with variables and standard is not too severe. (Evidence that this condition also held in Welford's experiment is provided by the low error rate of about 4% and the fast response times, which varied between 499 and 621 ms.) Conversely, the longest times observed by Welford are for responses to penultimate stimuli.

Again this finding appears to be consistent with the proposed model, though within what limits is not yet clear. Current simulation work suggests that well-spaced stimuli, combined with low target levels of confidence, may be even more conducive to producing the effects observed by Welford than the parameters exemplified in Fig. 109c. At any rate, very similar patterns have been observed by Welford (1971) for a variety of 8-choice experiments with and without central reference lines. Similar empirical patterns have also been reported by Smith (1977) and by Nettelbeck and Brewer (1976). It seems likely that further simulation studies will show these patterns to be consistent, at least in outline, with those produced by the adaptive process. If so, the parsimony in accounting for these effects without additional assumptions must surely be counted as a particular advantage of the proposed model.

## Effects of Preparation

### Empirical Evidence

A number of experiments, particularly those of Welford (1971, 1973, 1975), have studied the effects of instructing observers to concentrate attention on

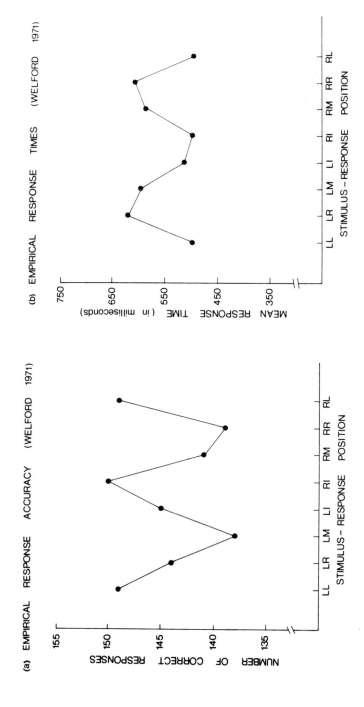

Fig. 110. Data from an 8-choice experiment by Welford (1971) plotted against stimulus-response (finger) position (i.e. left little, left ring, left middle, left index, right index, etc.). Figure 110a shows the total number of correct responses in experiment 1, while Fig. 110b shows the mean time taken to make a correct response.

a particular stimulus, or to be especially ready to respond when any one of a subset of stimuli appeared. Figure 111a, for example, shows the times for correct responses obtained by Welford (1973) in an 8-choice task in which observers were instructed to concentrate on the fifth or sixth stimulus in a horizontal array of neon lamps, with data for comparison from a condition in which no differentiating instructions were given. As can be seen from the figure, it was found that times for the stimulus concentrated on were considerably reduced, as were, to a lesser extent, times for responses to adjacent stimuli in the same half of the array. Conversely, times for responses in the other half of the array from the attended stimulus were increased, although times for responses to the very end stimuli remained virtually unchanged.

Analogous results were obtained by Welford (1973) in a similar experiment in which observers were instructed to concentrate either upon the left or upon the right of the stimulus array. The times obtained in this experiment are shown in Fig. 111b, along with those obtained in a control condition, in which no special attention was required. Again, responses to stimuli concentrated on are lower, while those to non-attended stimuli in the other half of the array are higher, than when no special instructions for differential preparation were given.

## The Pattern of Theoretical Measures: Preparation for One Response

At first sight, these results suggest that there may be a trade-off between the times taken for the correct identification of the attended stimulus (and perhaps its near neighbours) and those for the more distant, non-attended stimuli. Such a trade-off is indeed implied by most theoretical accounts embodying the notions of "preparation", "attention", "concentration", or "preparatory set". For example, according to the serial dichotomization model advocated by Welford, inspection may be "biased towards the attended light, which is reacted to faster, and away from others, which are reacted to more slowly, so that usually overall reaction time is little changed" (1968, p. 685). Similarly, in a model which assumes that an observer is either prepared for a stimulus or is unprepared, Falmagne (1965) has postulated that preparation is associated with short response times, and lack of preparation with long times. As a result, instructions to be ready to respond to a specific stimulus may be thought of as concentrating an otherwise random distribution of preparation, with the consequence that times for the prepared response will be lower, while those for the unprepared response will turn out to be higher than when no special instructions are given. In general, according to Audley, "any theory that gives a central role to expectancy, or a related concept, will predict that there will be a simple relation, often linear, between reaction times to the

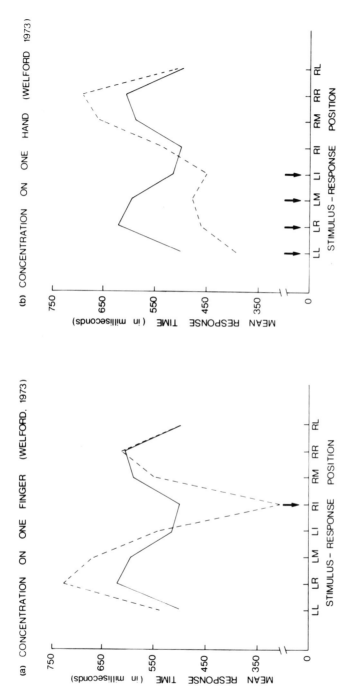

Fig. 111. Data from 8-choice studies by Welford (1973), plotted against stimulus-response (finger) position (i.e. left little, left ring, ... right ring, right little). The solid line in both figures represents the pattern of mean response times (already presented in Fig. 110b) when no special concentration was required. The broken line in Fig. 11a shows data when observers were asked to concentrate attention on the stimulus light corresponding to the right index finger (arrowed). In Fig. 111b the broken line shows results when observers were required to concentrate attention of the stimulus lights corresponding to the fingers of the left hand. (arrowed).

alternative stimuli, as these times are changed by the prior sequence of stimuli the subject has experienced" (1973, p. 516).

While the present adaptive model has a certain superficial resemblance to the preparation model of Falmagne, insofar as the response mechanism corresponding to each stimulus is regarded as an independent process, there are a number of important differences in conception and prediction. Perhaps the most obvious difference is that, in the adaptive model, the state of preparation for a response is not an all-or-none affair, but is continuously variable: using this approach an observer is thought of as being "more or less" prepared for any stimulus. A second, less obvious, difference is that the present approach enables us to distinguish between a general state of "fundamental" preparation (denoted by the value of target confidence set for a particular response) and a more "immediate" state of preparation (represented by the value of $k_e$ set for a particular trial or averaged over a series of trials). While the fundamental state of preparation may remain unchanged over a long series of trials, the immediate state of preparation (i.e. the value of $k_e$) will constitute the resultant between target confidence and such factors as the discriminability, probability and sequence of the various alternative stimuli. As such, its value may vary considerably within a series of trials, or between one series and another.

*Criterion values.*     One consequence of these differences is that, when the fundamental state of preparation for a particular response is intensified (by lowering the appropriate target level of confidence), then the immediate states of preparation for all of the response alternatives (i.e. the values of $k_e$) are free to redistribute themselves in quite a complex fashion. Figure 112a, for example, shows a typical pattern of criterion levels set for each of 8 responses in a simulation of the adaptive model of choice-reaction when the target level for one response is reduced below that for the others. As is to be expected, the criterion for the prepared response is decreased by an amount proportional to the reduction in the target level of confidence. However, the behaviour of the other criteria is not so simple. If the reduction in target confidence is relatively small, then criterion levels for adjacent responses may be slightly raised. However, as target confidence for the prepared response is lowered further, then criterion levels for immediately adjacent responses are also "pulled down", followed by those for more distant responses in the array. From the graphs, it appears that criteria for responses in the same half of the array as the prepared response are more sensitive to this downward attraction, while end stimuli (which in this case are also those farthest away) remain almost unaffected.

The interplay of factors underlying this pattern is exceedingly complex, and includes changes in the likelihood that each response will be made

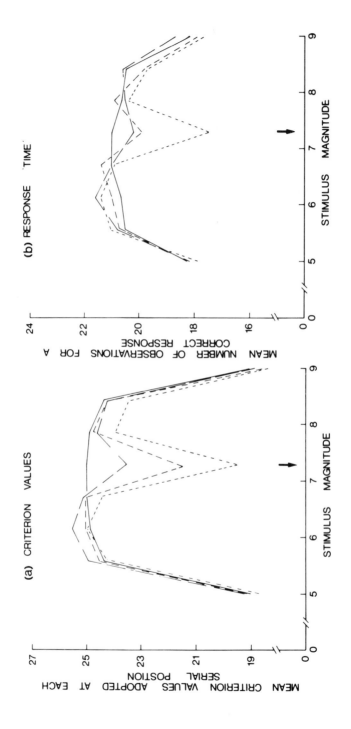

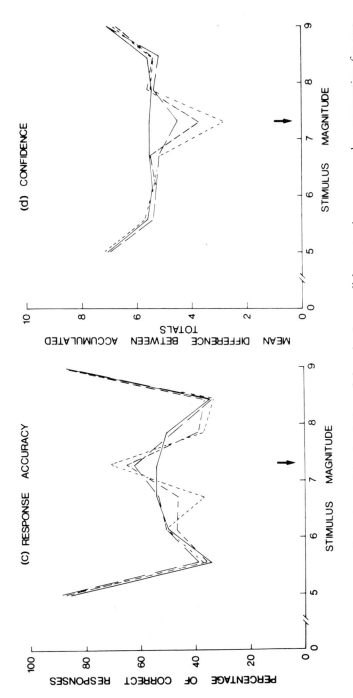

Fig. 112. Serial position effects obtained in simulation of the adaptive parallel eventuation process when preparation for one response (arrowed) is intensified by progressively lowering the target level of confidence for the identifying criterion from 5, through 4 and 3, down to 2, as indicated by lines composed of progressively shorter dashes. Figure 112a shows the pattern of values adopted by the identifying criteria, Fig. 112b that of response time, Fig. 112c that of response accuracy, while Fig. 112d shows the values of the hypothetical basis for confidence in each identifying response.

incorrectly in place of other alternatives, as well as changes in the proportion of slow, unconfident responses that are forestalled by the prepared response. While these factors could be teased out, their explication would be lengthy and is not essential to our immediate aim of establishing the face validity of the model within the context of choice-reaction. Perhaps, for the present, a useful shorthand conceptualization might be provided by the observation that the subtle pattern of inter-relationships between a set of parallel, independent modules, all operating in competition while attempting to maintain similar standards, is reminiscent of the behaviour of a miniature society: a slight drop in the norm adopted by one member provokes a defensive heightening of those of his neighbours, while a larger fall encourages a general relaxation of standards overall.

*Mean number of observations.* Given the distribution of criterion values, the mean numbers of observations taken by the simulated model follow a reassuringly similar pattern, though close inspection reveals some minor, but intriguing, differences. As can be seen from Fig. 112b, times for the prepared response are predictably lowered as target confidence for that response is reduced. Meanwhile, times tend to be lowered for adjacent responses in the same half of the array, but to be increased for those in the other half, with times for the end responses remaining virtually unchanged. As can be judged from Fig. 111a, there is a striking resemblance between the features of the theoretical times and those of the empirical data obtained by Welford (1973) in a similar task.

*Response frequency.* Figure 112c completes the picture of the predicted effects of intensifying preparation for a particular response. According to the model, the percentage of attended stimuli correctly identified increases as a function of the degree of preparation. Conversely, the proportions of correct responses achieved by the immediately adjacent modules decline. Both effects are clearly due to the prepared module "stealing a march" on its slower neighbours, even though the response is often incorrect.

## The Pattern of Theoretical Measures: Preparation for Several Responses

Simulations of the adaptive model have also been carried out to explore the effects of intensifying preparation for more than one response, as in the experiment by Welford (1973), the results of which are reproduced in Fig. 111b. Figures 113a and 113b, for example, illustrate the behaviour of the theoretical process when target confidence is lowered for all responses in one half of the array. The figures show that criterion values are generally reduced, but particularly so for the prepared half of the response array. When the reduction in target confidence is relatively low, then response times for the non-prepared half are increased, while those for the prepared half are predictably shortened. With larger reductions in target confidence, however, the times for non-prepared responses may not increase, and may even fall below those for the condition in which no special preparation is postulated. Meanwhile, the proportion of correct responses declines overall, particularly for certain serial positions, such as the second and fifth from the left.

Again, these predictions are strikingly similar in outline to those obtained in the 8-choice task by Welford (1973). This correspondence, together with the good account offered by the model of Welford's data (1971) for concentration on a particular response, provide eloquent testimony of the ability of the model to encompass the detailed changes in measures of response time and frequency at different serial positions that result from unequal preparation. At the same time, the theoretical possibility that the shorter times for prepared responses may not be compensated by lengthened times for non-prepared responses distinguishes the present model from that of Falmagne (1965). This gives the proposed adaptive process the advantage of being able to incorporate Welford's (1971) finding that times for end responses were not appreciably modified when observers were instructed to concentrate on a stimulus near the middle of the intervening range. In addition, only the adaptive model is consistent with Welford's finding (1971) that, although times for the prepared response in a 4-choice task were reduced, those for the other responses remained virtually unchanged.

As it stands, therefore, the proposed adaptive parallel eventuation model appears to offer a very accurate and comprehensive account of the main findings of experiments on choice-reaction, and would seem to be nicely consistent with Thomas' conclusion (1973) that expectancy is related both to the quality of the sensory information and to the speed–accuracy compromise adopted by an observer. In addition, it promises to account for some other, less central, aspects. For example, preliminary simulation work shows effects of variations in the probability and sequence of stimuli, with the added complication that these are not the same for all positions in the stimulus array. Indeed, it would be interesting to study the behaviour of the model when presented with sequences of given run structures. However, in view of the interaction of factors of discriminability (such as serial position, stimulus spacing, or the noise associated with variables and standards), a systematic analysis of these effects has not yet been undertaken. Instead, I shall conclude this chapter with an examination of one of the less complex, but more unexpected, properties of the adaptive identification process.

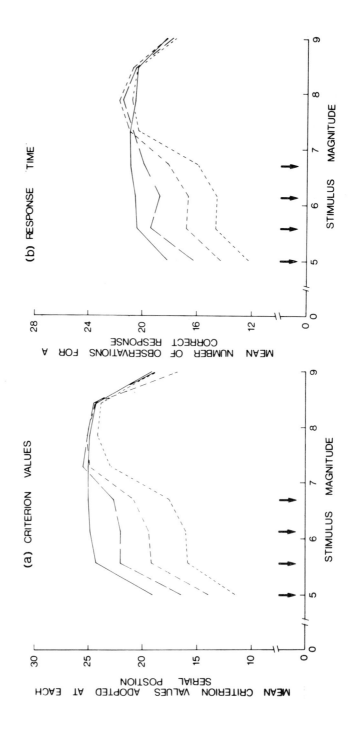

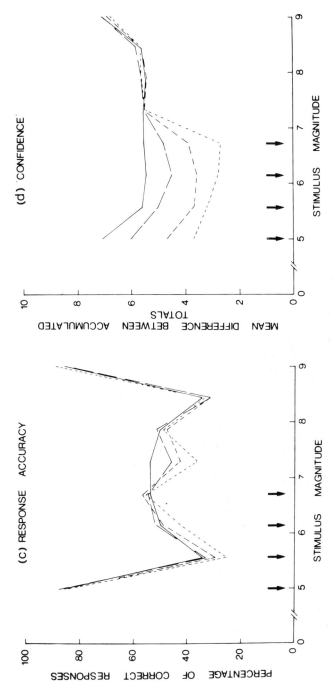

Fig. 113. Serial position effects obtained in simulation of the adaptive parallel eventuation process when preparation is intensified for responses in one half of the array (arrowed) by progressively lowering the target level of confidence for the identifying criterion from 5, through 4 and 3, down to 2, as indicated by lines composed of progressively shorter dashes. Figure 113a shows the pattern of values adopted by the identifying criteria, Fig. 113b that of response times, Fig. 113c that of response accuracy, while Fig. 113d shows the values of the hypothetical basis for confidence in each identifying response.

## Yerkes-Dodson Effects

### The Empirical Effects

In 1908, Yerkes and Dodson reported the results of a study in which mice were trained in a Yerkes box to discriminate between two shades of grey by being rewarded with food for a correct choice, and punished with electric shock for a wrong one. These authors found that, when the discrimination was easy (i.e. there was a large difference in brightness between the two discriminanda), then increasing the shock up to a certain point produced learning in fewer trials, but further increases beyond this peak led to progressively slower learning. Yerkes and Dodson also reported that the peak which produced optimum performance occurred at a lower shock intensity when the discrimination was difficult than when it was easy. Their findings are shown in Fig. 114a, which is redrawn from a graph prepared by Broadhurst (1959). These results have generally been taken to imply that there is an optimum level of arousal for any task, and the more difficult the task, the lower is this optimum.

While subsequent work on the topic was largely confirmatory, the complexities involved in any study of the influence of two interacting variables on a third may have been at least partly responsible for its comparative neglect until Eysenck (1955) drew attention to its relevance in the fields of personality and learning theory. Following Hebb's (1955) equation of arousal with a general drive state, a number of physiological psychologists pointed to a similar "inverted-U" relationship between activation and various measures of efficiency in human performance. A very readable summary of work up to 1958 consistent with the Yerkes–Dodson principles is given by Broadhurst (1959), while a theoretical interpretation using Hullian concepts has been proposed by Broen and Storms (1961). More recently, Broadbent (1965) has proposed an empirical generalization of the principle of an interaction between motivation and task difficulty, which is intended to apply to a corpus of experimental literature on the effects of noise and other stressors on efficiency. Meanwhile, Welford (1968) has drawn attention to wider applications of the principle in a variety of studies on human performance.

### The Response of the Adaptive Model to Increases in Noise

In considering how the present approach to stimulus identification might encompass the Yerkes–Dodson phenomena, it seems natural to regard the number of trials to learn as the counterpart of the number of observations required to make a response correctly, and to interpret shock intensity as

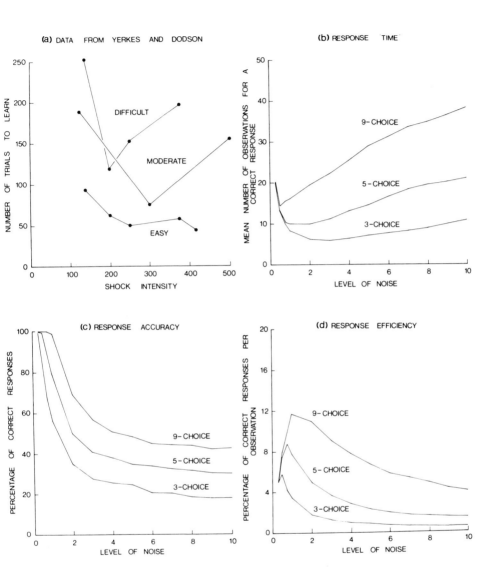

Fig. 114. Empirical and theoretical phenomena of optimality. Figure 114a shows learning data from Yerkes and Dodson plotted against the intensity of shock given as punishment for an incorrect response. Figures 114b, c and d show data obtained in simulation of the adaptive parallel eventuation process when the noise added to both variables and standards is increased from 0·3 up to $10\sigma_{(V-S)}$. The measure of response efficiency shown in Fig. 114d is obtained by dividing the percentage correct by the mean number of observations required for a correct response.

analogous in its arousing effects to a general increase in noise affecting both variables and standards equally (i.e. to an increase in both $\sigma_V$ and $\sigma_S$). At this point, the multiple constraints applied in developing the adaptive version of the parallel eventuation model combine to generate an unexpected dividend: whereas most attempts to account for the Yerkes–Dodson phenomena make special postulates, such as a ceiling for "effective reaction potential" (Broen and Storms, 1961), the present model exhibits a Yerkes–Dodson type of interaction between task difficulty and noise, without making any additional assumptions whatsoever.

To investigate the behaviour of the model when noise is increased, some 2000 trials of the hypothesized process were simulated for various degrees of choice from 3 up to 20, with 13 different levels of noise (with $\sigma_V = \sigma_S$), varying from 0·3 up to $10\sigma_{(V-S)}$. Each set of 2000 trials embodied the features of a typical choice-reaction task, with alternative stimuli being presented equiprobably and in random order. Target levels of confidence ($C_E$) were assumed to be equal for all responses, and all parameters of the model remained unchanged, irrespective of the noise level. Thus the behaviour of the simulated process reveals inherent features of the proposed model, rather than following from any specially postulated modification.

Figure 114b shows the number of observations required by the simulated model to make a correct response, at each of three degrees of choice, as the level of noise is increased from 0·3 up to 10 units. As the noise is increased beyond 0·3, the number of observations falls to a minimum, which is different for each degree of choice, and then begins to climb as the noise level increases further. The U-shaped patterns of response time predicted by the model are in line with Yerkes and Dodson's finding that, for a given task, there was an optimum level of activation at which the time taken to learn was at a minimum, and above or below which the number of trials to reach a criterion increased. Looking more closely at Fig. 114b, we notice that the optimum noise level (at which response time is at a minimum) occurs near 3 units for a 3-choice task, near 2 for a 5-choice task and near 0·5 units for a 9-choice task. This decrease in the optimum level of noise coincides nicely with Dodson's generalization (1915) that "the optimum intensity of shock varies inversely with the difficulty of discrimination".

While the reader may accept for the moment that the pattern of response times predicted by the model offers a good reflection of empirical findings, he may be troubled by the thought that, on most accounts, we should expect discrimination to be most accurate where both variables and standards are entirely free from noise, and accuracy of discrimination to fall steadily as progressively more noise is added. Indeed, the overall percentage of correct responses made by the simulated process does fall uninterruptedly when noise is increased, as is shown in Fig. 114c. Definite optimal levels of noise reappear only if we combine response frequency and time into a measure of efficiency, such as percentage of correct responses per observation made (Fig. 114d).

## Noise as a Necessary Condition for Identification

One of the basic steps towards understanding why the model responds in this manner to simple increases in noise appears to be the realization that, not only is adaptability an integral feature of the model, but the presence of noise in either the variable or the stored standards is essential for its operation. The latter statement may seem surprising, but it follows directly from the fact that the quantity tested by each intermediate accumulator is determined by the sum of the totals of the positive and negative differences between momentary values of the presented variable $V$ and the appropriate stored standard $S$ minus their modulus (i.e. a quantity of the form $(t_g + t_l) - |t_g - t_l|$). If the variable and the standard have exactly the same value and if both are entirely free from noise, then there are no differences to accumulate, the criterion $k_e$ for the intermediate accumulator will never be reached and no response can be issued. Given any noise, however slight, in either variable or standard, then, of course, the relevant intermediate accumulator will begin to fill up—slowly, when the variability is small, and more quickly as the variability is increased.

If we consider a module in which the mean value of the variable corresponds very closely with that of the standard with which it is being compared, and where there is only a slight variability in either variable or standard, then (as has just been mentioned) the intermediate accumulator will fill very slowly. On the other hand, little or no evidence will be accumulated by any other module in favour of identification with a different standard. When it does occur, therefore, the eventual identification will be made with maximum confidence. Now, if the variability is increased slightly, then the accumulator in question will reach its criterion more quickly, and responses will tend to be faster. At this stage, the slight decrease in confidence which follows does not appear to produce a sufficiently large upward revision of the criterion to offset the quickened rate of accumulation, and response time continues to decline. However, as soon as further increases in noise begin to result in an appreciable number of errors and confidence falls more frequently and severely below the pre-set target, then upward revisions of the criterion become substantial. From this point onwards, response times tend to rise as progressive increases in noise provoke further upward revisions of the criterion. This adaptation slows down, but does not completely arrest the increase in errors, and the proportion of correct responses continues to decline, though more gradually, towards an asymptote at the level of chance performance. Using this approach, the optimum level of noise represents a peak of efficiency, in which a quickened rate of accumulation is exactly balanced against an increased liability to error by an adaptive system attempting to slow down the inevitable deterioration in performance that comes with increased noise.

When the task is more difficult, then increasing noise results in the same increase in the rate of accumulation as for an easier task, but produces a faster increase in the error rate. As a result, the equilibrium point occurs earlier and the optimum level of noise is lower for the more difficult task. Changes in the target level of confidence will also affect the pattern. As is shown in Fig. 115a, a general increase in the target level of confidence will slow down the rate at which accuracy falls off as noise is increased. Meanwhile, response times will be higher and decrease more slowly to a minimum, but increase more rapidly afterwards (Fig. 115b). The net result is that, for any measure of overall efficiency such as percentage of correct responses per observation, the optimum level will be a joint function of noise, task difficulty and the target level of confidence set by an individual observer. Thus the behaviour of the model conforms nicely with Schlosberg's conclusion that "there is an optimum level of activation for each type of task, and perhaps for each subject" (1954).

## Conclusions

Although the properties of the adaptive parallel eventuation process have not yet been exhaustively catalogued or scrutinized in complete detail, it appears at present to offer an integrated and faithful account of a wide variety of otherwise only loosely related, and often complex, empirical phenomena.

Perhaps the most distinctive characteristics of the model are that it is necessarily adaptive, and that it presupposes the existence of sensory noise for its operation. In the case of the Yerkes–Dodson effects in particular, it is clear that the model not only works to counteract noise in the sensory input, but is absolutely dependent upon the existence of noise for its operation. There may appear to be a somewhat defiant air about a model for identification, which depends upon the variable and the standard being (at least momentarily) different. On the other hand, the existence of noise at all levels of the sensory system can be safely assumed: the condition in which all random activity had subsided in an organism would be approached only at the absolute zero of temperature. Despite the intricacy of its behaviour, however, if we regard the three-category accumulator process as an elementary decision module, readily capable of neurophysiological realiza-

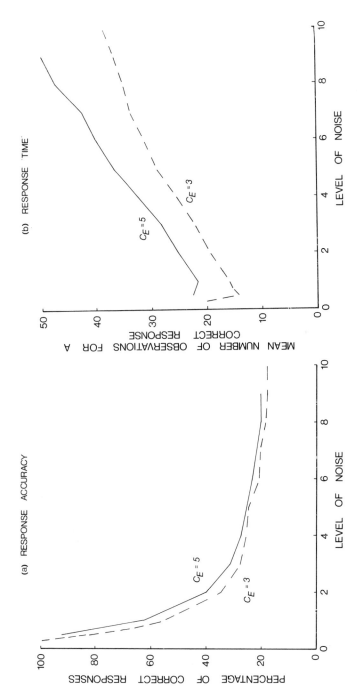

Fig. 115. The pattern of (a) response accuracy and (b) response times obtained in simulation of the adaptive parallel eventuation model as the noise associated with both variables and standards is increased from 0·3 up to 9σ$_{(V-S)}$. The solid lines show data obtained with a target level of confidence for the identification response set to 5, while the broken lines show data for a target level of 3.

(a) RESPONSE ACCURACY

(b) RESPONSE TIME

LEVEL OF NOISE

LEVEL OF NOISE

PERCENTAGE OF CORRECT RESPONSES

MEAN NUMBER OF OBSERVATIONS FOR A CORRECT RESPONSE

$C_E = 5$

$C_E = 3$

tion, then the adaptive parallel eventuation model can be seen as embodying one of its simplest evolutionary developments.

Meanwhile, it is probably unnecessary to dwell on the fact that even such a simple network of adaptive modules is capable of a rich variety of applications. Further predictions in several areas could be pursued without any major development of the model. For example, it seems that the identification of stimuli varying on several dimensions could probably be achieved simply by adding further modules for each dimension, with the model automatically showing a preference (through adaptively lowered criteria) for the more discriminable dimension(s), but capable, if "instructed" through changes in target confidence, of switching its reliance to other, less discriminable dimensions. It should also be possible to accommodate at least the structure of the selective reaction experiment by a relatively simple reallocation of overt responses to decision outcomes by the various modules. Again, as was noted earlier, it should be possible to utilize the redundant covert responses to generate new standards, or to allow the model to scale stimuli in terms of a small number of given standards. In general, the modular nature of the process makes it easy to maintain a morphological correspondence between the structure of the task and that of the model, so that its application to new tasks and situations is quite simple and straightforward.

Any one of these applications would be exciting in itself and, indeed, a certain problem arises as to which direction may be the most profitable and testing for further extensions of the modular approach to perception taken in this book so far. In a situation of this kind, however, it often happens that theoretical development is usefully guided by taking into consideration some more general constraints than those posed by the immediate problem. The following chapter, therefore, is not intended as a further exercise in devising a simple configuration of adaptive decision modules to account for some other elementary cognitive activity. Rather, it is an attempt to work from the molar to the molecular, and to view the process of perception in the reverse direction to the one we have followed up to this point. Although the intervening gap must remain frustratingly great, it is hoped that, by contemplating the possible destinations of the present approach, the general direction of its further development may be at least partly determined in advance.

# 9
## Perceptual Organization

*If only we could forget for a while about the beautiful and get down
instead to the dainty and the dumpy.*
J. L. Austin, "Philosophical Papers" (1961, p. 131.)

Up to this point we have followed a pattern of theoretical development, which, general considerations would suggest, resembles the evolution of the perceptual system itself. This strategy appears to have been successful to the extent that the linkage of elementary, self-regulating decision functions into more complex configurations promises to provide explanations for more advanced perceptual achievements that those we have considered so far. Rather than pursue these applications at this stage, however, the purpose of the present chapter is to provide a perspective for future developments, and to complement the argument by turning to a consideration of more molar aspects of perception, and examining the degree to which they too appear to imply the operation of decision processes of the kind we have inferred from more rudimentary perceptual tasks.

The present chapter, accordingly, begins from the provisional standpoint, put forward in Chapter 1, that the process of perception may be construed as the attempt to respond differentially to the inherent structure and topography of objects as these are revealed in the limited and not completely predictable presentation of the optical images reflected from them. From this standpoint, the chapter proceeds to consider the outstanding features of perceptual activity emphasized by several traditional approaches to perception. Although it is in no sense intended as an adequate review, the first section attempts to distil from each approach those conclusions which appear to be most strongly founded. The second then attempts to synthesize these conclusions into a schematic description of the minimum sequence of operations apparently involved in the perceptual organization of retinal excitations into a coherent picture of the environment. Following this synthesis, the third section tries to infer the functions which adaptive decision modules might play in the execution of such a sequence, and considers some evidence in support of the important theoretical role assigned to them. Finally, the last section explores the extent to which the operation of decision processes may be inferred from phenomena associated with changes in perceptual organization.

## Some Traditional Approaches to Perception

The aim of considering some of the established approaches to perception in this first section is not to subject them to an exhaustive, systematic evaluation, but to select from each those conclusions which appear to possess the greatest validity. Underlying this eclectic strategy is the conviction that what turns out to be most valuable in each will complement, rather than oppose or supplant, the insights afforded by the others. If this is so, then it should be possible by piecing them together to achieve a synthesis of traditional views on the perceptual organization of sensory information. With this aim in mind, therefore, the various approaches are examined in a sequence which reveals the need for a progressively finer articulation in our conception of different aspects of the perceptual process.

### Gibson's Theory of "Ecological Optics"

Of all the established views of the perceptual process, the one which is at first sight simplest is the anti-theoretical approach of Gibson (1950, 1966, 1972), which, starting from a phenomenological viewpoint, attempts to explain perception in terms of simple stimulus–response relations, without reference to any mediating processes whatsoever. Gibson's main interest lies in how an observer gains information about the position, size, shape, layout and movements of objects, and in how he perceives his own position and movements within the environment. The answer, according to Gibson, lies in the basic hypothesis that "for every aspect or property of the phenomenal world of an individual in contact with his environment, however subtle, there is a variable in the energy flux at his receptors, however complex, with which the phenomenal property would correspond if a psychophysical experiment could be performed" (1959, p. 465).

The initial impetus for this approach comes from the property of geometrical optics that an image may be generated at any so–called "station-point" in space at which light rays, reflected from surrounding surfaces, intersect. According to Gibson, all of the information needed to specify the position, size, layout and movements of objects in space is contained in images generated by the patterns of ambient light rays, which, over time, provide a binocular observer with a "textured optical array, supplemented by the transformations relating a simultaneous pair of them, and by the transformations relating a sequence of momentary arrays" (1959, p. 474). In Gibson's opinion, the visual system is capable of directly detecting specific patterns, and no further processes of "copying, storing, comparing, matching, deciding, etc." are regarded as necessary (1966, p. 39). The detection of these patterns is thought of as a very elementary, reflex-like response, sometimes characterized as the "pick-up" of information and sometimes as a process of "resonation", with different observers being more or less "tuned" to perceiving particular patterns. The chain of events envisaged by Gibson as giving rise to a detectable variation in physical energy is represented in Fig. 116.

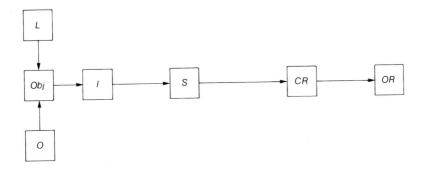

Fig. 116. Representation of Gibson's psychophysical hypothesis. The relations between the light source (L), object (Obj) and the observer (O) give rise to a structured optical image (I), which is transformed into a detectable stimulus (S). The relation between S and the covert perceptual response (CR) is quite direct, as, by implication, is that between CR and the overt response (OR).

As a result of the extreme generality of the basic hypothesis, the number of instances in which it can be tested is limited only by the variety of phenomenal properties which we can distinguish, and Gibson's signal contribution has been to suggest several detailed analyses of the optical information concerning the layout of the environment and the position of an observer within it. For example, according to Gibson, the stimulus for the perception of a surface consists of a clearly focussed, textured retinal image, while information about slant is given by the "texture gradient", i.e. by the rate of increase (or decrease) in the projected density of the tiny elements composing the microsctructure of the surface. Analyses are also offered concerning the perception of edges (Gibson, 1950), the translation and rotation of a rigid body (Gibson, 1955, 1957) and the perception of self-movement (Gibson, 1950). Meanwhile, more exact mathematical analyses of the perception of slant and approach have been proposed by Purdy (1958), Flock (1964), Braunstein and Payne (1969) and Schiff (1965).

The main criticisms levelled against the theory of ecological optics have taken the form of questioning the necessity or effectiveness of the critical features proposed by the theory, pointing to the importance of other factors than those championed by Gibson, questioning the veridicality of perception as claimed by him, or demonstrating the operation of judgmental or other mediating processes in perception. For example, among those advancing criticisms of the first kind, Epstein and Park (1964) have questioned whether visual texture is necessary for the perception of surface. In the same vein, a large number of studies contradict Gibson's assertion that texture is necessary for the perception of slant, and hence for that of depth (e.g. Clark et al., 1955; Gregory, 1966, 1970; Attneave and Frost, 1969; Olson, 1974). Meanwhile, several researchers have questioned whether other features of the visual array may not sometimes (or always) be more effective sources of information about slant than a gradient in texture-density (e.g. Gruber and Clark, 1956; Wohlwill, 1962; Flock and Moscatelli, 1964; Eriksson, 1964; Kraft and Winnick, 1967; Philips, 1970; Newman, 1970, 1971, 1973).

From these experiments, it is possible to draw two tentative conclusions. Firstly, the visual system appears to be sensitive to a rich variety of sources of information concerning the layout and movements of objects, with the effectiveness of any one depending to some extent upon the presence or absence of others. Secondly, there appears to be a preference for "simplicity" or "invariance" in perceptual organization, with outline figures, such as the inverted trapezoid of Clark et al. (1955), perceived in such a way as to be consistent with this simplicity. According to Gibson, such principles may operate in ambiguous or conflicting situations, in which there is inadequate, equivocal, reduced, or misleading information about depth. He argues, however, that such situations are usually artificially contrived and do not represent the normal functioning of the visual system. To a large extent, the starting point of the next approach to be considered lies in questioning the generality of this last reservation.

## The "Probabilistic Functionalism" of Brunswick

Although the two are often contrasted, Gibson's theory resembles the so-called "probabilistic functionalism" of Brunswick (1952, 1955) in that both place an "ecological" emphasis on the abundance of sources of visual information available to an organism. However, while Gibson asserts that such sources normally operate in a geometrically precise way to determine perceptions directly and automatically, Brunswick emphasizes the view that stimuli are typically insufficient, ambiguous, unreliable, or misleading. For example, a trapezoidal image on the retina may be caused by a tilted rectangle (as was concluded by the observers of Clark *et al.* (1955)), or by any one of a family of trapezia at different angles to the line of sight. Although the ambiguity in this case could be reduced by rotating the object, according to Brunswick, organisms are normally obliged to act quickly, and are forced to depend upon a variety of sources of partial and potentially misleading sensory information, which can be regarded as providing only probable "clues" or "cues" to the nature of the object from which they arise.

Despite the uncertain nature of these cues, the perceptual system, according to Brunswick, generally attains an end-result which is remarkably constant, and which corresponds closely to the objective situation in which the organism finds itself. Indeed, according to Brunswick, the primary function of perception is to bring about the adaptive stabilization of the perceptual environment in spite of varying proximal stimulation. This attainment is represented in terms of a so-called "lens model". In this model, the initial (distal) focus denotes some physical quality, which, due to various forms of interference, gives rise to various, not completely predictable effects at the receptors of an organism. These may be regarded as more or less reliable cues to the nature of the object, with the degree of correspondence between the proximal stimuli and the properties of objects being termed the "ecological validity" of the stimuli. Since each stimulus has a limited ecological validity, the organism is obliged to be selective and to weight it according to its experienced probability of producing a perceptual response with a high "functional validity", or veridicality. By varying the degree of "cue utilization", the organism seeks to achieve a constancy in perception which corresponds closely to the stabilities which characterize its physical environment. It is this convergent aspect of the mediating process which is described as "terminal focussing", and underlies the analogy of a lens.

Because the model is not specified in detail, but is advanced as a framework for experimental enquiry, criticisms of probabilistic functionalism have tended to be somewhat general (e.g. Postman, 1955; Hilgard, 1955; Krech, 1955; Feigl, 1955). In effect, Brunswick's model remains largely descriptive rather than explanatory, and the mediational process is conceived as a simple, stereotyped activity. Indeed, Brunswick argues that the lens model itself is a dynamically integrated system and should be taken to represent the fundamental effective unit of perceptual functioning (1952, p. 19; 1955, p. 206).

While such a level of analysis would seem to have been too molar to be useful, Brunswick's general approach is consistent with the conclusions drawn from our discussion of Gibson's views and, in addition, implies a more detailed conceptualization of the process of perception. An attempt to

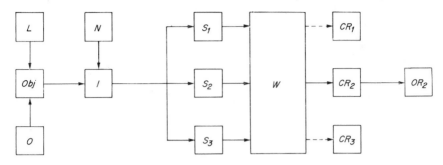

Fig. 117. Representation of Brunswick's probabilistic approach. As in Fig. 116, the relations between the light source ($L$), the object ($Obj$) and the observer ($O$) give rise to a structured optical image ($I$), which is disturbed by noise ($N$). The resulting stimuli ($S_1$, $S_2$, . . .) have only a probabilistic relationship to $I$ and are linked to various covert responses ($CR_1$, $CR_2$, . . .) by a weighting system ($W$), according to their experienced functional validity. The relationship between the covert and the overt response ($OR$) is assumed to be direct.

summarize this is presented in Fig. 117 and, as can be seen from a comparison of Figs 116 and 117, the second conceptualization is more comprehensive. The main additions are the recognition of sources of interference and ambiguity in the transmission of sensory information, and the inclusion of mediating processes characterized generally as tending towards some form of stabilization. However, beyond the assertion that these mediating processes take place, no really detailed specification can be arrived at on the basis of the evidence considered so far. In contrast, one of the main features of the next approach to be considered is that it attempted to provide a concrete analogy in terms of which these processes might be described.

## Gestalt Theory

Despite some profound differences, there are many tantalizing resemblances between the spirit and pronouncements of Gibson and those of the "gestalt" approach to perception. Like Gibson, the gestalt theorists are opposed to an atomistic approach, in which complex perceptions are constructed out of more elementary ones by shifts of attention, associative linkages, or more complex cognitive processes. Like Gibson, gestalt theorists have pointed to some striking phenomenological evidence for their contention that the primary perceptual activity is the perception of structure, pattern, or gestalt in the visual image. Like Gibson too, the gestalt theorists hold that perception of configuration is a very direct, unlearned process, while the perception of particular aspects is less direct, and is susceptible to change by practice and learning.

On the other hand, unlike Gibson, the gestalt theorists argue that the perception of structure, though automatic, is not necessarily veridical. Again, perhaps because of their association with the physical sciences, the gestalt theorists are not concerned primarily with lawful relations in the visual array, which specify the layout and movements of families of objects, but with the perception of any kind of structure, whether following from the geometry of reflection and refraction, or produced by any other physical process. As a result of their interest in stimuli structured by other than purely optical processes, the gestalt theorists are led to conclude that it is primarily the relations among visual features which determine which features become grouped together, rather than (as in Gibson's view) those between the observer and his environment. As Wertheimer points out, "the nervous system evolved under the influence of the biological environment; it is only natural that the gestalt tendencies which developed in the process reflect the orderly conditions of that environment." (Katz, 1951, p. 28).

Thus, while they recognize, along with Brunswick, the operation of a mediating process in perception, the gestalt theorists emphasize the importance of internal relations in the visual image, rather than the interpretative role of experience. According to the latter, the visual image is transformed by the sensory system into a three-dimensional cortical field of forces with certain dynamic properties. Like a field of physical or electromagnetic forces, this system tends towards a stationary state of equilibrium, in the course of which the arrangement of forces is redistributed. The redistribution is assumed to follow a tendency towards stability, regularity and simplicity, and this assumption—in the form of the law of prägnanz—is postulated as the basis for observed tendencies towards "goodness" in perceived configurations. Although the experiential aspect of perception is not analysed, the relation between a cortical field and a perceived configuration is assumed to be simple. According to Köhler, "our working hypothesis states that the specific arrangement of actual experience is an accurate reproduction of a dynamically functioning arrangement of corresponding brain processes" (Katz, 1951, p. 56).

Some of the main strengths and weaknesses in the gestalt approach have been pointed out by a number of writers (e.g. Helson, 1925a, b, 1926a, b, 1933, 1969; Hochberg, 1957; Asch, 1968; Avant and Helson, 1973). On the positive side, for example, the gestalt theorists' innovative investigations of conditions conducive to the perception of configuration were predominantly empirical in character, with the result that the principles of proximity, similarity, closure, common destiny and common movement have a general intuitive currency and are still in widespread use—at least as a kind of descriptive shorthand. Although the meaning of the various principles remains ambiguous, and although there are no clear reasons for choosing one principle rather than another, several attempts have been made within the last two decades to remedy these deficiencies. For instance, the "rules for the probability that a surface is seen as figure", originally enunciated in 1915 by Rubin (1958), have been considerably sharpened by a number of studies (e.g. Harrower, 1936; Oyama, 1950; Künnapas, 1957; Frisch and Julesz, 1966; Lindauer and Lindauer, 1970). Similarly, numerous other experiments have investigated the importance of various factors in producing discriminable groupings among arrays of simple elements (e.g. Hochberg and Silverstein, 1956; Green et al., 1959; Hochberg and Hardy, 1960; Lie, 1964; Beck, 1966a, b, 1967, 1972; Julesz, 1969; Olson and Attneave, 1970; Zahn, 1971; Jarvis, 1972; Beck and Ambler, 1972; Prytulak, 1974; O'Callaghan, 1974).

While these studies do not invalidate the gestalt principles, they do indicate the need to specify more precisely the constraints in the visual image to which human observers appear to be sensitive. In the meantime, however, the principles draw attention to the perception of structure which is produced by non-optical constraints. In particular, the two kinds of principle neatly parallel the two classes of constraint distinguished in the introductory chapter: those concerned with the formation of single processes and those having to do with the linkage of these processes into more complex configurations. As an acknowledgment of at least the objective counterpart of the gestalt principles, therefore, we would seem to be obliged to add two further sources of structure to our developing conception of the perceptual process. These are shown in Fig. 118.

On the other hand, the gestalt account of the mechanism whereby an observer responds to these constraints has met with less success, (c.f. Lashley et al., 1951; Sperry et al., 1955). A major difficulty is that the nature of the cortical fields is ambiguous and their properties incompletely specified, with the result that explanations of phenomena are often indistinguishable from further articulations of the theory. Again, even if the hypothetical fields could be supposed to maintain a fairly straightforward topological correspondence with the visual array, this would not provide a complete explanation of perceptual organization, since the system which "sees" and the process of "seeing" are still left unanalysed. Indeed, viewed from a much later vantage point, the hypothesis of cortical fields seems best regarded as a temporary metaphor in the search for a conceptual language which would more adequately capture what seem to be important features of the perceptual process: its dynamic, interactive properties, its propensity for minimizing some variable(s) of a high order and its tendency towards a state of equilibrium. As with the suggestively similar lens model of

Brunswick, the level of theoretical analysis would seem to be too molar to be useful. We next turn our attention, therefore, to a more molecular approach, which appears to have far-reaching implications, not only for the gestalt hypothesis of cortical fields, but for our whole pattern of theorizing about the processes underlying perceptual organization.

## Neurophysiological Evidence for "Feature-detecting" Systems

From the perspective of recent neurophysiological work it now appears that, not only are explanations of perceptual organization in terms of cortical fields quite untenable, but the picture of visual features establishing their own neuronal circuits from among a mass of undifferentiated cells is becoming increasingly implausible. In contrast, microelectrode studies carried out over the last twenty years underline the importance of the microanatomy of neural pathways and structures. While the possibility of developmental changes is not ruled out, the degree of localization and anatomical differentiation indicated by these studies suggests that organisms have evolved neural subsystems which respond only to a stimulus which is of some biological value. For example, Lettvin et al. (1961), have found evidence in recordings from individual ganglion cells that the visual world of the frog is sustained by the retinal registration of a small number of quite complex features, such as "moving contrast" or "convex edges".

These studies might be taken to suggest that in higher animals with more fully developed visual systems, even more complex data reduction would be performed at the earliest stages. However, the microelectrode studies by Kuffler (1953) and by Hubel and Wiesel (1961) on the ganglion cells of cats suggest that the level of processing carried out at the retinal level by higher mammals remains elementary. Indeed, as we ascend the phylogenetic scale, it seems that there is a progressive postponement of the detection of complex features, and the insertion of an increasing number of simpler feature detecting systems. As a result, it is only when we reach the cortical level in higher mammals that we find signs of less elementary systems. For example, in recordings from single cells in the visual cortex of the cat, Hubel and Wiesel (1962) found evidence for three main types of detector: simple, complex and hypercomplex cells. The simple cells have receptive fields averaging about 2° and are sensitive to lines of specific widths and orientations, to edges at specific orientations and frequently to edges and lines moving at particular rates and in particular directions. While complex cells are generally sensitive to the same kinds of feature which excite simple cells, their responses appear to be independent of the position of the feature within a much larger receptive field. Finally, hypercomplex cells appear to respond to the outputs of combinations of complex cells and are triggered,

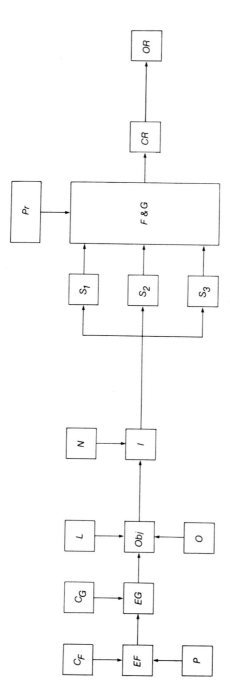

Fig. 118. Representation of the gestalt conception of the perceptual process. Certain primitive physical constituents (*P*) undergo element formation (*EF*) under the influence of certain physicochemical constraints (*C_F*). These elements in turn are grouped into larger processes (*EG*) under the influence of other constraints (*C_G*). Such a process may constitute an object (*Obj*), with the relations between it and the light source (*L*) and the observer (*O*) giving rise to a structured optical image (*I*). Disruption of this image by noise (*N*) gives rise to a variety of stimuli (*S₁*, *S₂* . . .), which undergo certain processes of figure–ground differentiation and grouping (*F* and *G*) in conformity with a general principle of prägnanz (*Pr*). The resulting covert response (*CR*) is assumed to be directly related to the overt response (*OR*).

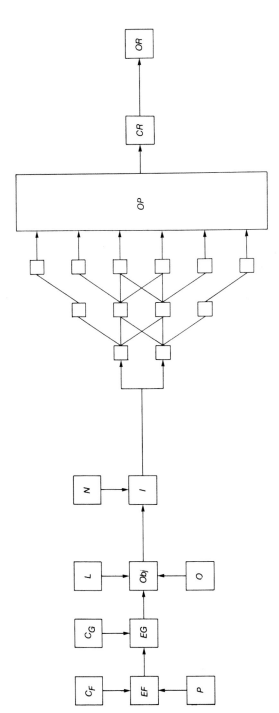

Fig. 119. The place of a hierarchy of feature-detecting systems (unlabelled boxes) in a developing conception of the perceptual process. With the exception of an unspecified organizing process (OP), the symbols retain the same denotation as in Fig. 118. The interconnections within the hierarchy are only suggestive and are not intended to be interpreted literally.

for example, by angles or corners situated anywhere within the corresponding receptive field.

To some extent this neurophysiological evidence is consistent with both
the Gibsonian and the gestalt contention that the perception of configuration
is a primary, quite immediate, perceptual activity. On the other hand, the
general implication is that perceptual organization is not represented by a
shifting pattern of activity within an otherwise homogeneous medium, and
this is diametrically opposed both to the concept of cortical fields propounded by the gestalt theorists and to Hebb's notion (1949) of differing
patterns of connectivity. Instead, perceptual activity appears to be sustained
by a hierarchical arrangement of precisely connected specialized cells, in
which a large number of units at lower levels simultaneously signal the
presence of a variety of elementary features. Through successive sequences
of generalization, followed by increased specificity, this information comes
to trigger fewer and fewer detectors, with each stage representing a higher
degree of organization in the information. At the same time, as Barlow
(1972) points out, it is important to recognize that this hierarchy may be
inverted, since the number of cortical neurons available for vision is several
orders of magnitude greater than that of the incoming fibres. Figure 119
illustrates the place of such a hierarchy in our developing conception of the
perceptual process.

Despite a certain sense of relief which comes with the realization that the
process of perception is enormously simplified by the operation of a large
number of relatively simple neural systems, each sensitized to detect some
particular feature of the environment, it is clear that certain problems
remain unanswered by the neurophysiological approach. As it stands, for
example, the supposed hierarchical organization of feature analysers is
conceived as a passive process, rather than as a system which seeks
stimulation and variation in input, and responds in a dynamic way that
reflects the properties of both current and past patterns of excitation. The
importance of the information-seeking properties of perceptual systems is
underlined by Gyr et al. (1966), while the necessity for some dynamic
feedback processes within the hierarchy is urged by Milner (1974), who
follows Minsky (1961) in arguing that a simple feature analysing system
would respond to all of the features in a visual array without indicating
which features belonged to which stimulus object.

Both these criticisms may be taken to imply the operation of very similar
principles. For example, Gyr et al. (1966) follow Platt (1962) and Gibson
(1963) in arguing that the perceptual system selects as features certain
properties of the visual input which remain invariant under the transformations of translation and rotation normally generated by eye, head and body
movements. Meanwhile, the gestalt law of prägnanz, according to which

the perceived configuration tends to be as simple as possible, may be viewed as an analogous principle, which seems particularly appropriate for the segmentation and grouping of features within a static array. It is tempting to try to subsume both tendencies under a single principle, and some attempts to do this, using approaches derived from information theory, are considered in the following section.

## Information-theory Approaches

The so-called "information-theory" approach in visual perception is derived from attempts to apply the measures developed by Shannon and Weaver (1949) for the quantification of information in an ideal communication system to an analysis of the processing of sensory information by human beings. In order to apply information measures usefully in this context, the elements in an experimental situation need to be explicitly identified with the corresponding terms in the communication channel model. According to the generally accepted version, the ideal communications system involves four main elements: (i) a *source*, which consists of a finite set of events (A), plus an ordering principle which produces an infinite sequence of signals from this set; (ii) an *encoder*, which transforms these signals into an input for (iii) the *communication channel*, which transmits the signals to a set of output terminals, where (iv) the *decoder* interprets them in terms of a finite set of events (B), which have a previously defined relationship with those in (A). The elements of this system are illustrated in Fig. 120.

In applying information measures to problems of visual perception, three main identifications have been implicit. In all three, the observer's responses have been identified with the set of events B, the main differences being whether whole stimuli or stimulus elements have been identified with the source, and whether the observer has been identified with the communica-

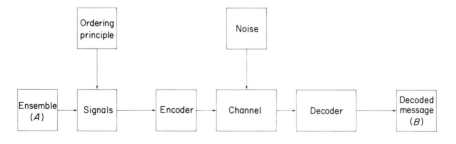

Fig. 120. The basic elements of a communications system.

tion channel or the decoder. Where the main objective, as in the present chapter, is to study the perceptual system as a mechanism whereby sensory inputs are organized or recorded into a different form, then it seems most appropriate to regard the observer as a decoder and the stimuli as signals in the channel. Although there are a number of conflicting expressions of it (e.g. Hochberg and McAlister, 1953, p. 361; Attneave, 1954, p. 189; Garner, 1962, pp. 183, 204), the most generally viable form of the (essentially psychological) "information-theory" hypothesis concerning perceptual organization is that a major function of the perceptual system is to recode sensory information into a more "economical" form.

Attneave's hypothesis (1954) was that figures which are "good" in the gestalt sense contain less information and are more redundant or organized and, consequently, easier to perceive. However, this approach has been subjected to a number of criticisms, notably by Green and Courtis (1966) and by Evans (1967). Among the difficulties faced by this approach are: (i) the fact that, when an observer is presented with just a single stimulus, it is not clear how much information (if any) is conveyed by this presentation; (ii) that a sequence of stimuli (or stimulus elements) inspected by an observer would not normally constitute an ergodic sequence; and (iii) the difficulty that information and redundancy are conceived of as being reciprocally related, so that to perceive a stimulus in terms of minimum information carries the paradoxical implication that this maximizes redundancy.

In an attempt to account for the perception of unique stimuli in the same terms as for sets of stimuli, I suggested (Vickers, 1967) that, as a result of eye movements and binocular vision, even a unique stimulus would generate a small subset of patterns and that, like a subset selected and presented by an experimenter, this subset would determine the actual information conveyed by a stimulus. In either case, I argued, observers could infer from constraints detected in the stimuli that the presented subset was not drawn from the total set of all possible stimuli embodying the same pattern elements. Instead, they might infer that the patterns were drawn from a subset which was as small as possible, consistent with the constraints detected in the observed subset. This suggestion is illustrated in Fig. 121. Using this approach, observers are free to perceive a stimulus as belonging to a constrained subset of stimuli without in any way changing the actual information conveyed by its presentation. Following Evans' distinction (1967) between "constraint" and "discrimination" redundancy, it would be predicted that stimuli from small inferred subsets would appear more constrained, or organized, but, at the same time, would be less discriminable from other stimuli within the same subset.

The conceptualization would seem to resolve a number of paradoxes confronting the analysis of perceptual organization in terms of information theory. Indeed, although he does not make use of the distinction between constraint and discrimination redundancy, Garner (1962, 1966, 1970, 1972, 1974) was the first to argue cogently that observers perceive single stimuli as belonging to inferred subsets, and to present several converging lines of evidence which showed clearly that the perceived properties of a single stimulus are determined by the nature of the subset from which it is presumed by the observer to have been drawn. In turn, however, this development results in two ironically opposed consequences.

One consequence is that the picture of the perceptual system as a decoder operating on signals in a channel, is considerably clarified. As is illustrated in Fig. 122, in the case of unique figures (or a sequence of views of a unique object), the total ensemble may be regarded as the set of all possible combinations of the stimulus elements in question, while the signal generating process can be thought of as consisting of two stages. In the first, the constraints jointly imposed by physical forces, by the growth and composition of objects, as well as the optical interactions between the source of light, the position of the observer, and the movement, rigidity, or elasticity of the object concerned, all combine to import a high degree of structure to any momentarily perceived stimulus, to any sequence of stimuli, or to any temporally continuous pattern of stimulation. In the second, a variety of intervening processes (such as physical obstacles, the deliberate manipulations of an experimenter, the movements of an observer, or variations in his arousal or attention) all serve to restrict the availability of the stimuli in question in ways which may often be quite unrelated to their inherent constraints. The decoding process embodied in the observer may thus be interpreted as an attempt to infer the nature of the organization responsible for the structure detected in a limited presentation. Such a view seems intuitively satisfying, and does not appear to do too much violence to the communication channel metaphor.

At the same time, unfortunately, the communication channel model becomes unworkable for the purposes of quantitative analysis within the context of perceptual organization. In the first place, when the observer is presented with a unique stimulus, or has access to a limited, though indeterminate, succession of views of a single object, the information conveyed by the unique presentation or the sequence of views becomes equally indeterminate. In any case, if the perceptual system is viewed as a decoding process, rather than as a communication channel, then the measurement of channel capacity (as in absolute judgment tasks) is no longer applicable, and the significance of assigning precise information values to stimuli (or to stimulus elements) is reduced, since the primary function of the stimulus becomes one of affording some opportunity for the

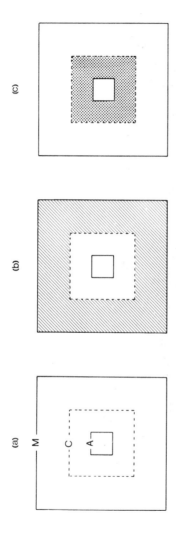

Fig. 121. Information analysis of visual stimuli proposed by myself (Vickers, 1967) and Evans (1967). The universe of all possible random combinations of stimulus elements (M) determines the maximum amount of information which can be conveyed by a stimulus composed of these elements. However, since these elements are usually combined according to certain constraints, the size of the constrained subset (C) is smaller and the potential information conveyed is less. In addition, certain principles of random selection may further reduce the size of the subset of stimuli presented (A) and this determines the actual information conveyed by any one stimulus. The shaded area in Fig. 121b denotes the difference between the size of the maximum set and the constrained subset and determines the amount of constraint redundancy, while the dotted area in Fig. 121b denotes the difference between the sizes of the constrained and the actual subset shown and determines the amount of discrimination redundancy.

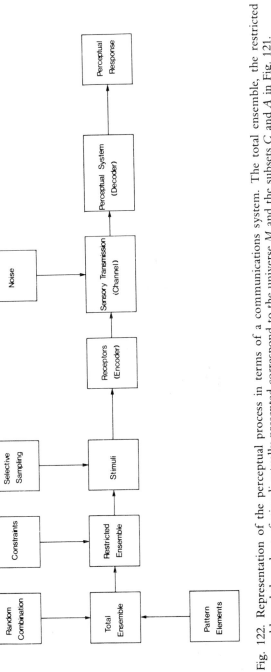

Fig. 122. Representation of the perceptual process in terms of a communications system. The total ensemble, the restricted ensemble and the subset of stimuli actually presented correspond to the universe $M$ and the subsets $C$ and $A$ in Fig. 121.

detection of structure or constraint. In the second place, except with certain well defined patterns, such as binary valued matrices, it is usually uncertain what constitutes a stimulus element, and it is never clear what neurophysiological limitations should be taken into account in assessing the size of the total set of all possible combinations of these elements. Hence, it becomes impossible to assign a maximum value to the amount of information that might be conveyed by any collection of these stimulus elements. In the third place, as Garner emphasizes, the striking feature of human perceptual organization is that observers behave as if stimuli were representatives of inferred subsets of constrained possibilities, and the nature and size of these subsets are matters for empirical investigation rather than something which can be quantified in advance. Moreover, in studies of this apparent inferential behaviour, observers seem to be differentially sensitive to various kinds of constraint, so that for the present at least, it seems more profitable to study the detection of those constraints, as Garner has done, in a piecemeal way, untrammelled by the concepts of information theory.

## A Tentative Synthesis

While I have far from exhausted the list of traditional theories of perception, it seems useful at this point to attempt to synthesize the main implications which are either directly consistent with all the approaches outlined above, or at least with some modified version suggested by the associated evidence. Beginning with an analysis of the environmental situation, therefore, I shall examine the extent to which some consensus can be reached concerning various other aspects of the process of perception. Following the development of a comprehensive conceptualization, I shall then conclude this section by considering some novel implications of this view.

### Elements of a Synthetic Approach

The requirements of the hypothetico-deductive method tend to sharpen differences between theoretical approaches, and the degree of consensus among those we have considered is much greater than is generally acknowledged. In trying to bring out these agreements, I shall consider various aspects of the perceptual process in turn.

### Analysis of the Objective Situation

In their conception of the objective environment, for example, all five approaches are consistent with the view, introduced in Chapter 1, that the constraints under which natural phenomena occur are embodied in their chemical composition and in the sizes, shapes, textures and overall organization of their component parts. In turn, all five share the view that this inherent structure is conveyed with great precision by the pattern of changes in the wavelength and intensity of reflected (or refracted) light rays. Similarly, they recognize that the interactions between the direction of the incident light, the layout, orientations and movements of objects, and the movements and position of an observer, combine to produce characteristic sets of geometrical transformations in the optical image. Finally, despite some difference of opinion as to their importance, all five approaches acknowledge the operation of intervening factors, which serve to restrict, degrade, or distort the information available to an organism from the sensory effects produced by such an image.

## Detection of Configuration

A second main focus of agreement is that the adult perceptual system is capable of directly detecting a variety of simple features, such as lines at particular orientations and configurations of lines intersecting at one point. Although Hebb (1949) would presumably argue that the detection of these features is a learned capability, the degree of localization and the precise anatomical differentiation indicated by the neurophysiological evidence argue in favour of regarding feature detecting systems as part of the genetic endowment of the system. From an evolutionary point of view it seems certain that the first constraints to which the vertebrate visual system would have become sensitive would have been of the most elementary kind (such as some inhomogeneity in the central portion of a field of otherwise diffuse illumination). Following this stage it seems that evolution could then proceed along either of two—not quite mutually exclusive—paths. The first alternative, followed by lower vertebrates (such as the frog), would be gradually to refine the receptors so as to respond to more specific aspects of the environment. The second alternative, which appears to have been that followed by the higher primates (including man), is not to specialize, but to multiply the number of functional units sensitive to the feature in question. This would in turn produce some selective stress towards the evolution of secondary neural systems (the so-called complex and hypercomplex cells), capable of responding to similarities and relations between the elementary features detected by the simpler, more peripheral cells.

## Figure-Ground Differentiation

Despite the detailed analysis of the sensory input which may be achieved by a hierarchical organization of feature detectors, the difficulties envisaged by Minsky (1961) and Milner (1974) still apply. Unless the visual system is to respond to all of the features in the visual array, irrespective of which features belong to which physical object, then some principles for combining features and for determining the appropriate level of analysis, appear to be necessary. Gibson, for example, takes the perception of the elements composing a texture for granted, while the other approaches conceive of figure–ground differentiation as an immediate, unlearned process. Even Hebb, for whom the learning component in perception is all-important, regards the unity and segregation implied in the operation of figure–ground differentiation as primitive products of "the pattern of sensory excitation and the inherited characteristics of the nervous system on which it acts" (1949, p. 19).

Meanwhile, if figure–ground differentiation is regarded as an innate process, then it seems necessary to suppose that this operation must have evolved in a piecemeal way, so that, at each stage in its development, it acted as an integrated, fully functioning system. Despite the tantalizing appearance of holistic principles (as has been emphasized by the gestalt and information theorists), it seems likely, therefore, that the initial stages of perceptual organization are mediated by a number of simple, independent processes, involving immediate responses rather than complex cognitive activity. In agreement with this view, the process of figure–ground differentiation has been regarded by many quite different perceptual theorists (such as Hebb and Garner) as being mediated by a small number of primitive principles, or "rules of thumb", automatically applied without regard to the structure or significance of the processed stimulus. Such principles, for example, might underlie the tendency for the lower face of a Necker cube (or other outline figure) to appear initially as the closer, or for the smaller of two adjacent areas to be perceived as figure, as in the case of the sectors of the Rubin cross shown later in Fig. 126.

## Constraint Detection

While it seems necessary to postulate the operation of these principles in order to get the process of perceptual organization "off the ground", the rules involved in the figure–ground differentiation of many patterns, such as Figs 123a and 123b, seem to be less simple. In these instances, quite complex constraints, such as periodicity or symmetry, appear to influence which elements are seen as figure. Since the average area of the white elements is in both cases equal to that of the black, it appears that the equivocal tendencies of a primitive organizing principle based on area have been resolved by the detection of further constraints associated with one particular organization. This suggests that, when a primitive figure–ground differentiation, based on area, leads to the detection of further constraints, this consequence is fed back as a reinforcing signal, making the perception of that particular organization more probable.

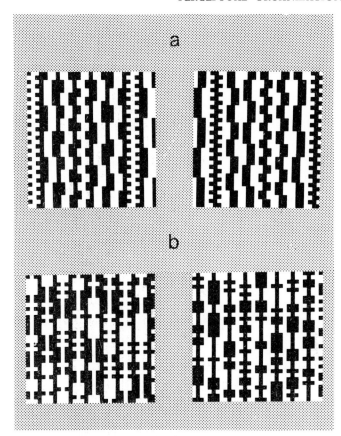

Fig. 123. Examples of patterns in which (a) periodicity and (b) symmetry operate to determine whether the black or the white columns tend to stand out as figure. Within each pattern the areas of black and white are equal.

In turn it seems likely that the figure–ground organization which predominates will also exert some selective influence over the output from the feature detectors, since the successful detection of constraint will depend to a large extent upon the differentiation of pattern elements at an appropriate level of complexity. In line with this expectation, the impressive pattern detection performance of the human visual system suggests that it does indeed possess the capability of following the phenomenologists' prescription to choose units of an appropriate order for analysis. This would suggest, therefore, that the output is enhanced from those feature detectors which provide the elements for a "successful" or "clear" figure–ground organization, while the output from others, less relevant, is attenuated.

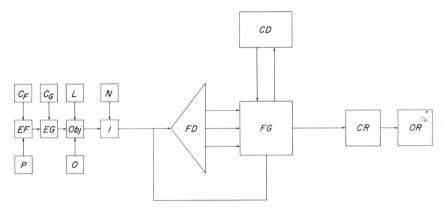

Fig. 124. Representation of the sequence of operations involved in figure–ground differentiation. As in Fig. 118, $P$ = primitive constituents, $EF$ = element formation, $C_F$ = constraints associated with element formation, $EG$ = element grouping, $C_G$ = constraints associated with element grouping, $L$ = light source, $Obj$ = object, $O$ = observer, $N$ = noise, $I$ = optical image, $CR$ = covert response and $OR$ = overt response. In addition, $FD$ represents a hierarchy of feature-detecting systems, $FG$ the process of figure–ground differentiation and $CD$ the associated process of constraint detection.

Figure 124 shows a tentative representation of the general sequence of operations envisaged in the above account of figure–ground differentiation. The process begins with stimulation of simple feature detectors. These elementary responses are then refined through successive stages of differentiation and generalization so as to make possible the detection of a rich variety of more complex features. At the same time, however, the original simple features are preserved, as are all the features detected in any intermediate stage. The most complex features then provide the initial "suggested" elements, for the primary organizing system. This decides which elements are to constitute figural components according to a small number of rules of thumb, selected during the course of a long evolution. The figural components are then tested for the presence or absence of various constraints. Any constraint detected serves to increase the likelihood of the particular organization in which the constraint was detected. At the same time, the predominant organization exerts some selective influence on the outputs from the various feature detectors. Hence, in principle, the effects of detecting a powerful, high-order constraint may be fed back via the figure–ground differentiation process to modify the features detected by the system in such a way as to increase the amount of constraint detected even more.

Grouping

Figure 124 represents a tentative sketch of a process of organization which is generally regarded as being the most elementary carried out by the visual system. As we have seen, a second organizing process, which is usually assumed to depend on figure–ground differentiation, seems to be implied by the gestalt principles of grouping. If this process does indeed succeed figure–ground differentiation, then the most economical hypothesis is that it operates in the same way. In order words, grouping also proceeds initially in accordance with certain heuristic principles, with the tendencies towards one grouping or another then being modified as a result of the detection of constraints in the various groupings. It also seems likely that successful groupings would exert some feedback influence over figure–ground differentiation. For example, the reverberating effects of such feedback would seem to be required to explain the sudden dramatic perceptual reorganizations experienced in situations such as the hidden figures tests devised by Leeper (1935).

The absence of elaborate cognitive functioning implied by this scheme harmonizes well with Garner's conclusions (1974) about perceptual organization. In particular, the data he presents from Royer and Garner (1966) show that, when presented with a continuous, cyclically repetitive sequence of signals and pauses, observers do not perceive all of the possible organizations. Instead, certain "organizational principles" appear evident, such as: (i) runs of identical elements are never broken; (ii) simple temporal progressions (increases or decreases in run length) are preferred; and (iii) mirror reflections of patterns are also preferred. Garner then goes on to suggest that each perceived organization may be viewed as a compound of the perceived organizations of two one-element patterns in which two more primitive principles operate, namely: (i) start the pattern with the longest run; and (ii) end the pattern with the longest gap. Which of the two one-element patterns is more effective in determining the structure of the composite two-element pattern does not appear to be determined by its structure, goodness, or simplicity of organization. Instead, the two elements appear to be segregated into figure and ground, then the perceived organization of the figure is determined by the relative lengths of the runs and the gaps. As Garner conclude, "this process of perceiving organization is quite straight-forward, and does not involve any very high level of cognitive processing at all" (1974, p. 66).

Transformation

Figure 125 presents a scheme in which the operation of grouping has been included. In addition, one further set of operations, those of transformation,

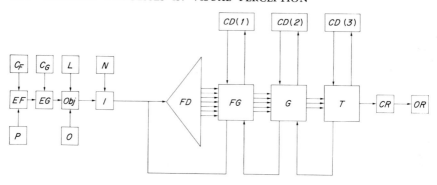

Fig. 125. Representation of the processes involved in perceptual organization. Elements suggested by the feature-detecting system (*FD*) are operated on by various figure–ground differentiation principles (*FG*) and suggested organizations tested by the constraint detection system, *CD*(1). A similar sequence is carried out by the operations of grouping (*G*) and transformation (*T*), together with their associated constraint detection systems, *CD*(2) and *CD*(3). The denotation of other symbols remains the same as that in Figs 124 and 118.

is represented. Among the reasons for this is the consideration that, over a long period, the detection of simple constraints would allow the organism to make a wider variety of informed responses to environmental situations. Among them would be a number of movements (whether of the whole organism or some part, such as the head or eyes), which would have the effect of increasing the input of certain of the simple constraint detection systems. (For example, elements could be perceived as being regularly spaced under a changed line of regard.) Eventually, it is suggested, the organism might develop the capability of "internalizing" some of these responses, i.e. of transforming the stimulus input in such a way as to maximize the amount of constraint detected.

As has been implied by Attneave (1972), the six transformations most likely to achieve this appear to be those of translation and rotation with respect to each of the three major axes. A further advantage of these operations is that the amount of transformation required could supply the organism with a three-dimensional specification of the distances, orientations and layout of objects in its environment. At the same time, however, if both element grouping and element transformation were also (independently) under the control of processes of constraint detection, then some equivocation might occur between transformed and untransformed arrays of elements. This consequence would seem to be consistent with Attneave's suggestion (1972) that the perceptual system may be "simultaneously trying to minimize distances from the frontal plane on the one hand, and differences between the logarithms of tridimensional lengths on the other, and that a compromise is reached at some equilibrium point" (1972, p. 297). In an earlier paper, I put forward a similar notion, namely, "that the impression of visual depth given by a pattern represents a compromise between the economy gained from making a tridimensional specification of the elements in the pattern and the possible cost of coding the information in this way" (1971, p. 23). The present conceptualization would appear to suggest an analogous hypothesis, namely, that perceptual organization in depth represents a balance between the tendency towards a transformation giving rise to the maximum constraint and the tendency towards an untransformed array, with the strength of the tendency in both cases being determined by the amount of constraint detected.

## General Considerations

As must now be clear, the analysis of the process of perceptual organization presented in Fig. 125 is closely analogous to our conception of the physical processes which give rise to a structured visual image. The physical processes of element formation, aggregation and movement are paralleled by hypothesized perceptual processes of figure–ground differentiation, grouping and transformation. Meanwhile, the constraints which operate in each physical process are assigned separate arrays of constraint detectors in the perceptual system. Although determined genetically, and not character-ized by any complex cognitive activity, this system is extremely flexible and, in its reconstruction of a stable perceptual picture of the environment from a multiplicity of independently sensed features, it is similar—in outline at least—to Brunswick's lens model. Before examining some implications of this approach, we shall briefly consider its relation to the traditional theories discussed above.

### Relation to Traditional Approaches

Although the schematic picture in Fig. 125 cannot be advanced as a complete synthesis of the traditional approaches summarized in the first section, it does embody most of the main ingredients. It shares Gibson's and Brunswick's insistence on the abundance of information available in the visual image, while distinguishing between the non-optical constraints emphasized by gestalt theorists and the optical constraints studied by Gibson and Brunswick. It embodies the notion—common to Gibson, gestalt theory and the neurophysiology of feature detection—that the perception of features, and the detection of constraints among those features, are relatively direct, unlearned processes. On the other hand, the processes of figure–ground differentiation, grouping and transformation are conceived as operations distinct from mere registration, albeit proceeding in accordance with elementary principles. These mediating processes are morphologically similar to the physical processes giving rise to structure in the visual image, and are controlled by the detection of constraints by neural systems which must be supposed to have evolved because they possessed what Brunswick would term a "high ecological validity".

At this stage, it would be premature to attempt to specify the nature of these constraints in detail. However, in keeping with the proposals of Gyr *et al.* (1966), it could be suggested that the constraint detection system which controls the process of transformation does so in such a way as to maximize the features within one class which remain invariant, with respect to certain dimensions, under transformations of translation and rotation. Similarly, the detection of constraints such as periodicity, progression, or symmetry might be supposed to be instrumental in controlling the operations of grouping and figure–ground differentiation. What seems important to emphasize at present is that, despite the appearance of holistic principles, such as a search for economy in coding, the constraint detection systems are perhaps best conceived of as numerous, independent and functioning in competition with each other for control of the organization of sensory information.

## Some Further Consequences and Possibilities

*"Unique" stimuli.*   While such a system allows for considerable flexibility in the organization of sensory information, no high level of quasi-rational inference is assumed. On this view, even Garner's hypothesis that observers infer a stimulus to be drawn from a subset of stimuli which is as small as possible, consistent with the constraints detected in the presented stimulus, may attribute more cognitive processing to the perceptual system than is strictly necessary. If a major function of the perceptual system is the detection of constraint, and if an object is seen simply as a configuration of elements which are organized according to certain constraints, then the detail in which the object is perceived will depend upon the number and variety of constraints detected. Strictly speaking, this means that, provided the constraints remain unaltered, the object in question should be indistinguishable from others also formed in accordance with the same constraints.

Of course it is true, as Leibniz pointed out, that "we should never find two leaves in a garden, nor two drops of water, which were perfectly alike", provided we can examine them (microscopically if need be) in sufficient detail (1956, p. 214). In these circumstances, however, it seems likely that we differentiate between the objects in question either by detecting some constraint in one which is not present in the other, or by detecting some difference in the degree of constraint. In other words, it would seem to be more economical to suppose that we never perceive unique stimuli (or unique objects, for that matter): we perceive only different combinations of multiple constraints. The ancient philosophical problem of how we generalize from particulars to universals need not arise for the perceptual system if we suppose that it responds only to constraint in the stimulus, and that generalization depends upon ignoring certain constraints (or differences in degree), while differentiation depends upon seeking out new constraints, or detecting differences in degree.

*The sequence of operations.* Up until now it has been assumed that the sequence of operations in perceptual organization repeats that of the processes in the natural world which give rise to a structured optical image. It has also been taken for granted that what is generally regarded as the most rudimentary operation (namely, figure–ground differentiation) should occur first, followed by grouping, and finally by the more sophisticated processes of transformation. However, it could be argued that this order is neither the most biologically advantageous nor the most plausible from an evolutionary point of view. One possible disadvantage, for example, is that operations succeeding figure–ground differentiation are limited by the outputs which it produces and, in contrast to those of the transformation process, it seems likely that many of these will reduce the availability of some information. If this is the case, then a more advantageous evolutionary strategy would be to postpone the selective, focussing effects of figure–ground differentiation for as long as possible, while interposing other, more advanced operations before it. Thus, the process of transformation may operate directly on the output from the feature detectors, followed by grouping processes (responsible, among other things, for the perception of surfaces), with figure–ground differentiation occurring as the final operation.

## Decision Processes in Figure–Ground Differentiation and Grouping

Faced with a system as complex as that in Fig. 125, the problem arises as to how it may be studied. The most useful approach seems to be to follow Garner's strategy (1974) of confining attention to situations in which other hypothesized processes need not be assumed to operate, or in which their operation is unequivocal. Under these circumstances, variations in performance (or "process limitations") can be attributed with some confidence to the particular operation in which we are interested. While it must be acknowledged that the success of such a strategy depends to a large extent upon the adequacy of the conceptual framework presupposed by it, in the present context at least, this approach suggests a quite specific role for decision mechanisms in the operation of figure–ground differentiation.

## Figure–Ground Differentiation

As an example, we may consider the perceptual organization of the Rubin circle in Fig. 126, in which the main factor that determines which of the two sets of sectors is seen as figure is the relative sizes of the sector angles (Oyama, 1950). Since most observers would be in close agreement as to what constitutes the elements of Fig. 126, we may assume that the feature detecting system operates unequivocally to define the eight sectors in terms of features such as arcs and straight line segments. The stage at which differences in organization emerge would seem to be the subsequent operation of figure–ground differentiation. At this point, as I have argued above, the process of organization seems to follow a primitive rule of thumb, according to which the smaller elements are classified as figural. There appear to be no further constraints to be detected, so we may assume that the associated constraint detection system (1) is not implicated.

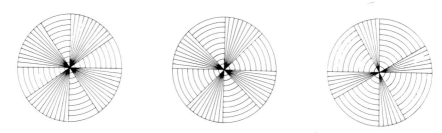

Fig. 126. Rubin circles composed of "radius" and "arc" sectors. The smaller the size of the sector angle, the more likely that set of sectors is to be perceived as figure against ground.

Following (or, perhaps, preceding) the organization into figure and ground, it seems likely that grouping of the sectors may occur on some criterion such as equal area. However, it seems implausible to suppose that this would produce differences in organization in this particular case (although it might, for example, where segments of one colour were all equal in area, while segments of the other colour were all different). Similarly, no further constraints appear to be associated with one of the two likely groupings rather than the other, so we may rule out the operation of the second constraint detection system (2). Finally, it seems unnecessary to suppose that either the process of transformation or its associated constraint detection system (3) is important here. Therefore, in this instance at least, it seems possible to hypothesize that perceptual organization is mediated by a simple process of discrimination, and that no other cognitive processes need be assumed to be involved. I shall first attempt to make this hypothesis more explicit, before examining some of the relevant evidence.

## Figure–Ground Differentiation as a Decision Process

If we suppose the operation of figure–ground differentiation to be mediated in this instance by a simple discrimination process, then, on the basis of the conclusions reached in the first two parts of this book, it is possible to specify in some detail the sequence of events presumed to take place. In particular, as in traditional psychophysical situations, we can suppose that unpredictability in responding is largely due to random variations in the perceived angular size of the $R$ ("radius") and the $A$ ("arc") sectors. As was argued in Chapter 2, the most convenient additional assumptions to make are that the distributions of perceived sizes are normal, and have equal variances. Again as in Chapter 3, we may suppose that the observer inspects the momentary $(R–A)$ differences, one at a time and at a steady rate, until he accumulates a criterion amount $k_g$ or $k_l$ of positive or negative difference respectively. If $k_l$ is reached first, then the organizational response is one of the form: "the $R$ sectors are figural elements". If, on the other hand, the $A$ sectors are judged to be smaller, the converse response is made.

With this approach, the primitive "rules of thumb" responsible for figure–ground differentiation are seen as elementary decision rules. Alternative organizations, indicated by different primitive rules, are accomplished by different decision mechanisms, operating independently and in competition, on relevant differences and equalities in features of the stimulus. The resulting organization depends upon the first mechanism to reach a decision, and may be supposed to persist until some alternative organization is initiated, either by the same or by a different decision mechanism. Meanwhile, the criterion values employed by each mechanism would be subject to control by some target level of confidence. As a result, in the simple situation where no further constraints are detected, the value of $k$ for the most confident organizational response would be lowered more than that for any other. Thus this response would occur even more rapidly and would come to dominate—or even monopolize—the input to any subsequent organizational operation.

In the same way, the detection of constraint (which must depend primarily on the recognition of differences and equalities as revealed by some particular organization) may also be supposed to be mediated by an array of elementary decision modules, operating in parallel. In turn, when some constraint is detected, it seems plausible to suppose that this might result in a decrease in the target level of confidence controlling the decision process which gave rise to the constrained organization in question. On the other hand, in order to preserve the stability of the system, it would seem to be necessary to assume that the target levels of confidence controlling the constraint detection mechanisms are themselves relatively immune to alteration by anything which happens during the process of perceptual organization. This means that, while the effects of a clear constraint might reverberate back through the system and result in a very stable organization, as soon as some feature of the stimulus is altered, the adaptive elements in the system would be capable of adjusting to this by revising either the primary criterion levels or the target levels controlling the basic organizing responses.

While a hypothesis of this kind may seem at first to be somewhat general, it is also capable of yielding some quite precise predictions, at least some of which are at odds with the implications of the traditional approaches discussed earlier. In particular, when applied in a restricted situation such as the perceptual organization of Fig. 126, the hypothesis leads to the following predictions:

*Response probability.*   As in simple psychophysical judgments, when the emergence of one or the other organizational response depends upon a difference in the values of two stimuli, or stimulus elements, along a single dimension, then the probability of that response should be a sigmoid (psychometric) function of the difference.

*Response time.*   As in psychophysical tasks, the time taken to achieve an organizational response should be inversely related to the degree of discriminability of the pattern elements along the relevant dimension.

*Variations in caution.*   As detailed in Chapters 2 to 5, tasks involving simple psychophysical judgments frequently show evidence of a trade-off between speed and accuracy. In terms of the present approach, a figural response to the larger of the two sectors in Fig. 126 would be analogous to an error in a simple discrimination task. If an observer adopted high criteria, therefore, we should expect him to take a longer time on average to achieve a perceptual organization, but to make fewer "errors" than at lower criterion values.

*Variations in bias.*   If the process of perceptual organization is mediated by the accumulation of criterion amounts of "evidence", then the values of $k$ adopted by an observer should be susceptible to manipulation by the same means which have proved successful in the control of criterion levels in simple psychophysical judgments (e.g. instructions, rewards, or punishments).

*Confidence.* Finally, we should expect that an observer would find it a meaningful task to report his confidence in the perceptual organization of a stimulus, and that the pattern of variations in confidence should resemble those obtained in simple psychophysical judgment.

## Evidence for the Operation of Decision Processes in Figure–Ground Differentiation

In order to test these predictions, an experiment (unpublished) was carried out by an Honours student, G. Humphris, supervised by myself. In this experiment, stimuli similar to those in Fig. 126 were presented to each of eight student observers, who were required to indicate, by pressing one of two keys, which of the two sets of sectors first appeared as "figure". Each observer made figural responses to a series of 500 stimuli, in which 10 different angular values for the sectors, ranging from 20° up to 70° in steps of 5°, were presented in random order. The results, together with some other relevant findings, fall naturally under the five headings employed above.

*Response probability.* As can be seen from Fig. 127, response probabilities were related as predicted to the angular difference between the sector elements. Results from a number of other studies also suggest a relationship of this kind (e.g. Frisch and Julesz, 1966; Künnapas, 1957; Oyama, 1950).

*Response time.* Figure 128 presents the pattern of response times, averaged over the two fastest, the two slowest and the two intermediate observers, and shows a striking resemblance to the pattern predicted by an accumulator model for two-category discrimination, as portrayed in Chapter 3 (Fig. 35). As is suggested by Fig. 128, response times for "incorrect" organizations tended to be longer than those for "correct" in 21 comparisons out of 30, with 6 of the 9 exceptions occurring in the case of the two fastest responders. These results are nicely consistent with the properties of an accumulator process, and are echoed by Künnapas' finding that "the dominant (correct) figure appears as figure very rapidly . . . The nondominant (incorrect) figure appears as figure more slowly" (1957, p. 38).

*Variations in caution.* When the total number of errors made by each observer was compared with the mean time taken for all responses, no significant correlation emerged and it seems likely that the expected relation

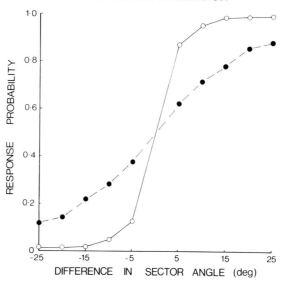

Fig. 127. Probability of responding "X is figure" obtained in an unpublished experiment by Humphris, employing the stimuli shown in Fig. 126. Filled circles represent the means of data for the four "least accurate" observers, while empty circles represent means for the four "most accurate". For each observer, the probability of identifying the "arc" sectors as figure for an angular difference of $x°$ has been averaged with that of identifying the "radius" sectors as figure for a difference of $-x°$. Hence the symmetry of the curves in this instance is artefactual. However, presentation in this form facilitates comparison with the simulated curves in Fig. 32.

may have been masked by other individual differences, such as the "noise" associated with the stimuli. However, when mean overall response times for this experiment were compared with those taken by the same observers in a second probabilistic discrimination task of a type previously employed (Vickers *et al.*, 1971), a highly significant positive correlation was obtained (Spearman rho = $0.833$; $p = 0.01$). This suggests that these observers adopted a similar pattern of criterion levels for the two tasks. The determination of response time by the decision criterion may well be responsible for the factor labelled "speed of judgment", extracted by Thurstone (1944) in a factorial study of 40 different tests of perceptual performance, and for a similar factor extracted in a later study by Künnapas (1969) and characterized by him as "decision speed".

*Variations in bias.*   Although the present experiment throws no light on this particular point, several other experiments have suggested that continued inspection of a related figure can change the relative likelihood of

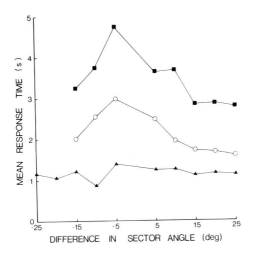

Fig. 128. The pattern of times taken to achieve a figural response in an unpublished experiment by Humphris. Filled triangles represent the means of data for the two fastest observers, empty circles those for the two intermediate and filled squares those for the two slowest observers. For each observer the mean time taken to identify the "arc" sectors as figure for an angular difference of $x°$ has been averaged with that taken to identify the "radius" sectors as figure for a difference of $-x°$. The curves for the slowest and intermediate observers are curtailed because no "errors" were made at differences of $-25°$ and $-20°$.

alternative interpretations of an ambiguous test figure presented subsequently (e.g. Harrower, 1936; Carlson, 1953; Adams, 1954; Cohen, 1959). Again, it has been shown that punishment of one interpretation of an ambiguous figure changes the likelihood of its being reported later as figure, even in situations where observers are assured that no punishment will be given (Schafer and Murphy, 1943; Mangan, 1959; Lie, 1965). While it cannot be certain, as Saugstad (1965) points out, that altered reports represent a real change in the appearance of a stimulus, these findings lend themselves naturally to an interpretation in terms of changes in the relative criterion values adopted for a simple decision process.

*Confidence and "perceptual clarity".*     Mean confidence ratings from the present experiment averaged over all eight observers are shown in Fig. 129, plotted against the corresponding difference in sector angle. With the exception of the first point, which, for each observer, is based on fewer measures than the others, mean confidence seems to bear a direct, monotonic relation to angular difference, similar to that found in simple discrimination. As expected, observers appear to experience varying degrees of confidence in their perceptual organization of a stimulus. Indeed, this aspect of perception seems closely analogous to the notion of "perceptual clarity" recently invoked by Haber (1969) and Dodwell (1971), to the notion of "figuredness" used by Künnapas (1957), to the attribute of "goodness" investigated by the Gestalt theorists, and to the outmoded concept of "attensity" employed by Titchener (1908). Their shared meaning seems to refer to the degree to which a given difference or pattern "stands out" in the observer's consciousness. Until cogent reasons are advanced to the contrary, therefore, a considerable economy of theory can be achieved by supposing that they have a common theoretical basis in the difference between the accumulated magnitudes of the signal differences at the moment of a decision. Among other implications, this view would account for Künnapas' report that "the dominant figure 'correctly perceived' as figure has always much greater clearness than the nondominant in the same role" (1957, p. 38).

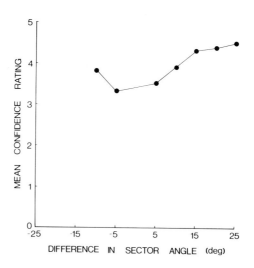

Fig. 129. Mean confidence ratings in figural responses obtained in an unpublished experiment by Humphris. Data represent the means for all 8 observers. For each observer the mean confidence in identifying the "arc" sectors as figure for an angular difference of $x°$ has been averaged with that in identifying the "radius" sectors as figure for a difference of $-x°$. The curve is curtailed at the left because some observers made no "errors" at differences of $-25°$ and $-20°$.

## Perceptual Grouping

When we turn to consider the operation of perceptual grouping, the picture which emerges is similar. As with figure–ground differentiation, the most useful strategy appears to be to study situations in which perceptual performance is limited by processes clearly involved in grouping, but in which the constraints imposed by other operations can be assumed to be minimal. Figure 130, for example, shows two examples of stimuli which I devised (Vickers, 1972b), for which grouping processes would seem to constitute the obvious limiting factors. In both figures, an array of dots has been randomly and independently "jittered" in the horizontal and vertical directions about the intersection points of an underlying (unseen) rectangular matrix, which in every respect is perfectly regular. Little or no ambiguity arises in the figural differentiation of the black dots from the white background. Similarly, since the array is seen unequivocally as lying in a plane at approximately right angles to the line of sight, we may assume that its perceptual organization is not limited by the operation of transformation. On the other hand, considerable uncertainty exists as to whether the dots are perceived as organized predominantly in a horizontal or in a vertical direction. In the case of Fig. 130a, where the amounts of horizontal and vertical jitter are held equal and constant, the prevailing organization depends upon whether the mean horizontal interdot distance is greater than the vertical, or vice versa. As the gestalt principle of proximity would suggest, the direction of the predominant organization corresponds to that of the smaller mean interdot distance.

Figure 130b illustrates a fairly similar situation, which is different only in that the mean horizontal and vertical interdot distances are held equal and constant, while the amount of jitter in the two directions is allowed to vary. In this case, the direction of predominant organization tends to be that of the greater amount of jitter.

In the case of either figure, the most straightforward interpretation seems to be that the observer applies some primitive grouping principle, based on proximity, to the dot elements. The grouping operation gives rise to an organizing decision which depends upon whether the measure of proximity is greater in the horizontal or in the vertical direction. As in the case of figure–ground differentiation, this response may be supposed to be mediated by a simple adaptive decision mechanism. Where (as in this case) there appear to be no further constraints determining the process of perceptual organization, this view leads to a similar set of predictions to those for figure–ground differentiation.

Some empirical results have indeed been obtained concerning the operation of grouping with arrays of the kind shown in Fig. 130. In two separate

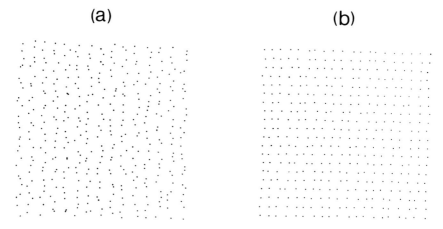

Fig. 130. Patterns of dots in which factors of proximity determine whether the array is perceived as organized in a predominantly vertical or horizontal direction. In Fig. 130a the mean interdot distance is greater in the horizontal than in the vertical direction. In Fig. 130b it is the amount of "jitter" in the horizontal direction which is greater.

experiments, both following the same design as that carried out by Humphris, Shephard (1972) instructed observers to indicate, by pressing one of two keys, whether each of a series of 500 stimuli appeared to be organized in a predominantly horizontal or vertical direction. The first experiment studied effects of varying mean horizontal and vertical proximity (interdot distance) in arrays like those of Fig. 130a. The second studied effects of holding horizontal and vertical proximity constant, while varying the relative amounts of jitter in the two directions. In both cases, the observed relationships between differences in proximity or in jitter on the one hand, and response probability and time on the other, amply justified the conclusion that, where elements are clearly defined, then perceptual organization by grouping would seem also to be mediated by a simple decision mechanism.

## Some General Implications

Clearly, a great deal of work remains to be done to specify this picture of perceptual organization in more detail. For example, we have had to gloss over the hypothesized process of transformation and the intriguing question of the exact sequence of these operations. For the present, however, perhaps enough has been said to indicate the general direction which further development might follow. I shall conclude this section, therefore, by considering some more immediate implications of the proposed approach.

In the first place, if the system outlined in Fig. 125 is realized by means of a multiplicity of adaptive decision modules, each operating on specialized inputs but capable of communicating, with, and influencing, other adaptive modules, then certain additional aspects of perceptual organization can be accommodated. For example, the "transactional" approach to perception, most commonly associated with the work of Ames (1951), Ittelson (1952, 1962) and Kilpatrick (1952) emphasizes that perception depends not only upon the stimulus conditions themselves, but upon certain transactions between sensory effects and the assumptions, expectations, interests, attitudes and motivation of the observer. While some of the transactional demonstrations are open to other interpretations based on some economy or simplicity principle, most researchers would concede that the readiness with which perceptual organizations emerge, or the aspects of a stimulus which appear most salient for an observer, are influenced to some extent by motivational factors and by the effects of past experience. Insofar as the present approach allows for the variation of target levels of confidence (and hence of criterion values) by the effects of past sensory input or by other motivational systems, it allows for the kinds of influence emphasized by the transactional theorists.

At the same time, the present approach rules out certain extreme interpretations suggested by proponents of transactionalism. For example, it is true that the proposed view of perception does imply that some real difference in experienced perceptual organization may result from the biassing effects of past experience or of motivational factors, rather than a simple change in an observer's readiness to please (or deceive) the experimenter by altering his reports of what he perceives. Nevertheless, the information upon which a perceived organization is based is neither occluded, distorted, nor generated by assumptions, expectations, or motivational variables. Any non-veridical organization which results from idiosyncratic biassing of target levels or criterion values carries with it all the information needed for its subsequent correction (in the form of a reduced basis for confidence in the particular perceptual decisions concerned). In other words, abundant sensory input is itself a source of correction and calibration in perception, and distorting forms of perceptual organization are likely to be sustained only by the continual biassing of target levels by some abnormally persistent motivational or higher control system.

In turn, this inherent "self-righting" property of the decision modules responsible for perceptual organization goes a long way towards accounting for some of the hitherto elusive properties of the perceptual process, such as the dynamic, interactive aspects and the tendency towards a state of equilibrium, emphasized by both Brunswick and the gestalt theorists. In addition, the employment of stabilizing negative feedback makes possible the kind of flexibility and adaptive control to which Helson (1964) draws attention. Again, as in Helson's view, perceptual organization depends upon the pooled effect of "focal", "contextual" and "organic" components. However, unlike the models of Brunswick or the gestalt theorists, the adaptability of the system is not solely a property of its overall organization, but is an inherent feature of each component subsystem. Such a view constitutes an important shift of emphasis away from theories implying elaborate cognitive processes, executed by complex configurations of very simple elements, towards one postulating a very restricted range of simple functions, carried out by elements which, although still quite simple, are endowed with all the basic properties generally ascribed to the whole perceptual system. In proposing the adaptive three-category decision module as the basic functional unit of perceptual activity, the present approach is in fundamental agreement with some current views in the field of artificial intelligence (e.g. Deutsch, 1968; von Foerster, 1969; Pask, 1970). Meanwhile, in the field of perception itself, the picture of a hierarchy of adaptive systems is closely similar in spirit, if not in detail, to Powers' (1973) notion of a hierarchy of feedback control, in which higher level control organizations counter disturbances by changing the reference level (or some other parameter) in the adaptive subsystems below them.

## Decision Processes Underlying Changes in Perceptual Organization

Despite requiring considerable development, the approach outlined in the first part of this chapter is evidently capable, even in its present state, of generating some quite precise predictions and of suggesting new ways of looking at old problems. One further problem, to which we now turn, concerns changes or fluctuations in perception and is obviously of crucial importance for an understanding of perceptual organization. Although empirically well-established, the phenomenon has until recently suffered from some theoretical neglect. Before discussing examples of two types of explanation, it is perhaps useful to begin by summarizing some of its main properties.

### Some General Properties of Changes in Perceptual Organization

As early as 1875 it was noticed by Urbantschitsch that, during prolonged attention to a faint stimulus, the stimulus seemed to disappear for quite long periods. Throughout the subsequent history of the study of perception a number of similar phenomena have been reported under the heading of "fluctuations", "oscillations", "reversals", or "rivalry". Besides the many ambiguous stimuli giving rise to these effects (which constitute the standard furniture of laboratory demonstrations in perception), other situations giving rise to changes in perceptual organization include near-threshold stimuli and cases where conflicting stimuli are presented separately to each eye. As Attneave (1968, 1971) points out, whether these changes are predominantly tridimensional or bidimensional, they all seem to involve the periodic replacement of one perceptual organization by another, which is markedly different, although not necessarily the unique converse of the first. Mefferd (1968a) has drawn attention to a number of similarities among the changes in organization which occur with a wide variety of stimuli, and I have suggested (Vickers, 1972c) that the phenomena might usefully be classified under the general heading of *perceptual alternation*. Some of the main characteristics of perceptual alternation have been summarized by Sadler and Mefferd (1970) and these are listed below, together with two other general features, (ii) and (vi), of my own addition (1972c, p. 32):

(i) "There are at least two distinct phases of a viewing session with 'ambigous' stimuli—a period of active orientation on O's part; and a subsequent phase in which occur the characteristic sudden complete reorganizations of percepts referred to here as fluctuations (Mefferd, 1968b). Undoubtedly a later Phase 3 exists in prolonged viewing sessions, as fatigue, boredom, reporting habits and the like modify O's reporting behaviour, fixation, blinking, etc.

(ii) "The average of the times during which a particular percept is seen is a direct function of the probability that that percept will occur first (Künnapas, 1957; Price, 1967a, 1967b; Sadler and Mefferd, 1970).

(iii) "These abrupt reorganizations of a percept occur spontaneously, requiring no volitional effort by O, and the new percept is maintained steadily for a period. While O can influence the *rate* of the fluctuation (Washburn et al., 1934; Ammons et al., 1959; Ulrich and Ammons, 1959; Adams, 1954; Gregory, 1966; Mefferd et al., 1968), he cannot completely prevent a fluctuation, elicit a specific initial percept, or induce a reversal at will.

(iv) "The *rate* is also susceptible to the influence of O's 'set', no matter how it may be established (e.g. Ammons et al., 1959; Leppmann and Mefferd, 1968; Mefferd et al., 1968).

(v) "The *rate* of fluctuation is also susceptible to influence by a variety of manipulations of stimulus properties, including its complexity (Gordon, 1903; Donahue and Griffitts, 1931; Porter, 1938; Ammons and Ammons, 1963, 1965; Wieland and Mefferd, 1966, 1967).

(vi) "The rate of alternation tends to increase as a function of viewing time (Brown, 1955; Price, 1969a, 1969b) for about the first 3 minutes, after which the rate becomes relatively stable. Towards the end of an extended 10–12 minute session the duration of alternate perceptions may become highly variable (Bruner et al., 1950; Torii, 1960; Price, 1968). Presumably this last phase corresponds to the third phase distinguished above by Sadler and Mefferd in section (i)."

## A Satiation Model

One of the first, and most widely accepted, hypotheses to account for perceptual alternations has been some form of "fatigue" or "satiation" theory, derived from the work of McDougal (1906), or from Köhler (1940) and Köhler and Wallach (1944). According to this approach, there is a steady build-up over time of "fatigue products", "resistance", or "excitation", associated with the perceptual organization actually experienced by an observer. When this cumulative effect reaches a certain critical level (satiation), the neural structures sustaining this particular organization cease to operate and a different set, representing the alternative organization, come into play. As soon as the perceptual mechanisms are occupied with this new organization, the "fatigue" or "inhibition" in the old one dissipates, so that, when the structures sustaining the new organization become satiated in turn, those subserving the former are ready to come into play again. The system will thus continue to switch from one state to the other indefinitely. A somewhat analogous electronic system is typified by the multi-vibrator circuit suggested as a model for figural reversals by Attneave (1971).

Unfortunately, while the satiation model can account for variations in alternation rate by assuming that values of the satiation threshold $S$ are appropriately sensitive to experimental manipulations of attitude, set, task difficulty and task length, as described in features (iii) to (vi), it fails to cope with what seem to be the basic characteristics of the process, as outlined in features (i) and (ii). For example, as it stands, the satiation model does not specify the process by which the initial organization emerges. As a result, there is no way of relating a longer duration for one percept with a higher probability that that percept will occur first. Again, the model does not show much promise in accounting for the great degree of variability observed in the durations of successive organizations (e.g. Mull et al., 1954; Sadler and Mefferd, 1970). For example, if it is assumed that the amount of fatigue accumulated in successive time intervals varies according to a normal distribution and that, after switching to an alternative organization, the fatigue associated with the satiated percept is immediately cleared, then it can be shown (following Cox, 1962, pp. 46–59) that the standard deviation in percept duration should vary as a direct function of the square root of the mean percept duration. As indicated below, this increase in variability appears to be too gradual to account for empirical data.

## A Model Based on Classical Psychophysics

The first study to suggest an alternative model capable of dealing with these difficulties, seems to have been an apparently neglected paper by Guilford (1927). Guilford first determined the 50% limens for the detection of a spot of light of low intensity by each of three observers. The fluctuations in visibility of the spot were then recorded by having observers press a key at the moment of disappearance, and lifting it as soon as the spot reappeared. The percentage of time the spot was visible to one observer is shown in Fig. 131a, plotted against stimulus intensity. The curve clearly resembles the psychometric function obtained when the percentage of *times* that a stimulus is reported is plotted against stimulus intensity (i.e. when the stimulus is presented repeatedly for a brief interval only). Further support for the hypothesis that the fluctuations are determined by the same factors which determine a psychological threshold is provided by Guilford's finding that the observer with the highest 50% limen gave the highest intensity at which the stimulus was visible 50% of the time and vice versa.

An alternative representation of Guilford's results is shown in Fig. 131b. The two sets of graphs in Fig. 131 provide a suggestive comparison with the results of a study of the reversals of the "cross" and "plus" percepts of a Rubin circle, conducted some 30 years later by Künnapas (1957) and reproduced in Fig. 132. Künnapas also obtained results which supported the notion that the relative duration of alternative percepts, fluctuation rate and thresholds were influenced in similar ways by the same factors. In the first place (Fig. 132a), the percentage of times one set of sectors (e.g. "cross") was seen first as figure was a sigmoid function of the difference in angular size between the two sets of sectors. In the second place (Fig. 132b), the average duration of the time for which one set was perceived as figure was a more or less direct (though not linear) function of the size of the difference in sector angle.

The similarity between these results and those of Guilford is striking and, indeed, a mechanism which might account for both sets of data was sketched in by Guilford, though not fully explained by him. Guilford's suggestion deserves to be quoted in full:

> The same stimulus, say at the limen, is perceived at one moment because a "chance" disposition of the factors on the whole favours it; it is not perceived at another moment because the "chance" disposition is on the whole against it. A fluctuating light or sound would then give us a continuous picture of the "chance" dispositions, perceptible when the balance of factors is favourable, and imperceptible when the balance of factors is unfavourable. (1927, p. 552).

If, as suggested by Guilford, the fluctuations of a weak stimulus give us a continuous picture of these "chance" factors, then it seems reasonable to suppose that an observer will (as he is instructed) report only those cases in which a chance factor gives rise to a percept which is different from the one favoured in the instant before. Thus, Guilford's suggestion can be seen as

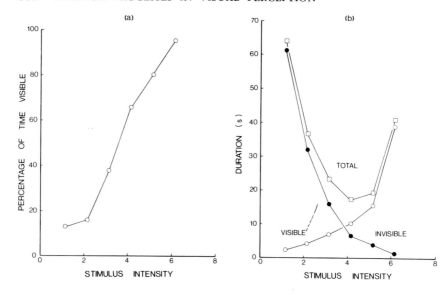

Fig. 131.  Data from Guilford (1927). Figure 131a shows the percentage of time the stimulus was visible as a function of intensity. Figure 131b shows the average duration at each intensity of the intervals of visibility and invisibility and the average duration of the total period (visible and invisible). (Intensity units represent readings on a Nagel adaptometer divided by 1000.)

tantamont to a cyclic repetition of a classical psychophysical process of judgment of the kind discussed in Chapter 2.

Such a model nearly links together the mechanism of a psychophysical threshold with the process underlying perceptual alternation. The average percept duration $\bar{D}_A$ is given by $\bar{D}_A = 1/Q$ where $\bar{D}_A$ is the average length of a run of successive responses of the same kind $(A)$, if each response is made independently of the previous one with a constant probability $P = 1 - Q$, and $Q$ is the probability of occurrence of the alternative response $B$. Predictions can also be made about the variance $\sigma^2_D$ in the duration of each percept, using the relations $\sigma^2_{D_A} = P/Q^2$ and $\sigma^2_{D_A} = Q/P^2$. Substitution of a few values for $P$ shows that the standard deviation $\sigma_{D_A}$ follows the mean $\bar{D}_A$ very closely, and is very well approximated by the equation $\sigma_{D_A} = \bar{D}_A - 0.5$.

The model is also capable of yielding some further predictions concerning the shape of the distribution of percept durations (Bush and Mosteller, 1955, pp. 315–316; Restle, 1961, p. 173; McGill, 1963, pp. 312–317), and the distribution of the number of reversals per unit of time (Restle, 1961, p. 173). Meanwhile, the predicted relation between stimulus difference (or intensity) and percept duration is very similar to the pattern obtained by Guilford and Künnapas, and shown in Figs 131b and 132b. Unfortunately

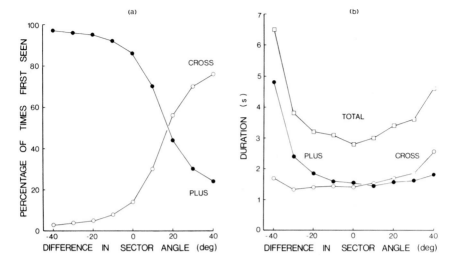

Fig. 132. Data from Künnapas (1957). Figure 132a shows the percentage of times each set of sectors in a Rubin circle was seen first as figure. Figure 132b shows the average duration of each of the alternative perceptions, together with the total period ("cross" and "plus") at each value of the difference in angle ("plus" minus "cross") between the two sets of sectors.

while the model accounts nicely for features (i) and (ii) listed above, it does not offer any explanation of the effects on alternation of attitude, set, or bias, stimulus complexity, or task difficulty and length, as summarized in features (iii) to (vi). For example, instructions to "hold" or "switch" can increase the mean duration of both percepts, but there is nothing in this classical model which can be altered so as to produce such changes.

## A Cyclic Accumulator Model of Perceptual Alternation

It would appear that the classical psychophysical model and the satiation model are complementary, and that a better account would be provided by some version of the classical model which contained a variable which behaved like the satiation threshold $s$. Since there are very close resemblances between the way $s$ is assumed to change and the way in which the criterion $k$ is varied in an accumulator model of psychophysical judgment, it would seem inevitable that better results would be obtained by substituting the cyclic repetition of an accumulator process for that of the classical mechanism. I have proposed a process of this kind (Vickers, 1972b, 1972c), which is illustrated in Fig. 133.

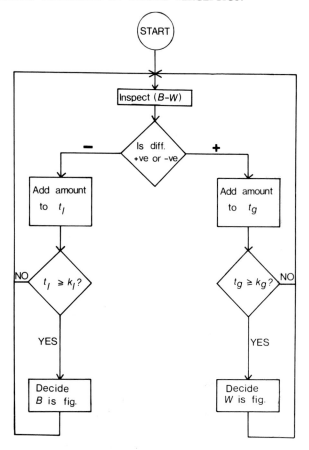

Fig. 133. Flow diagram of a cyclic accumulator process applied to organizing the black (*B*) and white (*W*) sectors of a Maltese cross design as figure and ground. (Adapted from Vickers, 1972b).

Such a system is very flexible, and has a great many interesting properties. Among the most relevant to the features of perceptual alternation outlined above are the following. (With the exception of the last, they correspond to the properties (i) to (vi) summarized above.)

## The Initial Phase

As outlined in the previous section, the probability of one percept being chosen before another, and the time taken for its emergence, should be related to the discriminability of the stimulus elements. Bias can be accommodated by supposing that the observer holds different values of $k$ for each alternative, while changes in the values of $k$ for both alternatives should be analogous to the speed–accuracy trade-off observed in simple psychophysical judgment. As we have seen, there is a considerable amount of evidence which confirms these predictions and supports the view that the initial emergence of a perceptual organization is mediated by the same kind of mechanism which underlies simple psychophysical judgments.

## Relations between the Initial Percept and the Subsequent Rate of Alternation

If we consider the case of a stimulus which gives rise to two equally probable percepts, and an observer who adopts equal values of $k$ for both alternatives, then, as with Guilford's model, the mean run length of successive organizational decisions of the same kind will be equal to $1/Q$ (i.e. $1/0·5 = 2$). If we also assume that the time required to translate an organizational response into overt form is quite small, then, under these circumstances, mean percept duration should on average be approximately twice as long as the time taken to achieve the initial organization (as appears to have been found by Künnapas (1957)). Moreover, an observer who adopts low values of $k$ should produce a fast organizational response in the initial phase, followed by alternating percepts of equal, but relatively short, average duration (i.e. a high rate of alternation). Times for the first organizational response from a more cautious observer, on the other hand, will be longer, and his subsequent rate of alternation lower. These predictions too are supported by Künnapas' finding (1969) of a significant negative correlation between the time required for the first figural response and the subsequent alternation rate, and by Lindauer and Lindauer's report (1970) that a decrease over trials in the time for the first figural response was accompanied by an increase in the rate of alternation.

In order to explore these relations in more detail I carried out a simulation of 15 "sessions", each of 500 cycles of the cyclic accumulator process, operating in non-adaptive, two-category mode on each of 21 normal distributions of differences, such as might be generated by a series of comparisons between the angular sizes of adjacent black and white sectors of a Rubin cross (Vickers, 1972c). Figure 134 shows the mean duration of one of the two alternative percepts obtained in these simulations for each of three values of the criteria $k_g = k_l$, plotted against the mean of the distribution of hypothesized subjective differences. It is clear that the theoretical curves closely resemble those obtained by Guilford (1927) and Künnapas (1957) (Figs 131 and 132).

Meanwhile, the pattern of standard deviations predicted by the proposed process was also examined (Vickers, 1972c) and is very similar to that of the

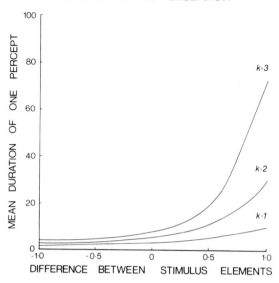

Fig. 134. The mean duration of one percept of the form "$V > S$" or "$S$ is figure" obtained in simulation of the cyclic repetition of a two-category accumulator process (Vickers, 1972c), plotted against the difference in units of $\sigma_{(V-S)}$ between the means of the two stimulus elements $V$ and $S$. Each curve represents data for a different value of the criteria $k_g = k_l$. Duration is measured in terms of the number of ($V-S$) differences inspected.

mean. A more detailed picture is provided by Fig. 135, which shows the typically linear relations between the standard deviation and the mean duration of one particular percept obtained in a series of 30 simulations, each of 500 cycles of the accumulator process, operating (again in non-adaptive, two-category mode) at each of 5 different levels of subjective difference ($\overline{V-S}$), ranging from $-1\sigma_{(V-S)}$, through 0, up to $1\sigma_{(V-S)}$. In this case, mean percept duration was varied by varying the levels of $k_g = k_l$ adopted for the two alternative responses from 1 to 6, in steps of 1. When ($\overline{V-S}$) departs from 0, the two alternative percepts become non-equiprobable, with responses to negative differences corresponding to errors in a simple discrimination task. As can be seen from Fig. 135, the coefficient of slope increases somewhat with increasingly positive values of ($\overline{V-S}$) and decreases as lower values are considered. In other words, the slope of the relation between the standard deviation and the mean percept duration is a function both of the response made and of the discriminability of the relevant stimulus elements.

When ($\overline{V-S}$) is zero and the percepts are equiprobable, the coefficient of slope is approximately 0·83. This accords well with Nettelbeck's finding (1972) that the standard deviation was a linear function of the mean percept

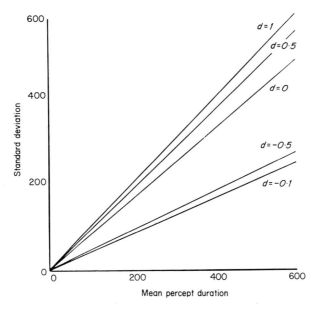

Fig. 135. The relations between the standard deviation and the mean percept duration obtained in simulation of the cyclic accumulator process for different degrees of discriminability $\overline{(V-S)} = d$. At each value of $d$ from $-1 \cdot 0$, through 0, to $1 \cdot 0$, the coefficients of slope are $0 \cdot 43$, $0 \cdot 46$, $0 \cdot 83$, $0 \cdot 94$ and $1 \cdot 0$ respectively.

duration, the coefficients of slope being $0 \cdot 93$ and $0 \cdot 90$ for each of the two alternative percepts of a Necker cube. Similar results have also be obtained in an unpublished study by White (1972). Though consistent with a cyclic accumulator process, these findings would appear to rule out the satiation model—at least in the form outlined above.

## The Control of Alternations

Turning to the ability of the proposed model to account for aspects of the data for which the satiation process seems particularly appropriate, we find that the introduction of adjustable criterion levels, as a counterpart to a satiation threshold, enables these features to be easily accommodated. For example, the cyclic repetition of an accumulator process would produce abrupt alternations between percepts and, since the factor ultimately governing their occurrence is the spontaneous random activity of the nervous system, these would required no volitional effort on the part of an observer. Meanwhile, although an observer could neither directly "prevent a fluctuation, elicit a specific initial percept, nor induce a reversal at will", he could be expected to influence the rate of alternation by raising or lowering

criterion values, by adopting unequal values of $k$ for alternative organizations, or—possibly—by directing his attention to different features of the
stimulus.

## Indirect Subjective Factors

Since variations in set can be accounted for in terms of changes in the value
of $k$ maintained for each alternative, the rate of alternation should be
susceptible to influence by any of the factors likely to change the set adopted
by an observer. In agreement with this, there is considerable evidence to
show that observers can control alternation rate in obedience to instructions
(e.g. Ammons et al., 1959, Leppman and Mefferd, 1968; Mefferd et al., 1968;
Pelton and Solley, 1968). Similarly, some evidence that the probabilities of
perceiving alternative organizations are affected by rewards and punishments is reviewed by Saugstad (1965). Unfortunately, the interpretation of
these experiments is complicated by the way in which the observer
perceives the "demand characteristics" of the experiment (Orne, 1962).

## Objective Factors

As noted above in (v), a number of experiments have reported that more
complex figures alternate more slowly. Although the notion of "complexity" is not precisely defined in these experiments, the Scripture blocks,
Beaunis cubes or Schröder staircase employed by Gordon (1903), Donahue
and Griffitts (1931) and Porter (1938) all constitute assemblies of several
elements or subpatterns. It seems reasonable to suppose, therefore, that an
observer's judgment concerning the whole array may be based on a series of
decisions concerning its elements (c.f. Goldstein, 1967; Pickett, 1970; Olson
and Attneave, 1970; Vickers, 1972b). This would be expected to take longer
and result in a slower decision cycle than a judgment based on a single
decision concerning only two elements.

## Spontaneous Changes in the Rate of Alternation

In order to accommodate changes in the rate of alternation throughout a
viewing session, it is necessary to assume that some adaptive version of the
decision process is operating, such as the one outlined in Chapter 7.
Predicted changes then depend upon the discriminability of the stimulus
elements, the initial (resting) values of the criteria $k_g$ and $k_l$ and the levels of
target confidence and $C_G$ and $C_L$. For example, when the stimulus elements
are indiscriminable, as in a Rubin cross with equal sectors, and the initial
criterion values high relative to the target levels of confidence, then the
initial organization will be slow and the percept durations relatively long.
As criteria are revised downwards to reduce overconfidence, percept

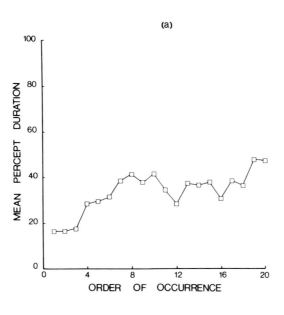

**(a)**

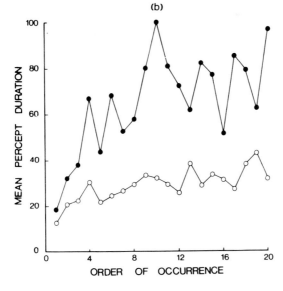

**(b)**

Fig. 136. Changes in mean percept duration as a function of the occasion on which the percept occurred as obtained in simulation of the cyclic accumulator process. Figure 136a shows the mean duration of one of the two equiprobable percepts when $(\overline{V-S}) = 0$. Figure 136b shows changes in the duration of the more probable "correct" percept (filled circles) and of the less probable "incorrect" percept (empty circles) when $(\overline{V-S}) = 0 \cdot 1 \sigma_{(V-S)}$.

durations will become shorter and alternation rate will increase, as noted above in (v). This indeed appears the most likely chain of events following exposure to a new stimulus. On the other hand, with repeated familiarity, a situation might arise in which criterion values were low relative to levels of target confidence. In this case, alternation rate should decrease when criteria are adjusted upwards. This less usual, but theoretically possible, effect is illustrated in Fig. 136a, which shows the results of a computer simulation of an adaptive two-category process, operating with a mean stimulus differ-ence $(\overline{V-S})$ of zero, initial criterion values of $k_g = k_l = 4$ and levels of target confidence $C_G = C_L = 3$.

In either case, provided initial criteria and target levels are equal, then any difference in the stimulus elements will produce a change in the relative durations of the "correct" and "incorrect" organizations. Figure 136b illustrates one set of simulation results where $(\overline{V-S}) = 0 \cdot 1 \, \sigma_{(V-S)}$, and where both criteria were initially relatively low. As is shown in the figure, the mean duration of the "correct" percept increases to a level around 80, about which it continues to fluctuate. Meanwhile, the mean duration of the "incorrect" percept increases very little and reaches a stable level just above 30. In other words, the hypothesized process tends to select one organiza-tion, and this preference becomes more marked with continued inspection of the stimulus until reaching a position of stability.

## Environmental Effects on the Rate of Alternation

Besides these spontaneous changes, a number of other factors may result in variations in the alternation rate. These I have termed "environmental" factors (Vickers, 1972c) and they include increases in alternation rate induced by stressors, such as heat, noise, fatigue, or drugs (e.g. Heath et al., 1963; Ash, 1914; Hollingworth, 1939; Tussing, 1941). Conversely, a number of studies have found that perceptual deprivation, or even sustained immobility, can produce decreases in alternation rate (Zubek et al., 1962; Ormiston, 1961; Freedman and Greenblatt, 1959; Zubek et al., 1963; Zubek and Wilgosh, 1963; Zubek and MacNeill, 1966; Zubek, 1969).

I have suggested (Vickers, 1972c) that these changes in alternation rate could be due to increases or decreases in criterion values in response to decreases or increases in arousal. The finding in Chapter 8 that the amount of noise added to the stimulus could produce faster or slower response times, according to whether it gave rise to significant adaptation on the part of the model, would suggest that perceptual alternation may be another phenomenon which is sensitive to optimum levels of noise or arousal. If this is so, it follows that, at more extreme states of arousal, alternation rate should start to decrease again if the phenomenon is to preserve a parallel with the Yerkes–Dodson effects discussed in Chapter 8. Unfortunately, no evidence is known concerning this prediction.

## Some Summary Conclusions

Although there is clearly considerable scope for further experimental investigation of the notions put forward in this chapter, there appears to be sufficient evidence to warrant the conclusion that simple decision mechanisms of the kind outlined in earlier chapters play a crucial role in the initial emergence of perceptual organization. At least in the case of figure–ground differentiation and grouping, the probability of an organizational response, the time taken to make it and the confidence or clarity attributed to it by an observer all conform to the pattern predicted by a simple decision mechanism, operating in response to variations in bias, caution and discriminability. Finally, the hypothesis that periodic changes in perceptual organization are mediated by a cyclic repetition of the decision mechanism underlying the initial organization of sensory input serves as a unifying approach, which integrates a large number of findings in two wide areas of study, while at the same time incorporating the most salient and sometimes opposing features of the perceptual process, such as stability and adaptability, or its sensitivity to subjective factors and its predominant tendency to veridicality.

Meanwhile, although most of the evidence reviewed above has been concerned with figure–ground differentiation, grouping, or perceptual alternation as they occur in comparatively simple, limiting situations, perhaps enough has been said to indicate the context in which the underlying decision mechanisms are thought of as operating, and the directions which further development of these ideas might follow. For example, among the questions which it seems might be tackled in these terms is the distinction by Garner (1974) between "integral" and "nonintegral" dimensions of sensory information, based on performance in tasks involving discrimination or judgments of similarity. Again, variations in the preference for (and degree of utilization of) constraint and discrimination redundancy would seem to suggest differences in the emphasis given to the identifying and discriminating functions of the general-purpose, adaptive, three-category decision module, which, it has been argued, is pervasively involved in the perceptual process. In the meantime, although we should doubtless remain wary of enticing and facile analogies, the picture of the perceptual process outlined in the present chapter seems at least to have the merit of showing a clear and plausible continuity between the most elementary processes of discrimination and identification and the most complex achievements of the perceptual system. In contrast to the approach of Gibson, with which the chapter opened, the present hypothesis would seem to answer squarely to Gyr's argument that the findings of current research imply a perceptual system which "does more than resonate, but, rather, compares and decides" (1972, p. 259).

# 10
## Further Developments

*In this act [of perceiving] I am conscious of myself as the perceiving subject and of an external reality as the object perceived; and I am conscious of both existences in the same indivisible moment of intuition.*
                    Sir William Hamilton: "Lectures on Metaphysics"
                                              (1859–60, Vol. I, p. 288.)

In its portrayal of perception as mediated by a sequence of arrays of adaptive decision modules, the previous chapter preserves a clear continuity between the most elementary achievements of discrimination and identification and the more complex, molar activity of perceptual organization. Of equal plausibility from an evolutionary point of view, the sequence of three main operations can be regarded as a mirror image of the sequence of physical processes (element formation, element linkage and movement) distinguished in the introductory chapter. This picture of the perceptual system is distinctive insofar as it views the quantitative analysis of sensory information as being mediated by a very small number of simple functions, carried out on a rich diversity of qualitatively and topographically differentiated information, by a single type of general-purpose module which embodies all the basic properties generally ascribed to the whole perceptual system. In both its simple and its complex applications this module must be assumed to possess some adaptive, self-regulating properties, while its successful operation presupposes an environment in which sources of random variation guarantee that—except, perhaps, momentarily—no two stimuli remain exactly the same in magnitude along any particular dimension. Differences in the processing of information can be explained by qualitative variations in the information upon which the modules are supposed to operate, or by changes in the assignment of responses to the decision outcomes reached by each module. Due to its modular construction, it is possible to maintain a fairly straightforward morphological correspondence between the structure of a given task and that of the configuration of decision modules hypothesized as underlying it. In the case of perceptual organization, at least, interaction between different modules seems to be evenly balanced between the transmission of information and the communication of control.

Meanwhile, the reference levels regulating the constraint detection system may be supposed to be susceptible to influence by motivational factors and by information held in long-term memory. Indeed, in view of its selective character, we may go so far as to speculate that motivational and learning factors might operate primarily (or even solely) on the constraint detection system associated with figure–ground differentiation, especially since the focussed output of this last operation is the most likely candidate to be matched against remembered information or against the specification of some desired input. Interactions between these factors and the reference levels prevailing in the constraint detection system could account for changes in the parts of a stimulus towards which attention is "directed", as well as variations in the detail with which an object is perceived. Although it might be questioned whether these factors are embodied in two separate systems, they are so represented in Fig. 137, which constitutes a tentative scheme of the perceptual process as developed in this book.

Even as it stands, Fig. 137 raises numerous questions concerning the general characteristics of this hypothetical system. For example, it might be asked whether there are any basic, limiting factors in the system, in terms of which it would be possible to determine human perceptual capacities, or to measure and understand individual differences in performance. Again, it might be doubted whether the processing of sensory information by the perceptual system would turn out to be regulated solely by a single type of reference level, corresponding to a certain acceptable "balance of evidence", confidence, or clarity in perceptual decisions. And, thirdly, it might be objected that this system still fails to account for an important subjective element: the specification of perceptual experience as witnessed by an observer—by an elusive, indefinable, insubstantial "I". Many other questions also arise, but to these at least some tentative answer is possible. I shall, therefore, conclude my exploration of the role of decision processes in visual perception by considering each of them in turn.

## Perceptual Indices of Performance

In the investigation of human information-processing, as in other contexts, it is often desirable to compare performance in terms of certain, well-defined, standard measures. One such index, for example, is the absolute threshold, while another is the index of detectability $d'$, proposed by signal detection theory. As we have seen in Chapters 2 and 5, however, the

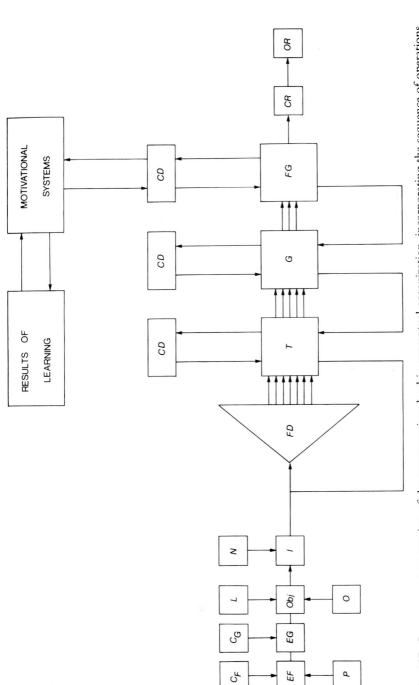

Fig. 137. Summary representation of the processes involved in perceptual organization, incorporating the sequence of operations suggested on p. 317 and indicating their possible relation to motivational and learning systems. The denotation of the symbols remains the same as for Figs 118, 124 and 125.

operation of subjective bias makes it impossible to interpret the absolute threshold as an unequivocal measure of sensitivity. Similarly, as we have also seen throughout Part I, the finding that observers seem to be able to counteract the effects of random variations in the sensory representation of stimuli makes it difficult to distinguish between differences in $d'$ due to changes in sensitivity and those attributable to varying degrees of caution. The question naturally arises, therefore, as to whether the present approach is capable of suggesting some alternative, analogous indices of perceptual performance.

Although the research reported in this book has been directed primarily towards developing a theoretical understanding of perceptual activity, rather than towards providing convenient measures or methods of calculation for use in applied contexts, it is not difficult to single out those parameters which appear likely to be responsible for individual differences or for changes in performance. Indeed, several potentially useful indices, have been proposed (Vickers *et al.*, 1972), based on the properties of the accumulator model of two-category discrimination outlined in Chapters 2 and 3. The indices in question include a measure of *inspection time* $\lambda$, a measure of *noise* $\sigma$, in index $\delta$ of the use of *immediate memory* and both a direct estimate $k$, and an indirect estimate $L$ (based on overall mean response time) of the degree of caution exercised by an observer. It seems most convenient to examine the definition, rationale and application of each of these indices in turn.

## Inspection Time, $\lambda$

If discrimination is mediated by an optional-stopping decision process in which evidence from a series of observations of $(V-S)$ differences is accumulated until it reaches a predetermined criterion $k_g$ or $k_l$ in favour of one or the other response, then, as values of $k$ are reduced, a situation will arise where either $k_g$ or $k_l$ will almost invariably be reached at the first observation. In the case of the runs, recruitment, and random walk models (where integer values are counted), this situation will clearly arise when $k_g = k_l = 1$. As can be seen from Fig. 35, this situation will also be approached in the case of the two-category accumulator process when the mean $(\overline{V-S})$ of the distribution of subjective differences is of the order of three times greater than the associated standard deviation $\sigma_{(V-S)}$, and when values of $k_g = k_l$ (expressed in the same units) do not exceed $\sigma_{(V-S)}$.

We attempted (Vickers *et al.*, 1972) to measure the minimum time $\lambda$ required for one observation of the sensory input by presenting observers with pairs of vertical lines, similar to those shown in Fig. 138a, and with a clear difference of 0·8° in length. This difference was 2·67 times the maximum of 0·3° estimated for $\sigma_{(v-s)}$ from the data of older observers at a stimulus exposure of 150 ms. At this level of discriminability, it was argued, the probability of observing a $(V-S)$ difference of the wrong sign should be less than 0·005. Provided that an observer was able to complete at least one observation of the sensory input, therefore, at least 99·5% of his responses should be correct, even if based solely on the sign of the inspected difference. Accordingly, one way of estimating the minimum time $\lambda$ required for a single inspection would be to determine the minimum interval necessary for performance at this degree of discriminability to attain some predetermined level of high accuracy.

a                           b                           c

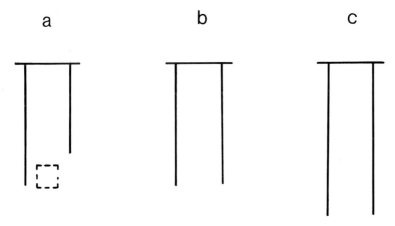

Fig. 138. Scale drawing of the types of stimulus display used by Vickers *et al.* (1972). Figure 138a shows a typical stimulus and the position of the square attention cue, which was presented beforehand. Figures 138b and 138c show the backward masks used in experiments 1 and 2 respectively.

In order to measure $\lambda$ in this way, we carried out two experiments, in both of which the same 10 observers (previously screened for visual acuity) were required to discriminate each of a series of 500 test stimuli, resembling those in Fig. 138a and with a constant difference of 0·8°. In the first experiment, 10 different exposure durations, ranging from 8 to 80 ms were employed in random order, while, in the second, the range extended from 12 to 120 ms. In both experiments, there was an equal number of occasions on which the longer line was on the left or the right. To prevent observers from accumulating further information from stored traces, stimuli in the two experiments were followed immediately with one of the backward masks shown in Figs 138b and 138c. Finally, in order to allow for other possible sources of error, due to momentary inattention or anticipation, a conservative limit of 97·5% was set as the criterion for virtually error-free performance.

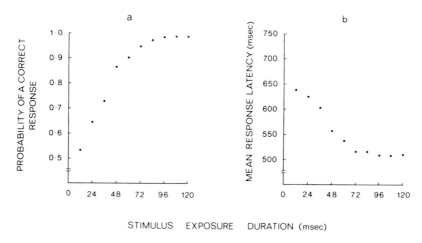

Fig. 139. Average patterns of empirical response probability and time (Vickers *et al.*, 1972, experiment 2), plotted against stimulus exposure duration.

Results from both experiments were closely similar, and the pattern of mean response frequencies and times obtained in the second is shown in Fig. 139, plotted against the corresponding duration for which the discriminanda were exposed. These results have several interesting aspects. In the first place, response times decrease as exposure duration increases; as already noted in Chapter 4, this relation is inconsistent with the notion that observers can control the length of time for which sensory input is fed to the decision mechanism. Secondly, the fact that the decrease begins to level out at the point (around 100 ms) where observers attain 97·5% accuracy suggests that this duration does in effect constitute a measure of λ. Thirdly, the fact that an observer requires a minimum inspection time of the order of 100 ms, and that shorter durations give rise to longer response times implies that, when a shorter exposure provides insufficient evidence (or none at all), the observer may be forced to rely upon further inspections of non-informative, noise-produced differences between the objectively equal lines comprising the backward mask in order to attain a criterion amount of evidence in favour of one response or the other.

We measured the group mean value of λ for the same 10 observers in both experiments. The two group means turned out to be very close (105 and 99 ms), as were the distributions of λ for individual observers which were not significantly different, but were highly correlated. Meanwhile, later comparisons of $\lambda$ with estimates of $\sigma$ and of $L$ showed no evidence of any correlation. These results suggest that $\lambda$ is a stable, independent and reliable index of performance.

In a further study, Nettlebeck and Lally (1976) confirmed the stability, independence and reliability of $\lambda$ and, in addition, found that there was a significant negative correlation between inspection time and several performance sub-tests in the Wechsler Adult Intelligence Scale (Wechsler, 1958). Similar results have also been obtained by Lally and Nettelbeck (1977), which are consistent with the view of O'Connor and Hermelin (1965) and of Savage (1970) that slowness or other limitations in sensory input constitute an important source of differences in intellectual ability. Meanwhile, on a more applied level, as Nettelbeck *et al.* (1978) point out, the finding that inspection times for 14 rehabilitees were inversely correlated with the total number of errors in an industrial sewing task has obvious implications for the rate of presentation of information in the industrial training of such people.

## *A Measure of Noise, σ*

As we have seen in Chapter 2, the phi–gamma hypothesis of classical psychophysics implies that a measure of the variability limiting discriminative performance should be given by the standard deviation $\sigma_{(v-s)}$ of the psychometric function obtained when the probability of making one response (e.g. "$V > S$") is plotted against the objective difference $(v-s)$ between the stimuli. As was also shown in both Chapters 2 and 3, the value of $\sigma_{(v-s)}$ cannot be taken as an unequivocal measure of discriminative capacity because it is subject to the degree of caution (or values of $k$) adopted by an observer. However, provided the observer is forced to adopt such low values of $k$ that he effectively bases his judgment upon a single observation of the subjective $(V-S)$ differences, then, as I have pointed out (Vickers, 1972a; Vickers *et al.*, 1972), the probability of sampling a positive $(V-S)$ difference will be given directly by the observer's proportion of responses of the form "$V > S$". In other words, under these circumstances, the value of $\sigma_{(v-s)}$ can be interpreted as a measure of the noise limiting discriminability. This may be achieved, they argue, by presenting observers with a range of stimulus differences, each for a time equivalent to a single inspection, and taking steps to prevent further data accumulation from stored traces. Taking 100 ms as a useful average of the various estimates of inspection time, an index of noise $\sigma$ was accordingly defined as "the standard deviation of the best-fitting normal ogive, calculated for the psychometric function obtained in a forced-choice discrimination task, using the method of constant stimuli, the discriminanda being presented for 100 ms, in random order, and followed by appropriate backward masking" (Vickers et al., 1972, p. 276).

In our third experiment, we presented the same 10 undergraduate observers with a random series of 500 stimuli resembling those in Fig. 138a, but with 10 differences in line length, each stimulus being presented for 100 ms, and followed by a backward mask resembling that in Fig. 138c. An estimate of $\sigma$ was obtained for each observer by calculating the standard deviation of the cumulative ogive (for a normal distribution with a mean of zero) that best fitted the proportion of correct responses made at each stimulus difference. These estimates averaged 0·32°, which is comparable to the figure of 0·30°, calculated for the older observers of Botwinick et al. (1958), who were presented with signals of 150 ms duration, but without backward masking. At the same time, as we have shown, it is some 3 to 15 times greater than the measures for young adults yielded by a number of other studies of discrimination performance in which some opportunity for multiple observations was allowed (Vickers et al., 1972, p. 276, Table I).

Since individual measures of $\sigma$ showed no significant difference when calculated for the first two and the last two experimental runs, but were significantly correlated, we concluded that, like $\lambda$, the measure $\sigma$ is a stable and reliable indicator of performance. Some indication that it is also a valid indicator is given by the close correspondence found by us between the measure of $\sigma$ calculated from responses in a previous experiment (Vickers, 1967), employing visual stimuli to which large, but controlled amounts of noise had been added, and the objectively estimated value of that noise. Also consistent with this conclusion are the results of a study by Nettelbeck (1972), in which 10 observers were given painful electric shocks at unpredictable intervals. The observers who were shocked showed an increased heart rate and gave higher ratings of anxiety in the experimental situation, than a control group who received no shocks. Although the blocks of trials in which shocks were administered were excluded from analysis, the experimental observers yielded an average value of 0·66° for $\sigma$, which was more than double the figure of 0·28° for the control group. Even during the first session, during which they received no shocks, but were told to expect some on the following session, the experimental observers yielded a very high value of 0·49°. These results provide good evidence for the proposed interpretation of $\sigma$ as an index of noise, or nonspecific random neural activity. Such variability, it has been argued, is an inherent feature of the sensory representation of stimuli and would therefore constitute a basic factor limiting discriminative capacity. In addition, however, these findings imply that it may be increased or diminished by the presence or absence of environmental stressors, such as heat, noise, or (in this case) conditions inducing anxiety.

## Estimates of the Degree of Caution

The indices of noise and inspection time examined by my colleagues and me (Vickers *et al.*, 1972) depend upon measuring the performance of the two-category mechanism of discrimination under certain limiting conditions, which nullify the possible effects of data accumulation or adaptability. Even under less restricting conditions, however, some consistency might be expected in the execution of an elementary decision process of this kind. For example, it might be surmised that values of $k$ (whether determined by a target level of confidence or by some other reference level) might turn out to be fairly characteristic of individual observers, and to represent fairly habitual—though modifiable—personal styles in processing sensory information. Although we did not attempt to assess its potential, we also proposed a fairly direct estimate of caution ($k$). Assuming that, under appropriate circumstances, observers will operate with equal (unbiassed) values of $k_g$ and $k_l$, we suggested that values of $k$ may be inferred from the psychometric function of an individual observer, provided that the noise limiting discriminability is independently known and can be regarded as approximately the same for different observers. A formula for calculating values of $k$ in terms of the units of objective stimulus difference has already been presented in Chapter 3 (p. 88). Such a procedure seems to yield an acceptable approximation with multi-element stimulus arrays, such as those in Fig. 25, where the external noise added to the array can be precisely controlled and is of sufficient magnitude to swamp any individual differences in internal (or "neural") noise.

Meanwhile, a less direct measure, which nevertheless emerges creditably from our experiments is that of mean overall response time $L$. Where values of $\lambda$ and $\sigma$ remain constant from one situation to the next, then the main determiner of changes in response time is the value of the criterion $k$ (again assuming $k_g = k_l$). At the same time, if it is supposed that observers tend to adopt characteristic criterion levels, then changes in criterion from one situation to another would be expected to be reflected by differences in $L$, although values of $L$ for individual observers could turn out to be correlated between the two sets of conditions. In agreement with this, we found that, while values of $\lambda$, $\sigma$ and $L$ were independent, measures of $L$ in experiments 1 and 2 were correlated, as were those between experiments 2 and 3, and 1 and 3. Meanwhile, although there was no significant difference in $L$ between the two similar experiments (1 and 2) designed to estimate inspection time by presenting only highly discriminable stimuli, there was a significant increase between experiment 2 and the third experiment (in which noise was determined by presenting a range of quite difficult discriminanda). These findings suggest that, like $\lambda$ and $\sigma$, the measure $L$ may serve as an independent, stable and reliable measure of performance, and may (albeit with some care) be interpreted as an approximate index of the degree of caution exercised by an observer.

Confirmation of the independence, stability and reliability of the index $L$ has been obtained by Nettelbeck (1973) and Nettelbeck and Lally (1976), while I have suggested (Vickers, 1972b, 1972c; Vickers et al., 1972) that changes in caution may underlie differences in a number of other perceptual indices which have not hitherto been clearly interrelated. As noted in Chapter 9, for example, values of $L$ for a study of the times required to achieve a figural organization of a Rubin circle were highly correlated with those taken to make a (superficially quite different) probabilistic discrimination. As also noted above, the interpretation of $L$ as an approximate index of the degree of caution employed by an observer seems to correspond to the factor labelled "speed of judgment" by Thurstone (1944) and to that characterized as "decision speed" by Künnapas, meaning "the readiness with which a choice is made when the response is not completely determined by the sensory input" (1969, p. 32). This factor, it was argued, is the main one responsible for the relations observed between reversal rate and the time required to achieve an initial organizational response. Similarly, as we have suggested (Vickers et al., 1972) the same factor of caution may be responsible for individual differences and changes in a number of other perceptual indices of performance, including critical flicker frequency, visual acuity and susceptibility to figural after-effect. If this interpretation is borne out by later specific investigations, it would allow these various ad hoc measures to be related within a single conceptual framework, and would set clear limits to the kind of interpretation that might be placed on them.

## Other Possible Indices

A number of other indices readily suggest themselves. For example, a further measure examined by my colleagues and me is the difference $\delta$ between the values of $\delta$ obtained with and without backward masking. Such a measure, we suggested, should indicate the varying extents to which different individuals benefit by the inspection of evidence from immediate memory. In a study of 40 undergraduates, for example, Nettelbeck (1973) found wide differences in the use made of temporarily stored information, with values of $\delta$ ranging from $0°$ up to $0.30°$, with a mean of $0.12°$. Variations of this kind would seem to be of obvious importance to an understanding of individual differences. In a similar vein, it would be surprising if some index of the relative preference for the "equals" response in three-category judgments did not turn out to be related to performance in a variety of other perceptual tasks, in which varying emphasis on discriminative and identifying functions might be adopted by individual observers.

At the same time, due recognition should be paid to the adaptive nature of the decision processes involved. As it stands, for instance, an adaptive decision mechanism is capable of assuming quite different levels of caution in response to changing experimental circumstances, while maintaining a constant value of target confidence (or of some other reference level). If it were possible, therefore, to isolate and measure these reference levels, then the resulting indices would be more general and powerful than a measure such as $L$. Again, it may be profitable to focus attention on the control characteristics of the decision process. For example, such factors as intermittency and coarseness in control might underlie the finding by Nettelbeck and Lally (1976) that, while mean values of $L$ for an intellectually retarded group of observers were not significantly different from those of an intellectually normal group and were unrelated to intelligence, standard deviations in $L$ for individual observers were negatively correlated with performance measures of I.Q. As was pointed out in Chapter 7, the tendency for coarse or intermittent control to produce violent fluctuations in criterion levels gives rise to a decrease in discriminative capacity overall. This would go some way towards explaining Baumeister and Kellas' generalization (1968) that increased variability in individual performance is an important attribute of retardation. As I have argued (Vickers, 1978), the behaviour of higher level control systems would be expected to show more constancy and generality than the systems regulated by them, and may therefore turn out to be more useful for the understanding of individual differences in performance.

## Other Control Processes

The notion that some subjective counterpart of reported confidence functions as a reference variable for the correction and control of perceptual activity would seem to be implied by apparent adjustments in criterion levels made by observers in response to changes in the discriminability of a stimulus sequence. Such a reference variable enables a rapid adjustment to be made to any change—even of short duration—in the sequence, and seems particularly suited to ensuring that the caution with which decisions are reached is appropriately geared to the current quality of the sensory information on which they are based. At the same time, however, the question arises as to whether perceptual activity might not be controlled by some other reference variables in addition to that of confidence or "perceptual clarity". Physiological functions, such as respiration and heart rate, are typically regulated by a number of different systems, and it seems reasonable to expect to find a similar complexity in the control of information processing. For example, intuitively at least, we sometimes seem to find ourselves reflecting after a decision that, had the evidence for the chosen response not been so clear, we should have been inclined to make the alternative response because that was what we had been expecting. Although it is far from being a necessary implication, this occasional subjective experience of conflict does raise the possibility that, in addition to being regulated by some *post hoc* assessment of the quality of sensory evidence in favour of each individual response, the parameters of the general decision mechanism might also be influenced by an *a priori* factor of expectation.

Some objective evidence that this may be the case has been obtained in a recent experiment (Vickers *et al.*, 1977). In this study, each of 26 observers was presented with a continuous sequence of 600 pairs of lines resembling those in Fig. 138a, but with a constant difference between them of only 1 mm (0·04°). Each observer was instructed to indicate whether the longer line appeared on the left (L) or the right (R) by pressing the left- or the right-hand of two keys. For half the observers, the longer line appeared to the left on 50 out of the first 100 trials, and to the right on the remaining 50. Over the next 100 trials, the number of occasions on which it appeared to the left was reduced to 41, this number being further reduced by 9 in each successive block of 100 trials. Within each block, the actual trials on which the longer line appeared to the left were randomly determined. The procedure followed for the other 13 observers was exactly similar, except that it was the number of occasions on which the longer line appeared to the right which was steadily reduced. Since each block of 100 trials followed those preceding it in an unbroken sequence, there was no sudden perceptible decrease in the probability of the less frequent stimulus from one block of trials to the next.

If performance in this task were controlled solely by some target level of confidence, then the expected pattern of response frequencies should resemble those of the adaptive model for signal detection in vigilance situations, which was outlined towards the end of Chapter 7 (pp. 231–232). Specifically, when the probability of the *l* ("left-hand longer") stimulus is reduced, then the proportion of the alternative *R* responses which turn out to be incorrect (and therefore to be made with relatively low confidence) will be smaller. In consequence, the adaptive model (whether of signal detection or of two-category discrimination) will reduce the criterion ($k_r$) controlling the *R* response. Conversely, the proportion of *L* responses which turn out to be incorrect (and hence to be made with low confidence) will be higher, so that the value of $k_l$ must be adjusted upwards in order to maintain, on average, the target level of confidence. As a result, when the probability of an $l$ stimulus is decreased, the conditional probability of making an $L$ response will also be decreased, while that of making an $R$ response will increase. A change of this kind, it was argued in Chapter 7, would account for the decline in the proportion of "hits" traditionally observed in vigilance experiments, where the objective probability of a signal during the test session is usually much lower than that prevailing during the initial demonstration and practice trials.

The results which we obtained (Vickers et al., 1977) however, turned out to be surprising. Figure 140 shows the pattern of conditional response probabilities observed in each successive block of 100 trials as the probability of one stimulus event is steadily reduced. (Data for the two groups of

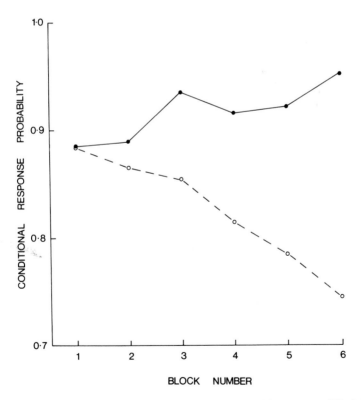

Fig. 140. Mean conditional probabilities of correct "signal" responses (filled circles) and "nonsignal" responses (empty circles) (Vickers et al., 1977).

observers have been appropriately averaged.) As can be seen from Fig. 140, the conditional probability of making a correct $L$ (or $R$) response increases, while that of making a correct $R$ (or $L$) response decreases, as the probability of the $l$ (or $r$) stimulus is reduced. This pattern is the direct opposite of that found in traditional vigilance tasks, and also of that predicted by an adaptive accumulator mechanism controlled solely by a target level of confidence.

In order to explain this somewhat paradoxical set of results, we argued that it is necessary to suppose that the observer maintains a record of the long-term probability $(H)$ of making a particular response $X$ over the entire length of a relevant sequence of trials, and that he periodically compares this with some representation of the immediately recent probability $(G)$ of making the $X$ response. The difference $(G-H)$, we pointed out, could serve as an error signal for the correction and control of some parameter of the decision process. In particular, the difference $(G-H)$ may be one factor which determines the value of the target level of confidence $C_x$ (which in turn controls the value of the criterion $k_x$ corresponding to the response in question). In other words, according to our results, decision processes may be subject to a *hierarchy of control*, in which the reference level (namely, target confidence) responsible for adjusting each of the criterion levels in the primary decision process is itself subject to control by another reference level (in this case, the cumulatively determined, long-term proportion of responses in each corresponding category).

This hypothesis leads to three interesting sets of predictions, which I shall consider briefly for the case of a simple, two-category discrimination task. In the first place, and of paramount importance for the fabric of the argument so far, provided that the *a priori* probabilities of the two alternative responses remain stable, then $(G-H)$ will tend to be equal to zero, and the target levels of confidence for the two responses will remain unchanged. Even if the *a priori* probabilities of the two responses are markedly different, no correction will be made to target levels of confidence as long as the recent and the long-term probabilities of each response remain the same. Under these circumstances, the behaviour of the adaptive decision model outlined in Chapter 7 will remain unaltered. Only when a change in the proportions of stimuli of one kind or the other foreshadows a discrepancy between the response proportions $G$ and $H$, will the behaviour of the adaptive decision mechanism differ from that depicted in Chapter 7.

One situation in which the behaviour of the decision mechanism will differ is exemplified by the experiment represented in Fig. 141 (Vickers *et al.*, 1977). In this situation a steady, progressive reduction in the *a priori* probability of one response $(X)$ will give rise to an increasing discrepancy between $G$ and $H$. In the case of $X$, the discrepancy takes the form of a

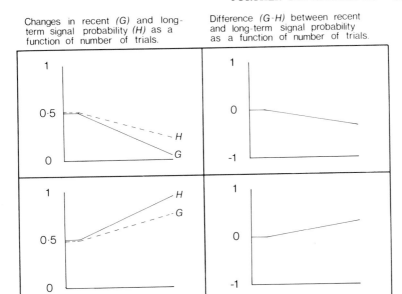

Fig. 141. The general form of changes in the recent (G) and the long-term probability (H) of a signal occurring in the experiment of Vickers *et al*. (1977), together with the associated changes in the difference (G–H). (Adapted from Vickers *et al*., 1977).

progressive decrease in the value of (G–H), while, in the case of the alternative response Y, it produces a progressive increase. As we have seen, according to the simple adaptive process outlined in Chapter 7, this situation should give rise to a decrease in the conditional probability of making a correct X response, and an increase in that of making a correct Y response. However, according to our hypothesis (Vickers *et al*., 1977), any decrease in (G–H) gives rise to a decrease in the target level $C_x$ controlling the X response and, simultaneously, to an increase in the level $C_y$ controlling the alternative Y. As a result, a progressive decrease in the *a priori* probability of an X response will give rise to a progressive decrease in the criterion $k_x$, and thence (as observed) to a steady increase in the conditional probability of making that response. An exactly converse change would of course be predicted in the case of the alternative Y response (as we also observed).

Such a state of affairs could not, of course, continue indefinitely, and Fig. 142 illustrates the pattern of values likely to be taken by G and H in the third main type of situation, in which the *a priori* probability of one response X is reduced abruptly and then remains unchanged. Such a pattern might be

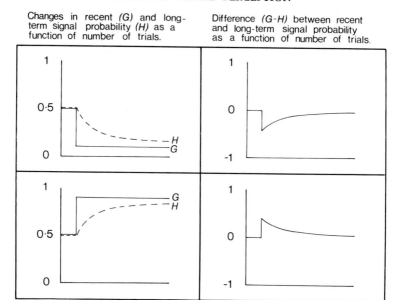

Fig. 142. The general form of changes in the recent $(G)$ and the long-term probability $(H)$ of a signal, when the recent probability undergoes an abrupt step change in value. (Adapted from Vickers *et al.*, 1977).

encountered in a vigilance experiment, for example, where the *a priori* probability of a "signal" response undergoes a step reduction from (say) 0·5 during demonstration and practice trials down to (say) 0·2 during the vigilance session proper, and then stays constant. The result, as can be seen from the graph of $(G-H)$, is likely to be a sudden discrepancy between the recent and the long-term probability of the response $X$. However, provided that the recent probability does not fall any further, the long-term probability will eventually "catch up" with it as it is revised by the inclusion of more recent trials. When this happens, the discrepancy between the recent and the long-term probability will return to zero. According to our hypothesis, this pattern of change in $(G-H)$ will be directly reflected by the target confidence $C_x$ (and inversely by that for the alternative response). As a result, there will be a rapid initial reduction in $k_x$, followed by a much more gradual increase as $C_x$ slowly returns to its previous value. In subjective terms, when an observer suddenly finds that he is making fewer $X$ responses than before, he suspects that he may be being too rigorous as to what constitutes an $x$ stimulus and so decreases his criterion for that response. Then, as the situation appears to stabilize, he gradually increases his criterion again.

According to our approach (Vickers *et al.*, 1977), it is this return to a stable criterion which is usually recorded as a vigilance decrement. An explanation of this kind, we argued, would account for the apparent effects of long-term probability observed by Baddeley and Colquhoun (1969), and would be consistent with evidence of conservatism from studies of probability estimation, learning and revision (e.g. Attneave, 1953; Vitz and Hazan, 1969). The recent and long-term probabilities could be registered by a simple cumulative mechanism of the kind encountered throughout this book. As Howell suggests, "a simple cumulative mechanism appears to be the more plausible way of explaining man's storage of frequency information", in conjunction with a more detailed record of responses, which is "heavily biassed towards recent events" (1970, pp. 213–214). The logic of this proposed expectancy model also has some similarities to a model suggested by Robinson (1964) and, more particularly, to a recent proposal by Indlin (1976), which was independently presented at the same time as that of our results (Vickers *et al.*, 1977). According to Indlin, the observer may be thought of as a system with feedback, in which the reference signal is the averaged proportion of the observer's responses over the entire experimental sequence, and the feedback signal is generated by comparing this long-term probability with "a moving proportion of the observer's responses of a certain type". The main difference between the last two approaches is that Indlin states that corrections are made directly to some parameter ($\beta$) in a signal detection model, whereas we envisage them as being made to the reference level of confidence which controls criteria in a primary accumulator process.

On this latter view, long-term probability functions as a reference variable in a higher-level control system. An overriding system of this kind would operate over a longer time scale and need only come into play when response probabilities change, for example by causing the adaptive system controlled by it to "hunt" temporarily for a signal which becomes infrequent, before reverting to its original target of confidence. As yet, this picture of a hierarchy of control is perhaps best regarded as only tentative. However, besides being plausible, it does allow our results (Vickers *et al.*, 1977) to be reconciled with the evidence surveyed in the rest of this book. In addition, as we shall see in the following section, it helps to put some venerable but otherwise baffling problems into a new perspective.

## *Choice, Control and Consciousness*

In the approach to perception sketched in above there is one aspect which I have so far refrained from touching upon. As Adrian remarks "there is still the one thing which does seem to lie outside that tidy and familiar framework . . . the "I" who does the perceiving and the thinking and acting" (1966, p. 240). While it has so far proved difficult to show conclusively that it is necessary to involve the concept of consciousness in order to explain any aspect of behaviour, Shallice (1972) has pointed out that many cognitive psychologists make use of the notion of consciousness (as well as allied concepts) in the design, conduct and interpretation of their experiments. Meanwhile, over the last fifteen years or so, there has been a growing conviction that the phenomena of consciousness represent an important unsolved problem in psychology (e.g. Thouless, 1963; Collier, 1964; Burt, 1964, 1968; Sperry, 1965, 1968, 1969, 1970; Eccles, 1966; Koestler and Smythies, 1969; Joynson, 1970, 1972, 1974; Mandler, 1975a, 1975b; Hilgard, 1977). Although it is clearly impossible to do justice to the topic in the few remaining pages of this book, it seems encumbent on me to try to indicate, at least in outline, how an approach derived from a consideration of the most elementary principles might be applied to what is generally regarded as the most mysterious aspect of perceptual activity. Accordingly, in this final section, I shall consider first how the theoretical approach developed up to this point might be applied to some of the behavioural correlates of variations in awareness. I shall then complete my analysis of the role of decision processes in perception by considering their relevance to the phenomenological aspects of consciousness.

## Behavioural Features of Variations in Awareness

If we accept the view that perception is mediated by a sequence of arrays of decision modules, which are in turn regulated by a hierarchy of reference levels, then some hypotheses concerning the behavioural aspects of consciousness suggest themselves quite readily. In the first place, there seem to be reasonable grounds for accepting the view of Miller (1962) and Peterfreund and Schwartz (1971) that only the final (or, possibly, the intermediate) results of mental activity are conscious. Where observers are not apprised beforehand of any requirement to introspect, then little—if anything—can be elicited by post-experimental questioning concerning the processes leading up to a perceptual decision, whether of the form "$V > S$", or one such as "Black is figure". As Audley (1964) points out, even in expanded judgment tasks, little or no information is retained regarding the sequence of stimulus events. Meanwhile, even when observers are instructed beforehand to introspect on their judgmental processes, the events leading up to the initial perception or recognition of a stimulus do not seem to be conscious. For example, commenting on observer's introspections concerning the process of comparing simultaneously presented stimuli of different brightness, Fernberger concluded that "the process consisted apparently in an immediate perceptual experience" (1918, p. 149). Although more extended judgmental processes involving lifted weights were accompanied by sensations of muscular tension, the immediate character of simple judgmental processes is confirmed by a similar phenomenological study by Wells (1927), who found that, like the perception of the warning signal itself, the initial recognition of stimulus words was simply preceded by a "momentary blank". Accordingly, while there is clearly no doubt that most (if not all) decision *outcomes* are conscious, we should seem to be justified in regarding the series of inspections upon which an outcome is based as unconscious. As such, they bear obvious resemblances to a number of other hypothesized processes, including the *petites perceptions* of Leibniz, as well as Stout's notion of "indiscernible differences", which account "by their accumulation for the difference which is ultimately noticed" (1938, p. 301).

Although there would seem to be good grounds for regarding the decision outcome itself as usually (perhaps invariably) conscious, it is not immediately clear, however, that this need be so in general. For example, in the case of the elementary systems depicted in Figs 3, 38 and 67, the simplest reactions that need be attributed to the system in response to inequalities in illumination would have the character of elementary reflexes. As in the case of the simple optomotor behaviour of the beetles studied by Reichardt and Hassenstein (Reichardt, 1961), such responses would seem to have invariant, automatic, involuntary characteristics not normally associated with human conscious experience. Accordingly, while the capacity to respond to stimulation is generally accepted as one necessary criterion for consciousness (e.g. Penfield and Roberts, 1959; Evans, 1970), since at least the time of James (1890) it has come to be generally accepted that the pattern of conscious responding should also exhibit the characteristics of adaptability and of goal-directedness (e.g. Joynson, 1970, 1972, 1974; Shallice, 1972; Mackay, 1966). If this is so, it suggests that decision outcomes need not be conscious unless they constitute the input to some higher control mechanism, responsible for regulating the parameters of the primary decision process itself. As has been suggested by Mandler (1975a, 1975b), consciousness may have something to do with "the simple addressing of complex structures". In this case, it may serve to differentiate whether a decision outcome is transmitted only to the relevant effector mechanisms or is also to serve as the input to some higher control mechanism.

A view of this kind would lead us to agree with Welford's general conclusion (1972) that responses subject to adaptive control are conscious, while those for which such monitoring is unnecessary or impossible tend to be automatic and their execution unconscious. More specifically, however, in the context of the proposed adaptive module for simple judgment, this view leads to some surprisingly detailed predictions. For example, if a trial is terminated before any decision has been reached, there should be no response to that trial and no awareness of it on the part of a hypothetical module (or on that of an observer). Normally, of course, the observer may be supposed to continue sampling from stored traces, or to "top up" the accumulators with noise-produced differences between the elements of a backward mask (Vickers *et al.*, 1972). However, when the material stored in temporary memory traces deteriorates rapidly, or when information in the accumulators themselves may be assumed to decay, then instances may arise where the sensory effects of a stimulus dissipate more rapidly than they accumulate, with the result that the criterion amount of evidence is never reached. Such a state of affairs would be particularly likely to arise whenever a high target level of confidence, possibly in combination with a very faint or improbable stimulus, resulted in the adoption of a very high criterion level for the corresponding response alternative.

Figures 143a and 143b illustrate the behaviour of the adaptive module (operating in two-category mode), when the *a priori* probability of the "$V > S$" response is reduced abruptly from 0·5 to 0·05, when the information in the "$V > S$" and "$V < S$" accumulators decays slowly and when trials are terminated either upon the achievement of a decision outcome or after a fixed number of observations (whichever occurs first). The figures are based on the results of a computer simulation of 40 repetitions in each of which a random series of 1000 stimulus differences with means $\overline{(V-S)}$ equal to either −0·5 or $0·5\sigma_{(V-S)}$, and with $\sigma_{(V-S)} = 1$, were presented to the proposed process. As has been assumed throughout the previous chapters, the accumulators were cleared only when the amount of evidence accumulated in one reached a critical total. In other words, if several successive trials occurred without any response being triggered, stimulus differences could be accumulated over these trials (within the limits of the decaying memory).

Such a mechanism has several interesting properties. As in Fig. 143, for example, if the proportion of "greater" to "lesser" stimuli is suddenly reduced, the criterion level for a "greater" response is adjusted upwards,

Fig. 143. The pattern of response of the adaptive two-category process to a step reduction in the *a priori* probability of a response of the form "$V > S$" from 0·5 to 0·05. In Fig. 143a the solid line represents the conditional probability of making a response of the form "$V > S$" correctly, while the broken line gives the conditional probability of making that response incorrectly. Similarly the solid line in Fig. 143b shows the mean number of observations taken to make the response "$V > S$" correctly, and the broken line shows the number taken to make it incorrectly. The asterisks in Fig. 143a show the probability that, on any trial, no response would be made by the time the trial terminated. Data have been averaged over successive blocks of 100 trials.

## (a) RESPONSE PROBABILITY

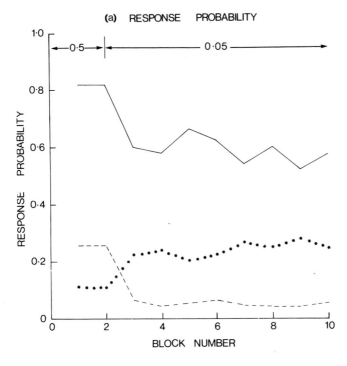

## (b) RESPONSE TIME

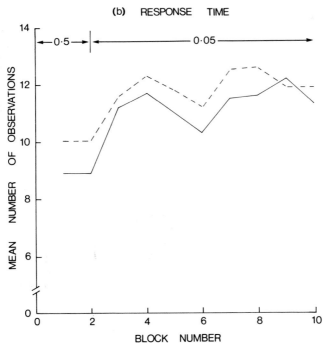

"greater" responses take longer and there is a rise in the proportion of trials which do not issue in any response. In terms of the specific hypothesis proposed above, when the accumulation of sensory evidence does not eventuate in a decision by the primary process, then there is no conscious input to any higher control mechanism, and the system remains "unaware" that a trial has occurred. On the other hand, since some at least of the accumulated evidence may remain until the start of a subsequent trial, it is possible to integrate evidence over several successive "sterile" trials until eventually the original criterion is reached. When this occurs, the response in question will tend to be made with a very high level of confidence, resulting in turn in a probable reduction of its criterion level. Immediately, subsequent greater stimuli will then be more rapidly detected and the proportion of missed trials will diminish. Thus, it is possible to restore the "wakefulness" of the system by presenting either one or two very clearly greater stimuli or else a succession of only slightly greater stimuli. Meanwhile, because of the integration of information over successive sterile trials, it is even possible for the system to respond occasionally to signals "in arrears". For example, it is possible for the system to fail to reach the "greater" criterion on a greater trial, but, with the help of the residue of evidence from that trial, to reach that criterion of a subsequent lesser trial.

Similar behaviour would be produced by the adaptive module (operating in two-category mode) when the maximum discriminability over a series of stimuli is severely reduced, as might happen, for example, when general illumination levels are decreased. In such a situation, it is true, it would be possible to counteract the tendency on the part of the system to "ignore" the occurrence of trials by supposing that target levels of confidence could be reduced. In this case, criteria in the primary process might not be adjusted upwards to such an extent that accumulated sensory information could leak away before it accumulated to trigger a response. However, this would reduce the accuracy of responding in a situation which called for increased caution, and could result in virtually random responding on the part of the primary decision process. If, instead, target levels of confidence were increased under such circumstances, then any discriminability could be exploited (where it existed). On the other hand, where it did not exist, or where decisions took so long that sensory information "faded" before a decision was reached, then the system would tend to remain inert and unresponsive. Indeed, if target levels of confidence were assumed to be subject to periodic slow fluctuations, which coincided in time (but varied inversely) with fluctuations in detectability and discriminability, then the adaptive module would show a cycle of responsiveness reminiscent of the diurnal rhythm of wakefulness exhibited by higher animals. This form of adaptation would have the biological advantage, for example, of preventing an animal from indulging in unnecessary random activity during periods of time when it would be vulnerable to attack by other animals, particularly those with a greater sensory sensitivity under these conditions, such as nocturnal animals.

Other applications of the notion of integrating degradable information over successive inconclusive trials readily suggest themselves. For example, the hypothesis that stimuli which do not give rise to conscious perception may nevertheless affect the perception of subsequent stimuli is clearly relevant to the problems of subliminal perception as lucidly outlined by Dixon (1971). Unfortunately, while such problems represent an obvious area for application of the present approach, an adequate treatment is beyond the scope of the present book. So far as the problem of consciousness in perception is concerned, it seems more important to conclude by considering one final aspect, which, although almost universally recognized, cannot yet be dealt with by the hypotheses developed so far.

## Phenomenal Aspects of Consciousness

The notion that consciousness is associated with the input from a primary decision process to some higher control mechanism has several close resemblances to Shallice's hypothesis (1972) that consciousness corresponds to the "selector input" which represents a certain state of affairs $X$, selects which "action system" is to be dominant and sets the goal of the action system. For example, as in the scheme envisaged by Shallice, "the speed and accuracy with which an action system operates depends on its level of activation, which can continuously vary" (1972, p. 387). One difference, however, is that the present conceptualization is based on experimental evidence of the operation of a hierarchy of at least two identifiable control mechanisms, embodying confidence (or perceptual clarity) and long-term response probability as reference levels. It thus represents a step towards the compilation of a dictionary of control mechanisms, in terms of which quite specific hypotheses about consciousness can be formulated. Another difference is that the selection (or, as conceived here, the "addressing") of a control mechanism is synonymous with the selection of a reference variable (or "goal"), since each control mechanism embodies only one reference variable. This less flexible conceptualization means that the principles that determine which control mechanism is currently regulating the operation of a primary decision mechanism may be quite simple, and a feasible subject of empirical investigation. Meanwhile, in agreement with Newell et al. (1958) and Miller et al. (1960), it pictures the processing of sensory information as taking place under the control of a hierarchy of regulating mechanisms, which, unlike the scheme proposed by Shallice, may be quite rigidly interrelated, at the lower levels at least. Unlike the schemes of Newell *et al.* and Miller *et al.*, however, all processing of information is carried out by the same primary decision process. The hierarchy in question is a pure hierarchy of *regulative control*, i.e. it entails the modification of some *parameter* only of a process lower in the hierarchy, rather than a change either in the information input to the process in question or in the operations performed on this information. This conception includes the idea of simultaneous operation over different time scales, with inputs to higher levels being less frequent than those to control mechanisms at lower levels. As Broadbent (1977) has recently pointed out, this picture of information-processing corresponds closely to some of the early ideas propounded by Bartlett (1942), Craik (1966) and Welford (1951).

At the same time, the above hypothesis regarding consciousness does not by itself account for the fact that one universally recognized character of normal conscious experience is that it takes the form of experience *of* a state of affairs *by* some observer or "self" (e.g. Hamilton, 1859–60; James, 1890; Sherrington, 1940; Adrian, 1966). Although the distinction of a "self" appears to be subject to continuous variations in clarity, and, possibly, to undergo qualitative changes as well, it almost always implies the registration of experience by a single observing system. Since I have identified the "content" of consciousness with those decision outcomes which constitute the input to a control mechanism, it seems natural to identify the "self" with this higher process. However, the conscious awareness of this "self" is more difficult to account for. In terms of the present approach, at least two (not necessarily inconsistent) possibilities suggest themselves. One possible hypothesis, which seems to capture the dynamic, regulatory aspects of the phenomenon, is that *consciousness is identifiable with a form of coding the outcome of a perceptual decision process in such a way as to specify, in some qualitative or topographically distinct manner, the locus of the highest mechanism of adaptive control which is currently regulating the process in question.*

The exact wording of this hypothesis is important, and would seem to make it an extremely powerful one. In the first place, the allocation of one goal or reference level to each control mechanism makes possible a fairly straightforward identification of "self" with the highest locus of adaptive control which is currently in operation. In the second, the representation of this locus in some qualitative or topographically distinct form of coding means that any decision outcome which serves as the input to a control mechanism is not coded simply in the form "$V > S$", but always in the form "$V > S$, as decided under the control of system $A$". On this view, conscious perceptions not only convey the results of decisions concerning incoming sensory information, but they also specify the regulating system, and it is the second aspect of this dual representation which corresponds to our subjective experience of a "self", an "I", or an "ego".

The above hypothesis has a fertility which can be only crudely summarized in the space remaining. Firstly, if it is usually the case that at any one time there is one highest locus of control, then, whether this follows from general considerations (as Shallice (1972) has argued), or is largely determined by genetic factors (as suggested above), it follows that conscious perception will include the awareness of a single, unique "self". On the other hand, in pathological cases, or in circumstances such as the split-brain studies of Sperry (1965, 1968, 1969, 1970), there may be multiple loci of control and multiple perceptions of "self". Secondly, since this view implies the possibility that primary decision processes may be regulated by a number of different mechanisms at a number of different levels, it is consistent with our increasing willingness, as observed by Armstrong (1968), to attribute consciousness to organisms higher on the phylogenetic scale. Similarly, it is consistent (though far from identical) with the view of Sperry (1969, 1970), Thorpe (1967) and others, that consciousness is an "emergent property", a product of the evolution of a particular level of complexity. Moreover, in its assignment of an addressing function to consciousness, the proposed hypothesis corresponds closely to James's uncannily perceptive view that consciousness is something "added for the sake of steering a nervous system grown too complex to regulate itself" (1890, *I*, p. 144).

On a more general level, since the hypothesis identifies an important aspect of consciousness with the representation of the highest locus of regulative control, it is only to be expected that the notion of "self" should be assigned an active, goal-directed, monitoring role (e.g. Penfield and Roberts, 1959; Thorpe, 1966; Evans, 1970). The notion of freewill can then be explained as arising both from the circumstance that the "self" does indeed exercise control over systems below it, and from the corollary that what is manipulated by the "self" is usually (perhaps always) some aim, or goal, constituting the reference level in a lower system. On the other hand, the operation of the highest level of adaptive control is (by definition) not subject to control by any other system. It is in this sense that the behaviour of the "self" can be construed as "free" or "undetermined". Ironically, of course, this highest locus must therefore be supposed to operate in a non-adaptive, purely automatic, stereotyped manner.

As the locus of control shifts from one level to another, so behaviour will be determined by standards which regulate activity over longer periods of time or by more immediate target levels. Indeed, logically there would seem to be no limit to the number of possible levels of control. On the other hand, however, the problem of infinite regress does not arise, since there is no reason why control should not stop at the first, second, or at any other level. It seems likely that limits to the highest level at which control can operate would be set jointly by the variety and difficulty of sensory decisions and by the number of neural units available. For example, if each response by a simple two-category decision process were controlled by a similar process, and each response by one of those first-level control processes were in turn controlled, then $2^{n+1}$ accumulator units would be necessary to sustain $n$ levels of control. Although it is not suggested that the structure of control in human information processing corresponds to such a simple pattern, this illustrates one way in which the quality and level of awareness and the conscious control exercised by an individual may be at least partly determined by the sheer number of available cortical neurons.

Meanwhile, on a more down-to-earth level, this proposed view of consciousness also appears to have some value in empirical terms. For example, if the reference levels of the adaptive decision module outlined in Chapter 7 are themselves regulated by a higher control mechanism, then not only will each outcome by the primary decision process be conscious, but the observer should be aware of the adjustments to the primary criterion levels, provided these form the input to some higher control mechanism. However, since these adjustments are not made following each response by the primary decision process, then the awareness of changes in criterion should be intermittent. Again, since such adjustments follow the achievement of a primary decision, the process of reporting their occurrence should not interfere with the operation of the primary process. If an observer were asked to report his awareness of such changes in caution, therefore, he should find it a meaningful task. Moreover, if he were asked to indicate his awareness simply by responding "yes" or "no" after each primary decision, this secondary introspective task should conform in all essential respects to a standard signal detection task. The only difference would be that, instead of reporting on the results of a primary decision about sensory information, the observer would be reporting on the occurrence or otherwise of a secondary decision concerning the operation of the primary process.

In order to test these predictions, and to explore the possibility of using controlled introspection of this kind, a quite simple experiment (as yet unpublished) was recently carried out by myself and Smith. In this study, each of 18 observers was presented with an unbroken series of 350 signal and 350 nonsignal stimuli of the kind employed by myself and Johnson, and illustrated in Fig. 61 (p. 158). The detectability of the signal stimuli remained constant throughout, and the primary task for the observers was to press one key in response to a "signal" stimulus, and the other in response to a "nonsignal" stimulus. Immediately afterwards, observers were required to press one of two keys to indicate whether on that particular trial they had experienced any change (in either direction) in their relative readiness to make either response. (The instructions were deliber-

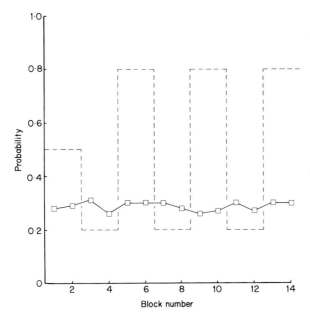

Fig. 144. The mean unconditional probability of reporting a change in readiness, recorded in an unpublished experiment by myself and Smith, plotted for each successive block of 50 trials during which objective signal probability varied in abrupt steps as indicated by the broken line.

ately left rather unspecific so as to avoid overloading the observer.) Finally, in an attempt to manipulate the activity of the controlling mechanism thought to be responsible for adjusting the criterion levels in the primary process, the *a priori* probability of the "signal" stimulus was varied in abrupt steps every 100 trials (Fig. 144).

Figure 144 shows the mean probability of reporting a change in readiness, given that a secondary response was made (which happened in about 95% of all trials). As hypothesized, observers found the task a meaningful one and, as predicted, awareness of change is quite intermittent, occurring on average every three trials or so. On the other hand, somewhat surprisingly, the frequency of experienced changes in readiness appears at first to be unrelated to the objective changes in signal probability.

A closer scrutiny of the data, however, reveals a quite different pattern. For example, Fig. 145a shows that the mean conditional probability of reporting a change in readiness *following a response of a particular kind* is lawfully related to objective signal probability. In particular, when objective signal probability decreases, the probability of reporting a change in readiness following a correct "signal" response increases and vice versa.

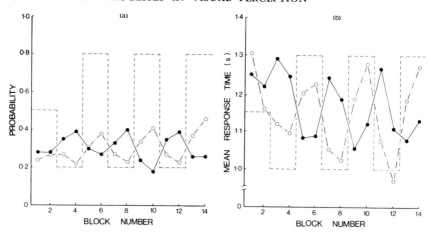

Fig. 145. Data from an unpublished experiment by myself and Smith. Figure 145a shows the mean probability of reporting a change in readiness conditional upon correctly responding "signal" (filled circles) or "nonsignal" (empty circles). Figure 145b shows the time taken to make a correct "signal" (filled circles) or "nonsignal" response (empty circles). As in Fig. 144, the broken line indicates the changes in objective signal probability.

Exactly complementary effects occur in the case of the "nonsignal" response. As is evident from Fig. 145b, these effects would appear to be related to systematic increases and decreases in the criterion levels adopted by observers. From these results it would appear, for example, that when a reduction in signal probability occasions an increase in the "signal" criterion, then correct "signal" responses are more likely to be followed by a conscious change in readiness than when signal probability is high and the "signal" criterion low. Such a result is to be expected on the proposed hypothesis, since the basis for confidence (or "balance of evidence") in the "signal" response will be enhanced when the "signal" criterion is high (and reduced when it is low). As with primary decisions, an enhanced input is more likely than a reduced one to give rise to an immediate response (in this case, a conscious adjustment to a primary criterion level).

Obviously, it would be desirable to proceed to require a more specific secondary response from the observer, so that indications by him of the direction of change in his readiness can be compared with those expected on theoretical grounds. Nevertheless, even as it stands, the above experiment seems to constitute a useful first step in the transformation of a very general hypothesis into a model of consciousness capable of making detailed, quantifiable predictions. At the very least, it seems to show that the "internal perceptions" of consciousness are amenable to experimental investigation by controlled introspective methods, and that the consciousness by an observer of changes in the operation of his primary decision processes is a lawful phenomenon, which is clearly related to variations in the stimulus input and to the outcomes reached by those primary processes. While it is true that these results also raise some further questions, the specific nature of these questions mean that in future it should be less difficult to design experiments to investigate them.

## Epilogue

The present book has followed the somewhat unfashionable strategy of attempting to construct a general theory of perceptual activity in terms of the combination and interconnection of a single type of perceptual (or cognitive) unit, distinguishable in terms of both structure and function, and capable of being given an elementary neurophysiological realization. Starting with the basic principles of discrimination, identification and self-regulation, the book has demonstrated how a general, adaptive decision module emerges from the multiple constraints which appear to operate in a variety of simple judgmental tasks. It was then shown that a rudimentary combination of these modules might evolve, which would be capable of executing a more complex judgmental task. Finally, a tentative synthesis of traditional approaches to perception was offered, in which an attempt is made to clarify the crucial and pervasive role of these modules in the overall activity of perceptual organization. As developed so far, this approach appears to have significant implications both for the understanding of individual differences and variations in perception, and for certain behavioural and phenomenological aspects of consciousness. Owing to its iterative, modular structure, there appear to be no obvious limits to its further development.

In contrast with most previous approaches in this vein, in which the simplicity of the hypothesized units has been outweighed by the complexity of the functional configurations into which they have been supposed to enter, the present approach proposes a perceptual or cognitive unit, which itself embodies all the basic principles essential for perception, and which is conceived of as acting in a quite uniform manner primarily on the output from units differentially sensitized to the varying features and topography of the environment. In effect, the overall activity of perceptual organization is pictured as mediated by a sequence of hetarchical arrays of adaptive decision modules, operating independently and in competition with each other, but modified in their operation according to the reference levels embodied in a hierarchical structure of similar modules, for which the sole function is that of regulation or control. Thus, to employ Deutsch's terminology, the present approach emphasizes the importance of "internal feedback or secondary messages", which have to do with "change in state of parts of the system" rather than being exclusively focussed on the more traditional problems associated with "the primary messages", which "move through the system in consequence of its interactions with the outside world" (1949, 1968, p. 394). While it seems advisable to remember that (like the feature detecting system discussed in Chapter 9) the hierarchy of control may be an inverted one, there seem to be some grounds for the opinion advanced by myself (Vickers, 1978) and by Broadbent (1977) that the behaviour of higher control systems may well turn out to be more constant, more important and more theoretically interesting than that of the processes regulated by them.

In the meantime, the role of consciousness in a system subject to multiple sources of control would seem to offer one of the most inviting and exciting avenues for further exploration. The significance of developing specific testable hypotheses about consciousness is perhaps most clearly brought out in two quotations which illustrate one of the great divisions which still exist in our thinking about human behaviour and experience. On the one hand, there is the empiricist view, epitomized by David Hume, who writes towards the end of the "Treatise on Human Nature":

> Whenever I enter most intimately into what I call *myself*, I always stumble on some particular perception or other, of heat or cold, light or shade, love or hatred, pain or pleasure. I never can catch *myself* at any time without a perception, and never can observe anything but the perception . . . [Now,] pain and pleasure, grief and joy, passions and sensations succeed each other, and never all exist at the same time. It cannot, therefore, be from any of these impressions, or from any other, that the idea of "self" is derived; and, consequently, there is no such idea (1874, *IV*, pp. 533–534).

On the other hand, we have the famous rationalist answer by Descartes to his own sceptical conclusions concerning knowledge gained from experience:

> Whilst I thus wished to think that all was false, it was absolutely necessary that *I*, who thus thought, should be somewhat; and as I observed that this truth, *I think, hence I am*, was so certain and of such evidence that no ground of doubt, however extravagant, could be . . . capable of shaking it, I concluded that I might, without scruple, accept it as the first principle of the philosophy of which I was in search ("Discourse on Method" (1912) IV, p. 26).

The historical contrast between these two philosophies could hardly be more dramatic. The concept of a conscious "self", regarded as meaningless by the empiricists, and outlawed by later behaviourist psychologists, served as the cornerstone of the rationalist philosophy of mind, which in turn gave rise to the structuralist psychology of Wundt and Titchener. To complete the irony, it was this latter movement, rather than more empiricist approaches, which first gave birth to experimentation but with an introspective methodology which was ill-suited to its purpose and its stage of development. Perhaps nothing illustrates the inadequacy of partial approaches more poignantly than the continuing history of this great division in our thinking. Whether it can be bridged by the proposed synthetic view, in which conscious experience is regarded both as representing environmental information and as specifying the regulatory, perceiving system remains to be seen. However, it seems unquestionable that it is only by making such an attempt that we can hope to gain some insight into the multifaceted complexities and contradictions that constitute human behaviour and experience.

# References

Adams, J. K. (1957). Behaviour without awareness. *Psychol. Bull.* **54**, 383–405.

Adams, J. K. amd Adams, P. A. (1961). Realism of confidence judgments. *Psychol. Rev.* **68**, 33–45.

Adams, P. A. (1954). The effect of past experience on the perspective reversal of a tridimensional figure. *Am. J. Psychol.* **57**, 708–710.

Adrian, E. D. (1966). Consciousness. *In* "Brain and Conscious Experience." (J. C. Eccles, Ed.) pp. 238–246. Springer–Verlag, New York.

Alexander, L., Eichen, L., Haselden, F. O., Pascucci, R. F. and Ross-Brown, D. M. (1974). Remote sensing: environmental and geotechnical applications. *Dames Moore Eng. Bull.* **44**, 1–50.

Alluisi, E. A. and Sidorsky, R. C. (1958). The empirical validity of equal discriminability scaling. *J. Exper. Psychol.* **55**, 86–94.

Ames, A. (1951). Visual perception and the rotating trapezoidal window. *Psychol. Monogr.* **65**, No. 324.

Ammons, C. H. and Ammons, R. B. (1963). Perspective reversal as affected by physical characteristics of Necker cube drawings. *Proc. Montana Acad. Sci.* **23**, 287–302.

Ammons, R. B. and Ammons, C. H. (1965). Learning and performance of rotary pursuit and reversals of perspective with continuous practice and a single rest. (Paper presented to Rocky Mountain Psychological Association, Albuquerque, N.M., May 1965.)

Ammons, R. B., Ulrich, P. and Ammons, C. H. (1959). Voluntary control of perception of depth in a two-dimensional drawing. *Proc. Montana Acad. Sci.* **19**, 160–168.

Anderson, D. A., Huntington, J. and Simonsen, E. (1966). Critical fusion frequency as a function of exposure time. *J. Optic. Soc. Am.* **56**, 1607–1611.

Angell, F. (1907). On judgments of "like" in discrimination experiments. *Am. J. Psychol.* **18**, 253–260.

Armstrong, D. M. (1968). "A Materialist Theory of Mind." Routledge and Kegan Paul, London.

Asch, S. E. (1968). Gestalt theory. *In* "International Encyclopaedia of the Social Sciences." (D. Sills, Ed.) Vol. 6, pp. 158–175. Macmillan & Free Press, New York.

Ash, I. E. (1914). Fatigue and its effects upon control. *Archs Psychol.* **31**, 1–61.

Attneave, F. (1953). Psychological probability as a function of perceived frequency. *J. Exper. Psychol.* **46**, 81–86.

Attneave, F. (1954). Some informational aspects of visual perception. *Psychol. Rev.* **61**, 183–193.

Attneave, F. (1968). Triangles as ambiguous figures. *Am. J. Psychol.* **81**, 447–453.

Attneave, F. (1971). Multistability in perception. *Sci. Am.* **225**, 62–71.

Attneave, F. (1972). Representation of physical space. *In* "Coding Processes in Human Memory." (A. W. Melton and E. Martin, Eds) pp. 283–306. V. H. Winston, Washington.

Attneave, F. and Frost, R. (1969). The determination of perceived tridimensional orientation by minimum criteria. *Percep. Psychophys.* **6**, 391–396.

Audley, R. J. (1960). A stochastic model for individual choice behaviour. *Psychol. Rev.* **67**, 1–15.

Audley, R. J. (1964). Decision-making. *Br. Med. Bull.* **20**, 27–31.

Audley, R. J. (1973). Some observations on theories of choice reaction time: tutorial review. *In* "Attention and Performance IV." (S. Kornblum, Ed.) pp. 509–545. Academic Press, New York and London.

Audley, R. J. and Mercer, A. (1968). The relation between decision time and relative response frequency in a blue-green discrimination. *Br. J. Math. Stat. Psychol.* **21**, 183–192.

Audley, R. J. and Pike, A. R. (1965). Some alternative stochastic models of choice. *Br. J. Math. Stat. Psychol.* **18**, 207–225.

Austin, J. L. (1961). A plea for excuses. *In* "Philosophical Papers." (J. O. Urmson and G. J. Warnock, Eds) pp. 123–152. Clarendon Press, Oxford.

Avant, L. and Helson, H. (1973). Theories of perception. *In* "Handbook of General Psychology." (B. B. Woolman, Ed.) pp. 419–448. Prentice Hall, Englewood Cliffs, N.J.

Baddeley, A. D. and Colquhoun, W. P. (1969). Signal probability and vigilance: a reappraisal of the "signal rate" effect. *Br. J. Psychol.* **60**, 169–178.

Bamber, D. (1969). Reaction times and error rates for "same-different" judgments of multidimensional stimuli. *Percep. Psychophys.* **6**, 169–174.

Barlow, H. B. (1956). Retinal noise and absolute threshold. *J. Optic. Soc. Am.* **46**, 634–639.

Barlow, H. B. (1972). Single units and sensation: a neuron doctrine for perceptual psychology? *Perception* **1**, 371–495.

Barlow, H. B. and Levick, W. R. (1969a). Three factors limiting the reliable detection of light by retinal ganglion cells of the cat. *J. Physiol.* **200**, 1–24.

Barlow, H. B. and Levick, W. R. (1969b). Changes in the maintained discharge with adaptation level in the cat retina. *J. Physiol.* **202**, 699–718.

Bartlett, F. C. (1942). Fatigue following highly skilled work. *Proc. Roy. Soc. Lond.* (B), **131**, 247–257.

Battersby, W. W. and Jaffe, R. (1953). Temporal factors influencing the perception of visual flicker. *J. Exper. Psychol.* **46**, 154–161.

Baumeister, A. A. and Kellas, G. (1968). Reaction time and mental retardation. *In* "International Review of Research in Mental Retardation." (N. R. Ellis, Ed.) Vol. 3, pp. 163–193. Academic Press, New York and London.

Beach, L. R. and Scopp, T. S. (1967). "Intuitive statistical inference about variances." L. R. Beach, (Mimeo), Seattle.

Beach, L. R. and Swensson, R. G. (1966). Intuitive estimation of means. *Psychonom. Sci.* **5**, 161–162.

Beck, J. (1966a). Effect of orientation and shape similarity on perceptual grouping. *Percep. Psychophys.* **1**, 300–302.

Beck, J. (1966b). Perceptual grouping produced by changes in orientation and shape. *Science* **154**, 538–540.

Beck, J. (1967). Perceptual grouping produced by line figures. *Percep. Psychophys.* **2**, 491–495.

Beck, J. (1972). Similarity grouping and peripheral discriminability under uncertainty. *Am. J. Psychol.* **85**, 1–20.

Beck, J. and Ambler, B. (1972). Discriminability of differences in line slope and in line arrangement as a function of mask delay. *Percep. Psychophys.* **12,** 33–38.

Berkson, J. A. (1944). Application of the logistic function to bio-assay. *J. Am. Stat. Ass.* **39,** 357–365.

Berkson, J. A. (1953). A statistically precise and relatively simple method of estimating the bio-assay with quantal response, based on the logistic function. *J. Am. Stat. Ass.* **48,** 565–599.

Bindra, D., Williams, J. A. and Wise, J. S. (1965). Judgments of sameness and difference: experiments on decision time. *Science* **150,** 1625–1627.

Bindra, D., Donderi, D. C. and Nishisato, S. (1968). Decision latencies of "same" and "different" judgments. *Percep. Psychophys.* **3,** 121–130.

Binford, J. R. and Loeb, M. (1966). Changes within and over repeated sessions in criterion and effective sensitivity in an auditory vigilance task. *J. Exper. Psychol.* **72,** 339–345.

Birren, J. E. and Botwinick, J. (1955). Speed of response as a function of perceptual difficulty and age. *J. Gerontol.* **10,** 433–436.

Boring, E. G. (1917). A chart of the psychometric function. *Am. J. Psychol.* **28,** 465–470.

Boring, E. G. (1920). The control of attitude in psychophysical experiments. *Psychol. Rev.* **27,** 440–452.

Boring, E. G. (1950). "A History of Experimental Psychology." (2nd ed.) Appleton-Century-Crofts, New York.

Boring, E. G., Langfeld, H. S. and Weld, H. P. (1948). "Foundations of Psychology." Wiley, New York.

Botwinick, J., Brinley, J. F. and Robbin, J. S. (1958). The interaction effects of perceptual difficulty and stimulus exposure time on age differences in speed and accuracy of response. *Gerontologia* **2,** 1–10.

Bower, G. H. (1959). Choice-point behaviour. *In* "Studies in Mathematical Learning Theory." (R. R. Bush and W. K. Estes, Eds) Chapter 6. Stanford University Press, Stanford.

Braun, H. W. and Heymann, S. P. (1958). Meaningfulness of material, distribution of practice, and serial position curves. *J. Exper. Psychol.* **56,** 146–150.

Braunstein, M. L. and Payne, J. W. (1969). Perspective and form ratio as determinants of relative slant judgments. *J. Exper. Psychol.* **81,** 584–590.

Briggs, G. E. and Blaha, J. (1969). Memory retrieval and central comparison times in information processing. *J. Exper. Psychol.* **79,** 395–402.

Broadbent, D. E. (1965). A reformulation of the Yerkes-Dodson law. *Br. J. Math. Stat. Psychol.* **18,** 145–157.

Broadbent, D. E. (1971). "Decision and Stress." Academic Press, London.

Broadbent, D. E. (1977). Levels, hierarchies, and the locus of control. *Q. J. Exper. Psychol.* **29,** 181–201.

Broadbent, D. E. and Gregory, M. (1965). Effects of noise and of signal rate upon vigilance analyzed by means of decision theory. *Hum. Factors* **7,** 155–162.

Broadhurst, P. L. (1959). The interaction of task difficulty and motivation: the Yerkes-Dodson law revived. *Acta Psychol.* **16,** 321–338.

Broen, W. E. and Storms, L. H. (1961). A reaction potential ceiling and response decrements in complex situations. *Psychol. Rev.* **68,** 405–415.

Brown, J. and Cane, V. R. (1959). An analysis of the limiting method. *Br. J. Stat. Psychol.* **12,** 119–126.

Brown, K. T. (1955). Rate of apparent change in a dynamic ambiguous figure as a function of observation time. *Am. J. Psychol.* **68,** 358–371.

Brown, W. (1910). The judgment of difference. *Univ. Calif. Publ. Psychol.* **1,** 1–71.

Bruner, J. S., Postman, L. and Mosteller, F. (1950). A note on the measurement of reversals of perspective. *Psychometrika* **15**, 63–72.

Brunswick, E. (1952). The conceptual framework of psychology. New York: "International Encyclopaedia of Unified Science." (O. Neurath, Ed.) (1, No. 10.) Univ. Chicago Press, Chicago.

Brunswick, E. (1955). Representative design and probabilistic theory in a functional psychology. *Psychol. Rev.* **62**, 193–217.

Buck, L. (1966). Reaction time as a measure of perceptual vigilance. *Psychol. Bull.* **65**, 291–308.

Bugelski, B. R. (1950). A remote association explanation of the relative difficulty of learning nonsense syllables in a serial list. *J. Exper. Psychol.* **40**, 336–348.

Burt, C. (1964). Consciousness and behaviourism. A reply. *Br. J. Psychol.* **55**, 93–96.

Burt, C. (1968). Brain and consciousness. *Br. J. Psychol.* **59**, 55–69.

Bush, R. R. (1963). Estimation and evaluation. *In* "Handbook of Mathematical Psychology." (R. R. Bush, E. Galanter and R. D. Luce, Eds) Vol. I, pp. 429–469. Wiley, New York.

Bush, R. R. and Mosteller, F. (1955). "Stochastic Models for Learning." John Wiley & Sons, Inc., New York.

Carlson, V. R. (1953). Satiation in a reversible perspective figure. *J. Exper. Psychol.* **45**, 442–448.

Carlson, W. R., Driver, R. C. and Preston, M. G. (1934). Judgment times for the method of constant stimuli. *J. Exper. Psychol.* **17**, 113–118.

Carterette, E. C., Friedman, M. P. and Cosmides, R. (1965). Reaction-time distributions in the detection of weak signals in noise. *J. Acoust. Soc. Am.* **38**, 531–542.

Cartwright, D. (1941). Relation of decision-time to the categories of response. *Am. J. Psychol.* **54**, 174–196.

Cartwright, D. and Festinger, L. (1943). A quantitative theory of decision. *Psychol. Rev.* **50**, 595–621.

Cattell, J. M. (1893). On errors of observation. *Am. J. Psychol.* **5**, 285–293.

Christie, L. S. and Luce, R. D. (1956). Decision structure and time relations in simple choice behaviour. *Bull. Math. Biophys.* **18**, 89–111.

Clark, W. C. (1966). The psyche in psychophysics: a sensory-decision theory analysis of the effect of instructions on flicker sensitivity and response bias. *Psychol. Bull.* **65**, 358–366.

Clark, W. C., Smith, A. H. and Rabe, A. (1955). Retinal gradients of outline as a stimulus for slant. *Canad. J. Psychol.* **9**, 247–253.

Clark, W. C., Brown, J. C. and Rutschmann, J. (1967). Flicker sensitivity and response bias in psychiatric patients and normal subjects. *J. Abnorm. Soc. Psychol.* **72**, 35–42.

Clynes, M. E. (1961). Unidirectional rate sensitivity: a biocybernetic law of reflex and humoral systems as physiologic channels of control and communication. *Anns N.Y. Acad. Sci.* **92**, 946–969.

Clynes, M. E. (1969). Implications of rein control in perceptual and conceptual organization. *Anns N.Y. Acad. Sci.* **156**, 629–670.

Cohen, L. (1959). Rate of apparent change of a Necker cube as a function of prior stimulation. *Am. J. Psychol.* **72**, 327–344.

Collier, R. M. (1964). Selected implications from a dynamic regulatory theory of consciousness. *Am. Psychol.* **19**, 265–269.

Colquhoun, W. P. (1966). Training for vigilance: a comparison of different techniques. *Hum. Factors* **8**, 7–12.

Colquhoun, W. P. (1969). Effects of raised ambient temperature and event rate on vigilance performance. *Aero. Med.* **40**, 413–417.

Colquhoun, W. P. and Baddeley, A. D. (1964). Role of pretest expectancy in vigilance decrement. *J. Exper. Psychol.* **68**, 156–160.

Colquhoun, W. P. and Baddeley, A. D. (1967). Influence of signal probability during pretraining on vigilance decrement. *J. Exper. Psychol.* **73**, 153–155.

Conolly, K. J. and Bruner, J. S. (1974). "The Growth of Competence." Academic Press, London and New York.

Cornsweet, T. N. (1970). "Visual Perception." Academic Press, New York and London.

Corso, J. F. (1967). "The Experimental Psychology of Sensory Behaviour." Holt, Rinehart & Winston, Inc., New York.

Cox, D. R. (1962). "Renewal Theory." Methuen, London.

Craik, K. J. W. (1966). "The Nature of Psychology." Cambridge University Press, Cambridge.

Cross, D. V. and Lane, H. L. (1962). On the discriminative control of concurrent responses: the relations among response frequency, latency, and topography in auditory generalization. *J. Exper. Analysis Behaviour* **5**, 487–496.

Crossman, E. R. F. W. (1953). Entropy and choice time: the effect of frequency imbalance on choice response. *Q. J. Exper. Psychol.* **5**, 41–51.

Crossman, E. R. F. W. (1955). The measurement of discriminability. *Q. J. Exper. Psychol.* **7**, 176–195.

Crossman, E. R. F. W. (1964). Reply to Dr. I. M. Hughes. *Q. J. Exper. Psychol.* **16**, 181–183.

Culler, E. (1926). Studies in psychometric theory. *Psychol. Monogr.* **35**, (2, whole No. 163).

Davies, D. R. and Tune, G. S. (1970). "Human Vigilance Performance." Staples Press, London.

Descartes, R. (1912). "Discourse on Method." (Trans. J. Veitch) J. M. Dent, London.

Deutsch, K. W. (1968). Towards a cybernetic model of man and society. *In* "Modern Systems Research for the Behavioural Scientist." (W. Buckley, Ed.) Aldine Publishing Co., Chicago.

de Vries, H. (1956). Physical aspects of the sense organs. *In* "Progress in Biophysics and Biophysical Chemistry." (J. A. V. Butler, Ed.) pp. 256–258. Pergamon, London.

Dixon, N. F. (1971). "Subliminal Perception: the Nature of a Controversy." McGraw Hill, London.

Docherty, M. E. (1968). Information and discriminability as determinants of absolute judgment choice reaction time. *Percep. Psychophys.* **3**, 1–4.

Dodwell, P. C. (1971). On perceptual clarity. *Psychol. Rev.* **78**, 275–289.

Donahue, W. T. and Griffitts, C. H. (1931). The influence of complicity on the fluctuations of the illusions of reversible perspective. *Am. J. Psychol.* **43**, 613–617.

Donders, F. C. (1969a). Two instruments for determining the time required for mental processes. *In* "Attention and Performance II." (W. G. Koster, Ed.) *Acta Psychol.* **30**, 432–435.

Donders, F. C. (1969b). On the speed of mental processes. *In* "Attention and Performance II" (W. G. Koster, Ed.) *Acta Psychol.* **30**, 412–431.

Eccles, J. C. (ed.) (1966). "Brain and Conscious Experience." Spinger-Verlag, New York.

Edwards, W. (1965). Optimal strategies for seeking information: models for statistics, choice reaction times, and human information processing. *J. Math. Psychol.* **2**, 312–329.

Egan, J. P. (1976). "ROC Analysis." Academic Press, New York and London.

Egan, J. P., Greenberg, G. L. and Schulman, A. I. (1961). Operating characteristics, signal detectability and the method of free response. *J. Acoust. Soc. Am.* **33**, 993–1007.

Embrey, D. E. (1975). Training the inspector's sensitivity and response strategy. *In* "Human Reliability in Quality Control." (C. G. Drury and J. G. Fox, Eds) pp. 123–131. Halsted Press, New York.

Emerson, R. W. (1903). "Essays." (Ser. 1.) Houghton Mifflin & Co., Boston.

Emmerich, D. S., Gray, J. L., Watson, C. S. and Tanis, D. C. (1972). Response latency, confidence and ROCs in auditory signal detection. *Percep. Psychophys.* **11**, 65–72.

Epstein, W. and Park, J. (1964). Examination of Gibson's psychophysical hypothesis. *Psychol. Bull.* **62**, 180–196.

Eriksen, C. W. and Hake, H. W. (1955). Multidimensional stimulus differences and accuracy of discrimination. *J. Exper. Psychol.* **50**, 153–160.

Eriksson, E. S. (1964). Monocular slant perception and the texture gradient concept. *Scand. J. Psychol.* **5**, 123–128.

Erlick, D. E. (1961). Judgments of the relative frequency of a sequential series of two events. *J. Exper. Psychol.* **62**, 105–112.

Estes, W. K. (1960). A random-walk model for choice behaviour. *In* "Mathematical Models in the Social Sciences." (K. J. Arrow, S. Karlin and P. Suppes, Eds) Stanford University Press, Stanford.

Evans, C. (1970). "The Subject of Consciousness." Allen and Unwin, London.

Evans, S. H. (1967). Redundancy as a variable in pattern perception. *Psychol. Bull.* **67**, 104–113.

Eysenck, H. J. (1955). A dynamic theory of anxiety and hysteria. *J. Mental Sci.* **101**, 28–51.

Falmagne, J. C. (1965). Stochastic models for choice-reaction time with applications to experimental results. *J. Math. Psychol.* **2**, 77–124.

Fechner, G. T. (1860). "Elements of Psychophysics." Vol. 1. New ed. publ. 1966 (Trans. H. E. Adler) Holt, Rinehart & Winston, New York.

Feigl, H. (1955). Functionalism, psychological theory, and the uniting sciences: some discussion remarks. *Psychol. Rev.* **62**, 232–235.

Feller, W. (1950). "An Introduction to Probability Theory and its Applications." Vol. I (3rd ed. publ. 1968) John Wiley & Sons, Inc., New York.

Fernberger, S. W. (1914). The effect of the attitude of the subject upon the measure of sensitivity. *Am. J. Psychol.* **25**, 538–543.

Fernberger, S. W. (1918). An introspective analysis of the process of comparing. *Psychol. Monogr.* **26**, (No. 6), 1–161.

Fernberger, S. W. (1930). The use of equality judgments in psychophysical procedures. *Psychol. Rev.* **37**, 107–112.

Fernberger, S. W. (1931). Instructions and the psychophysical limen. *Am. J. Psychol.* **43**, 361–376.

Fernberger, S. W. (1949). Coefficients of precision in the method of constant stimuli. *Am. J. Psychol.* **62**, 591–592.

Fernberger, S. W., Glass, E., Hoffman, I. and Willig, M. (1934). Judgment times of different psychophysical categories. *J. Exper. Psychol.* **17**, 286–293.

Festinger, L. (1943a). Studies in decision: I. Decision-time, relative frequency of judgment, and subjective confidence as related to physical stimulus difference. *J. Exper. Psychol.* **32**, 291–306.

Festinger, L. (1943b). Studies in decision: II. An empirical test of a quantitative theory of decision. *J. Exper. Psychol.* **32**, 411–423.

Fitts, P. M. (1966). Cognitive aspects of information processing: III. Set for speed versus accuracy. *J. Exper. Psychol.* **71**, 849–857.

Flock, H. R. (1964). A possible optical basis for monocular slant perception. *Psychol. Rev.* **71**, 380–391.

Flock, H. R. and Moscatelli, A. (1964). Variables of surface texture and accuracy of space perceptions. *Percep. Motor Skills* **19**, 327–334.

Foley, P. J. (1959). The expression of certainty. *Am. J. Psychol.* **72**, 614–615.

Ford, B. J. (1973). "The Revealing Lens: Mankind and the Microscope." Harrap, London.

Freedman, S. J. and Greenblatt, M. (1959). Studies in human isolation. W.A.D.C. Technical Report, pp. 59–266. Wright-Patterson Air Force Base, Ohio.

Frisch, H. L. and Julesz, B. (1966). Figure-ground perception and random geometry. *Percep. Psychophys.* **1**, 389–398.

Fritz, M. F. (1930). Experimental evidence in support of Professor Thurstone's criticism of the phi-gamma hypothesis. *J. Gen. Psychol.* **4**, 346–352.

Fullerton, G. S. and Cattell, J. M. (1892). On the perception of small differences. University of Pennsylvania Philosophy Series, No. 2.

Garner, W. R. (1953). An informational analysis of absolute judgments of loudness. *J. Exper. Psychol.* **46**, 373–380.

Garner, W. R. (1962). "Uncertainty and Structure as Psychological Concepts." Wiley & Sons, New York.

Garner, W. R. (1966). To perceive is to know. *Am. Psychol.* **21**, 11–19.

Garner, W. R. (1970). Good patterns have few alternatives. *Am. Sci.* **58**, 34–42.

Garner, W. R. (1972). Information integration and form of encoding. *In* "Coding Processes in Human Memory." (A. W. Melton and E. Martin, Eds), pp. 261–281. V. H. Winston, Washington.

Garner, W. R. (1974). "The Processing of Information and Structure." Lawrence Erlbaum, Potomac, Md.

Garrett, H. E. (1922). A study of the relation of accuracy to speed. *Archs Psychol.* **56**, 1–105.

George, S. S. (1917). Attitude in relation to the psychophysical judgment. *Am. J. Psychol.* **28**, 1–37.

Gescheider, G. A., Wright, J. H. and Evans, M. B. (1968). Reaction time in the detection of vibrotactile signals. *J. Exper. Psychol.* **77**, 501–504.

Gescheider, G. A., Wright, J. H., Weber, B. J., Kirchner, B. M. and Milligan, E. A. (1969). Reaction time as a function of the intensity and probability of occurrence of vibrotactile signals. *Percep. Psychophys.* **5**, 18–20.

Gescheider, G. A., Wright, J. H., Weber, B. J. and Barton, W. G. (1971). Absolute thresholds in vibrotactile signal detection. *Percep. Psychophys.* **10**, 413–417.

Gibson, J. J. (1950). "The Perception of the Visual World." Houghton Mifflin Co., Boston.

Gibson, J. J. (1955). "Optical Motions and Transformations as Stimuli for Visual Perception." Psychological Cinema Register, State College, Pa.

Gibson, J. J. (1957). Optical motions and transformations as stimuli for visual perception. *Psychol. Rev.* **64**, 288–295.

Gibson, J. J. (1959). Perception as a function of stimulation. *In* "Psychology: a Study of a Science." (S. Koch, Ed.) Vol. 1. McGraw Hill, New York.

Gibson, J. J. (1963). The useful dimensions of sensitivity. *Am. Psychol.* **18,** 1–16.

Gibson, J. J. (1966). "The Senses considered as Perceptual Systems." Allen & Unwin, London.

Gibson, J. J. (1972). Outline of a theory of direct visual perception. *In* "The Psychology of Knowing." (J. R. Royce and W. W. Rozeboom, Eds) Gordon and Breach, New York.

Ginsburg, N. (1970). Flicker fusion bibliography, 1953–1968. *Percep. Motor Skills* **30,** 427–482.

Goldstein, A. G. (1967). Gestalt similarity principle, difference thresholds, and pattern discriminability. *Percep. Psychophys.* **2,** 377–382.

Goodson, F. E. (1973). "The Evolutionary Foundations of Psychology." Holt, Rinehart & Winston, Inc., New York.

Gordon, K. (1903). Meaning in memory and attention. *Psychol. Rev.* **10,** 267–283.

Granit, R. and Hammond, E. L. (1931). Comparative studies on the peripheral and central retina: V. The sensation time curve and the time course of the fusion frequency of intermittent stimulation. *Am. J. Physiol.* **98,** 654–663.

Green, B. F., Wolf, A. K. and White, B. J. (1959). The detection of statistically defined patterns in a matrix of dots. *Am. J. Psychol.* **72,** 503–520.

Green, D. M. and Luce, R. D. (1973). Speed-accuracy trade-off in auditory detection. *In* "Attention and Performance IV." (S. Kornblum, Ed.) pp. 547–569. Academic Press, New York and London.

Green, D. M. and Swets, J. A. (1966). "Signal Detection Theory and Psychophysics." Wiley, New York.

Green, D. M., Birdsall, T. G. and Tanner, W. P. (1957). Signal detection as a function of signal intensity and duration. *J. Acoust. Soc. Am.* **29,** 523–531.

Green, R. T. and Courtis, M. C. (1966). Information theory: the metaphor that failed. *Acta Psycholo.* **25,** 12–36.

Greenberg, M. G. (1965). A modification of Thurstone's law of comparative judgment to accommodate a judgment category of "equal" or no difference. *Psychol. Bull.* **64,** 108–112.

Gregory, R. L. (1956). An experimental treatment of vision as an information source and noisy channel. *In* "Information theory. Third London Symposium." (E. C. Cherry, Ed. pp. 287–298. Butterworth, London.

Gregory, R. L. (1966). "Eye and Brain: the Psychology of Seeing." Weidenfeld and Nicolson, London.

Gregory, R. L. (1970). "The Intelligent Eye." Weidenfeld and Nicolson, London.

Grice, G. R. (1968). Stimulus intensity and response evocation. *Psychol. Rev.* **75,** 359–373.

Gruber, H. E. and Clark, W. C. (1956). Perception of slanted surfaces. *Percep. Motor Skills* **16,** 97–106.

Guilford, J. P. (1927). Fluctuations of attention with weak visual stimuli. *Am. J. Psychol.* **38,** 534–583.

Guilford, J. P. (1936). "Psychometric Methods." (2nd ed. publ. 1954) McGraw Hill, New York.

Guralnick, M. J. (1972). Observing responses and decision processes in vigilance. *J. Exper. Psychol.* **93,** 239–244.

Gyr, J. W. (1972). Is a theory of direct visual perception adequate? *Psychol. Bull.* **77,** 246–261.

Gyr, J. W., Brown, J. S., Willey, R. and Zivian, R. (1966). Computer simulation and psychological theories of perception. *Psychol. Bull.* **65,** 174–192.

Haber, R. N. (1969). Repetition as a determinant of perceptual recognition processes. *In* "Information Processing Approaches to Visual Perception." (R. N. Haber, Ed.). Holt, Rinehart and Winston, New York.

Haber, R. N. (1970). Note on how to choose a visual noise mask. *Psychol. Bull.* **74,** 373–376.

Hake, H. W. and Rodwan, A. S. (1966). Perception and recognition. *In* "Experimental Methods and Instrumentation in Psychology." (J. B. Sidowski, Ed.) McGraw Hill, New York.

Hale, D. J. (1968). The relation of correct and error responses in a serial choice reaction task. *Psychonom. Sci.* **13,** 299–300.

Hale, D. J. (1969). Speed-error trade-off in a three-choice serial reaction task. *J. Exper. Psychol.* **81,** 428–435.

Hamilton, W. (1859–60). "Lectures on Metaphysics." Blackwood, London.

Hammerton, M. (1959). A mathematical model for perception and a theoretical confusion function. *Nature, Lond.* **184,** 1668–1669.

Harrower, M. R. (1936). Some factors determining figure-ground articulation. *Br. J. Psychol.* **26,** 407–424.

Hawkins, H. L. (1969). Parallel processing in complex visual discrimination. *Percep. Psychophys.* **5,** 56–64.

Hays, W. L. (1963). "Statistics for Psychologists." Holt, Rinehart and Winston, New York.

Heath, H. A., Ehrlich, D. and Orbach, J. (1963). Reversibility of the Necker cube: II. effects of various activating conditions. *Percep. Motor Skills* **17,** 539–546.

Hebb, D. O. (1949). "The Organization of Behaviour." Wiley, New York.

Hebb, D. O. (1955). Drives and the CNS (conceptual nervous system). *Psychol. Rev.* **62,** 243–254.

Hecht, S., Shlaer, S. and Pirenne, M. H. (1942). Energy quanta and vision. *J. Gen. Physiol.* **25,** 819–840.

Helson, H. (1925a). The psychology of Gestalt. *Am. J. Psychol.* **36,** 342–370.

Helson, H. (1925b). The psychology of Gestalt. *Am. J. Psychol.* **36,** 494–526.

Helson, H. (1926a). The psychology of Gestalt. *Am. J. Psychol.* **37,** 25–62.

Helson, H. (1926b). The psychology of Gestalt. *Am. J. Psychol.* **37,** 189–223.

Helson, H. (1933). The fundamental propositions of Gestalt psychology. *Psychol. Rev.* **40,** 13–32.

Helson, H. (1964). "Adaptation-Level Theory." Harper & Row, New York.

Helson, H. (1969). Why did their precursors fail and the Gestalt psychologists succeed? Reflections on theories and theorists. *Am. Psychol.* **24,** 1006–1111.

Helson, H. (1971). Adaptation-level theory: 1970 and after. *In* "Adaptation-Level Theory." (M. H. Appley, Ed.). Academic Press, New York and London.

Henmon, V. A. C. (1906). The time of perception as a measure of differences in sensation. *Archs Phil. Psychol. Sci. Method* **8,** 1–75.

Henmon, V. A. C. (1911). The relation of the time of a judgment to its accuracy. *Psychol. Rev.* **18,** 186–201.

Hick, W. E. (1952a). Why the human operator? *Trans. Soc. Instr. Technol.* **4,** 67–77.

Hick, W. E. (1952b). On the rate of gain of information. *Q. J. Exper. Psychol.* **4,** 11–26.

Hilgard, E. R. (1955). Discussion of probabilistic functionalism. *Psychol. Rev.* **62,** 226–228.

Hilgard, E. R. (1977). Controversies over consciousness and the rise of cognitive psychology. *Austral. Psychol.* **12**, 7–26.

Hochberg, J. (1957). Effects of the gestalt revolution: the Cornell symposium on perception. *Psychol. Rev.* **64**, 73–84.

Hochberg, J. E. and Hardy, D. (1960). Brightness and proximity factors in grouping. *Percep. Motor Skills* **10**, 22.

Hochberg, J. E. and McAlister, E. (1953). A quantitative approach to figural "goodness". *J. Exper. Psychol.* **46**, 361–364.

Hochberg, J. E. and Silverstein, A. A. (1956). A quantitative index of stimulus similarity: proximity vs. difference in brightness. *Am. J. Psychol.* **69**, 456–458.

Hofstatter, P. R. (1939). Über die Schätzung von Gruppeneigenschaften, *Z. Psychol.* **145**, 1–44.

Holland, H. C. (1961). Judgments and the effects of instructions. *Acta Psychol.* **18**, 229–238.

Hollingworth, H. L. (1939). Perceptual fluctuation as a fatigue index. *J. Exper. Psychol.* **24**, 511–519.

Hopkins, G. M. (1972). "Poems and Prose." (W. H. Gardner, Ed.) Penguin Books, London.

Hornsby, P. (1968). A test of a model for choice-reaction times. (Unpublished thesis submitted for the degree of B.Sc., University of London.)

Howell, W. C. (1970). Intuitive "counting" and "tagging" in memory. *J. Exper. Psychol.* **85**, 210–215.

Howell, W. C. and Kriedler, D. L. (1963). Information processing under contradictory instructional sets. *J. Exper. Psychol.* **65**, 39–46.

Howland, D. (1958). An investigation of the performance of the human monitor. US Air Force, Wright Air Development Center Technical Report No. 57–431.

Hoyle, F. (1962). "Astronomy." MacDonald & Co., London.

Hubel, D. H. and Wiesel, T. N. (1961). Integrative action in the cat's lateral geniculate body. *J. Physiol.* **155**, 385–398.

Hubel, D. H. and Wiesel, T. N. (1962). Receptive fields, binocular interaction, and functional architecture in the cat's visual cortex. *J. Physiol.* **160**, 106–154.

Hughes, I. M. (1964). Crossman's confusion-function and multi-choice discrimination. *Q. J. Exper. Psychol.* **16**, 177–180.

Hull, C. L. (1943). "Principles of Behaviour." Appleton-Century-Crofts, New York.

Hull, C. L. (1948). Reactively heterogeneous compound trial-and-error learning with distributed trials and serial reinforcement. *J. Exper. Psychol.* **38**, 17–28.

Hume, D. (1874). "A Treatise of Human Nature." Vol. I. Longmans, Green, and Co., London.

Huntington, J. M. and Simonson, E. (1965). Critical flicker fusion frequency as a function of exposure time in two different age groups. *J. Gerontol.* **20**, 527–529.

Hyman, R. (1953). Stimulus information as a determinant of reaction time. *J. Exper. Psychol.* **45**, 188–196.

Indlin, Yu. A. (1976). The observer as a system with feedback. *In* "Advances in Psychophysics." (H. G. Geissler and Yu. M. Zabrodin, Eds) pp. 175–193. V. E. B. Deutscher Verlag der Wissenschaften, Berlin.

Irwin, F. W. and Smith, W. A. S. (1956). Further tests of theories of decision in an "expanded judgment" situation. *J. Exper. Psychol.* **52**, 345–348.

Irwin, F. W., Smith, W. A. S. and Mayfield, J. F. (1956). Tests of two theories of decision in an "expanded judgment" situation. *J. Exper. Psychol.* **51**, 261–268.

Ittelson, W. H. (1952). "The Ames Demonstrations in Perception." Princeton University Press, Princeton.

Ittelson, W. H. (1962). Perception and transactional psychology. In "Psychology: Study of a Science." (S. Koch, Ed.) pp. 660–704. McGraw Hill, New York.

James, W. (1890). "The Principles of Psychology." Henry Holt & Co., New York.

Jarvis, R. A. (1972). Clustering using a similarity based on shared near neighbours: visual image experiments. In "Pictorial Organisation and Shape." (J. F. O'Callaghan, Ed.) pp. 90–97. Division of Computing Research, C.S.I.R.O., Canberra, A.C.T.

Jastrow, J. (1888). A critique of psycho-physic methods. Am. J. Psychol. 1, 271–309.

Jerison, H. J. (1977). Vigilance: biology, psychology, theory, and practise. In "Vigilance: Theory, Operational Performance, and Physiological Correlates." (R. Mackie, Ed.) pp. 27–40. Plenum Press, New York.

Jerison, H. J., Pickett R. M. and Stenson, H. H. (1965). The elicited observing rate and decision processes in vigilance. Hum. Factors 7, 107–128.

John, I. D. (1969). Mediating processes in choice reaction tasks. In "Attention and Performance II." (W. G. Koster, Ed.) Acta Psychol. 30, 58–64.

Johnson, D. M. (1939). Confidence and speed in the two-category judgment. Archs Psychol. 34, 1–53.

Johnson, D. M. (1955). "The Psychology of Thought and Judgment." Harper, New York.

Jones, R. W. (1973). "Principles of Biological Regulation: An Introduction to Feedback Systems." Academic Press, New York and London.

Joynson, R. B. (1970). The breakdown of modern psychology. Bull. Br. Psychol. Soc. 23, 261–269.

Joynson, R. B. (1972). The return of mind. Bull. Br. Psychol. Soc. 25, 1–10.

Joynson, R. B. (1974). "Psychology and Common Sense." Routledge and Kegan Paul, London.

Julesz, B. (1962). Visual pattern discrimination. I. R. E. Trans. I. Theory, PGIT, IT-. 8, 84–92.

Julesz, B. (1969). Cluster formation at various perceptual levels. In "Methodologies of Pattern Recognition." (S. Watanabe, Ed.) Academic Press, New York and London.

Kalmus, H. (1966). "Regulation and Control in Living Systems." John Wiley and Sons, London.

Katona, P., Barnett, G. P. and Levison, W. H. (1967). Directional sensitivity of the carotid sinus reflex. Anns N.Y. Acad. Sci. 156, 779–786.

Katz, D. (1951). "Gestalt Psychology.' (Trans. R. Tyson). Methuen & Co., London.

Kellogg, W. N. (1930). An experimental evaluation of equality judgments in psychophysics. Archs Psychol. 112, 1–79.

Kellogg, W. N. (1931). Time of judgment in psychometric measures. Am. J. Psychol. 43, 65–86.

Kilpatrick, F. P. (1952). "Human Behaviour from the Transactional Point of View." Institute for Associated Research, Princeton.

Kendall, M. G. and Stuart, A. (1968). The Advanced Theory of Statistics." Vol. 1. Griffin, London.

Knox, G. W. (1945). The effect of practice, under the influence of various attitudes, on the CFF. J. Gen. Psychol. 33, 121–129.

Koestler, A. and Smythies, J. (1969). "Beyond Reductionism: the Alpbach Symposium." Hutchinson and Co., New York.

Köhler, W. (1940). "Dynamics in Psychology." Faber & Faber, London.

Köhler, W. and Wallach, H. (1944). Figural after-effects: an investigation of visual processes. *Proc. Am. Philosoph. Soc.* **88**, 269–357.

Koppell, S. (1976). The latency function hypothesis and Pike's multiple-observations model for latencies in signal detection. *Psychol. Rev.* **83**, 308–309.

Kraft, A. L. and Winnick, W. A. (1967). The effect of pattern and texture gradient on slant and shape judgments. *Percep. Psychophys.* **2**, 141–147.

Krech, D. (1955). Discussion: theory and reductionism. *Psychol. Rev.* **62**, 229–231.

Kuffler, S. W. (1953). Discharge patterns and functional organization of the mammalian retina. *J. Neurophysiol.* **16**, 37–68.

Kuffler, S. W., Fitzhugh, R. and Barlow, H. B. (1957). Maintained activity in the cat's retina in light and darkness. *J. Gen. Physiol.* **40**, 683–703.

Künnapas, T. M. (1957). Experiments on figural dominance. *J. Exper. Psychol.* **53**, 31–39.

Künnapas, T. M. (1969). Figural reversal rate and personal tempo. *Scand. J. Psychol.* **10**, 27–32.

La Berge, D. (1959). A model with neutral elements. In "Studies in Mathematical Learning Theory." (R. R. Bush and W. K. Estes, Eds) Chapter 2. Stanford University Press, Stanford.

La Berge, D. (1961). Generalization gradients in a discrimination situation. *J. Exper. Psychol.* **62**, 88–94.

La Berge, D. (1962). A recruitment theory of simple behaviour. *Psychometrika* **27**, 375–396.

Lally, M. and Nettelbeck, T. (1977). Intelligence, reaction time, and inspection time. *Am. J. Mental Def.* **82**, 273–281.

Laming, D. R. J. (1966). A new interpretation of the relation between choice-reaction time and the number of equiprobable alternatives. *Br. J. Math. Stat. Psychol.* **19**, 139–149.

Laming, D. R. J. (1968). "Information Theory of Choice-Reaction Times." Academic Press, New York and London.

Laming, D. R. J. (1969). Subjective probability in choice-reaction experiments. *J. Math. Psychol.* **6**, 81–120.

Landahl, H. D. (1938). A contribution to the mathematical biophysics of psychophysical discrimination. *Psychometrika* **3**, 107–125.

Landis, C. and Hamwi, V. (1954). Effects of certain physiological determinants on the flicker-fusion Threshold. *J. Appl. Physiol.* **6**, 566–572.

Lashley, K. S., Chow, K. L. and Semmes, J. (1951). An examination of the electrical field theory of cerebral integration. *Psychol. Rev.* **58**, 123–136.

Lathrop, R. G. (1967). Perceived variability. *J. Exper. Psychol.* **23**, 498–502.

Leeper, R. (1935). A study of a neglected portion of the field of learning: the development of sensory organization. *J. Genet. Psychol.* **46**, 42–75.

Leibniz, G. W. (1956). "Philosophical Writings." (Trans. M. Morris). J. M. Dent & Sons, London.

Lemmon, V. W. (1927). The relation of reaction time to measures of intelligence, memory, and learning. *Archs Psychol.* No. **94**.

Leppmann, P. K. and Mefferd, R. B. (1968). Validity of perceptual reports of experienced and inexperienced observers. *Percep. Motor Skills* **26**, 1167–1172.

Lettvin, J. Y., Maturana, H. R., Pitts, W. H. and McCulloch, W. S. (1961). Two remarks on the visual system of the frog. In "Sensory Communication." (W. A. Rosenblith, Ed.) pp. 757–776. M.I.T. Press, Cambridge, Mass.

Levine, J. (1966). The effects of values and costs on the detection and identification of signals in auditory vigilance. *Hum. Factors* **8**, 525–537.

Lewin, K. (1935). "A Dynamic Theory of Personality: Selected Papers." (Trans. D. K. Adams and K. E. Zener). McGraw-Hill, New York.

Lie, I. (1964). The factor of proximity. *Scand. J. Psychol.* **5**, 129–135.

Lie, I. (1965). Reward and punishment: a determinant in figure-ground perception? *Scand. J. Psychol.* **6**, 186–194.

Lindauer, M. S. and Lindauer, J. G. (1970). Brightness differences and the perception of figure-ground. *J. Exper. Psychol.* **84**, 291–295.

Link, S. W. (1975). The relative judgment theory of two choice response time. *J. Math. Psychol.* **12**, 114–135.

Link, S. W. (1978). The relative judgment theory of the psychometric function. *In* "Attention and Performance VII." (J. Requin, Ed.) pp. 619–630. Lawrence Erlbaum, Hillsdale, N. J.

Link, S. W. and Heath, R. A. (1974). A sequential theory of psychological discrimination. *Psychometrika* **40**, 77–105.

Link, S. W. and Tindall, A. D. (1971). Speed and accuracy in comparative judgments of line length. *Percep. Psychophys.* **9**, 284–288.

Loeb, M. and Binford, J. R. (1964). Vigilance for auditory intensity changes as a function of preliminary feedback and confidence level. *Hum. Factors* **7**, 445–458.

Loemker, L. E. (Ed. and Trans.) (1956). "The Philosophical Papers and Letters of G. W. Leibniz." D. Reidel Publishing Co., Dordrecht, Holland.

Luce, R. D. (1959). "Individual Choice Behaviour." Wiley, New York.

Luce, R. D. and Green, D. M. (1972). A neural timing theory for response times and the psychophysics of intensity. *Psychol. Rev.* **79**, 14–57.

Lufkin, H. M. (1928). The best fitting frequency function for Urban's lifted-weight results. *Am. J. Psychol.* **40**, 75–82.

Lund, F. H. (1926). Criteria of confidence. *Am. J. Psychol.* **37**, 372–381.

Mackay, D. M. (1966). Conscious control of action. *In* "Brain and Conscious Experience." (J. C. Eccles, Ed.) pp. 422–440. Springer-Verlag, New York.

Mackworth, J. F. (1965). Deterioration of signal detectability during a vigilance task as a function of background event rate. *Psychonom. Sci.* **3**, 421–422.

Macmillan, N. A. (1971). Detection and recognition of increments and decrements in auditory intensity. *Percep. Psychophys.* **10**, 233–238.

Mandler, G. (1975a). Consciousness: respectable, useful, and probably necessary. *In* "Information Processing and Cognition: the Loyola Symposium." (R. Solso, Ed.) pp. 229–254. Lawrence Erlbaum, Hillsdale, N.J.

Mandler, G. (1975b). "Mind and Emotion." John Wiley and Sons, New York.

Mangan, G. L. (1959). The role of punishment in figure-ground reorganization *J. Exper. Psychol.* **58**, 369–375.

McCrary, J. and Hunter, W. S. (1953). Serial position curves in verbal learning. *Science* **117**, 131–134.

McDougall, W. (1906). Physiological factors of the attention process: IV. *Mind* **15**, 329–359.

McFarland, D.J. (1971). "Feedback Mechanisms in Animal Behaviour." Academic Press, London and New York.

McGill, W. J. (1963). Stochastic latency mechanisms. *In* "Handbook of Mathematical Psychology." (R. D. Luce, R. R. Bush and E. Galanter, Eds) Vol. 1. Wiley, New York.

McNicol, D. (1972). "A Primer of Signal Detection Theory." Allen and Unwin, London.

McNicol, D. (1975). Feedback as a source of information and as a source of noise in absolute judgments of loudness. *J. Exper. Psychol., Hum. Percep. Perform.* **104**, 175–182.

Mefferd, R. B. (1968a). Perceptual fluctuations involving orientation and organization. *Percep. Motor Skills* **27**, 827–834.

Mefferd, R. B. (1968b). Fluctuations in perceptual organization and orientation and perception of apparent movement. *Percep. Motor Skills* **27**, 368–370.

Mefferd, R. B., Wieland, B. A., Greenstein, D. G. and Leppmann, P. K. (1968). Effects of pretraining and instructions on validity of perceptual reports by inexperienced observers. *Percep. Motor Skills* **27**, 1003–1006.

Merkel, J. (1885). Die zeitlichen Verhältnisse der Willensthätigkeit. *Philosoph. Stud.* **2**, 73–127.

Miller, G. A. (1962). "Psychology: the Science of Mental Life." Penguin, London.

Miller, G. A., Galanter, E. and Pribram, K. M. (1960). "Plans and the Structure of Behavior." Holt, Rinehart & Winston, New York.

Milner, P. M. (1974). A model for visual shape recognition. *Psychol. Rev.* **81**, 521–535.

Milsum, J. H. (1966). "Biological Control Systems Analysis." McGraw Hill, New York.

Minsky, M. (1961). Steps towards artificial intelligence. *Proc. I. R. E.* **49**, 8–30.

Morgan, B. B. and Alluisi, E. A. (1967). Effects of discriminability and irrelevant information on absolute judgment. *Percep. Psychophys.* **2**, 54–58.

Muenzinger, K. F. (1938). Vicarious trial and error. I. A general survey of the relation to learning efficiency. *J. Genet. Psychol.* **53**, 75–86.

Mull, H. K., Ord, N. and Locke, N. (1954). The effect of two brightness factors upon the rate of fluctuation of reversible perspectives. *Am. J. Psychol.* **67**, 341–342.

Murdock, B. B. (1960). The distinctiveness of stimuli. *Psychol. Rev.* **67**, 16–31.

Murray, H. G. (1970). Stimulus intensity and reaction time: evaluation of a decision-theory model. *J. Exper. Psychol.* **84**, 383–391.

Nettelbeck, T. (1972). The effects of shock-induced anxiety on noise in the visual system. *Perception* **1**, 297–304.

Nettelbeck, T. (1973). Individual differences in noise and associated perceptual indices of performance. *Perception* **2**, 11–21.

Nettelbeck, T. and Brewer, N. (1976). Effects of stimulus-response variables on the choice-reaction time of mildly retarded adults. *Am. J. Mental Def.* **81**, 85–92.

Nettelbeck, T. and Lally, M. (1976). Inspection time and measured intelligence. *B. J. Psychol.* **67**, 17–22.

Nettelbeck, T., Cheshire, F. and Lally, M. (1978). Intelligence, work performance, and inspection time. *Ergonomics* **22**, (in press).

Newell, A., Shaw, J. C. and Simon, H. A. (1958). Elements of a theory of human problem-solving. *Psychol. Rev.* **65**, 151–166.

Newman, C. V. (1970). The influence on texture density gradients on judgments of length. *Psychonom. Sci.* **20**, 333–334.

Newman, C. V. (1971). The influence of visual texture density gradients on relative distance judgments. *Q. J. Exper. Psychol.* **23**, 225–233.

Newman, C. V. (1972). The role of gradients of binocular disparity in Gibson's theory of space perception. *Percep. Psychophys.* **12**, 237–238.

Newman, C. V. (1973). Variations in size and judgements as a function of surface texture. Q. J. Exper. Psychol. **25,** 260–264.

Nickerson, R. S. (1965). Response times for "same–different" judgments. Percep. Motor Skills **20,** 15–18.

Nickerson, R. S. (1967). "Same–different" response times with multi-attribute stimulus differences. Percep. Motor Skills **24,** 543–554.

Nickerson, R. S. (1969). "Same–different" response times: a model and a preliminary test. In "Attention and Performance II. (W. G. Koster, Ed.) Acta Psychol. **30,** 257–275.

Nickerson, R. S. (1971). "Same–different" response times. A further test of a "counter and clock" model. Acta Psychol. **35,** 112–127.

Norman, D. A. and Wickelgren, W. A. (1969). Strength theory of decision rules and latency in short-term memory. J. Math. Psychol. **6,** 192–208.

O'Callaghan, J. F. (1974). Human perception of homogeneous dot patterns. Perception **3,** 33–45.

O'Connor, N. and Hermelin, B. (1965). Input restriction and immediate memory decay in normal and subnormal children. Q. J. Exper. Psychol. **17,** 323–328.

Ogilvie, J. C. and Creelman, C. L. (1968). Maximum likelihood estimation of receiver operating characteristic curve parameters. J. Math. Psychol. **5,** 377–391.

Ollman, R. T. (1966). Fast guesses in choice reaction time. Psychomet. Sci. **6,** 155–156.

Olson, C. L. and Ogilvie, J. C. (1972). The method of constant stimuli with two or more categories of response. J. Math. Psychol. **9,** 320–338.

Olson, R. K. (1974). Slant judgments from static and rotating trapezoids correspond to rules of perspective geometry. Percep. Psychophys. **15,** 509–516.

Olson, R. K. and Attneave, F. (1970). What variables produce similarity grouping? Am. J. Psychol. **83,** 1–21.

Ormiston, D. W. (1961). A methodological study of confinement. W.A.D.C. Technical Report, pp. 61–258, Wright-Patterson Air Force Base, Ohio.

Orne, M. T. (1962). On the social psychology of the psychological experiment, with particular reference to the demand characteristics and their implications. Am. Psychol. **17,** 776–783.

Oyama, T. (1950). Figure-ground dominance as a function of sector angle, brightness, hue, and orientation. J. Exper. Psychol. **60,** 299–305.

Pachella, R. G. and Fisher, D. F. (1969). Effect of stimulus degradation and similarity on the trade-off between speed and accuracy in absolute judgments. J. Exper. Psychol. **81,** 7–9.

Pachella, R. G. and Pew, R. W. (1968). Speed-accuracy trade-off in reaction time: effect of discrete criterion times. J. Exper. Psychol. **76,** 19–24.

Pachella, R. G., Fisher, D. F. and Karsh, R. (1968). Absolute judgments in speeded tasks: quantification of the trade-off between speed and accuracy. Psychonom. Sci. **12,** 225–226.

Pask, G. (1970). Cognitive systems. In "Cognition: a Multiple View." (P. L. Garvin, Ed.) pp. 349–405. Spartan Books, New York.

Pelton, L. H. and Solley, C. M. (1968). Acceleration of reversals of a Necker cube. Am. J. Psychol. **81,** 585–588.

Penfield, W. and Roberts, L. (1959). "Speech and Brain Mechanisms." Princeton University Press.

Peterfreund, E. and Schwartz, J. T. (1971). Information processing and the nature of conscious and unconscious processes. Psychol. Iss. **7,** 219–229.

Pew, R. W. (1969). The speed-accuracy operating characteristic. *In* "Attention and Performance II." (W. G. Koster, Ed.) *Acta Psychol.* **30**, 16–26.

Philip, B. R. (1936). The relationship between speed and accuracy in a motor task. *J. Exper. Psychol.* **19**, 24–50.

Philip, B. R. (1947). The relationship of exposure time and accuracy in a perceptual task. *J. Exper. Psychol.* **37**, 178–186.

Phillips, R. J. (1970). Stationary visual texture and the estimation of slant angle. *Q. J. Exper. Psychol.* **22**, 389–397.

Pickett, R. M. (1964). The perception of a visual texture. *J. Exper. Psychol.* **68**, 13–20.

Pickett, R. M. (1967). Response latency in a pattern perception situation. *In* "Attention and Performance I." (A. F. Sanders, Ed.) *Acta Psychol.* **27**, 160–169.

Pickett, R. M. (1968). The visual perception of random line segment texture. (Paper read at Ninth Meeting of the Psychonomic Society.)

Pickett, R. M. (1970). Visual analyses of texture in the detection and recognition of objects. *In* "Picture Processing and Psychopictorics." (B. S. Lipkin and A. Rosenfeld, Eds) Academic Press, New York.

Pierce, C. S. and Jastrow, J. (1885). On small differences in sensation. *Proc. Nat. Acad. Sci.* **3**, 75–83.

Pierrel, R. and Murray, C. S. (1963). Some relationships between comparative judgment confidence and decision-time in weight lifting. *Am. J. Psychol.* **76**, 28–38.

Pike, A. R. (1968). Latency and relative frequency of response in psycho-physical discrimination. *Br. J. Math. Stat. Psychol.* **21**, 161–182.

Pike, A. R. (1971). The latencies of correct and incorrect responses in discrimination and detection tasks: their interpretation in terms of a model based on simple counting. *Percep. Psychophys.* **9**, 455–460.

Pike, A. R. (1973). Response latency models for signal detection. *Psychol Rev.* **80** (1), 53–68

Pike, A. R. and Dalgleish, L. (1976). The components of latency of response in two models for auditory detection with deadlines. *Percep. Psychophys.* **19**, 231–239.

Pike, A. R. and Ryder, P. (1973). Response latencies in the yes/no detection task: an assessment of two basic models. *Percep. Psychophys.* **13**, 224–232.

Pike, A. R., McFarland, K. and Dalgleish, L. (1974). Speed–accuracy tradeoff models for auditory detection with deadlines. *Acta Psychol.* **38** (5), 379–399.

Pitz, G. F. (1970). On the processing of information: probabilistic and otherwise. *Acta Psychol.* **34**, 201–213.

Platt, J. R. (1962). Functional geometry and the determination of pattern in mosaic receptors. *Gen. Systems* **7**, 103–119.

Polyak, S. (1957). "The Vertebrate Visual System." University of Chicago Press, Chicago.

Porter, E. K. H. (1938). Factors in the fluctuations of fifteen ambiguous phenomena. *Psychol. Record* **2**, 231–253.

Posner, M. I. and Keele, S. W. (1967). Decay of visual information from a single letter. *Science* **158**, 137–139.

Posner, M. I. and Taylor, R. L. (1969). Subtractive method applied to separation of visual and name components of multi-letter arrays. *In* "Attention and Performance II." (W. G. Koster, Ed.) *Acta Psychol.* **30**, 104–114.

Posner, M. I., Boies, S. J., Eichelman, W. H. and Taylor, R. L. (1969). Retention of visual and name codes of single letters. *J. Exper. Psychol.* **79**, No. 3, Pt. 2 (Monograph), 1–16.

Postman, L. (1955). The probability approach and nomothetic theory. *Psychol. Rev.* **62**, 218–225.

Powers, W. T. (1973). "Behaviour: the Control of Perception." p. 296. Aldine, Chicago, Ill.

Price, J. R. (1967a). Two components of reversal for a rotating skeletal cube: "conditioned satiation". *Austral. J. Psychol.* **19**, 261–270.

Price, J. R. (1967b). Perspective duration of a plane reversible figure. *Psychonom. Sci.* **9**, 623–624.

Price, J. R. (1968). Studies of reversible figures. (unpublished Ph.D. thesis, University of Western Australia.)

Price, J. R. (1969a). Studies of reversible perspective: a methodological review. *Behav. Res. Meth. Instr.* **1**, 102–106.

Price, J. R. (1969b). Effect of extended observation on reversible perspective duration. *Psychonom. Sci.* **16**, 75–76.

Prytulak, L. S. (1974). Good continuation revisited. *J. Exper. Psychol.* **102**, 773–777.

Purdy, W. C. (1958). The Hypothesis of Psychophysical Correspondence in Space Perception. (Doctoral dissertation, Cornell University.) University Microfilms, No. 58–5594, Ann Arbor, Michigan.

Rabbitt, P. M. A. (1966). Errors and error correction in choice-response tasks. *J. Exper. Psychol.* **71**, 264–272.

Rabbitt, P. M. A. (1971). Times for the analysis of stimuli and for the selection of responses. *In* "Cognitive Psychology." (A. Summerfield, Ed.), *Br. Med. Bull.* **27**, 259–265.

Rapoport, A. (1959). A study of disjunctive reaction times. *Behavl Sci.* **4**, 299–315.

Reed, J. B. (1951). The speed and accuracy of discriminating differences in hue, brilliance, area, and shape. (Account given *in* D. M. Johnson, 1955, "The Psychology of Thought and Judgment." pp. 371–372, Harper, New York.)

Reichardt, W. (1961). Autocorrelation: a principle for the evaluation of sensory information by the central nervous system. *In* "Sensory Communication." (W. A. Rosenblith, Ed.) M.I.T. Press, Cambridge, Mass.

Restle, F. (1961). "Psychology of Judgment and Choice." John Wiley & Sons, Inc., New York.

Robinson, G. H. (1964). Continuous estimation of a time-varying probability. *Ergonomics* **7**, 7–21.

Royer, F. L. and Garner, W. R. (1966). Response uncertainty and perceptual difficulty of auditory temporal patterns. *Percep. Psychophys.* **1**, 41–47.

Rubin, E. (1915). "Synosplerede Figurer." Gyldendalske, Copenhagen. Trans. and abridged version (1958) *in* "Readings in Perception." (D. C. Beardslee and M. Wertheimer, Eds) pp. 194–203. Van Nostrand Co., Inc., New York.

Ryder, P., Pike, R. and Dalgleish, L. (1974). What is the signal in signal detection? *Percep. Psychophys.* **15**, 479–482.

Sadler, T. G. and Mefferd, R. B. (1970). Fluctuations of perceptual organization and orientation: stochastic (random) or steady state (satiation)? *Percep. Motor Skills* **31**, 739–749.

Sanders, A. F. and Ter Linden, W. (1967). Decision making during paced arrival of probabilistic information. *In* "Attention and Performance I." (A. F. Sanders, Ed.) *Acta Psychol.* **27**, 170–177.

Saugstad, P. (1965). Effect of reward and punishment on visual perception of figure-ground. *Scand. J. Psychol.* **6**, 225–236.

Savage, R. D. (1970). Intellectual assessment. *In* "The Psychological Assessment of

Mental and Physical Handicaps." (P. Mittler, Ed.) Methuen, London.

Schafer, R. and Murphy, G. (1943). The role of autism in visual figure-ground relationship. *J. Exper. Psychol.* **32**, 335–343.

Schiff, W. (1965). The preception of impending collision: a study of visually directed avoidant behaviour. *Psychol. Monogr.* **79**, (Whole No. 604.)

Schlosberg, H. (1954). Three dimensions of emotion. *Psychol. Rev.* **61**, 81–88.

Schouten, J. F. and Bekker, J. A. M. (1967). Reaction time and accuracy. *In* "Attention and Performance I." (A. F. Sanders, Ed.) *Acta Psychol.* **27**, 143–153.

Scripture, E. W. (1905). "The New Psychology." Walter Scott Publishing Co., London.

Sekuler, R. W. (1965). Signal detection, choice response times, and visual backward masking. *Canad. J. Psychol.* **19**, 118–132.

Shallice, T. (1964). The detection of change and the perceptual moment hypothesis. *Br. J. Stat. Psychol.* **17**, 113–135.

Shallice, T. (1972). Dual functions of consciousness. *Psychol. Rev.* **79**, 383–393.

Shannon, C. E. and Weaver, W. (1949). "The Mathematical Theory of Communication." University of Illinois Press, Urbana.

Shephard, M. S. (1972). Decision processes in perceptual organization: effects of proximity and regularity on response frequency and latency. *In* "Pictorial Organisation and Shape." (J. F. O'Callaghan, Ed.) pp. 80–89. Division of Computing Research, C.S.I.R.O., Canberra, A.C.T.

Sherrington, C. S. (1940). "Man on his Nature." Cambridge University Press, Cambridge.

Simon, H. J. (1962). The architecture of complexity. *Proc. Am. Philos. Soc.* **106**, No. 6.

Smith, E. E. (1968). Choice reaction time: an analysis of the major theoretical positions. *Psychol. Bull.* **69**, 77–110.

Smith, G. A. (1977). Studies of compatibility and a new model of choice reaction time. *In* "Attention and Performance VI." (S. Dornic, Ed.) pp. 27–48. Lawrence Erlbaum, Hillsdale, N.J.

Smith, L. A. and Barany, J. W. (1970). An elementary model of human performance on paced visual inspection tasks. *AIIE Trans.* **2**, 298–308.

Smith, P. T. (1972). Decision-making and organization in memory. (Paper read to British Psychological Society Meeting in Nottingham, April, 1972.)

Snodgrass, J. G., Luce, R. D. and Galanter, E. (1967). Some experiments on simple and choice reaction time. *J. Exper. Psychol.* **75**, 1–17.

Solomons, L. M. (1900). A new explanation of Weber's law. *Psychol. Rev.* **7**, 234–240.

Spearman, C. (1927). "The Abilities of Man." Macmillan, London.

Spence, K. W. (1954). The relation of response latency and speed to the intervening variables and N in S–R theory. *Psychol. Rev.* **61**, 209–216.

Spencer, J. (1961). Estimating averages. *Ergonomics* **4**, 317–328.

Spencer, J. A. (1963). A further study of estimating averages. *Ergonomics* **6**, 255–265.

Sperry, R. W. (1965). Brain bisection and mechanisms of consciousness. *In* "Brain and Conscious Experience." (J. C. Eccles, Ed.) Springer-Verlag, New York.

Sperry, R. W. (1968). Hemisphere deconnection and unity in conscious awareness. *Am. Psychol.* **23**, 723–733. Reprinted in Lingren *et al.* (1971).

Sperry, R. W. (1969). A modified concept of consciousness. *Psychol. Rev.* **76**, 532–536.

Sperry, R. W. (1970). An objective approach to subjective experience. Further explanation of a hypothesis. *Psychol. Rev.* **77**, 585–590.

Sperry, R. W., Miner, N. and Myers, R. E. (1955). Visual pattern perception following subpial splicing and tantalum wire implantations in the visual cortex. *J. Comp. Physiol. Psychol.* **48**, 50–58.

Sternberg, S. (1966). High-speed scanning in human memory. *Science* **153**, 652–654.

Sternberg, S. (1969). The discovery of processing stages: extensions of Donders' method. *In* "Attention and Performance II." (W. G. Koster, Ed.) *Acta Psychol.* **30**, 276–315.

Stevens, S. S., Morgan, C. T. and Volkmann, J. (1941). Theory of the neural quantum in the discrimination of loudness and pitch. *Am. J. Psychol.* **54**, 315–335.

Stone, M. (1960). Models for reaction time. *Psychometrika* **25**, 251–260.

Stout, G. F. (1938). "A Manual of Psychology." (5th ed.) University Tutorial Press, London.

Swanson, J. M. and Briggs, G. E. (1969). Information processing as a function of speed versus accuracy. *J. Exper. Psychol.* **81**, 223–229.

Swensson, R. G. (1972). The elusive trade-off: speed versus accuracy in visual discrimination tasks. *Percep. Psychophys.* **12**, 16–32.

Swets, J. A. (1977). Signal detection theory applied to vigilance. *In* "Vigilance: Theory, Operational Performance, and Physiological Correlates." (R. Mackie, Ed.) pp. 705–718. Plenum Press, New York.

Swets, J. A. and Birdsall, T. G. (1967). Deferred decision in human signal detection: a preliminary experiment. *Percep. Psychophys.* **2**, 15–28.

Swets, J. A. and Green, D. M. (1961). Sequential observations by human observers of signals in noise. *In* "Information Theory: Proceedings of the Fourth London Symposium." (C. Cherry, Ed.) pp. 177–195. Butterworths, London.

Swets, J. A., Shipley, E. F., McKey, M. J. and Green, D. M. (1959). Multiple observations of signals in noise. *J. Acoust. Soc. Am.* **31**, 514–521.

Swets, J. A., Tanner, W. P. and Birdsall, T. G. (1961). Decision processes in perception. *Psychol. Rev.* **68**, 301–340.

Tanner, W. P. and Swets, J. A. (1954). A decision-making theory of visual detection. *Psychol. Rev.* **61**, 401–409.

Taylor, A. E. (Trans.) (1956). Plato: "Philebus and Epinomis." Nelson and Sons, London.

Taylor, J. S. (1950). Reaction latency as a function of reaction potential and behaviour oscillation. *Psychol. Rev.* **57**, 375–389.

Taylor, M. M. (1965). Detectability measures in vigilance: comment on a paper by Wiener, Poock and Steele. *Percep. Motor Skills* **20**, 1217–1221.

Taylor, M. M., Lindsay, P. H. and Forbes, S. M. (1967). Quantification of shared capacity processing in auditory and visual discrimination. *In* "Attention and Performance I." (A. F. Sanders, Ed.) *Acta Psychol.* **27**, 223–229.

Teichner, W. (1954). Recent studies of simple reaction time. *Psychol. Bull.* **51**, 128–149.

Teichner, W. and Krebs, M. J. (1972). Laws of the simple visual reaction time. *Psychol. Rev.* **79**, 344–357.

Teichner, W. and Krebs, M. J. (1974). Laws of visual choice reaction time. *Psychol. Rev.* **81**, 75–98.

Thomas, E. A. C. (1973). On expectancy and the speed and accuracy of responses. *In* "Attention and Performance IV." (S. Kornblum, Ed.) pp. 613–626. Academic Press, London and New York.

Thomas, E. A. C. and Myers, J. L. (1972). Implications of latency data for threshold and nonthreshold models of signal detection. *J. Math. Psychol.* **9**, 253–285.

Thompson, D'Arcy, W. (1917). "On Growth and Form." Cambridge University Press, Cambridge.

Thomson, G. H. (1920). A new point of view in the interpretation of threshold measurements in psychophysics. *Psychol. Rev.* **27**, 300–307.

Thorpe, W. H. (1966). Ethology and consciousness. *In* "Brain and Conscious Experience." (J. C. Eccles, Ed.) pp. 470–495. Springer-Verlag, New York.

Thouless, R. H. (1963). "Mind and Consciousness in Experimental Psychology." Cambridge University Press, Cambridge.

Throsby, A. (1962). Proportion of light to cycle as a determinant of critical flicker-fusion. *Psychol. Bull.* **59**, 510–519.

Thurmond, J. B. and Alluisi, E. A. (1963). Choice time as a function of stimulus dissimilarity and discriminability. *Canad. J. Psychol.* **17**, 326–337.

Thurstone, L. L. (1927a). Psychophysical analysis. *Am. J. Psychol.* **38**, 368–389.

Thurstone, L. L. (1927b). A law of comparative judgment. *Psychol. Rev.* **34**, 273–286.

Thurstone, L. L. (1928). The phi-gamma hypothesis. *J. Exper. Psychol.* **11**, 293–305.

Thurstone, L. L. (1937). Ability, motivation, and speed. *Psychometrika* **2**, 249–254.

Thurstone, L. L. (1944). "A Factorial Study of Perception." University of Chicago Press, Chicago.

Thurstone, L. L. (1948). Psychophysical methods. *In* "Methods of Psychology." (T. G. Andrews, Ed.) pp. 124–157. Wiley, New York.

Titchener, E. B. (1905). "Experimental Psychology." Vol. II, part 2. Macmillan, London.

Titchener, E. B. (1908). "The Psychology of Feeling and Attention." Macmillan & Co., New York.

Titchener, E. B. (1909). "Experimental Psychology of the Higher Thought Processes." Macmillan, London.

Tolman, E. C. (1939). Prediction of vicarious trial and error by means of the schematic sowbug. *Psychol. Rev.* **46**, 318–336.

Torii, S. (1960). Figure-ground reversals under successively repeated observations. *Jap. Psychol. Res.* **9**, 25–37.

Treisman, M. (1964). Noise and Weber's law: the discrimination of brightness and other dimensions. *Psychol. Rev.* **71**, 314–330.

Treisman, M. (1973). Adaptation-level theory. (M. H. Appley, Ed.) *Q. J. Exper. Psychol.* **25**, 569–570.

Treisman, M. and Watts, T. R. (1966). Relation between signal detectability theory and the traditional procedures for measuring sensory thresholds: estimating $d'$ from results given by the method of constant stimuli. *Psychol. Bull.* **66**, 438–454.

Trow, W. C. (1923). The psychology of confidence. *Archs Psychol.* **67**, 47.

Tussing, L. (1941). Perceptual fluctuations of illusions as a possible fatigue index. *J. Exper. Psychol.* **29**, 85–88.

Ulrich, P. and Ammons, R. B. (1959). Voluntary control of perceived dimensionality (perspective) of three-dimensional objects. *Proc. Montana Acad. Sci.* **19**, 169–173.

Urban, F. M. (1910). The method of constant stimuli and its generalizations. *Psychol. Rev.* **17**, 229–259.

Vickers, D. (1967). Theories and experiments on visual discrimination and the perception of visual depth. (Unpublished Ph. D. thesis, Cambridge University.)

Vickers, D. (1970). Evidence for an accumulator model of psychophysical discrimination. *In* "Current Problems in Perception." (A. T. Welford and L. Houssiadas, Eds) *Ergonomics* **13**, 37–58.

Vickers, D. (1971). Perceptual economy and the impression of visual depth. *Percep. Psychophys.* **10**, 23–27.

Vickers, D. (1972a). Some general features of perceptual discrimination. *In* "Psychological Aspects of Driver Behaviour." (E. G. Asmussen, Ed.) Institute for Road Safety Research, S.W.O.V., Voorlung, The Netherlands.

Vickers, D. (1972b). Decision processes in perceptual organization. *In* "Pictorial Organization and Shape." (J. F. O'Callaghan, Ed.) Division of Computing Research, C.S.I.R.O., Canberra, A.C.T.

Vickers, D. (1972c). A cyclic decision model of perceptual alternation. *Perception* **1**, 31–48.

Vickers, D. (1975). Where Angell feared to tread: response time and frequency in three-category discrimination. *In* "Attention and Performance V." (P. M. A. Rabbitt and S. Dornic, Eds) pp. 455–469. Academic Press, London and New York.

Vickers, D. (1978). An adaptive module for simple judgments. *In* "Attention and Performance VII." (J. Requin, Ed.) pp. 599–618. Lawrence Erlbaum, Hillsdale, N. J.

Vickers, D., Caudrey, D. and Willson, R. J. (1971). Discriminating between the frequency of occurrence of two alternative events. *Acta Psychol.* **35**, 151–172.

Vickers, D., Nettelbeck, T. and Wilson, R. J. (1972). Perceptual indices of performance: the measurement of "inspection time" and "noise" in the visual system. *Perception* **1**, 263–295.

Vickers, D., Leary, J. and Barnes, P. (1977). Adaptation to decreasing signal probability. *In* "Vigilance: Theory, Operational Performance, and Physiological Correlates." (R. R. Mackie, Ed.) pp. 679–703. Plenum Press, New York.

Vitz, P. C. and Hazan, D. N. (1969). Memory during probability learning. *J. Exper. Psychol.* **80**, 52–58.

Volkmann, J. (1934). The relation of time of judgment to certainty of judgment. *Psychol. Bull.* **31**, 672–673.

von Foerster, H. (1969). What is memory that it may have hindsight and foresight as well? *In* "The Future of the Brain Sciences." (S. Bogoch, Ed.) pp. 19–64. Plenum Press, New York.

Wald, A. (1947). "Sequential Analysis." Wiley, New York.

Washburn, M. F., Reagan, C. and Thurstone, E. (1934). The comparative controllability of the fluctuations of simple and complex ambiguous perspective figures. *Am. J. Psychol.* **46**, 636–638.

Weaver, H. R. (1942). A study of discriminative serial reaction: manual response to colour. *J. Exper. Psychol.* **31**, 177–201.

Wechsler, D. (1958). "The Measurement and Appraisal of Adult Intelligence." (4th ed.) Williams and Watkins, Baltimore.

Weiss, P. A. (1969). The living system: determinism stratified. *In* "Beyond Reductionism: the Alpbach Symposium." (A. Koestler and J. Smythies, Eds) pp. 3–55. Hutchinson & Co., New York.

Welford, A. T. (1951). "Skill and Age." Oxford University Press, Oxford.

Welford, A. T. (1960). The measurement of sensory-motor performance. *Ergonomics* **3**, 189–230.

Welford, A. T. (1965). Performance, biological mechanisms, and age: a theoretical sketch. *In* "Behaviour, Ageing and the Nervous System." (A. T. Welford and J. E. Birren, Eds) pp. 3–20. Charles C. Thomas, Springfield, Ill.

Welford, A. T. (1968). "Fundamentals of Skill." Methuen, London.

Welford, A. T. (1971). What is the basis of choice-reaction time? *Ergonomics* **14**, 679–693.

Welford, A. T. (1972). The obtaining and processing of information: some basic issues relating to analysing inputs and making decisions. *Res. Q.* **43**, 295–311.

Welford, A. T. (1973). Attention, strategy, and reaction time: a tentative metric. *In* "Attention and Performance IV." (S. Kornblum, Ed.) pp. 37–53. Academic Press, London and New York.

Welford, A. T. (1975). Display layout, strategy, and reaction time: tests of a model. *In* "Attention and Performance V." (P. M. A. Rabitt and S. Dornic, Eds) pp. 470–484. Academic Press, London and New York.

Wells, H. M. (1927). The phenomenology of acts of choice. *Br. J. Psychol. Monogr. Suppl.* **4**, 1–149.

White, M. A. (1972). Individual differences in perceptual performance on inspecting an ambiguous figure. (unpublished Honours thesis, University of Adelaide.)

White, R. W. (1959). Motivation reconsidered: the concept of competence. *Psychol. Rev.* **66**, 297–333.

Whitfield, I. E. (1967). The response of the auditory nervous system to simple time-dependent acoustic stimuli. *Anns N. Y. Acad. Sci.* **156**, 671–677.

Wieland, B. A. and Mefferd, R. B. (1966). Effects of orientation, inclination, and length of diagonal on reversal rate of Necker cube. *Percep. Motor Skills* **23**, 823–826.

Wieland, B. A. and Mefferd, R. B. (1967). Individual differences in Necker cube reversal rates and perspective dominance. *Percep. Motor Skills* **24**, 923–930.

Wilding, J. M. (1971). The relation between latency and accuracy in the identification of visual stimuli: I. The effects of task difficulty. *Acta Psychol.* **35**, 378–398.

Wilding, J. M. (1974). Effects of stimulus discriminability on the latency distribution of identification responses. *Acta Psychol.* **38**, 483–500.

Williges, R. C. (1969). Within-session criterion changes compared to an ideal observer criterion in a visual monitoring task. *J. Exper. Psychol.* **81**, 61–66.

Williges, R. C. (1971). The role of payoffs and signal ratios in criterion changes during a monitoring task. *Hum. Factors* **13**, 261–267.

Williges, R. C. (1973). Manipulating the response criterion in visual monitoring. *Hum. Factors* **15**, 179–185.

Wohlwill, J. F. (1962). The perspective illusion: perceived size and distance in fields varying suggested depth. *J. Exper. Psychol.* **64**, 300–310.

Wolfendale, G. L. (1967). Decision times in signal detection. *In* "Attention and Performance I. (A. F. Sanders, Ed.) *Acta Psychol.* **27**, 154–159.

Woollen, K. A. (1963). Relationship between choice time and frequency during discrimination training and generalization tests. *J. Exper. Psychol.* **66**, 474–484.

Woodrow, M. (1928). Behaviour with repect to short temporal stimulus forms. *J. Exper. Psychol.* **11**, 167–193.

Woodworth, R. and Schlosberg, H. (1954). "Experimental Psychology." Holt, New York.

Wyckoff, L. B. (1952). The role of observing responses in discrimination learning: Part I. *Psychol. Rev.* **59**, 431–442.

Yellott, J. I. (1967). Correction for guessing in choice reaction time. *Psychonom. Sci.* **8**, 321–322.

Yellott, J. I. (1971). Correction for guessing and the speed–accuracy trade-off in choice reaction time. *J. Math. Psychol.* **8**, 159–199.

Yerkes, R. M. and Dodson, J. D. (1908). The relation of strength of stimulus to rapidity of habit-formation. *J. Comp. Neurol. Psychol.* **18,** 459–482.

Young, J. Z. (1965). The organization of a memory system. *Proc. Roy. Soc.* (B) **163,** 285–320.

Zahn, C. T. (1971). Graph-theoretical methods for detecting and describing Gestalt clusters. *IEEE Trans. Comp.* **20,** 68–86.

Zubek, J. P. (1969). Sensory and perceptual-motor processes. *In* "Sensory Deprivation: Fifteen years of Research." (J. P. Zubek, Ed.) Appleton-Century-Crofts, New York.

Zubek, J. P. and Macneill, M. (1966). Effects of immobilization: behavioural and EEG changes. *Canad. J. Psychol.* **20,** 316–336.

Zubek, J. P. and Wilgosh, L. (1963). Prolonged immobilization of the body: changes in performance and the electroencephalogram. *Science* **140,** 306–308.

Zubek, J. P., Aftanas, M., Hasek, J., Sansom, W., Schludermann, E., Wilgosh, L. and Winocur, G. (1962). Intellectual and perceptual changes during prolonged perceptual deprivation: low illumination and noise level. *Percep. Motor Skills* **15,** 171–198.

Zubek, J. P., Aftanas, M. Kovach, K., Wilgosh, L. and Winocur, G. (1963). Effect of severe immobilization of the body on intellectual and perceptual processes. *Canad. J. Psychol.* **17,** 118–133.

# Subject Index

# N

Neural clock, 106, 108–110, 151–152, 165

Neural timing model, signal detection, 147–151

Neurophysiology
evidence concerning perceptual organization, 299–303, 309
representation of theoretical models, 97–99, 166–167, 209, 234

No-decision, region of, 48–50, 53, 69, 104, 146, 147, 151, 153, 201

Noise
measure of, 349–352
in models for choice-reaction, 250, 252, 255, 257, 259, 263–268, 270–272, 281
in neural clock, 109, 152
optimum level of, 284–287
precondition for identification, 287–289
in sensory representation, 25–27, 33, 38–39, 41–42, 54, 81, 139–141, 322, 337, 348, 351, 362
added to stimuli, 50–52, 75–77, 102, 155, 157–158, 325–326, 350, 351
in transmission of image, 295, 296, 300, 303, 307, 312, 314, 345

Number of stimulus-response alternatives, 242–246, 251, 252, 254, 257–260, 263–272, 285–286

# O

Objective stimulus difference
effects in choice-reaction, 247–248, 251, 259, 273–276, 280–281, 284–285
effects on confidence, 49, 172–174, 182–184, 188–189
effects in perceptual organization, 318, 321–326, 329, 331–333, 335
effects in same–different judgment, 124–127, 130–134,
effects in signal detection, 145, 149–155, 158–160, 163–165
effects in three-category judgment, 24, 102–105, 107–110, 112, 117–118, 120–123

effects in two-category discrimination, 23, 25, 26, 29–30, 60–63, 67–68, 72–82, 91–93, 214–215, 350–352

Observation(s)
conscious *versus* unconscious, 55, 56, 111, 112, 135, 176–180, 360–365
in models for signal detection, 139, 140, 143, 144, 145, 146, 147, 151, 152, 155, 161, 162, 165
in models for three-category judgment, 105–107, 114
in models for two-category discrimination, 44, 45, 46, 47, 48–53, 54–56, 57–59, 64, 65, 68, 69, 70, 76, 77, 81, 82, 88, 89, 91, 94
non-informative, 48, 53, 69, 112, 146, 147, 152, 153, 154, 348
time required for a single, 56, 245–246, 346–349

Observing response, 55

Optimality
strategy in random walk model, 65
use of sensory information, 144
value for $\beta$ in signal detection, 140–141

Optional-stopping
and confidence, 176–180
and perceptual indices, 346
and speed–accuracy trade-off, 88–90
in theoretical models, 47, 50, 52, 55, 56, 101, 105–112, 125, 146, 147, 165

Overall probability, of intermediate response, 104, 118, 119, 129

Overt (*see* Covert)

# P

Parallel elimination model, choice-reaction, 246–254

Parallel eventuation model
choice-reaction, 254–283
Yerkes-Dodson effects, 284–289

Payoff(s), 38, 110, 140–142, 321, 323

Percept duration
empirical findings, 329–340
theoretical predictions, 330, 331, 332, 335–340